ROBINHO

KING OF THE CITY

ROBINHO
KING OF THE CITY

PETER SMITH

JOHN BLAKE

Published by John Blake Publishing Ltd,
3 Bramber Court, 2 Bramber Road,
London W14 9PB, England

www.johnblakepublishing.co.uk

First published in hardback in 2009

ISBN: 978-1-84454-829-3

British Library Cataloguing-in-Publication Data:

A catalogue record for this book is available from the British Library.

Design by www.envydesign.co.uk

Printed in the UK by CPI William Clowes Beccles NR34 7TL

1 3 5 7 9 10 8 6 4 2

Papers used by John Blake Publishing are natural, recyclable products
made from wood grown in sustainable forests. The manufacturing processes
conform to the environmental regulations of the country of origin.

Every attempt has been made to contact the relevant copyright-holders,
but some were unobtainable. We would be grateful if the appropriate
people could contact us.

CONTENTS

INTRODUCTION

On Saturday, 13 September 2008 the players of Manchester City and Chelsea walked out of the darkness of the City of Manchester Stadium tunnel into a bright, sun-bathed afternoon. As they followed the three officials towards the pitch the captains of each side, John Terry of Chelsea and Richard Dunne of City, each with a hand planted on the shoulder of a mascot, squinted as they looked out upon the fantastic arena.

Flashbulbs flickered around the ground which, since the end of the Commonwealth Games in 2002, was home to Manchester City. The noise created by the boisterous home support reached a crescendo as fans seated next to the tunnel leaned over the barriers above the players' heads with arms outstretched, desperate to touch their idols.

The scene was not unfamiliar to the experienced centre-backs. Everywhere they played around the country they were greeted with similar fanfare and adoration.

If, however, on this particular Saturday afternoon, Dunne or Terry had made eye-contact with the exuberant City supporters hanging their scarves over the tunnel above them, they would have seen the eyes of the supporters drifting down past them, back towards the changing rooms. Their gaze was not focused on their club captain, nor was it fixed on the captain of England, who was leading out the all-star names of the Chelsea team. Instead they squinted deep into the darkness of the tunnel to try and catch a glimpse of their new hero.

As the heads of the players continued to bob by underneath the fans, the clamour became more and more frantic. Stephen Ireland, the talented Manchester City midfielder and Alex, Chelsea's Brazilian centre-half, appeared to complete the end of the procession of players. But then, just as it seemed that perhaps he would not emerge with the rest of his new team-mates, a sudden cry went up from those fans with the best view into the darkness.

Still doing up the ties on his sky-blue shorts, City's new star sauntered out of the tunnel. As he emerged from the shadows and came into the view of the rest of the stadium, a roar flooded like a wave around the ground. The Brazilian glanced up, took one swift look around the stadium, broke into a jog as he came on to the pitch, crossed himself and then skipped round 360 degrees, a smile on his face, his arms in the air, applauding his new audience. Robinho had arrived.

The boy from Brazil, who couldn't afford the bus to football training as a child in one of the poorest districts of São Paulo, had just been signed by the world's richest club for a British transfer record-breaking sum of £32.5 million. The delighted City supporters, who had seen their club transformed overnight with the sudden and unexpected takeover by the Abu Dhabi United Group, ecstatically welcomed the first world star to Eastlands.

INTRODUCTION

As the last few hours of the 2008 summer transfer window drifted away and Robinho's proposed move to Chelsea stalled, City had snuck in under the cover of darkness to gazump Roman Abramovich's millions with a huge offer for the Brazilian star, once hailed by Pelé as 'my successor.'

The former Real Madrid forward was the perfect example of the 'fantasy football' City's new owners were hoping to play with the club as they looked to propel their team from mid-table mediocrity to European glory. The first piece of that puzzle was to sign a worldwide star, a player who, with his awesome talents, could drive the club forward towards success. Robinho was that player. His trickery with a football, devastating pace and eye for goal made him an exceptional signing for the newly wealthy Manchester club. A player they could only dream about before the arrival of their new investors.

Just 13 minutes into his debut, Robinho clipped a free kick into the top corner of the Chelsea net to put City ahead against the European giants. The City support went into raptures. Their new era had begun.

Since that moment it has not all been plain sailing for Robinho, although throughout his life he has endured anything but calm seas. From his journey out of the poverty of São Vicente to the abduction of his mother in 2004, Robinho's 25 years have been as dramatic and remarkable as City's sudden rise into the world of footballing superpowers.

He is now the Premier League's best paid player and one of its top entertainers. His dazzling footwork – which he has compared to dancing the samba – was clear for all to see at the Emirates stadium in February 2009, when his flickering feet bewildered the defenders of Italy as he scored his 23rd goal for Brazil.

His story, though, is a million miles away from the Lamborghinis, designer clothes and beautiful country mansions that now decorate his life as a megastar of the game.

CHAPTER 1

'AND GOD CREATED ROBINHO'

Like Garrincha, Rivaldo, the great Pelé and so many of the other brilliant Brazilian footballers he would later be compared to, Robson de Souza's story began in the poverty stricken streets of the country's eastern coast.

Robson was born on 25 January 1984 in São Vicente, to Marina de Souza and her husband Gilvan de Souza, a local sewage worker. They lived in a small home in the deprived area of Parque Bitaru – a distant world from the one he now enjoys, 25 years on, as one of the best-paid footballers in the world.

São Vicente sits within the shadow of Santos, on an island in a south-eastern district of São Paulo, and is home to 320,000 residents. Now reliant on the tourism and fishing trades to support its economy, the town, known as *Cellula Mater* – literally, 'Mother Cell' – was the first permanent settlement for Portuguese colonisers in 1532 and was established by the explorer Martim Afonso de Sousa. In the August of the same year the first City Council of all the Americas was democratically elected and established in the

1

town, making São Vicente the focal point for the Portuguese settlers' exploration into Brazil.

However, Santos, barely three miles to the east, soon surpassed São Vicente as the dominant city in the region of Baixada Santista. Santos is a vibrant, modern city with a beautiful coastline, home to the largest beachfront garden in the world. The city has been able to blossom thanks to its enormous shipping industry. Home to the largest seaport in Latin America, Santos is the route out of Brazil to the rest of the world for the country's biggest exports – steel, oil, bananas, cotton and, of course, coffee.

In the shadow of this powerful city, that counts over 1.4 million Brazilians within its metropolitan area, Robson grew up. From his small home in São Vicente, where he lived off meagre meals of fish and rice, Robson, as a child, would have dreamed of the wealth of Santos; the vibrant trading, the growing metropolis and its glorious beaches.

For Robson though, like so many of his countrymen, the path to wealth was barred by the rigid class system of Brazil. The clamped-down barriers forced his family to scratch a living: his father in the sewers, his mother as a maid. But in Brazil there is a key that unlocks those barriers; it is a key that can take a boy from the poverty stricken *favelas* (shanty towns) and can elevate him to the most luxurious of lifestyles, a key that can deliver him from a life plagued with paucity and allow him to shine on a stage in front of thousands. The key, as every Brazilian boy knows, is football.

For the majority of British people, sport simply provides mental relief and escape from the day-to-day rigours, monotony and constraints of work and modern life, but in Brazil it is viewed as so much more. Football can literally free a Brazilian from the cage of poverty that encapsulates the

10% of the population who are unemployed (about twice the rate in Britain) and the poorest 40%, who get by on less than £30 a month. However, with just one of the 1,000 aspiring players who attended Santos's public trials between 2000 and 2004 being taken on by the famous club, it is no easy task to play your way out of poverty. Indeed, even the lucky few who do sign professional contracts are not guaranteed riches and fame. Of the 12,000 Brazilians who ply their trade on the pitches of their homeland more than 80% earn less than £100 a month.

While the sprawling *favelas* surrounding Brazil's major cities may be viewed as nothing more than slums by British standards, the country's programme for developing footballers from a young age far outclasses our own. The image of bare-footed boys kicking make-do footballs around in dusty streets is somewhat mythical: the youth set-ups in Brazil are, in fact, very well-structured, reasonably well-funded and, as the nation's glorious history in the sport demonstrates, extremely effective.

The game in Brazil is the lifeblood of the country and, like the majority of Brazilian children, Robson was attempting to kick a ball as soon as he could stand. At the age of six he was taken by his father to play for the out-of-school club Beira-Mar. Like hundreds of other clubs across the country, the Beira-Mar club is part of the institutionalised drive by Brazil to encourage its youth to take up competitive sport from as young an age as possible. Coaches, organised leagues and well-maintained indoor venues provide an excellent platform for the young players to express themselves and develop the sport's key techniques. The indoor game is far more commonly played than it is in Britain and, with grass being difficult to maintain in the country's tropical climate, and with the densely populated cities short of space for full-size pitches, clubs like Beira-Mar play *Futsal*.

Futsal is, essentially, football, but played on a basketball court with a small ball that barely bounces. The idea is that the fast-paced game, designed to give the players as much time with the ball at their feet as possible, hones the youngsters' skills, encourages them to dribble, to pass along the ground and control the ball. Like Zico and Ronaldo before him, Robson has always stated that it was his time on the *Futsal* courts as a child that developed his extraordinary touch and flair which now light up the stadiums of Europe.

'It helped me a lot,' he recently said. 'A lot of the moves and stuff I do on the pitch today are things I learnt playing *Futsal*. It is a really enjoyable way of playing football and increasing your skills. Even now when I go home for my holidays I like to play.'

Despite his small stature – which had earned him the nickname of Robinho ('Little Robson') that would later adorn the national team's number 11 shirt and the thousands of replicas sold around the world – he was clearly an extremely talented youngster as his former coach Adroaldo Ricardo – affectionately known as Betinho – recalled to the *Sunday Time*s: 'The first time he got the ball we realised that he was different. He would make spectacular moves.'

In his first season with the team they were local champions and at the age of nine Robinho netted 73 goals in a single season with the team.

In 2006 Robinho's sponsors, Nike, followed him back to Santos and the Beira-Mar club and made a film about his return. He visits Betinho, who is delighted to see his protégé return.

'Robinho was different from the others,' Betinho recalls, as he digs out a tape of him playing for the club as an eight-year-old. 'He had no fear of his opponents.'

The tape begins with Robinho flashing a cheeky smile to the camera, surrounded by his team-mates. 'This video is priceless!' laughs the portly coach. The film then cuts to the match. Robinho, wearing the white shirt, blue shorts and blue socks of his club, lurks on the other side of the court as a throw-in from his team-mate loops over two defenders and a Beira-Mar player. In an instant the youngster pounces on the opportunity and fires a right-foot shot past the despairing keeper. Arms aloft, he dashes back to his own half before celebrating wildly with his friends. On the sofa, with Betinho and his father, Gilvan, Robinho smiles, his eyes fixed on the screen.

'We were having so much fun. We had no idea we were playing well,' recalls the forward.

'Robinho again – he really knows how to play!' exclaims the commentator, as Robinho cuts in from the left flank past his marker. The green shirts of his opponents might as well be traffic lights as Robinho drives straight past them without hindrance, the ball appearing magnetised to his feet. He evades another tackle and lays the ball off to a team-mate.

The film cuts to another match, this time against red-shirted victims. In the bottom corner of the screen is the date and time: 3.53pm, 5 August 1992. Surrounded by two markers, the gesticulating of the coaches on the sideline in his peripheral vision, Robinho places his foot on the ball. He holds off the challenge from behind, and, as another defender takes a wild swing at the ball, Robinho drags it back, spins and breaks away from the defensive duo. The other marker is teased into making a desperate lunge by another drag-back but left sprawling on his backside as little Robson dances away.

'People like to see dribbles, moves and skill,' says Betinho, as they watch Robinho torment another child. 'Our games were the last ones so people would stay to watch us play.'

Robinho is then seen listening intently to Betinho as the coach explains tactics to the boys. He was clearly a huge influence on the young star.

'Coach Betinho would say to me you have to have some moves, like knowing how to dance the Samba,' remembers Robinho, before we see the eight-year-old pull off some dance moves of his own after scoring again.

This brilliant talent was enthusiastically encouraged by Betinho and his fellow coordinators at Beira-Mar, who waived his £5 monthly club fee, given that Robinho could not afford the 10p bus fare to the hall and had been relying on a neighbour to supplement his travel to training.

In 1994 Robinho, now aged ten, was taken to the Associação Atlética dos Portuários club by another one of his coaches at the Beira-Mar, Antônio dos Santos. Situated on the eastern side of the Mass of St Vincent, the hillside separating São Vicente from Santos, the Associação Atlética dos Portuários is a dockworkers' club, where Robinho played on a full-size pitch for the first time. Here, playing against boys far older than himself, and becoming well-known at the club for his ability to outshine his opponents, despite his size, he developed rapidly. Two years later he was signed to play *Futebol de salão* in Santos's youth team.

Futebol de salão, like *Futsal*, is a reduced version of football. Players use a size 2 football – compared to the size 4 ball used in *Futsal* – but like *Futsal*, which has since become the more dominant reduced format, *Futebol de salão* has a heavy insistence on technique and control over power and strength.

6

It was during this time that Robinho began to play with Diego Ribas de Cunha. Diego, as he is more commonly known, grew up in Ribeirão Preto, a wealthy region of São Paulo, 200 miles to the north-west of Santos. However, living a long way from home at such an early age was tough for the aspiring player.

'In the beginning, it was very difficult. I thought I was going to give up when I had to choose between being alone or if I should come back to my family in Ribeirão Preto. However, with the encouragement of my parents and my coach Eduardo Jenner, I became settled at Santos. I was pretty well received by the people there and made many friends.'

Robinho took a particular shine to his team-mate and the pair struck up a good friendship. Their camaraderie would grow and strengthen in the next 10 years as their careers took similar paths to the top of the world game. While Robinho currently displays his skills in the English Premier League, central midfielder Diego is the playmaker and craftsman at Werder Bremen in the German Bundesliga.

Despite being a year younger than Robinho and equally as short as his friend from São Vicente, Diego was the one who initially caught the eye of the Santos scouts visiting the *Futebol de salão* team in search of new talent to introduce into their professional set-up. It did not take long, however, for Robinho's flair to also attract the attention of the club, and the pair began their progression through the Santos junior ranks.

For the friends this was the ideal era to be making a mark at junior level. Both players were fortunate to be at Santos at a time when club president Marcelo Teixeira, having spent millions of Brazilian *reais* on star names without success, decided to invest in the club's youth set-up, aiming to create a more sustainable platform to revive the former glory days. In recent seasons, the title wins of the past seemed like long-faded memories for the Santos fans.

The club is known around the world as being the club for which Pelé played in Brazil. With the great Brazilian up front, and the likes of Coutinho and Pepe in the side during the 1960s, Santos took eight state championships, six national championships, two continental championships (now the Copa Libertadores) and two intercontinental championships (now the Club World Cup). However, in recent years the club's dedicated supporters, who each week fill the 20,000-capacity Vila Belmiro stadium, had been denied any form of success. The club's last title, the São Paulo State Championship, came in 1984 and the last time Santos won the national title was 20 years before that. Recent league campaigns had not seen any sign of an end to that barren period either. Santos finished 18th, 15th and 11th in the 2000, 2001 and 1999 seasons respectively, and a distant third-place finish in 1998 was the closest the club had come to repeating their triumphs of yesteryear. Teixeira was determined to halt the era of failure at the club.

As well as Robinho and Diego, players such as the defender Léo, now of Benfica, Sevilla's defensive midfielder Renato and Robinho's Manchester City team-mate Elano, also benefited from this new approach.

However, after five years at Santos, it was Robinho who had developed the most envious of talents. By now, Robson was showing all the hallmarks of a player capable of making his way in the professional game. He was one of the quickest sprinters at the club and certainly the fastest runner with a ball at his feet; he had equally impressive agility and although his height (he is just 5'8" tall) and strength were a disadvantage, he was able to rely on his well-developed football skills to keep him clear of bruising centre-backs. His first touch was capable of cushioning the firmest of passes and could bring down the loftiest of long balls. His passing ability, long or short, was also impressive, as direct or as cute as necessary, and reliably landing at the feet of his team-mates.

Robinho was also determined character. As much as he was a practical joker and had the loudest laugh off the field, he was extremely focused on taking his talent as far as he could on the pitch. He was well aware that he was talented – his teasing trickery, crafty drag-backs and cheeky stepovers demonstrated confidence in his ability – but he also knew that he had to improve to fulfil his ambitions and he would eagerly listen to anyone willing to advise him on his game and how he could become a better player. Robinho was hugely fortunate that one of the people happy to help him develop was perhaps the greatest footballer of all time.

The incredible Pelé, who had played 412 times for Santos and scored 470 goals for the club, had agreed to return to the *Peixe* ('The Fish' as Santos are nicknamed) in 1999 to oversee the youth development programme. On his first day in the job Pelé noticed Robinho and saw in the fifteen-year-old a special talent. In fact, the footballer who has scored more goals than any other player in history and helped Brazil to three World Cups declared Robinho 'my successor'.

Since Pelé's retirement in 1977 Brazil have longed for another superstar to emerge and captivate the world like the former Santos star. As a result of this desperate search, dozens of emerging talents have been christened – and burdened – with the title of 'The New Pelé'. Even Robinho's friend at Santos, Diego, would later be called 'The White Pelé'. However, weighed down by the unrealistic demands that title brings, no player has yet eclipsed Pelé's achievements. Perhaps none ever will.

However, for Robinho this was not a label conjured up by an over-excited journalist. Pelé himself believed his protégé would emulate and exceed his legend. Such an accolade serves to highlight just how extraordinary Robinho's talents were at the age of fifteen. True, Robinho was a skinny, almost malnourished, black kid with a cheeky smile, who hailed from the poor districts of São Paulo, so he was always likely to resemble the young Pelé, who led Brazil to World Cup glory at the tender age of seventeen, but his touch, finesse and ability with a football also drew comparisons.

'Robinho can surpass my own achievements. We have to thank God that another Pelé has landed on Santos,' Pelé said. 'I never thought I'd meet the King of Football at that stage,' Robinho recalled in 2008. 'He said that if I had humility and calmness, I stood a very good chance of becoming a pro.'

Concerned that Robinho's circumstances at home might impair his development, Pelé asked him to bring his father to the next training session. Pelé wanted to give Robinho emotional as well as sporting guidance and insisted the young star ate all his meals in the Santos canteen. It was the first time Robinho had eaten three square meals a day.

'He said he was going to make a special effort with Robinho,' recalled Gilvan de Souza at the time. So there, in the safety and security of the Santos dormitories, with Pelé as a mentor and the best food and facilities at his disposal, Robinho continued to blossom.

However, Pelé's tenure as youth team coach was not a long one and shortly after his revelations about Robinho, the superstar parted company with the club. Business commitments took the former striker away from the club – and away from Robinho. It was, at the time, a terrific blow for the youngster as he had been thrust into the limelight and left to stand there alone. However, after the initial disappointment, Robinho refused to shirk the challenge or shy away from his new reputation. Instead, the self-belief Pelé's words had inspired in him spurred him on with renewed vigour and, under the guidance of the Santos coaching staff, he determinedly battled towards fulfilling his dream of becoming a professional footballer.

CHAPTER 2
THE PRINCE'S GRADUATION

In the spring of 2001 the talent of Santos's youth team was exemplified by their success in the U17 South American championship. It was a distinguished title for the club to win and re-affirmed the quality of the developing players in Santos's youth academies, justifying the decision of the Santos President, Marcelo Teixeira, to invest in them. The driving force behind the juniors' success was unquestionably the devastating duo of Robinho and Diego. The pair's rapid development in the junior ranks had eclipsed their contemporaries by such a degree that both youngsters were fast-tracked into the Santos senior squad for the 2002 season. It would prove to be a sensational for Robinho and the club.

The Brazilian league, unlike the English Premier League which, since its establishment in 1992 has only had four different champions, had seen seven different clubs take the title in the past ten years. Santos, though, had spent the previous three seasons languishing in mid-table. Their last Campeonato Brasileiro title came in 1968, when Pelé was the Peixe's star player. Reigning champions Atletico-PR had profited from the play-off system, re-established in 2001, to overhaul regular season winners São Caetano. The 'Big Blue', as São Caetano are known by their supporters, was only founded in 1989 and had capped a march through the national divisions by finishing eight points clear of Atletico after 27 league games.

Prior to 2000 this would have sealed the title for the new club, but in 2001 an end-of-season play-off system was used to determine the Campeonato winners. The top eight finishers in the Campeonato Brasileiro Serie A in 2001 would battle it out in a seeded play-off system. Atletico-PR squeezed past São Paulo and Fluminense before destroying São Caetano 4-2 in the first leg of the final and then sealed a 1-0 victory away from home to take the title from the league winners.

The format, running from August to December, did away with the home-and-away system in favour of teams playing each other just once, with the top eight sides qualifying for the post-season play-offs and the bottom four relegated to the second division. The idea behind the scheme was to keep mid-table sides competing until the end of the season, thereby creating a dramatic end to the season. Brazilian football was no stranger to these unusual and unconventional methods of deciding national championships, which seem so alien to the European standard 'home-and-away' league format. Indeed, in the previous 10 seasons, 10 different methods had been used to select the national champions, the most bizarre of which, in 2000, saw the top three sides in the three tiers of Brazilian football compete in a play-off to determine the country's best side. How a team which finished third in Serie C could justify themselves as, theoretically, the best team in Brazil is unfathomable, but São Caetano nearly upset the odds, reaching the post-season play-off final as a second tier side before losing to top-flight Vasco da Gama 5-2 on aggregate. 2002 would be the final year of the play-off format, with the conventional league system re-introduced in 2003.

The U17 victory breathed an air of confidence into the Peixe ahead of their 2002 campaign and among the fans and squad there was a genuine belief that they could produce something special after years of mediocrity.

Victory on the opening day of the season was to buoy that belief. Santos began the new season at home to Botafogo RJ on Saturday 10 August 2002. The opposition, from Rio de Janeiro, had struggled in 2001, only escaping the four relegation places to Serie B by two points, and Santos were therefore expected to comfortably overcome Botafogo.

In front of a sell-out and exuberant home crowd at the Vila Belmiro – Santos's 86-year-old home – two youngsters lined up before the game: the slight build of Robinho, whose bright white teeth shone from his face with satisfaction and delight, and his dark-haired team-mate, Diego. Proudly wearing the famous white Santos jersey, both were enjoying the realisation that finally all the sweat, hours of practice and toil had paid off: they had achieved their childhood dream of becoming professional footballers.

All guns blazing, the Peixe came out showing no signs of nerves or apprehension, and it was young Robinho who first tested the visitors' keeper. Stepping inside his man, he curled a right-foot effort at goal, which was tipped round the post. After just 4 minutes, though, 21-year-old midfielder Elano, who would later play alongside Robinho for Brazil and Manchester City, pounced in the six-yard box to put Santos ahead. Diego then marked his own debut with a goal on 43 minutes from the edge of the box, before ripping off his shirt in ecstatic celebration. A late strike from Ademilson, the Botafogo forward, proved nothing more than a consolation for the visitors, as Santos made an ideal start to 2002 – their youthful side brimming with confidence.

A 2-1 defeat away to Juventude the following Sunday 18 August somewhat dampened those spirits, but, three days later and back in front of their own fans, Santos fired three past newly-promoted Figueirense. The victory was set up by goals either side of the half-time interval – first, Leo nodding in from close range before a stunning strike from Renato rifled into the top corner. Robinho was on hand to set up the third, dribbling into the box before squaring the ball across the six-yard line for Jesus Douglas to complete the scoring. In a league with no return fixtures Santos's home form would be crucial. However, the next week Diego, who had taken the step up to professional football in his stride, scored what looked to be the winning goal at the Maracana stadium against Fluminense. It would have been an impressive scalp for the Peixe – Fluminense finished third in 2001 – but the home side equalised through Ronieliton dos Santos in the 90th minute to deny Santos maximum points.

On 21 August, Santos' first midweek game of the season, the Peixe were nearly caught out at home by Parana, a side who had not tasted victory since their opening-day win over São Caetano. An exquisite free kick from Maurílio a minute into the second half found the top corner and silenced the home fans, but Santos pulled level when a hopeful chip into the 18-yard area by future Chelsea centre-half Alex caused chaos in the Parana box. Leo was quickest to react to the loose ball and fired a left-foot shot past the despairing keeper to record his second of the season. The winner came through Santos's heroic young star Diego, who held his nerve from the penalty spot to convert his second goal in as many matches.

Santos, under the guidance of Emerson Leão, had made a good start to the season, taking 10 points from a possible 15 and winning all three of their home games. Away from the Vila Belmiro, the young guns were unable to continue their good form, though, and were crushed 3-0 by Internacional on 31 August. However, six days after the humiliation against Inter, Santos shocked Vitoria with two goals from Alberto within 10 minutes of kick-off, and when Robinho scored his first goal for the club on 42 minutes a Santos victory was sealed – their fourth straight win at home. The Peixe had netted ten times and conceded just twice at home. Their superb start to the season at the Vila Belmiro lifted Santos up to sixth in the table, making their play-off ambitions a serious possibility.

That run of victories ended against Atletico-PR on 8 September, but the reigning champions, who had also begun the season well, could only come away from Santos with a 2-2 draw after leading their hosts twice.

Santos's away form continued at high-flying Coritiba when, after racing into a two-goal lead before the half-hour, thanks to Diego, the Peixe capitulated to a 4-2 defeat. The result re-affirmed Leão's side's woeful form on the road, which was in complete contrast to their displays at home. While Santos managed to take just 1 point from a possible 12 away from home another victory at the Vila Belmiro against the strong outfit of Gremio – who finished 2001 in fifth spot – improved the club's record as hosts. Now they had played 6, won 5, drawn 1, scored 14 goals, and conceded 4.

Finally, on 18 September, at the fifth attempt, Santos snatched all three points as visitors. Vasco Da Gama were on a run of patchy home form and Elano took advantage of some poor marking to put Santos ahead early on. Souza levelled for the 2000 champions, but Alex headed Santos back in front and Leão's boys held on for their first away win of 2002.

Two weeks later, following two disappointing draws, Robinho hit his second goal for the club against Palmeiras on 29 September. The young forward was played in from the right flank, drove into the penalty area and unleashed a thunderous left-foot shot that flew into the top corner of the near post. Palmeiras keeper Marcos was left rooted to the spot; stunned and completely unprepared for the velocity and accuracy of Robinho's strike. Minutes later, Robinho could have had his second. This time, teed up by Elano, he turned his marker before firing a right-foot effort at goal, only to be parried away by Marcos. Santos were relentless in their assault of the Palmeiras goal, with Diego's long-range effort turned round the post, a left-foot drive from Robinho well-stopped and Leo denied from close range among the numerous opportunities carved out by the home side. However, they could not find another route past 2002 World Cup winner Marcos and Francisco Arce, the visitors' right-back, stole a draw for Palmeiras with a beautiful free kick right at the death. Although a third consecutive draw for Santos, the match proved that Robinho was finally getting a foothold in professional football and beginning to demonstrate his natural talent on the competitive stage.

The goal against Palmeiras sparked Robinho into form and the diminutive forward netted two more goals in the next three games. A wondrous bicycle-kick from Alberto set Santos on course for a comfortable 4-2 victory away to Corinthians before, on 9 October, Robinho struck a crucial third goal in a 3-2 win over Atletico Mineiro.

Four days later Santos met play-off rivals Cruzeiro and Robinho hit the fourth strike of his debut season. A brace from Elano, either side of a well-taken header from Luvs, set up a secure lead for the visitors when Robinho was played through for a one-on-one with the Cruzeiro keeper on the hour mark. He made no mistake with his finish, neatly tucking the ball into the bottom corner which, despite a superb late strike by Joãozinho, secured Santos's third victory in a row. The Peixe were back on course for a post-season adventure.

Top-of-the-table São Paulo denied Santos a deserved point at the Morumbi stadium the following Wednesday when Ricardinho hit a 90th-minute winner after Diego levelled the match at 2-2, with 7 minutes to play. Two goals in the space of a minute had given São Paulo a decent cushion after half-time, but when Robert pulled one back for the visitors 3 minutes later and Diego equalised late on, Ricardiho's winner was a cruel blow for the valiant Santos. The defeat ended Santos's unbeaten run of eight games and instigated a shaky run of form for the Peixe. Three days later, Santos conceded their undefeated home record to Portuguesa 2-1 before going down by the same scoreline at Paysandu on 23 October.

Unaccustomed to defeat, the young side refused to give up on their play-off ambitions, and with just five games to go, they burst into life at the Vila Belmiro on Saturday, 26 October. Within half an hour William, Robert and Robinho had fired the Peixe to a commanding lead over Flamengo to get the squad back on track. Santos followed up this victory with an equally important 1-1 draw with Bahia, Leo stealing the vital 90th-minute equaliser. Santos's play-off ambitions were all but assured when, two days after the late show at Bahia, Diego put his team ahead at Guarani before Robinho pounced on a loose ball in the penalty box – the footage so reminiscent of his goal for the Beira Mar 10 years earlier – to seal a 2-0 win.

The victories allowed Santos to take their foot off the pedal for the final two games of the season, safe in the knowledge that Cruzeiro would be unable to assail their points total and were unlikely to better their goal difference. Robinho notched up one more goal in the regular season, hitting Santos's only goal in a 3-1 defeat at home to mid-table Ponte Preta on 9 November before a 3-2 defeat away to second-placed São Caetano brought the regular season to a close on 17 November 2002.

Emerson Leão had guided his young side to the post-season play-offs, finishing in the eighth and final qualifying spot. By claiming eighth place, the Peixe would have to face top-of-the-table São Paulo – Santos's local rivals – in the first round of the two-leg play-offs. Topping the table by 5 points from São Caetano, São Paulo were a difficult prospect for the young, but ambitious Santos side. São Paulo had won 16 of their 25 league games, giving them a hugely impressive win percentage of 69.3%, which dwarfed Santos's 52%. Santos's rivals had also comfortably out-scored every other side in the league, hitting 57 goals in the regular season.

In the other play-offs São Caetano would face seventh-placed Fluminense, while Corinthians, who had recovered from their demolition by Santos to finish third, would meet Atletico-MG. The last quarter-final would be played out by fourth-placed Juventude and Gremio. Despite being the lowest seed in the play-offs, Santos's young squad had little to fear as they went into the post-season: they had defeated Atletico-MG and Gremio at home, taken 3 points at Corinthians, been denied victory at Fluminense by a last-minute leveller and lost three tough ties away to São

Caetano, São Paulo and Juventude by just one goal. The Peixe would also host the league winners, São Paulo, in the first leg of the contest at the Vila Belmiro on 25 November.

Packed into the 20,000-capacity stadium, the Santos supporters created an electric atmosphere before the game. Black-and-white banners, in the colours of Santos, hung all around the ground and supporters waved flags, whirled scarves and tossed inflatable whales (the club mascot) around the stands as their chanting and singing reached fever pitch. In the dressing room Leão did his best to motivate his players – he reminded them of what they were capable of on their own ground, how dearly the fans wanted them to beat their rivals and that they had the talent to overcome their opponents. Meanwhile, the music and announcements over the Tannoy system in the stadium and the growing wall of noise from the supporters outside began to drown out his speech. With the growing intensity of their supporters, the Peixe emerged from the tunnel, determination in their eyes, fire in their bellies.

Santos's exuberant fans were sent into ecstasy half an hour after kick-off when Diego, trying to set himself up in the penalty box, lost control of the ball but managed to poke a pass to Alberto, who slid in a left-foot shot across the face of the goal. Wrong-footing Rogerio Ceni in the São Paulo goal, it flew into the bottom corner. Against all the odds Santos had upset the favourites and taken a vital lead. At the heart of the São Paulo midfield, however, was a young player who had been named Brazilian Player of the Year in 2002. Within five years of this quarter-final, he would be hailed as the greatest player on the planet. He was Ricardo Izecson dos Santos Leite, more commonly known simply as Kaka.

The future AC Milan star began to impose himself on the

game, nullifying Santos's attacks, nonchalantly flicking the ball over his opponents' heads and single-handedly driving São Paulo back into the match. Picking up the ball on the left-hand side of the pitch, a quick swivel relinquished the future Brazil star of his marker. He continued his storming run towards the Santos goal, his surprising speed taking him away from his pursuers before firing a fierce left-foot drive into the near top corner from just inside the penalty box.

A spectacular goal, it was testament to the midfielder's exceptional talent. The São Paulo number 8's sensational strike came right on the stroke of half-time, sending the visitors in at the break with the momentum all theirs. However, just 6 minutes into the second period, Santos's mercurial young star produced an equally stunning response. Receiving the ball on the edge of the box, Robinho teed the ball up with his first touch before rifling it into the roof of the net to fire Santos back in front.

Kaka continued to orchestrate attacks for São Paulo at the other end, but with Santos' keeper Fabio Costa in fine form the visitors could find no way through. And then, in the 66th minute, when a flick on from Leo found Alberto in the box, the tall forward coolly lay the ball back to the edge of the area for Diego to angle a fine shot into the corner of the goal to give Santos a vital two-goal cushion. The seventeen-year-old wheeled away in celebration in front of the ecstatic home crowd. Breaking away from his team-mates he was joined by best friend Robinho, the two lapping up the applause of the crowd. Between them they had led Santos to a stunning, and unexpected, victory. After all the expectation and hype surrounding the pair at the start of the season, both had justified Leão's support of young, hungry players and rewarded Teixeira's investment in youth.

Four days later on 29 November the sides met again in the return leg at São Paulo's imposing Morumbi Stadium. Immediately São Paulo looked to claw back Santos's advantage and, with just 4 minutes played, Fabiano, the season's top scorer, headed his 19th goal of the campaign to reduce Santos's lead to one goal on aggregate. Robinho, the hero of the first leg, nearly netted an equaliser in the second period, but his left-foot effort was well stopped by Ceni. Minutes later, though, he was again the focal point of the Santos attack and played a crucial role in the Peixe's leveller. Just before the hour mark, Leo, surrounded by four São Paulo players, released the ball to Robinho, who quickly trapped the pass and in one movement slid the ball back to the striker who had continued his run into the box, free from his markers. The forward made no mistake with the simple chance Robinho's quick feet had created, restoring the visitors' vital two-goal cushion.

In desperate search of another goal, São Paulo rattled the Santos bar twice, but in the final minute, with the home side pushing forward, Robinho dribbled clear, checked in field and fed a pass square to Diego. The Santos star slipped into the penalty box before calmly despatching the finish to seal the tie. Santos had won 2-1 at São Paulo, defeating the league winners 5-2 on aggregate, and it had been the young duo of Robinho and Diego conducting the underdogs' destruction of the championship favourites.

Robinho, however, was just warming up. On 2 December in the semi-finals at home to Gremio, who had snatched a 1-0 aggregate win over Juventude, the youngster stepped up another gear and the confidence gained from his superb display in tandem with Diego against São Paulo was evident for all to see. Clever drag-backs and cute flicks epitomised his exceptional form and a fine exchange with Alberto on the edge of the Gremio box nearly saw the youngster hit the opener, but his effort flew straight at the visitors' keeper. Santos were completely on top and, on 37 minutes, Alberto rocketed a left-foot shot into the top corner to give the Peixe the breakthrough they thoroughly deserved.

Early on in the second half, Robinho uncharacteristically wasted a good chance, but a cheeky back-heel from Alberto a minute later put Santos two clear and in complete control of the contest. Robinho continued to dribble and tease the Gremio defence with his trickery, drawing two rash tackles from Anderson Polga that resulted in the Brazil defender being sent off. Robinho responded to the assaults by latching onto a chip from Alex to expertly lob the Gremio keeper Danreli with an intelligent one-touch volley that sealed Santos's comfortable 3-0 win to all but assure them of a place in the championship final. Robinho's strike, his second in post-season games, was an exceptional combination of the skill and audacity that was quickly becoming the hallmark of his flamboyant play.

The Santos celebrations after the game were soured, however, when Gremio players accused the Peixe's young star of 'anti-football' and said that his mocking trickery could see him becoming seriously injured. Danreli was at the forefront of the accusations, bluntly stating: 'Players get angry when they get dribbled all the time. He could end up having his leg broken.'

Ironically, in a country famed for its flamboyant football, several Brazilian players paid for their flair in 2002. Jaba, the Coritibia striker, was sensationally cautioned by referee Leonardo Garciba for provoking defenders with his dummying and dribbling, while in October of that year a second-division player was chased from the pitch by opponents for performing kick-ups on the halfway line to run down the clock. As well as having a reputation for producing artistic and creative forwards, Brazilian football is also renowned for its tough-tackling defenders. The unsavoury threat could easily have upset and concerned eighteen-year-old Robinho. He was unrepentant, though, and dismissed Danreli's bitter remarks: 'I'm not changing my style. Danreli didn't mean what he said; he was still angry at the defeat.'

Regardless of the controversy, Santos had sealed an impressive win over Gremio and marched on to the second leg safe in the knowledge that they had the upper hand in the tie. And so it proved, with a back-post volley from Rodrigo Fabri being the only goal of the game. It was Fabri's 19th of the season and placed him joint top of the goal-scoring rankings with Fabiano of São Paulo, but essentially this was not enough – Santos had qualified for the final of the Brazilian Championship and would face Corinthians over two legs at the Morumbi stadium. The result also gave the team a tilt at South America's equivalent of the Champions League – the Copa Libertadores – for the first time in 18 years.

Corinthians, who had also clinched the Rio-São Paulo Tournament and Brazil Cup in 2002, had made it to the final after a thrilling 3-2 victory over Fluminense following their defeat of Atletico-MG in their first play-off game. Like Santos, Corinthians rose from mid-table in 2001 and proved to be a formidable outfit that season. Despite coming unstuck against Santos earlier in the year, they had a strong squad and pundits were stretched to predict the championship winner.

It was the young guns of Santos who made the breakthrough in front of over 58,000 fans and in pouring rain at the showpiece Morumbi Stadium on 8 December. The

Peixe took the lead after just 15 minutes following a flowing movement up the centre of the pitch, which concluded with Robinho laying the ball off to Diego who, from just inside the Corinthians half, played an exquisite slide-rule pass between two defenders to release Alberto. The tall forward finished in typical style to put Santos ahead. Despite Corinthians' best efforts, Santos held off their challenge and doubled the advantage in the 90th minute. Robinho intercepted a poor pass across the Corinthians back line and skilfully lifted the ball over the onrushing defenders to release Renato, the Santos forward, to chip the advancing Corinthians keeper. Advantage Santos.

All Leão's side had to do was produce a repeat performance of their defensive display in the second leg against Gremio and then, for the first time in 34 years, the Brazilian title would be theirs. However, Carlos Alberto Parreira, the Corinthians boss who secured the World Cup with Brazil in 1994, was still hopeful of a reversal. 'It's going to be hard, but not impossible to revert Santos's advantage,' he said. Meanwhile, while Santos legend Pelé was lauding the current side, seventeen-year-old Diego was quick to temper expectations and remind the jubilant supporters that they still faced a tough battle to overcome the double-cup winners and take the title. 'Today's victory was an important step,' he observed, 'but we still have to play hard in the next game.'

However, Diego himself was the one on the end of 'hard' play. The young midfield maestro was forced off the field with a thigh injury just 1 minute into the second leg. With their chief creative player crocked and a two-goal advantage in hand, Santos might have been expected to put ten men behind the ball and desperately defend their aggregate lead. However, with 74,500 fans crammed into the Morumbi

Stadium – set to be the showpiece ground of the 2014 World Cup – the youthful side, with an average age of just 22, couldn't resist attacking Corinthians. Typically, Robinho led the charge, and on 35 minutes he performed a series of moves that would elevate him to the status of national star.

Receiving the ball on the left-flank, the eighteen-year-old dribbled at his marker, the veteran defender Rogerio Pinheiro. Backing off from the explosive and unpredictable forward, Pinheiro continued to retreat towards his own box. Robinho then unleashed his now trademark 'pedala' – a series of lightning-quick stepovers (seven in total) that tied Rogerio up in knots. As Robinho burst out of the manoeuvre and darted past Rogerio into the Corinthians box the defender flailed a hopeful leg at the forward, but brought Robinho down and gave away a penalty. It was a mesmerising piece of skill that dumbfounded one of Brazil's most respected centre-halves. The electricity, precision and success of the move more than demonstrated the dribbling capabilities of Robinho and the crowd erupted with applause at the play. Robinho picked himself up off the floor to convert the penalty and give Santos a seemingly unassailable lead.

However, with fifteen minutes to play Deivid pulled one back for Corinthians before, on 84 minutes Anderson put Corinthians within one goal of taking the title (due to their better season record they would win if the two-leg aggregate scores were level). But once again, Robinho took hold of the game. With two minutes to play, he skipped away from his marker, cut into the box and teed Elano up for a simple finish. The Santos fans exploded into celebration, knowing the title was now theirs. As play resumed, Corinthians won a corner and threw eight men into the box in an attempt to save the championship. However, the corner was a poor one and was cleared downfield to the only Santos player outside his own penalty box – Robinho. Trapping the ball, he then teased his two markers. He turned and dummied, and eventually released the ball to Leo, who had surged forward to join him. The striker fired emphatically into the top corner to crown Santos Brazilian Champions for the first time since 1964.

'We fought hard for this, we really deserve it,' Robinho said following his match-winning performance. 'I was aware of my responsibility to the team, especially after Diego left, so I decided to take it into my own hands.' It was Santos's first major title since the São Paulo state crown in 1984 and manager Leão believed this was only the beginning of his team's rejuvenation. 'They can produce a lot more,' he stated. 'We were down 2-1 and we didn't get nervous. The kids can really play.'

It was a sensational way for Santos to celebrate their 90th anniversary and Robinho had, especially in the latter stages of the season, eclipsed all expectation in his debut season.

CHAPTER 3

SECOND IS THE FIRST LOSER

Santos's victory in the national championship was an exceptional achievement for a team that had spent so many years in the doldrums. The organisation that bills itself as the best club of the 20th century in the Americas had long seemed like a fallen giant which had lost its way in the modern game.

Santos had spent the desolate years since their glorious era in the late 1960s throwing big-money wages at big-name players, who simply hadn't produced success on the field. With the side struggling to re-capture its glory days, the Santos supporters, who craved more titles, chanted for former greats such as Pelé, Coutinho and Pepe. The Santos board responded to the fans' desperate pleas by waving even more *reais* in the faces of star names – who, in the latter stages of their careers, could not reproduce the performances that had earned them their reputation.

It was a brave move from Marcelo Teixeira and coach Emerson Leão to end this regime and put their faith in Santos's respected youth academy. Their judgement was validated, however, with the remarkable performances of the young squad – the side earning much credit for their superb temperament in the high-pressure games in the post-season when they were holding onto a slender advantage or needing to create openings against some of the best sides in Brazil.

The team's attitude to the game also won the club new admirers. With all the courageous naivety of youth, Santos played the 2002 season with wonderful attacking flair, netting 59 goals in 54 regular and post-season games. The quick, dribbling wingers, Robinho and William, danced past their markers; the artistic middle men, Elano and Diego, carved out chances, slipped inch-perfect passes to the strikers and surged forward at every opportunity while the forwards were clinical in front of goal: Alberto with his thunderous left foot and the crafty Leo, nipping in to beat his marker to the ball in the box time and time again – a deadly duo. Leading this team with their virtuoso performances, Robinho and Diego quickly became the star names at Santos. Leão said of the pair: 'Diego organises the attack better than Zico – Robinho dribbles better than Pelé' – not bad accolades for seventeen- and eighteen-year-olds in their first season as professionals.

Reflecting in 2008 on his first season at Santos, Robinho believes his determination to succeed was key to him securing a place in the team: 'I really took my chance when I had it. There were a lot of other good players but when I was eighteen I was handed my debut for Santos, and I took my chance in the first team and showed my best football.'

But it wasn't just the Santos coaches celebrating the class of 2002: pundits and former pros alike lauded praise on the young guns from the east coast. 'The excitement about this team is they are so incredibly young,' said Alex Bellos, the British author of *Futebol: The Brazilian Way*. 'They dribble

all over the place.' Eduardo Tostão, who played with Pelé for
Brazil and is now a football writer, was also full of praise for
the Peixe: 'It's not just players with ability, but the collective,
the ability of these youngsters combining with a good team
structure. Santos, after Pelé's generation, became a team
without force, without what it takes to win. It is important
that Santos become a team [of recognition] again.'

Another league title for Santos after the long wait since the
days of Pelé was always likely to provoke comparisons
between the current Santos squad and the great players of the
1960s, when the club took five national championship titles
in a row. Fernando Santos, director-general of Santos, was
quick to quash comparisons, but did state his belief that the
squad was exceptional among their contemporaries and
highlighted Robinho as the embodiment of the current side.
'You can't compare these players with Pelé, who was a
complete athlete, complete in all areas of the game,' he
commented. 'But these guys have special qualities and do
things normal players can't do. They play with *alegria*
[happiness], it's spectacular football. Everyone enjoys
Robinho dribbling; he doesn't even have to score a goal.'

Robinho has also been dismissive of the comparisons with
Pelé – despite the legend himself highlighting the similarities.
He told *Four Four Two* magazine: 'I agree that our
physiognomy is very much alike. I've been compared to Pelé
in a thousand ways. But Pelé is unmatchable. People always
want to find a new Pelé. They can't.'

Next Pelé or not, Robinho's sensational debut season, and
particularly his form towards the end of the year, earned him
many plaudits as the Brazilian press sensed a star had been
born. 'A top-line player, a genius.' raved César Seabra in an
article for sports paper *Lance*. 'A rare precious stone who,

without exaggerating, reminds us of the King [Pelé].' Fernando Calazans of *El Globo* was also in awe of the young boy from São Vicente: 'Robinho's artistic football has made him the heir to Pelé's throne at the Vila Belmiro.'

It was not just the Brazilian people who were getting excited about Robinho either. As well as featuring in numerous 'ones to watch' articles in the British press, Robinho had also attracted the attention of scouts from Europe's top clubs. A report at the time suggested Karl-Heinz Rummenigge, the chairman of 2001 European Champions Bayern Munich, watched Robinho on a trip to South America and was impressed with what he had seen. Meanwhile, the press circulated rumours AC Milan and Barcelona – the club Robinho had allegedly supported as a child – were set to offer £20 million for the eighteen-year-old forward.

Robinho, sensibly, stated his intention to remain at Santos to develop as a player and as a person, though hinted at a favoured future move to the Nou Camp: 'If one day I am able to choose where I go, I prefer Barcelona, but for now there's still a lot more to come from me. You haven't seen anything yet. Ronaldo got where he is because he knows how to handle himself, on and off the field. I'm too young to leave the country or be far from my family.'

Robinho's close relationship with his family – and his mother in particular – resonates throughout his story. Indeed, when transfer speculation linking him to Europe arose, Maria was moved to dismiss the claims about her son: 'It's too early for him to be playing abroad. But if he is sold, his father will stay in Brazil and I will go with him. Wherever he goes, I will take care of him. He is my only son and has never lived alone.'

Talk of a transfer to a European giant after just one season for Santos was also rejected by Fernando Santos, who declared the club was not a production line for the likes of Barcelona and Milan, but intent on building a successful new era for themselves. 'Our objective is winning titles, not selling players,' he said. 'We did not develop Diego and Robinho to sell them. We find players at 13 and 14 years old, who don't have agents, and we develop them. For this, we have nutritionists, psychologists, physical trainers, so that today we not only develop an athlete but a citizen.' However, Santos conceded that if the sums involved could be used to further the club as a whole he might have to listen to offers: 'Football is a business and if we have to sell our patrimony it is so we can reinvest it in improving the stadium and bringing in new players.'

It is a plague on Brazilian football that, despite consistently having one of the strongest national teams in the world, their club football has never been able to offer the riches, glamour and prestige associated with the European game. Since the late 1980s Brazilian clubs have had to stand by as droves of national talent pack their bags for Spain, Italy and England. The case of Robinho highlighted those problems and sparked Pelé to call for a scheme or system to be established that would encourage young talent to remain in Brazil: 'We need to work so that these young talents stay here. Youngsters like Robinho cannot leave Brazil this early. This generation has everything to shine at the next World Cup.'

The road to the World Cup 2006 in Germany seemed set to begin for Robinho at the 2003 South American Youth Championships in Uruguay, where Brazil would be aiming to defend their 2001 title. Held every two years in January, the Under-20s tournament is used as the South American qualification system for the FIFA U20 World Cup, which takes place the following December. Robinho and his Santos teammate Diego were both predicted to shine in their first international tournament. After Teixeira suggested neither player was fit enough to play, however, it was revealed by Brazil Under-20 boss Jose Claudinei that the pair were simply too good for that level of football: 'They're above the average of the other players in the category and are already to play for the Under-23 team, which will dispute the Gold Cup in the middle of the year. Besides, Santos is playing in Libertadores, the most important [tournament] among clubs on this continent.'

Despite the compliment of being too good for his age level, Robinho was disappointed to miss out on his first opportunity to pull on the famous yellow national team shirt. 'It's a pity not to be called,' he was quoted as saying on Pelé's website, *Pelé.net*. 'I was really hoping to be on the team. But no problem, leave it for next time.' Eventually, Brazil finished second behind Argentina in the round-robin tournament, but with the promise of an opportunity to shine on the international stage at the Gold Cup, later on in the year, Robinho could look ahead to a promising 2003 season, aware his chance would come in time.

It was to be a bumper year for Santos. In winning the Campeonato Brasileiro, the Peixe qualified for the Copa Libertadores – the South American equivalent of Europe's Champions League. Their quest to be crowned champions of their continent, and thereby go on to contest the Club World Cup against the winners of the Champions League, was set to begin in February with a home-and-away group stage format. Just a month after the start of the Libertadores, the Brazilian league was also due to begin – in an entirely new format to the previous year.

SECOND IS THE FIRST LOSER

Although a historic success for the club, Santos's victory in the 2002 Campeonato was criticised in many quarters. The play-off system had allowed a side which had finished the regular campaign 13 points behind top-of-the-table São Paulo to build momentum in the post-season and come away with the crown. Brazil has traditionally used a hybrid system of league and knockout contests to determine its national champion, but in 2003 the authorities opted to use the European-style league format, based solely on points amassed over the season. Each of the 24 clubs would meet home and away over a nine-month contest, including 552 matches.

Although instigated to level the playing field, many club directors opposed the move, aware that the knockout rounds not only heighten fan interest, but, just as importantly, increase revenue. Vasco da Gama President Eurico Miranda, whose side finished 15th in 2002, described the points system as 'alien to Brazilian culture', but it was one the players knew they must adapt to. Santos would have finished well out of contention for the title and Libertadores qualification spots, had the 2002 season been based on the points system and Diego was well aware of the need for his young squad to develop their consistency: 'We know we'll need a better campaign than last year. We never played under the points system, but we know that every game will be decisive.'

First up for Santos, though, were the opening rounds of the Libertadores. They were drawn in Group 3 alongside Colombian powerhouse America de Cali, Ecuador's El Nacional and 12 de Octubre of Paraguay for the four-team group stage, from which two sides would qualify for the Round of 16.

Santos began their campaign with a visit to America de Cali on 5 February 2003. The Red Devils had taken the

Colombian title for a third straight season and, with Santos billed as favourites for their group, were expected to challenge El Nacional for the second qualifying place. However, those ambitions took a serious blow with the arrival of Santos. America wasted three good opportunities to take the lead and were made to pay when Leo converted from close range. A scrambled leveller from America pegged Santos back, but a thunderous Alex free kick from 30 yards put the Brazilians back in control. From then on it was the Robinho show: displaying all of the tricks in his armoury, the winger mesmerised the crowd and dumfounded America's defenders. His shimmies, dummies and darting runs easily exposed the Colombian side's defence as Robinho tore the opposition apart, creating glorious openings for his team-mates. He capped off his performance by blasting the ball into the roof of the net. Santos ran out 5-1 victors and Robinho, substituted just before the end, received a standing ovation from the America supporters. Now his talents were on show for all of South America to appreciate.

The Paraguayan outfit 12 de Octubre scored a surprise 3-1 victory at home to El Nacional. Two weeks later, on 20 February, the top two sides in Group 3 met at the Vila Belmiro. Octubre coach Alicio Solalinde admitted before the game to knowing little about Santos – other than that 'with Robinho as an explosive element for the goal, we'll have to take our precautions.' Robinho's performance against America was clearly going to make him a marked man. The dazzling winger, though, picked up where he left off against the Colombians. Latching on to a Diego back-heel, Robinho, in acres of space, delivered an inch-perfect cross for Elano to pull Santos level after a defensive mix-up allowed Octubre striker Bareiro to put the visitors ahead. A powerful penalty from Santos's Ricardo Oliveira and a superb free kick from Nene sealed the win for the Peixe and secured their place at the top of Group 3. After just two games Santos's superb form had pundits ear-marking them for their first Libertadores since 1963.

A 0-0 draw at El Nacional on 12 March put the undefeated Santos on the verge of qualification for the second round, with the home tie against America de Cali on 19 March to come. However, since the opening day defeat America had secured a 1-1 draw with El Nacional and hammered 12 de Octubre 4-1, results that drew cautious comments from Leão ahead of the fixture. 'That game was atypical,' he said. 'They're changing their line-up and it won't be an easy game.'

Robinho was equally concerned about an America backlash. The forward, who had instigated the demolition in Colombia, said: 'They know us, and we know they'll mark us closely. We'll have to vary our play to score. Our production really has fallen off a little in recent games, but we have to recover our full potential now. We'll play at home and that is an added incentive.' Fernando Castro, the America coach, was also confident of a reversal. 'America is very different from the team that Santos beat badly. The team has raised its level of play, is in a good phase and can get revenge,' he predicted.

Two minutes after kick-off at the Vila Belmiro, though, it was clear Santos were not going to give America much chance of revenge. Diego's right-foot shot on 2 minutes beat the America keeper and when Robinho hit Santos's second from inside the box 20 minutes later the match was as good as over. Oliveira netted a third late on to seal a comfortable win for the Peixe and ensure Santos qualified for the next round.

Santos continued that emphatic start to the Copa Libertadores by routing 12 de Octubre 4-1 in Paraguay on 25 March, with Robinho again finding the back of the net as the Brazilians hit their 15th goal in just five games, a mark of their superb early-season form. With the Brazilian league kicking off just five days later, Santos seemed ideally placed to begin their defence of the national championship against Parana.

Touted by many as favourites to retain their title, despite the new league format and with the ever-growing reputation of its star players – Robinho, Diego, Alex and Elano – Santos's superb start to their first Libertadores campaign in over 20 years only re-affirmed the general opinion that the Peixe would repeat their success of 2002.

On 30 March, just 28 minutes into the new season, question marks over their title credentials were raised, though, as Santos went 2-0 down at the Vila Belmiro against Parana, a side who had narrowly avoided relegation in 2002 by just one point. Renaldo silenced the home crowd on 13 minutes before Marquinhos doubled the visitors' advantage just 15 minutes later. Robinho, though, carried his excellent goal-scoring form in the Libertadores into the league and began Santos's comeback with a well-taken goal just before the break to drag the Peixe back into the game. Parana held onto their slender advantage and it wasn't until 15 minutes from the end that Santos midfielder Nene was able to level the scores.

Fortunately for Santos their shaky start coincided with a bizarre week in the Brazilian Championship. Perhaps it was first-day nerves, or the fact that the clubs were unsure how to approach the new marathon-long season, but eight of the twelve opening day fixtures ended in draws. Santos's slip-up therefore did little damage to their league aspirations.

However, a scoreless draw with Atletico Mineiro the following weekend proved more costly as two of Santos's biggest rivals for the title, São Caetano and Cruzeiro, secured impressive wins. Five days later, the Peixe's start to the championship went from bad to worse when Paysandu, who had finished 2002 in 20th spot out of 26, recovered from Robinho's opener to run out winners after Velber fired in two second-half goals. Santos eventually got their first win of the season the following Saturday with Elano and Oliveira helping the club to victory over Figueirense. The Peixe support breathed a sigh of relief and returned to the Libertadores.

Oliveira was again on the scoresheet on 16 April, hitting his sixth goal of the Copa Libertadores as Santos finished their group stage fixtures with a 1-1 draw at home to El Nacional. Leão had successfully guided Santos to the top of Group 3 without any real trouble. The Brazilians had looked the best side by far and tore their opposition to pieces on several occasions, most notably in the opening day rout of America de Cali in Colombia. America responded well, though, and qualified in second spot, four points behind Santos, with El Nacional and 12 de Octubre well off the pace.

Robinho had shone for Santos. The youngster had netted three goals in six appearances and, particularly in the encounters with America and Octubre, had run the show for Santos – his mazy runs, swift counter-attacking play and keenness to create openings for his team-mates all major factors in Santos's cruise to qualification.

The Group 3 victory paired Santos in the last 16 with Group 6 runners-up, and three-times winners of the Copa Libertadores: Nacional from Uruguay. On 23 April following a good victory away in the Campeonato to

Flamengo, who had themselves made a good start in the championship, Santos flew out to Uruguay knowing a tough encounter lay ahead.

The Peixe, though, got off to the best possible start at Nacional's Parque Central Stadium, when Alex nodded in from close range after a goal-mouth scramble with just five minutes on the clock. Oliveira then fired Santos into dreamland with a superb shot into the top corner just before half-time. Gabriel Alvez pulled one back for Nacional, but Santos were once again two clear when Robinho scored with a fine header on 65 minutes. With a 3-1 lead, Santos seemed certain to qualify for the next round; however, a double salvo from Nacional saw Horacio Peralta and Diego Scotti pulled the hosts level. Dramatically, Santos were then awarded a penalty with just 6 minutes to play. Robinho stepped up and coolly converted the spot-kick to surely seal victory for the Brazilians. However, Nacional were not done and a sensational game was brought to a close with Benoit hitting an equaliser in the fifth minute of injury time. Unbelievably, despite leading 3-1 and then 4-3, Santos managed to come away with a 4-4 draw, a result which, in the opinion of Nacional coach Daniel Carreno, gave the advantage to the side from Uruguay.

'We presume that they, playing at home, will try to pressure our defence and score a quick goal,' he said. 'If we can stop them, they will get desperate and that will only help us. We can exploit the defensive deficiencies of Santos with Alvez.'

Robinho's double did not go unnoticed either. Carlos Alberto Parreira, the Brazilian national coach, called the young star into his squad ahead of Brazil's friendly with Mexico, following the withdrawal of Rivaldo through injury. Diego had made the initial squad a week earlier but many believed that with the likes of Rivaldo, Ronaldinho and Ronaldo – who had all shone at the 2002 World Cup as the famous three Rs – Robinho would have to wait at least until the Gold Cup in the summer for an international call-up, when Brazil were fielding an U23 team in the North American competition. However, when Rivaldo injured his right thigh while training with AC Milan, Parreira decided to give Robinho his first opportunity to experience life in the Brazil squad.

The nineteen-year-old was apparently asleep enjoying a siesta when his mother woke him to tell him of the news. 'He jumped for joy,' she delightedly told reporters. Following a disappointing 0-0 draw with China and 2-1 defeat to Portugal earlier in the year, Parreira named a strong squad for the trip to Mexico, hoping a decent victory would restore the public's confidence in him as he tried to maintain Brazil's reputation for being the best team in the world following their success in Japan and South Korea in the 2002 World Cup. Alongside Robinho would be the likes of Dida, the AC Milan goalkeeper, Gilberto Silva, Arsenal's dynamic midfielder, the magical Ronaldinho, who had been delighting European crowds for Paris SG, and Ronaldo, one of Robinho's idols as he was growing up and Real Madrid's star striker. Also with him on his first tour would be Diego. Just as when they graduated into the Santos first team together, now they would be stepping onto the international stage both as friends and as two great hopes for Brazilian football.

Returning to the Brazilian league between the two legs with Nacional, Santos, with their new international stars, showed their forward play was in exceptional form as they hit four without reply against Fortaleza on 27 April. Following the game, Robinho and Diego met up with the

Brazilian squad before flying out the following Monday to Guadalajara, Mexico. On the Tuesday they trained together with the World Cup winners – a special moment for Robinho. The Santos pair were both selected for the match-day squad and spent the first half eagerly awaiting a nod or call from Parreira to prepare themselves to enter the action. On the pitch, though, the game was far from a classic. In a dour match, Brazil rarely threatened Mexico. Ronaldo nearly put the visitors ahead on the hour mark but the Real Madrid man fired tamely over the bar. Six minutes from time Diego was brought on to make his international debut in front of 60,000 fans. Robinho, meanwhile, remained glued to the bench, looking on and accepting his moment would have to wait for another day.

Along with the newly-capped Diego, he returned to Santos and helped the Peixe put three past Criciuma on 4 May. Robinho hit the crucial second in the 3-1 away win, a goal that demonstrated the forward's new-found ability to regularly hit the back of the net. In his debut season he had wowed supporters with his jinking runs and trickery, but in 2003, he was showing signs of adding a more lethal finish to his movement – something he put down to hard work on the training ground. He told Pelé.net: 'I'm improving in this area. I've been training a lot individually and I hope to put in a few balls against Nacional.'

However, it was Oliveira who put in the first ball against Nacional in the return leg on 7 May. In front of a sell-out crowd at the Vila Belmiro the Santos striker headed in an Elano cross after just 9 minutes to put the Peixe ahead. Oliveira had signed for Santos at the start of 2003 and was already looking like a shrewd purchase – that goal was his ninth of the competition so far. However, Nacional were determined not to lie down and a stunning bicycle kick from Sebastian Eguren levelled the scores on 37 minutes before Fabian O'Neill's free kick, just 4 minutes later, put the visitors in front. Santos, unbeaten in the Libertadores, profited from some fortune, though, when Eguren made a mess of a dangerous Elano free kick and headed into his own goal. With the scores level at full-time, the match went to penalties to decide the tie. Penalty shoot-outs create heroes and villains every time they take place. Fortunately for Santos their goalkeeper, Fabio Costa, emerged as the hero, saving three penalties while Oliveira, Elano and Renato made no mistake with their efforts. Santos's reward for their narrow victory over Nacional was a quarter-final match up with Mexico's Cruz Azul, kicking off with an away leg on 21 May at the famous Azteca Stadium.

Santos's exertions in overcoming Nacional perhaps came back to haunt them the following weekend when they crashed to a 2-0 defeat at home to Cruzeiro – a result which, come the end of the season, would prove crucial – while a 1-1 draw away to Juventude, thanks to an own goal by Brazil international Mineiro, was not exactly an ideal warm-up for the tough test against Cruz Azul that awaited Robinho and his team three days later.

In front of 95,000 fans Santos kicked off their quarter-final tie at the Azteca Stadium, hoping a more convincing and comfortable passage than the nail-biting and error-strewn contest with Nacional awaited them. This time, though, it was the hosts, not Santos, throwing away crucial leads in the first leg. A powerful shot from Francisco Palencia on 18 minutes was cancelled out by Renato before the Cruz Azul striker again put the home side ahead just after the break. The second equaliser from Santos was nothing short of sensational, however. Receiving a poor clearance from Cruz Azul keeper Oscar Perez, Diego immediately fired the ball back towards goal and somehow beat the stopper from all of 35 yards to level the tie.

It was a good performance from Santos and the scoreline drew optimism from the Peixe camp, especially as their Mexican opponents had struggled so much in their group stage away from home. Cruz Azul didn't pick up a single point on the road in Group 8 and Robinho summed up Santos's desire to qualify and determination to prevail at home against the Mexicans – whatever the cost.

'Whether we give a show or not, we want the victory. If it comes with dribbles, touch-passing and beautiful goals, fine. If not, it will be with desire and determination,' stated the young Brazilian. Desire and determination it was for Santos – Robinho himself personified his team's attitude by jumping on a mistake by Cruz Azul keeper Oscar Perez to slot into an empty net after the keeper fumbled on the edge of his area. Although Santos lacked their usual impetus, partly due to the absence of top scorer Oliveira through injury, the solitary goal was enough to seal the win for Santos and book a semi-final meeting with Medellin on 4 June. Medellin are a Colombian outfit and had knocked out Gremio in the previous round.

Medellin had topped Group 7 ahead of the highly-rated Boca Juniors and were real contenders for the Libertadores that year; however, with Robinho driving the team forward, Santos proved themselves to be a match for any side in the competition. Over the past twelve months Robinho had drawn many plaudits for his wizardry with the ball, but Tim Vickery, writing for the *Independent* newspaper on 31 May 2003, was quick to point out that, following the win over Cruz Azul, Robinho should also be applauded for his work rate: 'Robinho is a lightweight figure whose great strength is his ability to beat his marker on either side. For the first time in his short career he has run into problems. He has lost form, and is suddenly struggling to get past his opponent. Rather than slink into despondency, his reaction has been to work himself into the ground.'

Santos's reliance on its creative forward players, such as Elano, Diego and, of course, Robinho, was called into question by the Medellin coach Victor Luna, who saw the Brazilian club's lack of tactical knowledge as a major weakness ahead of the sides' semi-final Libertadores meeting.

'Gremio has a more balanced formation, is more tactical than Santos [and] has greater weight,' he said. 'When you don't let them play, they get desperate.'

Despite remaining undefeated in the tournament, Luna picked up on the fact that Santos had won just one game of the previous four after an impressive display in the group stages: 'Santos started very well but soon declined, and that's very serious in the Copa. The teams that go from less to more, as is Medellin's case, almost always are finalists.'

The mood at Santos, though, following victories over Internacional and a thrilling 3-2 defeat of local rivals São Paulo, was very upbeat ahead of the semi-final. 'The victories in the national tournament and the Libertadores have lifted the entire club,' Diego reported. 'Winning a derby before a semi-final motivates us. We're more confident.' However, the more experienced defender Leo cleverly tried to temper the optimism in the young squad. 'There are no naive teams, especially in the semi-finals,' he said. 'From the midfield forward they are very fast and deserve attention. The simple fact that they eliminated Gremio shows their strength.'

Santos it was, though, who demonstrated their strength in

the first leg at the Vila Belmiro. Despite failing to convert any of their four good chances in the first period, Santos emerged victorious thanks to a goal from substitute Nene, who rifled a powerful effort across the face of goal and into the far corner. The single goal advantage handed the initiative to the Brazilian club, especially as Medellin proved to be anything but free-scoring at home after notching just four in three during the group phase.

Luna, the Medellin coach, was just as confident after the game as he had been before it, though, and warned Santos the tie was not yet finished. 'The 1-0 score is surmountable with the strength that we'll put forth to obtain revenge.' The coach also declared he would be willing to risk Mauricio Molina and Felipe Baloy, his injured duo who had had to sit out the first leg.

Santos returned to the league on 7 June with an added air of confidence and scored two quick goals to earn a reverse over Guarani, but their preparations for the crucial semi-final second-leg in Colombia took a blow when São Caetano stole a late win at the Vila Belmiro, thanks to an 80th-minute goal from Marcinho.

That result seemed to have taken its toll on Santos when Medellin took just 13 minutes to erase Santos's first-leg advantage – Tressor Moreno cleverly lobbing Fabio Costa to break the deadlock. However, centre-half Alex rose highest on 36 minutes to head home a deep free kick to swing the momentum back Santos's way and the Peixe sealed their advantage when Fabiano fired into the bottom corner just after the hour mark. The returning Molina capitalised on an error from keeper Costa on 80 minutes, but Leo secured Santos's place in the final with a late tap-in. Santos emerged victorious, overcoming the Colombian side 4-2 on aggregate.

They were now on course to become the first team since 1978 to have gone unbeaten throughout the Libertadores.

On the other side of the draw Boca Juniors, despite finishing second to Medellin in the group phase, had progressed with ease through the knockout rounds. After a dominant home performance against Brazilian outfit Paysandu secured a 4-3 aggregate win in the first round and two 2-1 wins over Chilean side Cobreloa in the quarter-finals, the Argentinean club met America de Cali in the semi-finals. The huge gap in class prevailed and Boca, after a comfortable 2-0 win in Colombia, routed America in the return leg 4-0 to complete the passage to their two-leg final against Santos, kicking off on 25 June at Boca's notorious La Bombonera Stadium.

With the defence of their league crown on hold, Santos began preparations for the trip to Argentina. Boca had been deadly at home in the Libertadores, only losing to Paysandu in the Round of 16. The pitch at La Bombonera is the minimum size under FIFA regulations and this, coupled with the unique atmosphere generated in the stadium by the 54,000 fans seated close to the pitch, has made Boca's home an infamously difficult venue to visit. However, Santos captain Paulo Almeida showed little concern ahead of the tie and insisted his side would not be forced to change their style by the stadium, the fans or their opposition, who had collected four red cards and 22 bookings during the competition. 'Whoever thinks that we are going to be hiding on defence the entire time is wrong,' he said adamantly. 'We will look to push forward like we always do.'

The two sides hadn't met each other since a friendly in 1971, which Santos won 3-0, but more significantly, they did meet in the final of the Copa Libertadores in 1963, in which Santos, with the help of Pelé, overcame Boca and Diego Maradona to win over two legs 5-3 and retain their title. Forty years on from that momentous occasion, it seemed the stage was set for Robinho to walk in the footsteps of his idol and emulate the great Pelé by delivering the Copa Libertadores for the Santos fans. Boca, though, had their own young star, who had been capturing the hearts of their supporters just as Maradona had all those years ago: Carlos Tevez.

The atmosphere with La Bombonera was, as ever, electric. Here, Jeff Rusnak describes the scene for the *Sun-Sentinel*: 'A thick rain fell in the hour leading up to the match, but it would have taken hail and a swarm of locusts to drive the blue-and-yellow-clad Boca fanaticos from their seats. As the teams entered the field like heavyweights poised for a title fight, streams of paper cascaded from three tiers of seating, flares and smoke bombs were set off, and a chorus of singing that was sustained for the next 90 minutes began. Imagine nearly 60,000 people who have been incarcerated for several months, who are told they have one day to live and they will spend that day watching Boca Juniors play a cup final at Bombonera. That's a hint of the atmosphere Santos was challenged by in its first Copa Libertadores final since Pelé produced a title 40 years ago.'

Despite the atmosphere, on the confetti-strewn field Santos took control of the first 30 minutes. However, after being unable to carve out any real chances, Santos were shell-shocked by a fantastic strike by Marcelo Delgado. The Argentina forward, who had represented his country in the 1998 World Cup and was playing his final game at La Bombonera before a move to Mexican side Cruz Azul, beat Fabio Costa in the Santos goal with a lethally accurate drive from the edge of the box. Robinho could have levelled the match just before the break but he uncharacteristically fired over the bar when one-on-one with the Boca keeper, Roberto Abbondanzieri. As predicted before the game, wild tackles flew in from both sides and on 82 minutes Santos's Reignaldo Araujo was sent off for rough play. Just 60 seconds later the Brazilian club's deficit was doubled as a free kick from Delgado bounced awkwardly in the box and deceived Costa to give the 2000 and 2001 Libertadores winners the upper hand at the final's halfway stage. Under heavy rainfall Robinho and Diego struggled to get into the match as Santos not only saw their unbeaten run come to an end, but also failed to find the back of the net for the first time in the 2003 Libertadores.

After the game Diego Cagna, the Boca captain, believed his side still had much to do to secure the title, fully aware of Santos's attacking ability and the different prospect the Brazilians would be at home.

'This win hardly gives us any breathing room. Santos is easily capable of scoring two goals in Brazil,' he said.

Emerson Leão, though, was furious at the game's outcome. The Santos coach said: 'Boca wasn't the best team we faced. They were the luckiest,' while Diego also declared the result 'unjust'. Regardless of their opinions on Araujo's dismissal and Delgado's fortuitous second strike, Santos were 2-0 down and had to form a plan to break down the Boca backline in the second leg – a mountain Boca's coach Carlos Bianchi was certain would be too high for the young guns to surmount: 'We have obligated Santos to beat us by more than two goals and it won't be easy to score three goals against us' – the Argentinean side hadn't lost in the Libertadores by a three-goal margin since 2001.

Santos, though, were afforded some shooting practice at

the hands of Bahia in the Brazilian national league, smashing four past their visitors, and the Brazilians were also buoyed by Elano returning from a knee injury that had kept him out of the first leg. Ahead of the second leg of the final, Robinho was confident: 'I trust in my team and in my potential. I'm going to score against Boca Juniors.' However, this would be no easy task. Despite Santos failing to break down his side in the first leg, Bianchi set his side up to defend their lead – opting for just the one lone striker: future Manchester United forward, Carlos Tevez.

On 2 July Santos, re-located to the 75,000-capacity Morumbi stadium, burst out from their starting blocks with all guns blazing and their diminutive duo, Robinho and Diego, doing what they do best – electrifying home support. Robinho, tearing down the wings, jinked inside his marker while Diego continued to thread exquisite passes to the Santos frontline as the Peixe sought out an early goal. However, the Boca defence, strong on numbers and stubbornly content with their first-leg advantage, held firm. Eventually, though, the Argentinean side burst forward with a swift counter-attack up the centre of the field. Midfielder Sebastian Battaglia slipped a pass into the feet of Tevez who, with great strength, held off Santos's towering centre-half Alex. Tevez laid the ball off to Battaglia, who had continued his run, Alex followed the ball and when the midfielder intelligently played a reverse pass back to the unmarked Tevez, the Argentina striker was left with a simple finish past Fabio Costa. It was a fantastic move between the two Boca players and gave the visitors a surely unassailable advantage.

Santos continued to pour forward in the desperate hope of finding the goals required to drag back Boca's huge advantage, and it was Alex who made up for his earlier mistake – hitting a thunderous strike from 30 yards out into bottom corner on 74 minutes. Santos's rejuvenation did not last long, though. Delgado, the hero of the first leg, was found all alone by a defensive clearance, and with Costa playing almost as a sweeper and frantically trying to close him down, the forward coolly fired into the vacant goal from just inside the Santos half. A penalty kick in injury time was converted by Boca defender Rolando Schiavi to complete Santos's demolition and seal a 5-1 aggregate victory for the Juniors. The travelling Boca support, along with the club's players and staff, celebrated jubilantly at the final whistle and as they received the coveted trophy. For Santos the dream of recapturing the Libertadores, 40 years on from their last win in the competition, was over. 'We did what we could, but it wasn't to be,' Diego said after the game. 'We will get them next time.' Leão was also dignified in defeat, saying: 'There is nothing to do but congratulate Boca Juniors. They outplayed us and deserved the title'. Now he and his players would have to re-focus their attentions on the Campeonato Brasileiro. However, they would return to the national league minus Robinho and Diego – following their first taste of continental football the pair had been selected in an U23 Brazil team, which had been invited to the Gold Cup in North America.

The tournament brings together the 10 CONCACAF international teams of North America, namely USA, Mexico, Honduras, Guatemala, Jamaica, El Salvador, Martinique, Costa Rica, Canada and Cuba as well as two guest teams from South America – Brazil and Colombia. The contest, similar to the European Championships held every four years between UEFA national teams, is organised into a group phase with the top two sides qualifying for the knockout rounds. For the first time since 1993, the 2003 edition was not held entirely in the USA. Mexico City was selected to co-host the tournament with venues in Miami, Florida and Foxboro, Massachusetts.

Brazil were drawn with Mexico and Honduras in Group A with their first game, against Mexico in the Azteca Stadium, the highlight of the opening round of fixtures. Not only was this a repeat of the friendly held three months earlier, but an opportunity for Brazil's young side to demonstrate what they could do against solid international opposition. For Mexico, and their under-fire coach, this was a chance to score a victory against Brazil and ensure their progress to the next round of a competition they had every possibility of winning. Since his appointment after the World Cup Argentine coach Ricardo Lavolpe had endured a rough ride in the Mexican managerial hot-seat, suffering four defeats and earning two draws in his seven games in charge. Prior to the match he stated his belief that his side would rise to the challenge of Brazil, but from the kick-off the South Americans took charge. Robinho started up front, with Diego and the São Paulo duo Kaka and Julio Baptista supporting him. He nearly capped his first start in the famous yellow Brazil shirt with a goal on 22 minutes, but after racing clear of two markers, the Santos star pulled his shot just wide of the goal from close-range. Kaka, too, could have put the guests ahead, but he was denied by a controversial slide tackle from Mexico keeper Oswaldo Sanchez that had the Brazilian support appealing for a foul. Despite out-playing their hosts, Brazil ended the game defeated – a powerful header from Jared Borgetti in the 79th minute proving to be the decisive goal.

For Robinho it had been a decent debut; he had shown flourishes of what he could do and was fearless in the face of international opponents. His adaptation to professional football had been such a smooth transition that his play so often belied his age. Confidence to run at defences and try again if he failed earned him much praise in 2002. His rapid and continued development in 2003 had seen him bring not only a deadly finishing streak to his attacking play, but also a determination – and progressive enough fitness level – to work hard for his side, going forwards or backwards. And now, against a strong Mexican outfit he proved that he could also produce on the international stage, in just his second year as a professional and at the tender age of nineteen, when so many of his contemporaries were only just being eased into club football.

The defeat against Mexico left Brazil needing victory over Honduras to ensure they proceeded to the knockout stages. Although this should have been a formality against a small Central American nation with a modest football history, in recent times their opponents had been riding the crest of a wave, sparked off by a victory over Brazil two years previously in the 2001 Copa America. The previous September Honduras had risen to 20 in the FIFA world rankings and the mood in the underdogs' camp was one of confidence and excitement at the challenge of needing just one point against Brazil at the Azteca Stadium to keep their hopes of qualification alive. However, despite the best efforts of Honduras stopper Victor Coello, who had to repeatedly parry away the best efforts of Kaka, Diego and Robinho, his valiant side went down 2-1 to Brazil, thanks to a 15th-minute goal from Maicon before Diego netted his first international goal with 5 minutes to play, latching onto a cross from Robinho's second-half substitute Thiago Motta.

The result, combined with Mexico and Honduras'

scoreless draw in the final Group A game, sent Brazil through to the second phase of the Gold Cup, where they met Group B winners, and fellow South American guests, Colombia in Miami on 19 July. Colombia had comfortably come through their group by beating Jamaica 1-0 and then seeing out a predictable 2-0 win over Guatemala, however, against Brazil, the South Americans were expected to step up a gear and, for the tournament organisers, the clash of the two guest sides in the second round was ideal. They were also blessed by the fact that Brazil's Under-23 side had brought Kaka along in centre-midfield. The São Paulo playmaker, who had looked impressive against Mexico and Honduras, was sensational in the quarter-final tie with Colombia, breaking the deadlock in the first half after a crowd-pleasing dribble from Robinho and sealing the victory with a left-footed curling effort from outside the box in the second period. From the first whistle he controlled the game, spraying passes wide and through the centre, dribbling past his marker and clinically finishing his chances. 'I am happy and pleased... Today, everything went well,' he mused modestly after the game.

Elsewhere Mexico smashed five unanswered goals past Jamaica while the USA did the same to Cuba, both sides re-affirming their seriousness about taking the Gold Cup crown. The other quarter-final was also a lively affair – Costa Rica, inspired by a Centeno hat-trick to a 5-2 victory over El Salvador.

Next up for Brazil were co-hosts USA in Miami on 23 July. The Americans were the current holders of the title after seeing off Costa Rica in the 2002 final. That year, driven by Landon Donovan, who had hit four past Cuba in the previous round, and guided by the respected and long-serving manager Bruce Arena, the Americans were confident of retaining their title – regardless of Kaka's form. Arena was cautious, however, of Robinho. When the Santos forward came up in the press conference, he remarked: 'He's always putting defenders on their heels. If he breaks just one of those plays, then the opposition is going to be in trouble.'

Brazil began brightly and within 20 minutes the visitors could have been a couple of goals to the good. However, Nilmar, the Internacional striker, saw his fine strike ruled out for an earlier hand ball while Kaka fired against the post when he had Kasey Keller beaten in the USA goal. The USA took heart from their good fortune and, against the run of play, Carlos Bocanegra latched onto a Claudio Reyna free kick to head home from close range. Nilmar, Diego, Kaka and Robinho all had good chances to get on the scoresheet, but with Keller in inspired form none of the highly-rated forwards could find the back of the net. On the hour mark, following a Diego free kick, Nilmar did appear to pull Brazil level. The Santos midfielder struck the crossbar with a fine effort, but when Nilmar tapped in the rebound his celebrations were cut short by the linesman flagging for offside. The USA seemed to have fortune on their side, their incredible record of not conceding since the opening game of the 2002 Gold Cup seemed safe and Brazil's Under-23 experiment looked to be at an end. However, with only a minute left to play, Brazil's Ewerthon danced into the USA box and fired a shot at Keller. The keeper couldn't hold onto the strike and the rebound fell kindly for Kaka to slam home. With the scores level on the final whistle the game went to extra time, when a costly mistake from USA defender Cory Gibbs handed Brazil a penalty. Gibbs had handled in his own box, so Diego stepped up and struck home the vital goal to put the Brazilians in control of the semi-final.

Despite only using the tournament to test Brazil's young stars of tomorrow, coach Ricardo Gomes had led the South Americans to victory over a strong American side, beaten Colombia and narrowly lost out to Mexico. In the process they had bettered their previous effort when they were guests in 1998 and finished third, following a defeat to the USA – and all of that with the likes of Romario, Edmundo and Ze Maria leading the team. Brazil had enjoyed a fine run to the final and now had another opportunity to overcome Mexico, a result which would not only confirm the Under-23s as potential world-beaters but also somewhat show up the senior side that had floundered since their World Cup win.

Back in Mexico City for the final, on 27 July, the home side were roared on by 70,000 fans as they dominated proceedings. Mexico had not leaked a goal in the entire tournament, and as the game drifted on, they looked far more likely to find the winner than Brazil. Jared Borgetti nearly found a way through with 3 minutes on the clock after Luis Perez and Jesus Arellano had gone close and Rafael Garcia had been denied by some desperate defending from Alex. The young Brazilians held out for the 90 minutes, but just 7 minutes into extra-time they were undone by Daniel Osorno's strike from 15 yards. After doing so well to reach the final Brazil were unable to assert themselves on the contest – perhaps it was nerves. Their coach Gomes suggested that the players, who would form the basis of Brazil's 2004 Olympic team, had not been able to train together ahead of the competition, while Robinho pointed to the altitude problems of play in Mexico City. 'We were not good. The altitude affected us,' he conceded after the game.

SECOND IS THE FIRST LOSER

The Gold Cup Final finished on 26 July and so Robinho, Alex and Diego headed back to Brazil with the rest of the squad to re-join Santos for the remainder of its 2003 Brazilian League campaign. In the absence of the trio Santos had been going well under Emerson Leão and keeping pace with league leaders Cruzeiro. There didn't seem to be any hangover from the disappointing defeat to Boca Juniors in the final of the Copa Libertadores, initially with Santos sweeping aside Coritiba at the Vila Belmiro 3-1 after the visitors had Williams sent off on 6 July. However, with the backlog of fixtures piling up due to Santos's Libertadores exploits, and the absence of three of their star players stretching the squad, the club began to struggle to maintain their form. Three days after the victory at home to Coritiba, Corinthians took advantage of Santos's tiring legs to snatch a 90th-minute equaliser and deny Leão's boys what looked like a hard-fought victory. On the road at Vitoria there was more pain to come, when two more late goals stole the points for the home side when Santos looked as though they had done enough to earn a draw. However, the Peixe eventually got back on track with a 2-1 win in the Vila Belmiro against Ponte Preta on 17 July. Just after the half-hour mark the visitors had took the lead, but goals either side of the half-time interval from Oliveira and Luis put Santos back in control and the home side held on to seal the win. That victory sparked a run of good form for the São Paulo State side. Santos hit four past struggling Fluminense with Elano, Nene, Oliveira and Jerri on target for the Peixe before playing out a thrilling 3-3 draw at home to Goias on 24 July – Nene, Oliveira and Jerri all on the scoresheet once again. In their final game before the internationals returned, Santos fought back from a goal down against Vasco da Gama, with

Daniel hitting a 78th-minute winner for the home side as they stretched their unbeaten run to four games.

This left Santos in third place in the Campeonato Brasileiro, with 41 points from 21 games. Ahead of them, having played a game more, sat São Paulo with 42 points while Cruzeiro led the way with 46 points, also from 22 games. Following Santos's distractions in the Libertadores they had done extremely well to keep up their Campeonato charge and, with 25 games still to go, the Peixe were well in contention to retain their title.

Robinho's first game back for Santos was on 30 July, in a 2-0 victory over Atletico-PR, where he was on hand to set up the moves for Nene and Renato to fire the Peixe to three points. The victory, Santos's game in hand over the two sides ahead of them, was enough to propel Leão's side into second spot, two points clear of São Paulo and two points behind the leaders, Cruzeiro.

However, Santos's title ambitions were hit when, just a day after the victory away to Atletico, Ricardo Oliveira sealed a move to Rafa Benitez's Valencia in Spain. Despite his exploits being overshadowed in the Brazilian press by the emergence of Robinho and Diego, the forward had topped the Libertadores goal scoring charts with nine strikes and was a key part of Leão's side. Real Betis had been keen to move for the Brazilian striker but, after being put off by a sell-on clause in Oliveira's contract, it was Valencia who won the forward's signature.

It was no surprise when Santos, deprived of their marksman, looked blunt and without a focal point when they visited Gremio two days after Oliveira's sale. The home side scored early and ran out 2-0 winners to end Santos's unbeaten run. However, Leão's side, who finished top of the goal-scoring charts in the Libertadores, were back to their usual ways a week later at the Vila Belmiro. Elano capped a magnificent performance with two strikes in the space of 10 minutes as Santos played out a dramatic 3-3 draw against Ateltico-Mineiro on 7 August. A double from Alex in the next game, though, was enough to secure a victory for the Peixe away to Parana – a vital win for Santos's title hopes as league leaders Cruzeiro went down 2-0 to São Caetano on the same day.

The following Wednesday Santos played their first game of the Copa Sudamericana, an international contest for South American clubs on a par with the UEFA Cup in Europe. Twelve Brazilian clubs are split into four groups of three, with the top side in each group going into a play-off to decide which two teams would meet the other South American qualifiers in the quarter-finals. Santos were grouped with Flamengo and their first opponents, Internacional. The Peixe were rescued by a late Fabiano header as they scraped a 1-1 draw at home to Internacional on 13 August and were fortunate to get away with a point. However, the tie could have swung the other way had Robinho, who seemed to have lost his knack of hitting the back of the net, missed an open goal on the hour mark. After recovering from a league defeat to Figueirense to beat Paysandu and Flamengo in the Vila Belmiro and then hold Fortaleza to a goalless draw away from home Santos were in far better shape when they met Flamengo for their second Copa Sudamericana fixture on 4 September. Their hosts had been defeated 3-1 by Internacional in their first fixture and Santos, needing a 3-0 victory to better Internacional's goal difference, handed Flamengo another thrashing, despite missing Elano, Diego and Renato through injury. Their crucial three-goal difference was sealed late on when Leo hit a low, left-footed shot into the bottom corner with time running out.

Santos maintained that momentum in the league, routing Criciuma 5-2 at the Vila Belmiro on 13 September. The creativity of Robinho, Diego and Elano was in full flow as William scored a hat-trick and Renato hit a brace. Their reward for topping Group 1 in the Copa Sudamericana was a final preliminary round against São Caetano to determine who would progress to the international stage from Brazil, along with São Paulo, who had won the other tie against Fluminense. São Caetano had one of Brazil's best defences that season, allowing only 24 goals in 30 games in the national competition, with just the one goal conceded in the Copa Sudamericana, to Cruzeiro. The Big Blue had drawn with Cruzeiro 1-1 before beating Palmeiras 3-0 in their other fixture. 'It will be tough to get a good result,' predicted the defender Leo, Santos's hero from the previous round. 'We will need to do our best.'

Santos's coach Leão was of a similar frame of mind, keen to do well in the contest after coming so close to an international trophy in the Copa Libertadores. He decided not to rest any regular starters against São Caetano even though Santos were to face Cruzeiro in a crucial match in the national championship three days after the first leg. 'Our intention is to play with our top players,' he said. 'We need to make an effort to do well in this competition.'

The gamble paid off with Robinho hitting the only goal of the game from the penalty spot at the Antacleto Campanella stadium. São Caetano dominated most of the match, but failed to capitalise on the scoring opportunities and when Diego was felled in the box by Marcelo Mattos, Robinho coolly converted from 12 yards.

SECOND IS THE FIRST LOSER

The tactic had worked as far as the Copa Sudamericana was concerned; however, going into the decisive clash with Cruzeiro, it was unclear how much the tough battle with São Caetano would have affected Leão's spirited young side. Santos were level on points with Cruzeiro, who topped the table due to their superior goal difference, and a win would see Santos take first place for the first time in 2003. When the sides met in May, earlier in the season, Cruzeiro emerged victorious after second-half strikes from Victor Aristizabal and Mota. The game had been a lively encounter and many pundits expected an equally exciting exchange at Cruzeiro.

Nearly 70,000 people were packed into the Mineirão Stadium to see the top-of-the-table clash and the home fans were the ones celebrating after just 14 minutes when, following a foul on Cruzeiro midfielder Wendell in the Santos box, Colombian striker Aristizabal converted the resulting penalty. The game ebbed and flowed from end to end throughout the remainder of the first half and continued at a relentless pace after the interval. Robinho carved out several chances for himself, including a winding dribble that eventually saw him denied by Cruzeiro (and future Tottenham Hotspur) stopper Heurelho Gomes, before the keeper pulled off a wonderful save to push away Robinho's dipping free kick. However, in the 65th minute, Santos forward Fabiano was sent from the field for an alleged elbow on a Cruzeiro player. Leão and his coaching staff were furious with the harsh decision but their protestations were adjudged to be too strong and Leão was subsequently sent from the dug out. After that frantic 5-minute spell Cruzeiro made their extra man tell, and within 4 minutes of Fabiano's dismissal they doubled their advantage when Felipe Mello's shot was deflected past Fabio Costa. Aristizabal headed in his second of the game to secure the win for Cruzeiro, for whom the result solidified their place at the top of the league, moving them three points clear of Santos and five ahead of third-place Coritiba, with São Paulo close behind.

For Leão's side, the defeat was a tough one to take. Not only had they felt hard done by with the decision to send off Fabiano, but they were also of the view that the result could have been very different had they taken their opportunities. Nonetheless, Santos were only three points adrift with 15 games still to play. Despite their double defeat to Cruzeiro, the title was not out of their grasp.

They also maintained their cup ambitions with a solid 1-1 draw in the Copa Sudamericana at home to São Caetano on the first day of October, sealing a place in the quarter-finals of the competition. The game was hardly a thrilling affair, with Santos intent on defending their one-goal advantage, and will be remembered only for the fact that it was the first time a female referee took charge of an international competition match in South America. Silvia Regina de Oliveira, a Brazilian woman who regularly officiates in Brazilian league games, marked the occasion by showing a red card to São Caetano's Marcelo Mattos for fighting.

Santos avoided a rematch with Boca Juniors in the international draw, instead facing a two-leg tie with Peruvian outfit Cienciano, who had qualified through the Peru/Chile regional preliminary rounds.

They returned to league action on 25 September with a 1-1 draw with Juventude , William hitting the equaliser for the Peixe with just 15 minutes to play, much to the relief of the Vila Belmiro faithful. The goal was a crucial one, as at the same time on the other side of São Paulo, Corinthians had just been defeated by Cruzeiro, Maurinho hitting the winner for the league leaders. However, two days later Santos were not so fortuitous when they visited Internacional. The hosts' very own Diego struck a fine second-half goal, but despite the valiant attempts of Robinho and Nene there was no late equaliser for the visitors. The next day, a Sunday, the Santos players would have to sit and watch Cruzeiro come away with another solid, if uninspiring 1-0 victory, this time at home to Vitoria. Mota struck at the start of the second half for Cruzeiro who, coupled with Santos's results had now extended their lead at the top of the table to 8 points. Their commanding goal difference (15 goals better off than Santos) effectively made the gap nine points. São Paulo had also moved up the league and now sat just behind Santos in third spot with 59 points, the same number as the reigning champions.

In an ironic coincidence the very next week, on 4 October – after Kaka's São Paulo pulled level with Santos – the two clubs met in the Campeonato at São Paulo's Morumbi Stadium.

The contest was a heated affair with both sides desperate to establish themselves as the number-one contender to displace Cruzeiro as league leaders. Crucially William, Santos's striker, got the first goal for the visitors when he headed in Diego's corner on 45 minutes. The Morumbi stadium played host to many crucial Santos games in 2002 and the Peixe looked at home as they attacked their opponents and doubled their advantage 10 minutes later. Robinho controlled a long pass, teased his marker as he waited for support before flicking a pass into the onrushing Nene. The midfielder's shot was well stopped by Rogerio Ceni, São Paulo's stopper, but he could only parry the shot up into the air. William reacted quickest and nodded in the rebound. Luis Fabiano, the league's top scorer with 23 goals, struck late on for São Paulo to finish off a swift counter-attacking move, but it was not enough and Santos reclaimed sole possession of second place. Unsurprisingly São Paulo were frustrated to have let their opportunity pass and, in the build-up to both goals, goalkeeper Ceni was critical of the referee. 'William was offside in the first goal and Robinho touched the ball with his hand in the second,' he claimed after the match. Nonetheless, the victory halted Santos's three-game winless streak. Santos's first three-point haul since mid-September, though, only prevented Cruzeiro from pulling further clear as the league leaders showed no sign of letting up their rampant pace, winning their sixth straight match 3-1 with a second-half comeback after trailing Criciuma 1-0 at the break.

Unfortunately for Santos the victory over São Paulo was not the ignition they hoped it might be. Another disjointed performance in what, during the 2002 season, had been their fortress – the Vila Belmiro – was rescued by a late equalising header from Alex, while in the dying seconds Andre Luis, the Santos midfielder, summed up the team's frustrations, seeing red for a rash challenge. Leão surely craved the consistency produced by Cruzeiro, who yet again punished Santos by taking maximum points, this time from Flamengo.

The following Saturday, 11 October, Santos seemed intent on victory. From the referee's first whistle the Peixe burst forward and Robinho, catching the São Caetano defenders sleeping, slipped in his fourth goal of the Brazil Championship, and remarkably his first since May. After brilliant performances in the Libertadores at the start of the year, where he was not only lighting up the South American stage with his pace and trickery but also with his goal-scoring feats, the forward's barren spell of goals in the league was surprising. Coupled with the sending-off of São Caetano's Adhemar after just 23 minutes, the goal seemed to assure Santos of victory but, in a feisty encounter, Santos defender Pereira lost his head 10 minutes later and was also sent from the field.

With ten playing ten the game opened up and both sides had chances to score, with Robinho looking particularly encouraged after hitting the back of the net early on. However, São Caetano pulled level just after the hour, Marcinho converting a penalty for the hosts. Renato, Santos's influential midfielder, whose absence from the team through injury had contributed to the Peixe's wobble, thought he had won the game for the visitors, firing past the São Caetano keeper on 81 minutes, but just 2 minutes later that lead was wiped out: Marcinho again with the equaliser.

Needless to say, the Cruzeiro express rolled on with another 1-0 win away from home against Atletico Mineiro, their lead over Santos stretched to a commanding 12 points. São Paulo also hit winning ways, putting three past Corinthians despite going down to ten men on the hour mark. That victory promoted São Paulo to second in the league, a point ahead of struggling Santos.

Santos again failed to capitalise with their opposition down to ten men, when they met Peru's Cienciano at the Vila Belmiro on 17 October. The visitors went a man down on 41 minutes in the Copa Sudamericana quarter-final first leg, when midfielder César Ccahuantico saw red for a bad tackle on Diego. Despite Santos piling on the pressure they could not capitalise on the one-man advantage and wasted numerous scoring opportunities. The Peruvians then got on the board themselves when Alex fluffed a clearance into his own net in the 71st minute. Luckily for the Peixe, Robinho followed up his effort away to São Caetano with a powerful shot from outside the box 5 minutes later to level the scores, but Santos were unable to find the crucial winning goal in the final 10 minutes. The result gave Cienciano a huge advantage going into their home tie, knowing a victory in Peru would send them through to the semi-finals.

Santos's home fans must surely have been wondering what had happened to their champions when, 4 minutes into their match with Atletico-PR the following weekend, Ferdandinho put the visitors ahead with an angled drive from the edge of the box. However, whether Santos's players felt enough was enough, Leão had uttered some choice words or the dismay of the home support spurred them on, the Peixe bit back fiercely. First, 5 minutes after Atletico had taken the lead, Alex rose highest in the box to glance Diego's corner inside the far post before the midfielder himself got on the scoresheet. Diego was tumbled in the box and got up to convert the penalty himself, 5 minutes before half-time. Atletico clearly hadn't learnt their lesson, bringing Fabiano down inside the penalty area on 51 minutes, the striker gladly getting up to slot home the spot-kick. A header from Atletico's Santos reduced the deficit but the Peixe held on for a crucial home win which, following São Paulo's defeat the previous evening, put them back in second place. Crucially, Cruzeiro had finally slipped up as well, Juventude ending their run of eight victories with an away win. Cruzeiro's lead had been cut to nine points. Could Santos pull off a remarkable comeback with nine games to go?

The reigning champions certainly demonstrated they believed this was possible when they visited bottom-of-the-table Bahia the following Wednesday. They were merciless in their forward play. Santos slipped behind on 8 minutes, but then Robinho hit an amazing volley from 25 yards that looped over the Bahia keeper to level the scores 5 minutes later. It was a sensational strike from a player who looked as if he had re-found his confidence following his league goal against São Caetano. The lightning-quick winger then crossed for Leo to put Santos in the lead with a header.

Unbelievably, Santos allowed the basement team back into the match, Didi profiting from a mix-up in the Peixe defence. However, when Robinho nipped in to meet Renato's cross Santos seemed back in control. Sensationally the first-half scoring was not over yet – Bahia again levelling the scores, thanks to a good header from Cicero. The hosts then took the lead on 51 minutes when Pretto guided a free kick into the bottom corner past Fabio Costa. Santos refused to give in, however, and a brace from Diego – his first a fine drive from outside the box, his second a simple volley from Robinho's inch-perfect cross after the wide man mesmerised his marker with the *pedala* – followed by a tap in from William and a penalty from Fabiano fired the Peixe to a remarkable 7-4 victory.

The sensational win was made even more sweet for the travelling Santos fans when the news broke that Cruzeiro had gone down 1-0 at Internacional. For all the critics of the conventional league season, fearing supporters were being denied a thrilling end to the season, the battle between Santos, São Paulo and the wobbling Cruzeiro was a remarkable advertisement for the new system. Two weeks earlier, Cruzeiro had looked certain for the title when they were 12 points clear, but having lost two in a row, that lead was halved by an improving Santos, who found their rhythm again after a difficult mid-season.

That improvement, make no mistake, was in a large part

thanks to the rejuvenation of their nineteen-year-old star, Robinho. His display against Bahia, his superbly-taken first goal, his determined second, and his confidence and creativity that sparked Santos's fifth had seemingly vanished from his game after the Gold Cup. With Robinho now firing on all cylinders and again driving the Peixe forward, there was a renewed belief in the Santos camp that they could retain the coveted league title.

Santos continued their attacking renaissance three days later at Coritiba, a side vying for one of the top five places that would qualify them for the Copa Libertadores, with Robinho once again the star man for Santos. He opened the scoring for the visitors with a deadly finish after robbing the Coritiba right-back of possession and darting into the opposition box. Leo slotted in another before the break as Santos took control of the match and then, 5 minutes into the second half, Robinho pulled off a flamboyant drag back, deceiving his two markers who expected a pass down the line, cut into the box and curled the ball into the far corner to seal the points for Santos – another piece of genius from the young maverick. An outrageous free kick from Andre Luis, curling in from 30 yards out, completed the Santos scoring as the visitors romped to a 4-0 away win to reiterate their ambitions for the league title.

Just four days later the league title was all Santos had to aim at. Ten thousand feet above sea level in the Andes, Cienciano dominated play from the start in the second leg of the Copa Sudamericana quarter-final at the Garzilaso Stadium. German Carty gave the Peruvians a deserved lead after 11 minutes, hooking in a left-footed shot that gave Santos keeper Fabio Costa no chance. Although Elano tied the match 2 minutes later with a powerful shot from just outside the box, Cienciano were the dominant side and Carty headed in his second to give the Peruvians a 2-1 lead at the break. Both sides missed good opportunities in the second period, but with the score unchanged, Cienciano progressed to a semi-final against Colombia's Atletico Nacional, while Santos returned to Brazil with the focus solely on the defence of their league title.

With that renewed aim, Santos returned to the scene of their league victory of 2002 and, despite an early setback, they defeated Corinthians 3-1 at the Vila Belmiro on 2 November. After a ferocious strike from Fabricio put the visitors ahead, Robinho struck back with an equally impressive curling effort from the edge of the box for his fifth goal in his previous three league games; the number 7 truly on fire for Santos at that time. Second-half strikes from Pereira and Fabiano sealed the win for Santos, while Cruzeiro and São Paulo also came out on top in their matches.

There was a flurry of second-half goals in Santos's next fixture on 5 November, at home to Vitoria, with the Peixe coming out on top of the shoot-out, 3-1. São Paulo and Cruzeiro continued to pick up wins to keep the pressure on Leão's side, but all Santos could do was keep beating the teams put in front of them, which they did once again the following weekend, away to Ponte Preta. Both teams exchanged the lead with a double from Diego giving Santos a 3-2 advantage on the hour. However, Santos needed a Renato strike 10 minutes from time to take the three points after Vieira levelled for Ponte Preta.

With four games to play, and still six points adrift of Cruzeiro, Santos were required to win their remaining games and hope the league leaders succumbed to a couple of defeats. A defeat for Santos at home to Fluminense and a victory for Cruzeiro away to Parana would seal the title for the table-toppers, but Santos had no intention of giving up their crown that easily. Despite a nervous first half and falling behind quickly after the interval, three goals in the space of 10 minutes from the ever-reliable trio of Diego, Alex and Fabiano led to a 3-1 victory for the home side – which matched the scoreline at Parana, where Cruzeiro had defeated their hosts. Santos lived to fight another week but they were unable to maintain their winning streak and on 30 November they finally conceded their crown to Cruzeiro. The Peixe went down 3-0 at Copa Sudamericana qualifiers Goias, while Cruzeiro did the business at home to Paysandu, comfortably winning 2-1 to clinch their first Brazilian league title.

Santos concluded the season with a couple of score draws to clinch second spot, finishing 13 points behind Cruzeiro and 9 clear of third-placed São Paulo. Cruzeiro had enjoyed an amazing season, finishing on 100 points from 46 games and scoring 106 goals in the process. Santos, though, had put up a valiant defence of their crown. After being heavily criticised for taking the 2002 title due to a run of form at the end of the campaign, they had proved in 2003 that over the course of 46 matches they had the staying power and could produce the consistency and dominance to justify their position as one of the best teams in the country.

The Libertadores journey far exceeded the wildest dreams of the players and fans, and perhaps this had taken its toll on Santos's campaign. The slow start to the season could be put down to their pre-season qualifying rounds in the Libertadores while there was clearly a hangover from the defeat to Boca Juniors in the league, with a spell of three out of four games after that final seeing Santos players concede late goals and miss out on valuable points. The Peixe were also unlucky to lose their two key players, Robinho and Diego, to the Gold Cup tournament midway through their campaign. That, however, was the price to be paid for unearthing two fantastic talents who, within 12 months of their debuts, were contending for spots in the Brazil squad and revered as critical to the country's defence of its World Cup.

As a mark of the exceptional season that the pair had had, and perhaps a signifier of how much Santos missed the duo, both Robinho and Diego were named in the sports journalists' South American Team of the Year, with Boca's Carlos Tevez scooping the Player of the Year award. It was evident for all to see that when Robinho was in full flow, as he was against Bahia and Coritiba in October, how devastating he could be to defences. He netted nine goals in the league of 2003, but with crucial strikes in the Libertadores, many assists throughout both campaigns and, of course, his contribution to Brazil's Under-23 side making the final of the Gold Cup, it was a year in which he re-affirmed his status as a fast-developing superstar. The 2004 season, though, would prove to be even more eventful for both Robinho himself, Santos and his family.

CHAPTER 4

TROPHIES, TRANSFERS AND ABDUCTIONS

The following January was a disappointing one for Robinho. After the superb efforts of the Brazil Under-23 side in the Gold Cup of 2003 they were hot favourites, along with Argentina, to progress through the Olympic Games qualification tournament. Many expected them to go on to claim the only football title that they had yet to win, at the 2004 Athens Games.

The tournament includes Under-23 sides from all 10 South American countries, with two teams qualifying for the Olympics. In 2004, the contest was held in Chile and the teams split into two groups based on previous performances in the competition.

The Samba Boys got off to a fine start, beating Venezuela at Concepcion by four goals and then over-powering Paraguay in a 3-0 win at the same venue, with Robinho scoring from the penalty spot in both games. He then netted Brazil's equaliser against Uruguay in a 1-1 draw, his marvellous end-of-season form showing no sign of letting up. Another 1-1 draw, in the final group game against Chile, meant Brazil finished second in Group A on 8 points, 2 behind Chile who had dropped just 2 points from their four matches. This meant the Gold Cup finalists would face a play-off against Group B's third-placed side, Colombia, in Valparaíso on 18 January 2004. It was a comfortable game for the Brazilians who, thanks to goals from Alex, Marcel and Dudu, ran out 3-0 winners, progressing to the final qualification group with Paraguay, who had defeated Ecuador in the other play-off match, and the two group winners, Chile and Argentina.

In a tight match, just three days after their play-off game, Brazil lost by a single goal to Argentina, who netted through Gonzalo Rodriguez 13 minutes from time. A comprehensive victory over Chile, though, in their next match, with Diego rounding off a 3-0 victory, seemed to assure the Samba Boys of a place in Athens. However, Paraguay, who the Brazilians had breezed past in earlier rounds, scored on the half-hour mark in the final round of group games and clung onto their lead to finish in second spot with 6 points. The Paraguayans snatched a late win over Chile with two goals in the last 10 minutes and, with a run of form in the latter stages of the contest and with the help of some clinical finishing, clinched an unexpected place at the Olympics. Argentina drew their final game to top the group and book their place on the flight to Greece, where eight months later, they destroyed their opposition and took the gold medal. Under their coach, Marcelo Bielsa, they did not concede a single goal in the tournament, and Carlos Tevez was the star of the show, netting eight goals including a hat-trick in the 4-0 quarter-final rout of Costa Rica and the winning goal in the final over Paraguay.

While Robinho had little to show for his efforts in 2003, in terms of silverware, after losing in the final of the Copa Libertadores to Boca Juniors, finishing runners-up in the Gold Cup with the Brazil youth team, coming second in the league to Cruzeiro and losing out in the quarter-finals of the Copa Sudamericana, he still shone in a fantastic second season that re-affirmed and increased his reputation as one of Brazil's hottest talents.

He did receive individual recognition for his fine form, though, not only being named in the Copa Libertadores Team of the Year, but also being nominated for the Laureus World Sports Awards for the Newcomer of the Year, alongside the likes of Spanish Formula 1 driver Fernando Alonso and sixteen-year-old Russian tennis player Maria Sharapova. Distinguished company indeed.

Back on duty for Santos in April 2004, Robinho's best efforts were not enough to keep them from crashing out of the São Paulo state championship semi-finals with a 7-3 aggregate defeat to local rivals São Caetano. The tournament is often seen as a good marker for how the Brazilian clubs will perform in the coming season, though with the dawn of the new full-league season, with its marathon of home-and-away matches, the importance of the state championship as a pre-season indicator of form was somewhat diminished, although it was a contest still held dear by the fans of the São Paulo state clubs and one that Emerson Leão would have been keen to win after failing to collect silverware when well-placed in the Libertadores, league and Copa Sudamericana.

To address this problem, and in the hope of finding the missing ingredient that would ensure the Peixe did not fall short at the crucial moments in 2004, an impressive squad was made stronger with four new signings. Paulo César arrived from Paris Saint-Germain, returning to Brazil just one year after moving to the French club, and defensive midfielder Clayton, who had shipped 60 goals in 46 games last season in the Campeonato Brasileiro, arrived from Internacional to fortify Santos's defence.

The 2002 league winners also signed up striker Leandro Machado. At the age of twenty-eight, he made Santos his eleventh club after stints at Flamengo, Sporting Lisbon and Dynamo Kiev. A young forward, Basilio, was also added to the powerful attack the Peixe had in place.

Santos were, however, forced to see a key player leave the club. Alex was signed for £5million by Chelsea in January 2004, but due to work permit problems had to be 'parked' at PSV Eindhoven until, three years later, Chelsea invoked a clause in his contract to sign him for the grand sum of 50p from PSV, who acted as a feeder club for the goal-scoring centre-half. It was a blow to lose Alex, but the defender was able to remain at Santos until the end of the regular season in Europe as the Peixe prepared for the 2004 Libertadores.

After coming so close to landing the title in 2003 and following their good run of form at the end of the year in the league, Santos were among the favourites for the South American club contest and began their campaign with a trip to Bolivia's Jorge Wilstermann on 5 February. The Bolivian league runners-up were conquered, though, by Brazil's national runners-up, with Santos running out 3-2 winners. An injury to Elano was a disappointing blow for the Peixe but their first victory in that year's competition buoyed the side and put them in second spot behind Barcelona of Ecuador who, after two games, were on 4 points.

But, on 18 February Santos were unable to capitalise on their game in hand, drawing 2-2 with Guarani of Paraguay at the Vila Belmiro – the visitors salvaging a point in the last minute, thanks to striker Lopes' header, which beat Santos keeper Nelson Bernal.

The draw was a disappointing result for Santos and the team's young stars came under fire from some quarters for not taking the games seriously and were accused of being distracted by offers from Europe. If they had been distracted by giants from abroad against Guarani, they were certainly more focused on the task at hand when they travelled to Ecuador in the next round on 3 March to meet Group 7 rivals Barcelona. The Brazilians dominated the first period with new signing Basilio – who had notched eight goals in the Libertadores and São Paulo State Championship since his pre-season move – and Robinho driving the Brazilians forward. Renato opened the scoring just before the break with a long-range effort and Basilio scored shortly after half-time on the counter-attack. Rodrigo Texeira pulled one back for the Ecuadorean side, but Robinho rounded off the win when he beat Jose Cevallos in the 85th minute to seal a 3-1 victory for Santos that put the Brazil's on top of their group.

Eight days later, Robinho scored the game-winning goal in the reverse tie before being sent off for the first time in his career. The young striker had a goal disallowed just before the interval but eventually found the net in the second half, heading in a cross from Marco Aurelio for his second goal in two games. However, his evening was marred by a late challenge that earned him his second yellow card with 4 minutes to play. The victory, though, opened up a 6-point lead for the Brazilians at the top of the table, practically ensuring a spot in the second round, meaning the absence of Robinho through suspension was unlikely to be devastating to their qualification hopes.

Indeed, Santos were able to maintain their winning form

with a 2-1 win away to Guarani on 25 March, Basilio and Robson each finding the net in Paraguay to ensure Santos's safe passage to the knockout stages. Santos's group games were completed with a 5-0 drubbing of Jorge Wilstermann at the Vila Belmiro on 14 April, where midfielder Diego capped a superb performance by netting a brace as the returning Robinho closed the scoring with a well-placed penalty, with 2 minutes to play.

Santos closed their group phase with five wins and one draw from their six ties, giving them the highest points total of all the other qualifiers. Now, with three weeks until their First Round match against Liga Deportiva Universitaria (LDU), they re-focused their attentions on the Campeonato Brasileiro that recommenced on 21 April 2004.

Favourites for the title after last season's league finish and their impressive run in the Libertadores, Santos were caught cold by hosts Parana in their first game of the season. Galvão slotted into the Santos net with less than a minute on the clock to stun the visitors to the Estádio Vila Capanema. The Peixe equalised through their adventurous full-back Leo, but were once again behind on 41 minutes, Carlinho ensuring the home side took a goal-advantage into the half-time break. Santos's task wasn't made any easier when defender Luis was sent off in the second half and the hosts made their numerical advantage pay, hitting their third shortly after the dismissal. Robinho did make it onto the scoresheet late on to kick-start his goal-scoring record for the season, but this was not enough to prevent last year's runners-up from slipping to a disappointing defeat.

A brace from Diego in a 2-0 win over Botafogo in the next round of league games, on 25 April, seemed to see Santos back on track, but the following Wednesday Figueirense, who had been an early-season surprise package with wins over Internacional and an away-day mauling of Atletico, beat the Peixe 2-1. Robinho again found the net with a real poacher's goal, but his strike came between efforts from Fernandes and Sergio Manuel that gave the hosts their third straight win and put them top of the standings. For the second game of the season Santos also had to battle on with just ten men, with new signing Clayton red-carded for a second bookable offence just before the hour mark.

It was poor start from Santos and, after their lacklustre opening in 2003 that saw them fall well behind the early pace set by the likes of São Paulo and eventual winners Cruzeiro, the Peixe would have to quickly find a solution to get back on track and back up with the league leaders.

The defeat and extra exertions of covering for the dismissed Clayton clearly took their toll and Santos came unstuck again in the league. This time, on 2 May, at the Vila Belmiro, it was reigning champions Cruzeiro doing the damage and eventually emerging 3-1 winners. Diego struck for the home side on 62 minutes, but by then Santos were 2-0 down and Dudu completed his brace for the visitors in the final minute to give Cruzeiro a 3-1 win and deliver a psychological blow to the players, supporters and staff at Santos, who had been confident of surpassing last season's league winners.

The encounter was a far from ideal way of preparing the Peixe for their next match – their vital Round of 16 encounter with LDU on 6 May. At least the tie gave Leão's side a chance to forget the Brazilian championship for a while, where three defeats in four games had seen the 2002 champions slump to seventh from bottom. Returning to the Libertadores, Santos were the standout side of the group stages: they were unbeaten in six games and netted 16 times in their six matches to amass the best points total of the competition. 'We can't lower our heads now,' Robinho told the press before the first leg match, knowing that a slip-up at this stage of the Libertadores would be far more damaging than their poor run of form in the league which could be accounted for over the remaining 42 matches. Santos's Libertadores hopes would not be so easily resurrected with a bad display in Ecuador on 11 May. LDU had come through a strong group in second spot behind São Paulo, but having hit 13 goals and conceded just 3, they were unlikely to give Santos a comfortable passage into the quarter-finals – and so it proved.

Santos, released from the pressure and expectation that seemed to haunt them in their national league, exploded into action from the first whistle in Quito. Robinho, picking up a loose ball on the edge of the LDU area, unleashed a phenomenal drive into the top corner, giving the home side's keeper absolutely no chance as the ball swerved away from his flailing arms and into the net – putting Santos ahead after just 2 minutes. Sensationally that lead was doubled by Elano, 2 minutes later. Robinho, again involved in the move, pushed a pass towards Elano, who stepped inside his man before slotting past the keeper.

However, Santos disastrously and criminally threw away their advantage. LDU hit their first reply through Paul Ambrossi, who headed in a long pass on 17 minutes. Santos held their lead until half-time but then the floodgates opened and Patricio Urrutia levelled the scores in the 47th minute before Ambrossi got his second and Franklin Salas capped the victory in the 84th minute with a header. From a 2-0 lead inside the first 5 minutes, which should have ensured a victory for Santos, not just in the first leg but in the entire tie, the Peixe capitulated to a scoreline which gave LDU a fantastic chance of sealing a place in the quarter-finals at the Vila Belmiro.

Coupled with the team's poor start in the league, their hammering in Ecuador enraged the club's board and shortly after the match it was announced that Emerson Leão had resigned as coach.

In his two years at the club he had led Santos to their first national championship since the days of Pelé and to the Libertadores Cup final in 2003, but now the coach had decided he was no longer the man to lead Santos. 'The marriage is over,' Santos's director of football Francisco Lopes told *Jovem Pan* radio station after the 4-2 defeat to the Ecuadorean champions.

Leão, a Brazil goalkeeper in the 1974 and 1978 World Cups and national team coach for eight months before being sacked in 2001, had fallen victim to the volatile world of Brazilian coaching, where it takes only a short run of relatively poor results to undo a manager's previous good work.

'It was a friendly separation,' insisted Lopes. 'The team had become used to victories and we were under pressure.' Despite the poor start to the season, though, it would have been hard to imagine Leão not turning Santos's campaign around as he had done in 2003, but supporters had also been demanding his resignation at the Vila Belmiro the previous weekend when the side lost 3-1 to Cruzeiro.

Within days Leão was back in work, though. His talents and revival of Santos had clearly not gone unnoticed at Cruzeiro, the club he had pushed all the way in the Brazilian league previous season and who had ironically spelled the end of his reign at Santos by defeating his side in front of the club's supporters. Strangely, his agreement to join Cruzeiro came within a matter of hours after former Cruzeiro boss Vanderli Luxemburgo agreed to join Santos – the two top teams of 2003 effectively swapping managers for the 2004 campaign.

Luxemburgo's arrival was the shake-up Santos needed and they put in a good performance in their return leg against LDU. Diego put Santos within one goal of LDU with an accurate volley before Robinho teed the midfielder up for his second from the edge of the box. The 2-0 win took the tie to penalties, which Santos edged 5-3 after the series finished 4-4 on aggregate. It was a lucky escape for Santos, but the victory merely papered over the cracks of their dismal start to 2004.

Another defeat in the league came away to Atletico-PR before Santos hosted Colombia's Once Caldas in the Libertadores quarter-final on 20 May. Knowing a decent run in the Libertadores was needed to keep their disenchanted support appeased, Santos put on a much-improved display at the Vila Belmiro in the first leg encounter. Just 2 minutes into the match, Robinho had a good chance, but his right-foot shot from inside the box flew just wide, while Santos's best opportunity of the half fell to striker Deivid, but his header smashed against the upright. Santos made life difficult for themselves on 54 minutes when Leo saw red for a second bookable offence. However, half-time replacement Basilio finally put the home side ahead on 83 minutes, slamming home from six yards out. The goal seemed enough to ensure Santos took a lead into their tricky second leg in Colombia, but Once hadn't given up and Arnulfo Valentierra netted the equaliser with just 3 minutes to play after a lapse of concentration from Peixe defender Pereira.

The score draw was not ideal for Santos, who in front of their home fans had been so strong in this competition over the previous two seasons. With the volatile and intimidating atmosphere created in stadiums across South America, obtaining a result away from home is a particularly difficult achievement but Luxemburgo's new charges would have to do just that. A morale-sapping 4-0 defeat at home, three days later in the Campeonato, didn't help much either. Santos, hosting Palmeiras, had already slipped behind to goals from Vagner Love and Mucoz when Pereira saw red for a reckless challenge. Inevitably the game slipped away from Santos, and in front of an irate crowd they slumped to their fourth defeat in five games in the league.

Unsurprisingly Santos were unable to continue their habit of belying their league form in the Libertadores and on 27 May could not produce the victory they needed in Colombia, eventually going down to a second-half free kick from Once's hero of the first leg, Valentierra, after their host's keeper Juan Carlo Henão denied Diego on several occasions.

For Santos, the dream of replicating the run to the final they achieved in 2003 was over. Although disappointing for the players, who came so close to taking the prestigious title against Boca the previous season, it was perhaps just as well because Santos really couldn't afford any distractions from the league if they still harboured any real hopes of the title, or at least a finish that would ensure them a place in the Copa Libertadores 2005.

Santos returned to league action with a draw away to Atletico Miniero on 30 May. Robinho missed a first-half penalty for the visitors as they battled for their seventh point from eight games, a poor return that left them in 20th place in the league. However, they finally got back on track with a victory away to Vitoria. The win seemed to breathe confidence into the young side and Robinho inspired another win three days later at the Vila Belmiro against Internacional, incredibly overcoming the height difference he conceded to the visiting defence to rise highest and head home Diego's corner for Santos's first. The Peixe went on to win 3-0, a result followed up with their third win in a row at home to Guarani.

Their title hopes, however, took a huge blow when Robinho's friend and Santos's key midfielder Diego signed for Portugal's Porto. The European champions signed the superb nineteen-year-old for £4.5 million on 30 July 2004. It was a sad day for Santos, but for Diego this was an opportunity to continue his development in Europe. Unfortunately for the midfielder he was unable to blossom at the Portuguese giants and is now far more settled at German side Werder Bremen.

However, there was no let-up in Santos's run of wins. Corinthians, Ponte Preta and their great rivals São Paulo all fell at the hands of the improving Santos and when Robinho and Basilio netted within the last five minutes against Flamengo on 14 July, the run of seven straight victories had propelled the Peixe into top spot in the Campeonato.

Eventually that fantastic run of results came to an end at Fluminense, when Marcelo struck a winner for the hosts. However, it did not take long for Santos to overcome the setback and three days later on 21 July Robinho netted a pair of goals as they routed Criciuma 5-2 to re-take the lead in the Brazilian championship.

Palmeiras, who had taken advantage of Santos's slip-up at Fluminense, had fallen to their first defeat in 10 games while reigning champions Cruzeiro were also beaten, by Vasco de Gama.

Robinho was again on the scoresheet at Goias. Rediscovering his goal scoring form, the young forward put the visitors ahead with an early header to kick off a thrilling exchange of goals between the sides, which eventually concluded 3-3. Santos, who had won the title in 2002, thanks to their exceptional attacking play, were top scorers in the league with 37 goals from 18 matches and that ratio leapt up in their next game, at home to Coritiba, where a brace from Elano and goals from Deivid and Basilio fired them to a comprehensive 4-2 win.

Three days later the crowds at the Vila Belmiro were treated to another flurry of goals from the Peixe, this time routing a reasonable Paysandu side 6-0. Robinho took his recent run of goals to five in the last four with a fantastic double. His first came about after the diminutive forward squeezed between two defenders before dribbling round keeper Paulo Musse to slot into the empty net. After Elano and Ricardinho finished off good moves, Robinho nodded home at the back post to give the hosts an unassailable half-time lead of 4-0. After the interval Basilio slotted in a fifth before Robinho appeared to seal his hat-trick with a thunderous strike from outside the box. However, replays showed his effort in fact cannoned off the post, back onto the diving goalkeeper and in off the back of Musse's head for an extraordinary own goal – the club's 18th in their last four games. Nonetheless the feast of goals served up for Santos's support secured the Peixe's tenth win in 12 matches, propelling Santos 3 points clear of their nearest rivals, São Paulo, as the season approached the halfway mark. Two successive defeats brought Santos back down to earth before Robinho struck an 82nd-minute winner against Vasco in a 3-2 win at São Januario Stadium on 12 August.

The revelation under Luxemburgo had been immense: the side was transformed from a team that looked under pressure and unable to cope with the demand of expectation into an outfit full of self-belief. The transformation was complete when, on 15 August, their dismal opening day defeat to Parana was avenged by taking the visitors apart at the Vila Belmiro. Once again, Robinho found the net twice, kicking off the scoring after just 2 minutes with a long-range effort before hitting his side's fourth after a smart 1-2 with Basilio, who also scored two. Leo was also on the scoresheet as Santos routed bottom-of-the-league Parana 5-1 to gain first place in the Brazilian championship. It was no coincidence that with Robinho hitting top gear – smashing six goals in his last seven games to take second place in the goal-scoring charts with 13 overall – Santos, too, were also excelling in the league.

The big wins kept coming at the Vila Belmiro, which had suddenly become every team's least favourite place to visit. This time it was Figueirense who suffered the full fury of the Peixe attack. Robinho was again the catalyst. First, the forward dribbled past two defenders and fired a powerful shot into the top left corner before hitting the visitors on the counter-attack in the second half, easily slotting in from close range after good work from Deivid. It was a reversal of the third goal, for which Robinho teed up his fellow striker after Elano got the ball running for Santos with a neat finish early on. The brace came just days after Robinho was confirmed as a member of Brazil's national team squad to play Bolivia in a World Cup qualifier on 5 September – recognition of his superb season and another sign that the twenty-year-old, who for the past three years had been crucial to Santos's exploits, was rapidly being embraced by the national side as well.

Robinho, aged 18, celebrates with his Santos team-mates after their 2002 Campeonato victory. They beat Corinthians 3-2.

Robinho in action for Santos during the 2003 Campeonato campaign.

Above: Celebrating Santos's win over Independiente in the 2003 Copa Libertadores semi-final second leg.

Below: Robinho training with Brazil team-mates Kaka, Diego and Julio Baptista prior to their appearance in the 2003 CONCACAF Gold Cup against Honduras in Mexico City.

Above left: Robinho relaxes with his friend and team-mate Diego at Brazil's training camp during the 2004 Under-23 South American tournament.

Above right: Celebrating after scoring a goal against Uruguay in Brazil's Group A match.

Below: Robinho kisses the Brazilian Championship trophy after Santos beat Vasco da Gama 2-1 to clinch their second Campeonato in three years.

A visibly emotional Robinho makes a plea for his mother's safe return after her kidnap in November 2004.

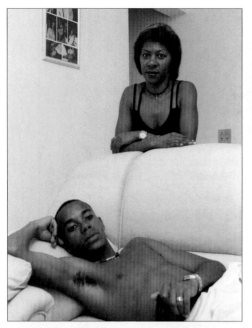

Above left: Robinho at home with his mother, Marina da Souza. She was eventually released by her kidnappers after being held for six weeks. A ransom of $120,000 (£100,000) was reportedly paid.

Above right: Celebrating with Brazil coach Carlos Alberto Parreira after scoring in Brazil's World Cup qualifier against Paraguay in 2005.

Below left: Robinho scored twice against Paraguay in another impressive performance for his country.

Below right: Showing off his skills during a Brazil training session.

Above: Robinho lines up with his Brazil team-mates ahead of another World Cup qualifying game.

Below: Santos fans show their support for Robinho in his final match for the club before his move to Real Madrid. The banner reads 'Robinho, you will be in our hearts, always'.

Robinho in action for Real Madrid in their 2005 Champions League campaign.
He made the move to Spain in a €24 million move.

Prior to heading off on international duty the striker hit two more in a sensational 4-4 draw at Cruzeiro before playing a pivotal role in Santos's 2-1 win away to Juventude on 2 September.

Brazil's victories over Bolivia and friendly with Germany kept him out of action for Santos when they met Atletico-PR in their next league game. Their visitors shared the league lead with Santos and a 1-1 draw was enough to ensure that, despite both clubs having 52 points from 29 games, the Peixe remained top of the pile, thanks to a greater win percentage. Atletico, the 2001 champions, had emerged from nowhere, putting together an 11-game unbeaten run to soar up the table.

With Robinho, Elano and Deivid returning to the fold after their international commitments, Santos followed up that draw with a crucial victory away to title rivals Palmeiras. Striker Deivid and midfielder Elano scored a goal each as Santos took advantage of Palmeiras' recent dip in form to emerge 2-1 winners.

Unsurprisingly, Robinho's exceptional season was attracting attention from overseas, as well as within Brazil. On 16 September 2004 it was reported Chelsea had made a £8 million offer for the highly-rated Brazilian midfielder. However, Jose Mourinho's bid was rejected and Robinho's representative Wagner Ribeiro admitted that it was not even considered. 'After the 2006 World Cup in Germany, Robinho is going to cost more than £30 million. He is the best player in Brazil,' he boasted. 'I didn't consider it [the Chelsea offer] from the beginning because they had offered only £12 million and that isn't enough for a player who is young and has a great future.'

In response to the speculation, Brazilian press reported that

Robinho had in fact signed a new contract with Santos to stay with the Brazilian league leaders at least until the summer of 2006. Robinho also came out to reassure his supporters. 'I am still very young and I have many things to learn,' he said. 'At the moment I am only thinking of winning the Copa Libertadores next year with Santos and taking Brazil to the World Cup.' More tellingly, though, he did reveal some of his future plans: 'When I decide to leave Santos I want to go to a big team that will appreciate what I have done during my career. I am not interested in going to a small team, even if I am paid more money.'

Santos president Marcelo Teixeira also stated his desire for Robinho to remain with the club. He said: 'Chelsea offered £8m for Robinho but I told them we cannot even talk for that price. It made no difference though, they are still pressuring us.

'We want to keep Robinho – that's why we extended his contract for another eight months.'

Two days later, however, Robinho seemed to have warmed to the offer from the London club, who were busy building a fresh era at Stamford Bridge under new owner Roman Abramovich. The twenty-year-old admitted the move might increase his stature in the national team, which, ahead of the 2006 World Cup, was a distinct priority for the young forward. He revealed: 'Chelsea's interest excites me, especially because of the conditions. I am paving my way into the Brazil team, so a transfer to a team like them would help. I hope we can take all possible steps in order not to close the door on the transfer.' It was hardly a resounding declaration of commitment to Santos.

His brace against Vitoria the following weekend in another 4-1 rout at the Vila Belmiro may well have been a signal of his desire to succeed with his first club, though some perceived his display as an advertisement to foreign eyes.

Santos continued to pick up vital points in their league as their title chase intensified, a 4-0 drubbing of Ponte Preta on 16 October was another example of how strong the Peixe were compared to their fellow top-flight clubs. However, three days after a 1-0 Derby Day defeat at São Paulo it was sensationally revealed by the Portuguese daily sports newspaper *The Record*, and reported by *Agence France Presse* on 27 October that: 'Benfica have signed 20-year-old Santos striker Robinho. The player will join the Portuguese league leaders during the January transfer window for an undisclosed fee.'

Wagner Ribeiro, Robinho's agent, later confirmed that contact had been made with the Portuguese club but denied an agreement had been reached, as stated by *The Record* and *AFP*. Ribeiro, though, did admit the move would be ideal for his client: 'They speak Portuguese, as in Brazil, the climate is mild and the Portuguese are like brothers.'

The following day it emerged that the move to Benfica would, in fact, be simply a stepping stone on Robinho's path to London. Chelsea were likely to replicate their purchase of former Santos centre-half Alex, by signing Robinho at a relatively cheap price – reportedly £10 million – and would avoid work permit issues by 'loaning' him to Benfica for a couple of seasons. The Portuguese side could not afford to sign Robinho on their own, but with Chelsea's help they would be able to benefit from the Brazilian for a limited time.

However, with no official confirmation from either party it seemed the move was still in the balance and Ribeiro confirmed talks were still going on with other clubs. 'Jose Veiga [Benfica's chairman] phoned me for talks, but we did not reach any conclusion because there are offers from two other clubs,' he said. 'They are the Dutch [PSV] and the other is Italian [Inter Milan].'

Robinho, though, refused to be drawn on the speculation. 'We are going to see,' said the youngster. 'My objective is to close the year well and help the Saints conquer the title. I want to continue playing well.'

The rumours and false stories of Robinho's departure frustrated Santos president Marcelo Teixeira, who was adamant his player would be staying put. 'I have already said clearly that we don't have any interest in negotiating Robinho at this moment,' he insisted. 'I have already warned Ribeiro about this and told him not to tell us about any offer at least until the end of the year.

'I want him [Robinho] fully concentrated on the Brazilian Championship and the Copa Sudamericana so I will not permit any interference from agents.' However, the Santos supremo did not deny a deal with Chelsea could take place in the near future, with the December finish to the Brazilian season tying in nicely with Europe's January transfer window. 'That's a rumour, but it could be true – I don't know and really don't care at this moment,' he said dismissively. 'I have also heard that the player would be bought by Benfica or loaned to PSV Eindhoven, but that's not something that we care about at this moment because we want the player to stay here.'

Meanwhile, Robinho continued to demonstrate his worth to Santos – and indeed his potential benefit to the likes of Chelsea – with another fine display in Santos's 5-0 victory over Fluminense on 30 October. He struck another two goals – one, a low right-foot effort from inside the box after just 7 minutes and his second, a powerful first-time strike in the second half – as Santos breezed past their opponents, striker Deivid hitting the net twice after Fluminense's Laercio bundled a Robinho cross into his own net.

Robinho's performance did nothing other than exaggerate the hype and rumour surrounding his move to Europe, and a new name emerged in the affair – Real Madrid.

Following reports Ribeiro had met Real Madrid's director of marketing, Jose Angel Sanchez – the man who sealed the move of David Beckham from Manchester United to the Spanish capital – to discuss a possible transfer, the agent told Spanish national agency EFE: 'The player definitely wants to play for Real Madrid, they are one of the best clubs in the world, and they are interested in the situation of the player. At the moment, he's considered to be Pelé's successor.' However, Ribeiro also revealed that Benfica, PSV Eindhoven and Chelsea had now also tabled offers, with the English Premiership side apparently matching the offer from the Spanish giants. 'In the coming season he's definitely going to be playing for one of the top clubs in Europe, one that's in the Champions League,' he added.

Dreams of the historic trophies on offer in Europe, the wealthy contracts and the glamorous lifestyle on offer at clubs such as Real Madrid were dramatically put on hold for Robinho on 6 November, however.

The twenty-year-old sensation, Santos's top scorer with 21 goals in 2004, was sent home from the team's hotel in southern Santa Catarina state, where his side were preparing for a game against Criciuma, to deal with a devastating family matter.

His mother, Marina Lima de Souza, had been enjoying a Saturday afternoon barbecue with friends and relatives at her home in the costal town of Praia Grande, 45 miles from São

Paulo. Two armed men climbed over the house's boundary wall and, at gunpoint, ordered all the guests into the house. They locked Marina's guests in the bathroom and took her through the house and back outside, where they forced her into her Mercedes, before driving away. Naturally, the news filled Robinho with fear. The forward had always been close to his mother and her kidnapping left him unable to eat or sleep. Sadly, in South America kidnappings are rife, and the growing wages and wealth of the footballers saw an increasing trend in the abduction of players' relatives.

Juan Roman Riquelme, the Argentinean playmaker of Boca Juniors, had one of his younger brothers kidnapped in April 2002. The seventeen-year-old, Christian Riquelme, was eventually released after a reported $160,000 (£84,500) was paid. Juan Roman promptly left to join Barcelona after continued threats to his family.

Then the father of brothers Gabriel Milito, who plays for Independiente, and Diego Milito, who plays for Racing Club, was also kidnapped. Gabriel moved to Real Zaragoza and Diego joined Genoa in Italy, relocating their young families away from the threats and dangers posed by the kidnappers of South America. But it is not just the players who are in danger. In May 2003 the nineteen-year-old half-sister of Mauricio Macri, the president of Boca Juniors and a member of one of Argentina's wealthiest families, was kidnapped. It caused one of the biggest sensations since Mauricio himself was kidnapped in 1991. Florencia Macri, who had been snatched as she left a theatre in a busy part of Buenos Aires, was eventually released after a reported $1.5 million (£800,000) had been paid. Two months later, in July 2003, Leonardo Astrada, the coach of River Plate, had his father kidnapped.

'We already know through intermediaries from the Santos team that Robinho is calm and confident about our work,' Alberto Corazza, the Santos police officer in charge of the investigation, told reporters shortly after the player's return home.

Three days later Robinho appealed for his family to be left in peace as he spoke in public for the first time since his mother was kidnapped. 'You're outside my house all the time and this is getting in the way,' the twenty-year-old said, clearly upset. Later that week police dropped their investigation into the abduction on the request of Robinho, so that he could negotiate direct with his mother's captors.

While his multi-million pound transfer to Europe was not the first thing on his mind at this time, his agent Ribeiro was quick to point out that a move to the likes of Real Madrid would free him and his family of such concerns. 'He wants to live a quiet life and he believes the only way to do so is to leave Brazil,' the agent said.

Meanwhile, his other agent, Juan Figger, continued to organise a deal with Real Madrid, informing Spain's well-known sports daily *Marca* that: 'What Real Madrid wants is to reach an agreement to give it first option on signing Robinho in June. The agreement is very close but there are a few details remaining.'

'Which player in the world doesn't want to be with Real Madrid? None. I have no doubts, Robinho is good enough to play for Real Madrid,' Ribeiro told Spanish papers. 'He's having a bad time. It would be painful for anyone to have their mother kidnapped. He is very close to her and he's suffering a lot. I wanted to go back to Brazil to help him, but he has asked me to stay here to sort out his move to Real Madrid before returning to Brazil.'

While Robson de Souza's personal life was in turmoil Robinho, the footballer was still top of the agenda for the press – and news broke on 21 November that Chelsea had jumped the queue to land the Brazilian ace with a £14 million bid. The move was welcomed by Ribeiro: 'He is not scared of going to England – a country very different to Brazil. He's excited and the Chelsea offer is encouraging.'

Robinho, though, was in no mood to speak of such negotiations. 'Real Madrid are the best club in the world. Any footballer dreams about playing there and I am no different. I would like to play in Spain and I hope that can happen one day, but I haven't got the head to deal with this right now,' he said. 'I hope this is over as quickly as possible, that my mother comes back home and that I can go back to playing football. I won't play until she is home.'

Forty days after her disappearance Robinho finally received the news he had been waiting to hear during the past, incredibly painful, month. His mother had been freed by her kidnappers. Forty days after being seized at gunpoint Marina was discovered knocking on the door of a house in Perus, on the outskirts of São Paulo, after being released from captivity. Later, local media claimed a £100,000 ransom had been paid by Robinho for her safe return.

'She said they told her to get out of the car and disappear,' Jose Bernardo, the man who discovered Robinho's mother, said in a television interview. 'But she didn't look scared and wasn't trembling.'

The police were called and Marina was taken to hospital for a check-up where doctors said that, despite losing 4kg (8.8lbs) she was in good condition. She was then driven home and reunited with her son. 'There is nothing better than seeing your mother happy and laughing,' the young striker said. 'I can have a happy Christmas with my family, whether or not we win the title. I've had trouble sleeping. You have lunch but you don't know if your mother is having lunch; when you have dinner, you don't know if she's having dinner. I was so happy to see my mum. She cried, and hugged me, and kissed me. And a mother's hug is all a kid wants in life.'

On behalf of the club, Santos's president Teixeira was equally delighted at the news: 'God has been generous because he has brought Dona Marina home. It's been traumatic for the players and they've missed Robinho's happiness and his contagious smile. This is a very happy day for Santos.'

With his family back together, the huge weight of fear, dread and panic lifted from his shoulders, Robinho had only one thing on his mind: 'Now all I want to do is play ball.'

The release of Marina dos Santos came just two days before Santos's final game of the season against Vasco da Gama, and Robinho was determined to be a part of the celebrations.

'I am very happy that Robinho is once again available for selection,' said Luxemburgo at the team hotel in São Jose do Rio Preto before the game. Robinho had last played for Santos nearly two months ago, in the 5-0 win over Fluminense on 31 October, when he scored twice.

Without him Santos had slipped to second spot in the league, two points off the pace set by Atletico-PR. However, the team were still in contention for the title and trounced already-relegated Gremio 5-1 in São Jose do Rio Preto to keep up with the leaders.

Everything, though, was against the Peixe. They were forced to play in São Jose do Rio Preto, 100 miles away from the Vila Belmiro, as punishment for their fans throwing objects onto the field in a clash with Vitoria earlier in the year. The 2002 champions and 2003 runners-up needed to win their final two matches and hope Vasco or Botafogo could hold Atletico to a draw without Robinho, who had been out of action for six league games since his mother's kidnap. Although the São Paulo-based side maintained second place, they had become noticeably weaker without their star man. However, on 13 December they were finally able to reclaim the coveted top spot. Santos surged into first place in the national championship with a victory over São Caetano as Atletico slipped to a surprise defeat to Vasco da Gama – the team Santos now had to beat to take the title for the second time in three years.

Thousands of fans wearing the team's black-and-white jerseys poured onto the streets and beaches of Santos on the Sunday evening after the victory over the Big Blue, commemorating a title that the team still hadn't quite guaranteed. For Luxemburgo, who had rescued Santos from their disastrous start, this would be his record fifth national title – and, as he told Pelé's website, the most satisfying of all: 'This championship was special. I think it would be the most difficult title of my career. We lost some of our top players during the season and had to remodel our team. Everything was against us. We were seriously hurt by some refereeing decisions. Even so, we're still strong and fighting for the title.'

Luxemburgo had won the championship twice with Palmeiras in 1993 and 1994, with Corinthians in 1998 and, of course, with Cruzeiro in 2003, when he denied Santos consecutive titles. His influence was greatly respected by all the players.

'He had to radically change the team during the competition and we still have quality soccer,' said striker

Basilio, who moved into Robinho's vacant slot in the starting line-up when the young forward's mother was kidnapped.

Remarkably he remained top goalscorer throughout his time away from the club, with 21 goals, with only Deivid managing to match the twenty-year-old's tally. Now he was back.

Robinho's return on 19 December 2004 was a joyful day for Santos. Midfielders Ricardinho and Elano scored a goal each as the Peixe defeated Vasco 2-1 to win its second Brazilian championship in three years. Minutes after the final whistle, fans poured onto the streets and beaches of Santos to celebrate the team's second national title since the Pelé era, while nearly 40,000 fans, who had made the 250-mile trip from Santos to São Jose do Rio Preto, were ecstatic in the stands.

Santos ended with 89 points from 46 matches, three points clear of Atletico-PR, who had drawn their final game against Botafogo 1-1 at home.

'We had many problems in the season but we never lost confidence in our abilities,' a delighted Robinho said after the game. Defender Leo agreed: 'We worked hard all year for this, now it's time to celebrate! I imagine people are going crazy in Santos right now.'

Indeed they were – several streets in downtown Santos had to be closed to accommodate the throngs of fans as tens of thousands took part in the celebrations throughout the night.

It was a sensational campaign from Santos. First, there was the recovery from the poor start under Leão and the injury problems with Elano, while the sale of Diego and Renato dogged the mid-season and their departure was only compounded when the club lost its driving force, Robinho. However, under Luxemburgo's guidance they had dealt with all their difficulties and sealed a fantastic title. 'I assure you,' the coach said after the victory, 'this is the most important title in my career. People near to us know what we had to endure and how hard we had to work all season long.'

Meanwhile, following the release of his mother, speculation about Robinho's transfer to Europe began to intensify once again. This escalated with the dramatic move of Luxemburgo to Real Madrid on 30 December. The Brazilian's achievements at Santos and with Cruzeiro in 2003 had caught the eye of the Spanish giants and he was appointed to take charge of Madrid for the remainder of the 2004/05 season. He became their third coach in six months when his predecessor, Mariano Garcia Remon, appeared to pay the price for questioning David Beckham's place in the starting line-up. Brazilian media quoted Santos Vice President Norberto Moreira da Silva as saying: 'He [Luxemburgo] told us he had an offer he could not refuse and asked to be freed from his commitment to Santos. It was his dream, so we thought it best to let him go.'

Replacing him at Santos would be Oswaldo de Oliveira, the former Vitoria coach, who was fired after only 14 games earlier in 2004.

With Robinho's good relationship with Luxemburgo clearly evident and likely to be a key lever in the deal, Real Madrid president Florentino Perez again announced his intention to bring the young star to the Bernabeu: 'There are no new developments. We have an interest in acquiring an option to buy him in June next year, but we did not want to take any further action because of the unfortunate recent events. Robinho is one of those great players who has that extra bit of magic that we think is important for Real Madrid. We will be talking more about the matter as of next week.'

Just days later, Madrid appeared to have secured the 'first option' deal with Santos, when Robinho conceded the talks had progressed favourably. 'The transfer negotiations with Real Madrid are advanced, but I cannot talk of Real Madrid out of respect for my current team Santos,' he said. This was followed up by Ribeiro, who implied a move at the end of the European season in June was preferable for both parties. 'We have said no to Chelsea, who would have paid 10 million euros, and to Benfica. All we could say is the player will participate with Santos in Libertadores Cup. His relation with the new Real Madrid coach, Brazilian Vanderlei Luxemburgo, has always been excellent. But there is nothing yet,' the agent insisted.

'I'm not interested in what people are saying,' Robinho told reporters as the growing speculation continued to mount around him. 'I want to stay at Santos. The move was good for Vanderlei and I am very happy for him but I want to help Santos in the Libertadores Cup.'

CHAPTER 5

THE REAL DEAL

In the winter of 2004/05, Robinho was hot property. Despite missing the last six games of the competition because of the traumatic kidnapping of his mother, he had just finished third in the goal rankings in the Brazilian league with 21 strikes. He had also broken into the Brazilian national team squad after impressing in the Under-23 side and had been a key figure in Santos's second league title in three years. His superb season had seen him win the Balo de Ouro, the prestigious trophy awarded to the best player in Brazil, based on an accumulated points ranking. With his attacking play – inspirational to team-mates, devastating to defences – he had made a name for himself in Brazil as one of the most exciting players with a ball at his feet in South America. After the initial eulogies from Pelé, his talents now won him praise from some of Brazil's finest recent stars.

'He is the greatest example of Brazilian fantasy football,' the former World Cup-winning captain Carlos Alberto said about him. Roberto Carlos, the Real Madrid left-back, whose adventurous play had led him to be considered by many as the best full-back in the world in his prime, said: 'It's my prediction that, within a maximum of two years, everyone will recognise him as the best player in the world. He's brought verve, happiness and spectacle back into the Brazilian national team.' Meanwhile, former Brazil striker Romario, who is a modern-day legend in Brazil after claiming to have scored over 1,000 goals in his career, said: 'Robinho is the inheritor of a line which flows from me to Ronaldinho through Rivaldo and Ronaldo – this boy will become the world's best footballer.' All those views were strengthened with the support of current Brazil boss, Carlos Alberto Parreira: 'Robinho's got no limits whatsoever. He's mature and he's got skill to spare. He'll become the best – perhaps the greatest ever.'

He also won the plaudits of Tostão, Brazil's industrious striker in their legendary 1970 World Cup-winning team. Tostão played alongside Pelé and is now a commentator and newspaper columnist; and in 2005 he had no doubt Robinho would hit the heights as a player. 'Robinho is an exceptional player, the best player in Brazil right now,' he said.

No wonder Real Madrid and Chelsea were falling over themselves to get his signature.

Of his potential transfer Tostão was sure a move would come sooner or later and that, when it did, Robinho would be more than capable of living up to his reputation. 'No one doubts his talent, but he is playing in Brazil, where the standard is not as high as in Europe. The question is, can he go to Europe and still turn it on? I think he can. He has so much potential.

'Going to Real would be the best move he could make. He could work with a manager who knows him and who he gets along with. He should only leave Brazil to go to a big team like Manchester United, Arsenal, Real Madrid, etc. If he goes to one of those teams and has a manager who knows how to use him, he'll become one of the best players in the world.'

Meanwhile, Santos's other starlets were being snapped up by European sides. Elano, Santos's goal-scoring playmaker was sold in January 2005 to Ukraine's Shakhtar Donetsk for £7 million. The midfielder, who would later be picked up by Sven-Göran Eriksson at Manchester City, joined Santos as a teenager in 2001 and burst onto the national stage two years later after he had been one of the key elements in the Peixe's 2002 title-winning campaign. Elano had always been less flamboyant than Diego and Robinho, but he had won admiration from Brazil coach Carlos Alberto Parreira for his solid and effective play as well as his versatility in midfield.

The exit of Elano, following the 2004 departures of Diego to Porto, Alex to PSV and Renato to Sevilla, was a blow to Santos President Marcelo Teixeira, who was hoping to persuade Robinho to remain at the club by building a successful squad that would see Santos dominate the Brazilian league and Copa Libertadores. However, with his hand forced by lucrative transfer fees from Europe's elite in the cases of Elano, Diego, Alex and Renato, it seemed only a matter of time before a club offered a package beneficial enough to tempt young Robinho away from the Vila Belmiro.

Robinho's separation from his former team-mate and good friend Elano did not last long, however. The pair were called up for Brazil's first international of 2005 – a friendly away to Hong Kong. The Brazilian FA had attracted criticism from home for agreeing to the fixture, reportedly accepting a million-dollar match fee for sending a strong team to play the Asian nation. For Brazilian manger Parreira, however, it was an ideal opportunity for his Samba

Boys to get back on track following an unexpected and worrying defeat against Venezuela before Christmas in their World Cup qualifying campaign.

Unsurprisingly the hosts could put up little resistance to their visitor's relentless attacks – orchestrated by World Player of the Year and Barcelona star Ronaldinho. The flamboyant forward, renowned for his toothy smile, gave a dazzling display as Brazil thrashed the minnows 7-1. Ronaldinho scored a cheeky lob and produced some inspired moments of play with his extravagant flicks and dummies. Ricardo Oliveira hit the back of the net twice while Roberto Carlos, Alex and Lucio also got on the scoresheet. Robinho teed up Lucio for the opening goal with a pin-point cross and put Ronaldinho through for his strike, before rounding off the scoring himself for his first international goal.

Playing only his second international match, the Santos star nodded in a cross from Oliveira to complete the rout and cap a performance that drew plaudits from his manager and team-mates. Parreira picked out the young striker for special praise after the match. 'Robinho is a very talented player,' he said. 'We think that he'll be a very good player for the future. He's very talented and he's only twenty-one, yet he showed a lot of quality.'

Experienced midfielder Ze Roberto also applauded the play of his colleague: 'With Robinho the team found more spaces because he moves so much,' the Bayern Munich man told Pelé's website.

While his career with Brazil was taking off, Robinho's team-mates at Santos were stalling ahead of the new Brazilian season. Following the departure of Vanderlei Luxemburgo to Real Madrid, Oswaldo de Oliveira was struggling to live up to his predecessor's reputation and was increasingly criticised in the press and by the Santos fans. Oliveira, who had been considered one of Brazil's most successful coaches, was booed by most of the 7,000 people in the crowd at Vila Belmiro stadium during the team's disappointing 0-0 draw against Guarani in the São Paulo state championship – a result that meant Santos had taken just 5 points from a possible 12 in their last four games and were left well off the pace in the local tournament. The club hadn't won at home in over a month and their razor-sharp attack appeared somewhat blunt in their recent outings.

'We have to stay behind Oswaldo,' insisted Santos defender Leo to reporters from *Lance*, a local newspaper. 'The result against Guarani wasn't good, but at no time did the team fail to go after the win.'

De Oliveira did manage to appease the support in their next clash against local rivals Corinthians, though. Corinthians, in a new regime of spending big on South America's star talent with the help of super-agent Kia Joorabchian, had purchased Boca Juniors' star man, South America's Player of the Year 2003 and Latin America Player of the Year 2004: Carlos Tevez. The signing created a furore in Brazil when he was acquired for more than £15 million in December 2004. It was the most expensive transfer fee paid by a Brazilian club and the duel between Santos's home-grown Robinho and Corinthians' Argentine import, Tevez, was eagerly anticipated by fans and neutrals alike.

Tevez had netted twice in his three previous games, but it was Robinho who came out on top. The Santos star scored a pair of second-half goals to fire his side to a 3-0 victory. Throughout the match, in front of a capacity crowd of nearly 20,000 fans in the Vila Belmiro stadium, Robinho was outstanding. 'Tevez is a great player, but this time I had the advantage against him,' a delighted Robinho told reporters after the game.

That victory, though, was not the kick-start de Oliveira was hoping for and, in his first Copa Libertadores game as coach of Santos on 16 February, the new boss could only look on as the 2003 finalists crashed to an opening-day defeat at the hands of Boliva's Bolivar. Cristian Zermatten struck three times for the hosts at the Estadio Hernando Siles as Santos went down 4-3 in the first game in Group 2. Robinho broke free to score a superb solo goal in the 89th minute for the visitors, but by then, the damage had been done and his strike was nothing more than a consolation. It was a poor start against the unfancied Bolivians and piled yet more pressure on de Oliveira, who was seemingly unable to reproduce Luxemburgo's magic.

Robinho, though, was making a superb start to 2005 and the striker netted his first professional hat-trick in a 5-1 drubbing of Rio Branco in the São Paulo State Championship. The three goals took Robinho's tally to nine goals in nine games in the pre-season contest, putting him top of the goal-scoring charts in the tournament along with America's Finazzi.

'That's the first time I've done that as a professional, but I hope to do even better in the future,' Robinho proudly told the Agencia Estado news wire after the match. 'I want to score three again, or maybe four. Hopefully we'll win the championship, but I'll be more than happy to end up as the top scorer.'

With a return to the Libertadores, though, came a return of their previous poor form. Midfielder Ricardinho stole a 3-2 win at the Vila Belmiro for the home side on 3 March, but their performance was less than convincing against Danubio, a weak outfit from Uruguay. Robinho, who had been struggling with a back injury before the match hit the equaliser on 70 minutes to score his second of the competition with a shot from six yards out, before Ricardinho hit the winner from the spot to mark his 50th game for the Peixe.

The win was an important one for Santos, who moved into a three-way tie for first spot in their group, along with Danubio and Bolvar, with LDU trailing after two defeats. The performance was a poor one and it hadn't gone unnoticed by the fans, including Pelé, who had attended the Vila Belmiro clash. 'I was worried when Danubio scored early,' Pelé told the local *Agencia Placar* sports news service. 'I was really suffering here.' Match-winner Ricardinho echoed Pelé's concerns and highlighted the importance of the result. 'We really needed this victory,' the midfielder said. 'We could not afford to lose any points today.'

Pelé, despite his disappointment at the general performance from Santos, was pleased to see his young protégé developing nicely. 'I'm glad he did that,' he remarked about Robinho's celebration after his goal. The twenty-one-year-old, not only resembling Pelé in stature and skill, celebrated his goal with a punch in the air, reminiscent of the Brazilian legend. Asked about Robinho's future, Pelé admitted he was disappointed that the forward was unlikely to remain at Santos, where he would certainly become a club hero just as he had done so himself, but he understood the youngster's desires to test himself in the major leagues of Europe. 'When I stayed with Santos I was able to bring more people to the stadium. If Robinho also stays, he will do the same. When I was 19 and already a World Cup winner Madrid made an incredible offer to me, but Santos made sure they improved my contract and

I stayed. I wish he could stay with Santos his entire career but I know it's hard to keep him here. I just wish him the best luck wherever he goes.'

A 2-0 win over lowly União Barbarense at the Vila Belmiro stadium following a 3-1 defeat to Palmeiras kept Santos in touch with the São Paulo State championship leaders São Paulo, but when the Peixe stumbled to a disappointing 3-3 draw at home to America to fall seven points behind their rivals the pressure on Oswaldo de Oliveira, who was supposedly in charge of Brazil's best club side, became overwhelming.

The day after their draw with America, the Brazilian champions fired their coach. 'We talked with Oswaldo this morning and decided to make it official,' Santos Director of Football Luiz Henrique de Menezes told *Pelé.net*.

Santos were quick to install former Luxemburgo assistant Alexandre Tadeu Gallo as their new coach following the departure of de Oliveira. Gallo had been in charge of Portuguesa, who had also struggled in the São Paulo State Championship, but was popular with fans, having been a commanding defensive midfield player for the club in 1995, when they finished runners-up in the league.

When Luxemburgo left for Real Madrid he had suggested Gallo as an ideal replacement to continue his work, and now it seemed his assistant would get a chance to prove him right. 'He is my master,' Gallo said of Luxemburgo. 'But I have my own personality and my own style.' The thirty-seven-year-old also denied reports that he was hired only as cover until Santos could find a more renowned coach. 'I would never accept that,' he insisted. 'I didn't come to stay only for a short period of time.'

While turmoil grew at the Vila Belmiro, Robinho

continued to blossom on the international stage. Called up to the national squad for their World Cup qualifiers in March 2005, against Peru and Uruguay, the forward, who was only added to the squad as a late replacement for the injured Inter Milan striker Adriano, continued to impress his team-mates, many of whom were rallying for him to get a starting spot. Parreira considered dropping experienced Lyon midfielder Juninho Pernambucano to accommodate the Santos man. 'I'm actually one of Robinho's fans, I wished we could play together,' Juninho said of the speculation. 'It's unusual we have to fight for a position.'

Robinho was also diplomatic about the situation, perhaps safe in the knowledge that sooner or later his time to shine for Brazil would arrive. 'I'm sure whoever gets to play will give all he has to the team,' he said. 'I'm happy to be on the national team. It's a great privilege.'

Parreira eventually opted to go for the more experienced and established Juninho. However, the five-times World Cup champions struggled to break through Peru's tight defence and only threatened their visitors when Robinho was introduced from the bench. More than 50,000 fans at Serra Dourada stadium had been chanting Robinho's name, imploring the coach to unleash the diminutive dribbler throughout the lacklustre first half. The trick worked and Kaka made the breakthrough for the home team on 74 minutes to secure a vital win in the 2006 World Cup qualification campaign for Brazil. 'Robinho played well,' Parreira acknowledged after the game. 'He was important because he added speed.'

However, despite the accolades Robinho found himself once again warming the bench three days later against Uruguay. Brazil fell behind to a strike from former

Manchester United centre-forward Diego Forlan just after half-time. Robinho was eventually introduced in Montevideo on 62 minutes. Six minutes later Emerson hit an equaliser as Brazil secured a draw with Uruguay to leave the Brazilians second behind Argentina in the South American World Cup qualifying race.

At Santos Gallo's reputation may not have been as distinguished as some of the managers the Peixe fans hoped to see at the helm, but he, like Luxemburgo, certainly had an immediate impact on his new charges. In his first game as manager of the Peixe on 6 April he looked on as one of the last remaining jewels from Santos's 2002 season ran riot against LDU in the Copa Libertadores. Robinho smashed two past Santos's Ecuadorian opponents as the Brazilians came from behind to beat the Colombians 3-1.

As well as being a match-winning contribution, the brace also moved the standout striker closer to Pelé's all-time scoring record for Santos in the Copa Libertadores. The two strikes against LDU sealed his place as Santos's second-best all-time scorer in the Latin American club championship with 12 goals. Pelé had hit the net 17 times during his time with the club.

Robinho's display at the Vila Belmiro, and his march towards the Pelé goal-scoring record, prompted fans once again to compare him with the master. 'Pelé is back,' the 20,000 fans chanted in unison, as Robinho dribbled past two defenders and fired an unstoppable low shot from the edge of the box for his first goal of the night. His fourth of the competition followed when he connected with a diving header from close range.

Including the 20-team pre-season São Paulo State Championship, Robinho had already recorded 15 goals in 17 matches in the 2005 season, with the Campeonato still yet to get underway. Despite his superb start to the year, he remained modest, though. 'It wasn't even my best match,' he said after the 3-1 victory. 'I just did what I know.' He also gave some words of encouragement for the supporters who idolised him and implored him to remain at the club. 'I hope I'll be able to make history with Santos. I don't know what will happen in my future, but I can say that I want to stay in the club for a long time.'

Another victory in the Libertadores followed on 20 April, 2-1 away at Danubio, before Santos re-focused their attentions on retaining the league title. Not only were the club aiming to repeat their 2004 victory but they also had the added challenge of trying to convince Robinho not to leave for Spain and Real Madrid. Once again the young star was set to be the main attraction of the 2005 tournament and, shortly after his apparent declaration of commitment to Santos, conceded: 'I think that Spain is the ideal country for me, but only God knows which club I will play for. Real Madrid are a great club and any football player would want to play there. Vanderlei Luxemburgo is a coach that I know well and who likes the way I play. He is special: he was with me every minute when my mother was kidnapped until she was released. He gave me tremendous support at a horrible time. Barcelona are also a very well-liked club in Brazil due to the success of our players like Romario, Ronaldo, Rivaldo and Ronaldinho.'

Santos, the favourites for the crown, kicked off their season in cavalier mode, routing Paysandu 4-1 on the opening day of the season – despite playing behind closed doors. As punishment for Santos fans who threw objects onto the field in 2004, the club was forced to begin 2005 without any supporters in the stands. Fortunately for Santos, though, their strike force did show up. Deivid opened the scoring for the hosts after just 5 minutes before Robinho, true to form, scored his 41st goal in 99 matches in the Brazilian league with a penalty after a Paysandu defender deflected the ball with his hand inside the penalty box. Further goals from substitute midfielder Edmilson and a second from Deivid, after Leonardo scored an own goal, sealed the win for Santos.

Three days later Robinho was again on the scoresheet, as Santos came from behind to beat Coritiba 3-2 at the Couto Pereira stadium. The victory sparked a run of fine results in the Copa Libertadores for Santos, who went on to win their final two group games, including a 6-0 drubbing of Bolivar, to top Group 2 and seal a meeting with Universidad de Chile in the first knockout round.

The Chileans had come second in Group 3, behind São Paulo, and had impressed defensively. After conceding four to São Paulo in their second match, they went on to concede just three more times in their next four games.

That defence held firm against Santos's renowned attack and Diego Rivarola put the hosts ahead just after the break. However, Ricardinho equalised for Santos before Patricio Galaz scored a late goal to give Universidad de Chile a crucial one-goal lead going into the second leg at the Vila Belmiro.

Between the legs Santos faced Atletico Mineiro in the Brazilian Championship. Among the packed crowds at the Vila Belmiro were scouts from Arsenal, sitting with Wagner Ribeiro. Robinho put on quite a show for his onlookers, as a double from Ricardinho helped Santos to a comfortable 3-0 win. However, the main story from the evening was that Arsène Wenger's spies were keeping an eye on Robinho. However, the twenty-one-year-old dismissed the rumours, instead preferring to focus on his team. 'The Arsenal scouts were there to look at the soccer in general,' he said. 'Not only Santos and not only me.' He added: 'I prefer to stay at Santos and win the Copa Libertadores. I want to give my best to help Santos become champions. What will be better for everybody will be better for me as well.'

The next step in pursuit of that elusive South American title came at the Vila Belmiro with the arrival of Universidad de Chile for the second leg of their Round of 16 tie. The resounding win over Atletico had clearly boosted morale in the Santos camp and the hosts destroyed their opponents. Robinho picked up another brace as Santos ran out 3-0 victors over Universidad de Chile, securing a 4-2 aggregate win and booking a place in the quarter-finals of the Copa Libertadores.

Following Flavio's opener, Robinho doubled the lead in the 71st minute when he connected with a cross from Bovio. After eluding two defenders, the forward then drew a foul in the box and picked himself up to convert the spot-kick with a minute left to play. The goals took Robinho's tally to 20 so far in the season, with 13 in the Libertadores. Santos's victory also ensured their 21-year unbeaten streak at the Vila Belmiro in the Libertadores remained intact and sealed a meeting with Brazilian side Atletico Paranaense in the next round.

Paranaense, who had finished runners-up to Santos in the 2004 Campeonato Brasileiro, had qualified from a tough group, scraping into the knockout phases. In their final group game they crumbled at home to group winners Medellin of Colombia, losing 4-0. America de Cali would have taken second spot in the group from the Brazilians had they drawn at home with bottom-of-the-table Libertad of Paraguay, but they blew their opportunity, losing 1-0 at the Estadio Pascual Guerrero after previously winning both their home fixtures. Atletico then edged past Cerro Porteno of Paraguay on penalties after the away sides in both legs pinched 2-1 victories.

The draw was a favourable won for the reigning Brazilian Champions – Atletico suffered a dismal start to the 2005 domestic season and were bottom of the league after six games with no points on the board.

However, league form counts for little in the knockout stages of a competition as intensely fought over as the Libertadores. Santos, fourth in the Brazilian league, came unstuck away in the first leg, with Paranaense striker Lima netting a winner in the 70th minute to secure a 3-2 win for the 10-man home side.

The match began with both teams creating good chances at the Kyocera Arena in Curitiba, and Santos took the lead when Ricardinho put Santos ahead with a right-foot shot inside the penalty area just 12 minutes in. Fifteen minutes later midfielder Evandro equalised for the home side, but when Atletico's Alan Bahia saw a straight red for a heavy challenge on Robinho it seemed Santos would take control of the match. Atletico, though, stole the initiative and took the lead on 40 minutes through midfielder Marcão. The advantage didn't last long, though, and Deivid levelled the tie with a header from Robinho's pin-point cross. However, Atletico – whose coach Antonio Lopes was in charge of his first game at the club and were missing regular defenders Vladimir Marin of Colombia and Felipe Baloy of Panama through international commitments – responded better than Santos in the second half. Deivid's leveller did not fire Santos into life and Atletico, despite their numerical disadvantage, took a one-goal lead into the second leg, meaning they would only need a draw to progress to the semi-finals of the Latin American club championship.

The task for Santos was made all the more difficult as the second leg would have to be played without Robinho and defender Leo, who both had to return to the national team to compete in two vital World Cup qualifying matches and the Confederations Cup in Germany, after being released from the Brazil camp to play in the first leg. Midfielder Fabinho and defender Paulo César would also miss the crucial quarter-final match-up, both players suffering with injuries.

Those absences were to prove crucial as Aloisio scored two goals for the visiting Atletico Paranaense in the second leg, sealing a 5-2 aggregate victory over their Brazilian rivals.

It was a sign of how much Santos were relying on their key men, particularly Robinho, following the departure of Diego, Alex and Elano. A view certainly held by Santos skipper Ricardinho: 'We could say that if we had Robinho and Leo we would have advanced,' he conceded after the game.

Meanwhile, on the international stage, Robinho was set to be handed his first-ever start in Brazil's home clash with Paraguay at Porto Alegre. 'I have been called up before, but mostly to stay on the bench,' he told the Agencia Placar news service ahead of the game. Realising, with the depth of talent in Brazil's frontline, that this opportunity in a competitive game would be vital to his future for Brazil and perhaps his hopes of a regular place in the team leading up to the World Cup, he insisted he was determined to make the most of the opening: 'Now that I get a chance to start, I'll go after the defenders to try to show what I can do.'

He was also heartened to hear the support of his coach, Parreira, prior to the game, who insisted his player was capable of competing, aged twenty-one, against the best in the world. 'Robinho has matured a lot,' Parreira said. 'He's been the top player in all national competitions, and I already feel confident enough to let him start in a game like this.'

His protégé didn't let him down. The youngster, who replaced one of his idols – Ronaldo – in the starting line-up, netted in the 81st minute and teed Ronaldinho up for his second strike in a superb full debut for Brazil on 5 June 2005. Ronaldinho's double, along with strikes from Robinho and Ze Roberto helped the Samba Boys ease to a 4-1 win over Paraguay, which lifted them to second place in the South American qualifying table.

Brazil netted just twice in their last four games and took only five points against Peru, Colombia, Ecuador and Uruguay, but the introduction of Robinho seemed to have sparked Parreira's side into life. Alex Bellos wrote in the *Guardian*: 'In Brazil's first competitive game with Robinho in the starting line-up, against Paraguay on Sunday, the world champions played their most fluent and exciting football since winning the World Cup three years ago.'

Robinho was also pleased with his first start for Brazil. 'We played well, it was a great victory and we leave here happy,' said the twenty-one-year-old striker, preferring to focus on his team's achievement. However, he received words of encouragement from World Player of the Year, Ronaldinho, who said: 'He is getting better and better with every game. People say he is one for the future but I think he has already arrived.' Brazil's left-back Roberto Carlos was also not shy about praising the youngster. 'Robinho is today's Garrincha. I am absolutely certain that Robinho will soon be the best in the world,' he went on, before – unhelpfully for Santos – reigniting the debate about Robinho furthering his career in Spain. 'I would go,' the Real Madrid wing-back told Pelé's website. 'If he goes to Real Madrid, he'll have every chance to work towards that goal. Robinho is coming to a great club, which has an immense infrastructure. Real is different from other clubs and Robinho will play better there than he did at Santos.'

Back on the field, though, Robinho was unable to influence the outcome against Brazil's bitter rivals. Argentina secured a place at Germany 2006 with a stunning first-half performance as they scored three times before the break to beat Brazil 3-1. Two goals by Hernan Crespo and one from Juan Roman Riquelme stunned the world champions, who fought back in the second half and replied with a trademark free kick from Roberto Carlos. Despite the loss, Brazil remained second in the 10-nation South American group on 27 points from 15 games and were still almost certain to advance as one of the four South American sides to progress automatically, maintaining their proud record as the only country to have played at every finals.

For the first time Brazil had tested a strike force pairing of Robinho and Inter Milan forward Adriano. Although the fledgling relationship did not produce any goals for the Brazilians Adriando insisted that with time it could bear fruit: 'I believe the association with Robinho, Kaka and Ronaldinho [the so-called "fantastic quartet"] has all the makings to be a success. But the pairing with Robinho needs time playing together to create an understanding, When you form a strike pairing things don't necessarily click from the word go. But Robinho and I are fully aware of the responsibility we have – we know that people are waiting for goals from us. I am very calm because we're working hard to make sure it succeeds.'

Following the mixed performance in the qualifying double-header, there was no let-up in international competition for Robinho. With the rest of the Brazil squad, he flew to Germany, to once again prepare himself to shine for the national team – and this time under the eyes of Europe's elite clubs in the pre-World Cup warm-up tournament, the Confederations Cup. The competition allows the host nation to test procedures a year prior to their staging of the biggest football tournament in the world, but is also taken very seriously by the teams involved – all holders of regional titles.

The 2005 Confederations Cup brought together the winners of the 2002 World Cup (Brazil), 2004 European Cup (Greece), 2003 CONCACAF Gold Cup (Mexico), 2004 African Cup of Nations (Tunisia), 2004 Asian Cup (Japan) and 2004 Oceania Nations Cup (Australia). Argentina were also invited to represent the 2004 Copa America, as the tournament winners, Brazil, had already qualified via their World Cup win, and the runners-up of the World Cup, Germany, had qualified as hosts.

Brazil were grouped with Greece, Japan and Mexico in the first phase of the contest and they kicked off their campaign with a comfortable victory over the European Champions in Leipzig, with Robinho once again putting on a superb display for his country. Adriano hit a stunning strike from 30 yards to open the scoring before Robinho tapped in at the far post to double the World Champions advantage just after the break. A year earlier, the Greeks had stunned Europe's major nations when their direct football saw them win Euro 2004, but they could not cope with Brazil and Juninho Pernambucano sealed the match with an expertly executed free kick from just outside the box.

After the match, Robinho's display drew a glowing tribute from his coach. 'It is a treasure for us to have such a player, with such a personality and such skills,' said Parreira. Once again, though, the youngster was more interested in praising his colleagues. 'It was not an easy game for us, but the instruction from the coach was to pass the ball very fast and that is how we played. I think it worked,' Robinho said. 'I was happy to score but I am even happier that we started the tournament with a win.'

However, Brazil lived up to their less-than-complementary reputation as 'the firefly' – handed to them by some supporters because their talent flickered on and off. This was highlighted three days after the drubbing of Greece, when their stars failed to shine in a 1-0 defeat to Mexico.

And Brazil made hard work of qualifying for the second round in their third match of the competition against Japan. The world champions had to thwart a late fightback from the Asian champions and held on for a 2-2 draw to seal a semi-final game against hosts Germany on 25 June. Robinho bounced back from a poor performance against Mexico to put his country ahead after just 10 minutes when he was set up by Ronaldinho. He then returned the favour to set up the Barcelona midfielder to hit Brazil's second before Akira Kaji and Mitsuo Ogasawara pulled Japan back into the match.

The return to form of Robinho sparked more transfer rumours and Brazil coach Parreira responded to talk of the Santos star heading to Real Madrid, or even Arsenal. 'I think it is high time to end the hypocrisy in all of this,' he said. 'This story about the transfer of Robinho has been running since December. I think it is inevitable that, sooner or later, Robinho will be another Brazilian player to leave the country.'

Reports suggested both Arsenal and Real Madrid had lodged bids for the Brazil forward, having watched him in the

Confederations Cup. On 27 June 2005 his agent, Ribeiro, even claimed Madrid had laid down an ultimatum for the Brazilian club. 'If Santos doesn't accept the proposal by July 8, Madrid will issue a statement saying that the club is no longer interested in the player,' Ribeiro told Pelé's website. With Arsenal unveiling Alexander Hleb – a new signing from Stuttgart – the next day, it seemed Real were now favourites to land Robinho's signature and even Ronaldo was hoping the transfer would go through. 'I'm hoping he signs with Real,' said Robinho's Brazilian team-mate. 'Robinho is worth any kind of investment, he is a great player.'

On the pitch it was Adriano and Ronaldinho hitting the headlines, though, the pair netting three goals between them as Brazil, having shaken off the shackles restricting them against Mexico and Japan, defeated hosts Germany 3-2 in Frankfurt to progress to a final against Argentina.

With the momentum now with them, and Argentina having stolen through to the final on penalties against Mexico, Brazil were tipped to take the title, and so it proved.

Ronaldinho, Kaka, Adriano and Robinho were becoming known as the 'Fantastic Four' in Brazil and four goals from three-quarters of the quartet crushed Argentina in the Confederations Cup final on 29 June. Stocky right-back Cicinho, replacing veteran full-back Cafu, also played a key role in all four strikes, teeing up Adriano twice and Ronaldinho for his strike, before playing a pivotal role in the move that put Kaka in for a simple finish as Brazil completed a rout of their fierce rivals, who just two weeks earlier had beaten them in the World Cup qualifiers.

With the title won and the tournament over, Robinho could now focus on dealing with the transfer speculation that had followed him throughout his successful tournament in

Germany. After the final, he told a German TV channel that he now hoped the Santos President Marcelo Teixeira would help him realise his dream by selling him to Real Madrid. 'The moment has come to leave Santos,' he stated. 'I'll go back to Brazil and talk with the Santos president. I expect he understands me. I wish to play for Real Madrid. It is the best club for a Brazilian to play for, where you can find the best players in the world. I know coach Vanderlei Luxemburgo and his work. Also, I am thinking of the security of my family,' said the twenty-one-year-old, the kidnapping incident involving his mother clearly still playing on his mind and perhaps a stimulant, speeding up his departure from Santos.

'I am very thankful with Santos, where I won two Brazilian titles, for what it did for me,' he continued, his love for the Peixe never having been in doubt. 'I would have liked a lot to have reached the Copa Libertadores final, but that was not possible. Now we have to see the future.'

This mutual respect, though, turned sour when, after his return to Brazil it appeared that Santos were not so eager as Robinho to seal his move to Madrid. Robinho and Leo, Santos's duo who had been a part of the Confederations Cup winning squad, returned to their homeland early on Friday, 1 July, and were told to go straight to training so that they were available for Santos's Campeonato fixture with Juventude on the following Sunday. However, Robinho did not appear at the Santos training ground and was fined for his failure to attend. 'I spoke to him earlier and he said he would take part in the training session, but he didn't turn up,' said Santos coach Gallo after the session. 'We're counting on him for practice on Saturday morning. If he goes absent again, we'll hand the matter to the directors.'

The matter was hardly helped by Real Madrid sporting

director Emilio Butragueno declaring their hopes for Robinho at the Bernabeu. 'Robinho,' he said, 'has been the soccer sensation of the past year. Although he is very young, his contribution to Real Madrid can be spectacular.'

On 4 July, ironically Independence Day in America, there seemed no progress in Robinho's release from Santos. The forward had not returned to training as Gallo requested and Wagner Ribeiro claimed that Teixeira was now intent on keeping the youngster at the club for another year. 'The problem isn't the money anymore, but the refusal by Marcelo Teixeira to let him go until next year,' Ribeiro told news agency EFE. Robinho, determined to play for Real Madrid, called on Teixeira to 'keep his promise' and allow him to transfer. 'If I'll play for Santos again, I don't know,' he told reporters. 'I want to leave Brazil. I think this is my moment.'

Reports suggested Robinho said Teixeira agreed to release him for 21 million euros the previous year. 'I didn't think there would be all this hoopla when I got my first concrete offer to leave Brazil,' a frustrated Robinho admitted. 'I never had a problem with President Marcelo Teixeira. He promised something... I hope he keeps his promise. It's hard for me to say I don't want to play any more for Santos, but the intelligent fan understands that I have a right to go to Real, the best club in the world.'

As a disgruntled Robinho missed training again on the Tuesday, Gallo confirmed he had passed the matter on to the directors, before Robinho's former boss, Luxemburgo, told reporters the move was definitely on. 'I think he's going to come,' he said. 'The move could be completed in the next few days.'

Robinho's father, Gilvan de Souza, also stated his belief that the transfer would not be long in coming. 'Teixeira promised us to let him [Robinho] decide about his future after the Liberators Cup. I don't know why he did not meet his word. But I expect the issue to be decided as soon as possible,' de Souza told local media. 'Madrid is a place that allows him to have better living conditions than São Paulo. There language also helps and there is more security, which is always important for a family,' he continued.

De Souza also confirmed that, despite Robinho's desire to join Real, there were other offers in the pipeline for the diminutive star. 'English clubs Arsenal and Chelsea, Holland's PSV Eindhoven and Benfica of Portugal have been interested in my son. But considering the hard work that Real Madrid has done, Robinho is sure that Real is the only club he would like to play with.' Gilvan also revealed that Robinho was prepared to give up his fee in the transfer to help speed the deal along. 'I agree with my son,' he said. 'We would like to give up some percentage we would receive for the transfer. Maybe this would make it easier for Robinho to leave for Spain.'

The saga showed little sign of coming to a quick conclusion, though. Fourteen days after his return from the Confederations Cup, Robinho was still not attending training sessions with Santos – and continued to be fined for each day of his absence. 'He still is Santos's employee,' club spokesman Aldo Neto reasoned. 'We will keep fining him for missing work until he decides to show up again.' However, this hard-line approach was not taken with all players. Leo, Santos's key defender, had sealed a move to Benfica after returning to Santos from the Confederations Cup and striker Deivid, who had enjoyed an impressive start to the 2005 season, was also locked in transfer negotiations with a number of clubs, including his eventual buyers, Sporting Lisbon of Portugal.

Santos, though, were stubbornly refusing to release Robinho – the final jewel in their crown after the departure of so many of their star names in the previous 12 months.

Few could blame them for their desperate desire to hold onto the inspirational Brazilian. Without him their league form had plummeted and the success Emerson Leão and Luxemburgo crafted in 2002 and 2004 was crumbling. Seven months after claiming a second title in three years, Santos were well off the pace in the Brazilian championship. Stripped of its best players and coach, the team was once again slipping back towards mid-table mediocrity. A 1-0 home defeat to Ponte Preta summed up Santos's demise. The result dropped the Peixe into fifth place in the standings, with 24 points from 15 matches. Fans jeered, and demanded the resignation of coach Tadeu Gallo. 'We are unusually nervous, we are not used to losing,' a concerned Gallo told local sports daily, *Lance*. 'The players are trying to do everything right, but they end up making too many mistakes.'

The Ponte Preta defeat for Santos, who fielded a team that mainly warmed the bench for stars such as Diego and Alex in the previous campaign, was their third in a row and sixth in their last 13.

'The team is psychologically discouraged,' reported midfielder Giovanni, one of the few additions made to Santos's roster in 2005, to the *Gazeta Esportiva* website. 'It's been hard, but we need to keep believing. There's still a long way to go.'

After missing 11 games and seeing his club slip down the league, Robinho reportedly offered his services ahead of the clash with local rivals Corinthians in return for a transfer to Madrid. It seemed at first that Santos would turn down the forward's offer, but on the eve of the game it was announced that a deal had been struck with Real Madrid for the transfer. On 30 July Real Madrid issued the following announcement on their website: 'Real Madrid and Santos have today signed an agreement that Robinho will be a Madrid player from August 25. The player will sign a contract which will link him with Real Madrid for the next five seasons.'

'I am sure that Robinho will adapt rapidly to the team,' Luxemburgo proudly told Real's website, following the breakthrough. 'He is a young player brimming with promise, who will be of great help to us.'

A fee was not announced on the Real Madrid website but the *Daily Mail* suggested the figure was 'around £20 million'. The paper also reported Robinho's side of the story following his return from the Confederations Cup. 'The President of Santos came to me and said that if I didn't move last summer and stayed to play Copa Libertadores football, then the club would let me move, without a problem, when the tournament ended,' Robinho explained. 'That same month, September 2004, Real Madrid came in and made a firm offer which both Santos and I accepted, so long as the move was not until this summer. Then I was just waiting for Santos to keep the firm promise that they made to me. This is a guy [Marcelo Teixeira] who, up until recently, had always treated me like one of his sons. During the 40 terrible days when my mother was kidnapped, this man was by my side supporting me all the time. I won't forget that, but nor can I forget the fact that when Real Madrid came in with their offer for me, he made a firm promise about when I could move to play in the Bernabeu. I've no idea why President Teixeira was being so unfair to me or why he was breaking his word. But I'm a man of my word. I'm honest and loyal and I've kept my bargain with Santos. The reason I refused to train with the club after coming home from the Confederations Cup was that I needed to have my situation totally cleared up. I wasn't acting like a baby – I was just looking for Santos to stick to the promise they made me.'

With the transfer cleared up, Santos took Robinho up on his offer and recorded their first win in four games, slamming four past Corinthians in a comprehensive victory. Although Robinho's return was the main headline of the day, the forward clearly suffered from his lack of match fitness after missing 11 matches for Santos. Instead it was midfielder Giovanni who was the decisive player, netting twice in the 4-2 victory. Robinho was also given a lukewarm reception from his previously devoted fans and when he missed an open goal during the second half it seemed his decision to return to the Santos fold was not so wise after all.

However, after the game Pelé was once again willing to offer words of encouragement and admiration for his protégé. 'It will be difficult to find a replacement for Robinho, as he has charisma and good soccer,' the Brazilian legend observed. 'I think that, in the future, Brazil will have players to replace him, but not now. I confess I don't see anyone', he added.

Following a 1-1 draw with third-placed Parana in their next game on 7 August, Robinho conceded he was not up to full strength. 'I'm still only about 80 per cent in shape. But the more I play, the better I feel.'

His final game for the club that had nurtured his talents was against Figuirense at the Vila Belmiro Stadium – which for so long had been like a theatre to his show. 'Nothing against the people of Belem, but I would very much like to say farewell at Vila Belmiro. To tell the truth, I don't like farewells, but I expect to return to Santos in the future,' said the striker.

Thousands of fans crammed into Santos's small stadium on 21 August to bid their hero farewell and the young maverick did not disappoint. He scored twice for the Peixe as the home side overcame their opponents in a thrilling 4-3 victory.

'The fans always supported me, and I'm grateful for the kindness of all,' he emotionally told reporters after the game. 'I wanted to say farewell to the Vila with a victory.'

As Robinho tied up the loose ends on the field the trouble that had quickened his departure also came to a head. It wasn't announced on the eve of his final game that Brazilian police had arrested the mastermind behind the abduction of Robinho's mother, one of Brazil's most-wanted criminals. Celio Marcelo da Silva was caught on the previous Friday night following a car chase and a brief gun battle in a southern section of São Paulo. Da Silva opened fire as officers approached the car he was in with his girlfriend. However, police overpowered the criminal. The accused, it was discovered, had, like a criminal in a movie, escaped from São Paulo prison in 2003 before kidnapping Marina by tunnelling his way out of the compound, where he was serving a 38-year sentence for murder and robbery.

Now, though, Robinho could dream ahead to a new future in Spain's capital city. 'I've always dreamed of playing in Europe, and in particular Spain, because the league there suits my style and is the closest to the type of football played in Brazil,' the twenty-one-year-old wonder kid told Spanish sports newspaper *AS*. 'In Spain, they tend to pass the ball around a lot and play in space, and that will be perfect for me.' The presence of former Santos coach Vanderlei Luxemburgo was also predicted to be ideal for settling the Brazilian in Europe. 'Luxemburgo knows me perfectly, and I know how he works,' Robinho said of his former (and now new) boss. 'I have got a particular style and technique, and Luxemburgo has always put me in positions where I'm used to playing.'

CHAPTER 6
THE MAVERICK OF MADRID

More than 8,000 fanatical Real Madrid supporters flooded into the Santiago Bernabeu stadium as Robinho was unveiled in August 2005, after signing a five-year contract with the Spanish club. The £20-million signing was the latest world star to arrive in the Spanish capital as part of Real Madrid president Florentino Perez's vision of a team of 'galacticos'. Madrid, for the past four seasons, had been spending big money on big names: David Beckham, Zinedine Zidane, Ronaldo and Luis Figo were just a few of the renowned players on the expensively assembled, star-studded Real Madrid roster of 2005.

Robinho was brought in alongside these modern-day megastars to add sparkle and flair, his trickery and dribbling skills intended to add even more bravado and flamboyancy to Madrid's play. 'Football can be many things but one of the most important is the spectacle it provides,' Perez told reporters at Robinho's presentation. 'It is in this aspect of fantasy football that Robinho excels.' Fantasy football, indeed. While thousands of supporters across Britain and

Europe began each season by compiling 'dream teams' for newspaper competitions, Perez was compiling his own dream team for real at Real.

Significantly, indicating the respect and high esteem in which his new employers held him, the twenty-one-year-old Brazilian striker was given the legendary No. 10 shirt. In South American football, and particularly for the national teams, the number 10 is a sacred shirt. Worn by the great Pelé and Diego Maradona for their countries, the shirt became synonymous with creativity, flair, and the team's most exciting player. In 2007 there was much commotion in Brazil when Ronaldinho, who had previously sported the No. 10 shirt, and who had dazzled fans with his flamboyant play, saw the number given to AC Milan's Kaka. Ronaldinho's powers had taken a dip and Kaka, emerging as one of the best players in the world, was awarded the No. 10 shirt in the Brazil team. Many regarded it as a symbol of Brazil looking to a new leader and, somewhat remorselessly, discarding their former talisman.

At Madrid, the number also held significant meaning. It had been worn by Argentina and Spain forward Alfredo Di Stefano, one of the most talented players of all time. Di Stefano was a major part of Real's dominance of European football in the 1950s, when they won five consecutive European Cups, with Di Stefano scoring in all of the finals. 'I wish you well, we expect a lot of you,' Di Stefano told Robinho at the presentation.

Robinho was also eager to deliver. 'Brazilian football is spectacular and entertaining and a lot of its players have succeeded here and I want to do the same,' he said at the ceremony, his words almost drowned out by the singing and cheering of the gathered supporters. 'There are a lot of similarities between Spanish and Brazilian football and I hope to adapt rapidly. It is a great honour for me to be here.'

Later Robinho insisted money wasn't the driving factor for his departure from Santos. In fact, he revealed, he had received far better financial offers from other clubs – though Real Madrid's prestige always made it his preferred destination. 'People said I chose Real because of their economic power, but that is not true. I had better offers from clubs such as Arsenal, Barcelona and Inter Milan. I could have made more money by going elsewhere.'

And so a new era began for Robinho. His task now, after achieving his dream of becoming a professional footballer for Santos, was to establish himself in one of the best teams in the world.

He was named in the squad for the first game of the Spanish season – where Real travelled to coastal club Cadiz on 28 August. The team based in the south of Spain had been promoted to La Liga after finishing second in the Segunda Division in the 2004/05 season. The encounter with Real immediately threw them in at the deep end of top-flight Spanish football, but it was a challenge they were relishing. This was the type of match-up their fans had been dreaming about all summer.

Reality brought them swiftly down to earth when, after just five minutes, Ronaldo fired a low shot into the bottom corner of the Cadiz goal to put Real ahead.

The home side, to their credit, battled strongly and incredibly levelled the scores midway through the second half. Luxemburgo, whose side, in their first game of the season, had seemed short of ideas up until that point, looked to Robinho.

The Brazilian's emergence on the touchline, stripped from

his tracksuit and now standing beside the fourth official in the majestic all-white strip of Real Madrid, drew loud cheers from the travelling support. It did not take long for Robinho to settle into the pace of the game. Real's new number 10 announced his arrival in Spain with a neat flick over an opponent's head – a move dubbed the 'sombrero' by the Spanish – with his very first touch of the ball and proceeded to revitalise the Real attack. Filled with confidence and a desire to impress his new supporters and team-mates, Robinho dazzled the Cadiz defence with unrelenting dribbles, his *pedala* wowing the travelling support and mystifying his opponents. With the game seemingly drifting to a draw, the forward then controlled a lofted pass from David Beckham with his head, swivelled across the edge of the area, played in Ronaldo, who burst into the box and teed up Raul to poke home the winner into the empty net with an inch-perfect pass.

'And God Created Robinho!' bellowed daily sports paper *AS* the next day after the forward's sensational 20-minute display. All the promises Real had been making about Robinho throughout the pursuit of the forward – that he was capable of becoming the best in the world, that his skill and talent were exceptional – seemed confirmed by that 20-minute cameo in Cadiz.

Later that month Robinho was also rewarded with a starting spot for Brazil, when Ronaldinho missed out because of suspension. It seemed Robinho's ability to conjure chances for his side against stubborn defences was key to his promotion from impact-substitute to starter. 'Chile will play tight on defence, and that's why we chose Robinho,' Brazil coach Carlos Alberto Parreira said. 'We have to use the dribble to get them off-balance so, Robinho.'

The hype and excitement, which continued to flourish with his move to Real Madrid, may have drawn jealous glances from former 'next big things' but it was a signal of the São Vicente-born star's popularity among his team-mates that they were happy for him, rather than envious of the attention and praise he received. 'It happened to me once. But I'm not jealous. It's time to talk about Robinho,' said AC Milan's Kaka while World Cup veteran Roberto Carlos, who had continually praised the young forward throughout his rise to fame commented: 'I have no doubt that next year Robinho will be chosen the world's best player. He has more than enough talent to do it. It's rare to see a player do the things he does with the ball.'

Parreira, although a fan of the former Santos striker, was cautious not to let the hyperbole get too out of hand. 'There's a tremendous marketing campaign around Robinho,' he said. 'I worry about this exaggeration over what he is, what he will be. Things should go a little slower, more normal, because his career is just starting.'

However, Robinho did little to help Parreira quell the wave of optimism surrounding him, seizing his opportunity as a starter for Brazil and playing a key role in a 5-0 demolition of Chile that guaranteed the 2002 World Cup winners a spot in Germany 2006. Robinho, notably wearing the No. 10 shirt for his national side in the absence of Ronaldinho, scored a goal and set up two for Adriano, demonstrating his strong work ethic by tracking back to defend. He also took the Man of the Match award. 'The No. 10 has found its owner,' declared the Rio sporting daily *Lance*.

However, this thrilling start to life at Madrid, further publicised by Robinho's shining performance for Brazil, made him a marked man when Real faced Celta Vigo. A 3-2 home defeat – a rarity at the Bernabeu – shocked the Madrid supporters. 'We worked hard, suffered and just got the piece of luck that you need to win games like this. It was a dream to win here and we have realised it. We closed down the spaces, which limited the number of passes that could get to Robinho,' commented Celta coach Fernando Vazquez after masterminding the victory.

Another shock result followed in the Champions League – Robinho's first experience of Europe's premier club competition was not to be a happy one. Instead it was another Brazil midfielder, Juninho Pernambucano, who took the headlines, scoring one goal and setting up another as his French side Lyon beat Real Madrid 3-0 in Group F on 13 September. Three goals in the first 30 minutes stunned the Spanish side, who couldn't find a way back into the match, despite second-half long-range efforts from Raul and Robinho.

The bizarre recent results, though, appeared to be simply a blip, and Robinho netted his first goal for Real in a 3-1 win over Athletic Bilbão the following week. Unusually for the small striker his goal came through a well-taken header after an inch-perfect cross from David Beckham. However, the game would be remembered for the sensational debut of England defender Jonathan Woodgate.

In the summer of 2004 the former Leeds United centre-half had signed for Real from Newcastle for £13.4 million, and had had to wait over a year to make his debut, after missing all of his first season with the club through injury. In his first game in the white shirt of Madrid, against Bilbão, he managed to score an own goal and was sent off for a second yellow card. 'I just can't believe I got sent off and scored an own goal on my debut,' the Middlesbrough-born defender told reporters. 'That's not the way that I dreamed my debut would be. I am in shock. At least things can only get better...' Fortunately for Woodgate, Robinho and Raul were on hand to erase his errors and seal a victory for Real, in bizarre circumstances.

In October 2005 Brazil rounded off their marathon qualification campaign of 18 matches with a 1-1 draw away to Bolivia and a 3-0 home win over Venezuela. The four points from their final round of fixtures was enough to seal first place in the CONMEBOL World Cup Qualifying standings, ahead of rivals Argentina on goal difference. Ecuador and Paraguay also progressed to the finals, while Uruguay took fifth spot in the table, booking a play-off match against Australia, which they eventually lost on penalties.

So Brazil had booked their spot on a plane to Germany the following summer and for Robinho it seemed the opportunity of representing Brazil at a major international tournament was just around the corner. His chances of making the squad – considered by many to be a certainty after his vibrant displays of the past year and a half for club and country – were bolstered on 13 October when he was named by FIFA on the shortlist for the 2005 World Player of the Year award. Alongside the all-star names of Ronaldo, Thierry Henry, Frank Lampard, Paolo Maldini, Andriy Shevchenko, Zinedine Zidane, Michael Ballack and last year's winner Ronaldinho, Robinho's name proudly sat at home among the best players in the world.

Real Madrid returned to Premier League action a week later and, following a 2-1 win over Olympiakos in September, lined up against Norway's Rosenborg at the Bernabeu on 19 October. It turned into a stroll for Los Blancos, who routed their visitors 4-1, with Woodgate making up for his disastrous debut by heading in the opener from a Beckham cross in his first European game for the Spanish giants.

The victory kick-started Real's season and 10 days later they moved to the summit of the Primera Liga after goals from Robinho, his second in the white of Madrid, and Alvaro Mejia gave them a 2-0 win over struggling Real Betis. Robinho opened the scoring by curling in a left-footed shot, a crucial strike considering Real played the game without Brazilian pair Ronaldo and Julio Baptista, Beckham and Zidane through injury.

Robinho then hit top gear in Norway as Real assured their progress in the Champions League with a 2-0 win over Rosenborg on 28 September. Robinho fired a dangerous cross across the face of goal in the 26th minute, which was deflected past Rosenborg goalkeeper Espen Johnsen by defender Mikael Dorsin before another Robinho dash into the box just before the break teed up Guti for the decisive second.

Robinho had enjoyed a decent start to his time at Real, his agility and trickery causing Spanish sides the same problems Santos's opponents had previously had to endure. However, Robinho revealed his physique was being addressed by the Real medical team, who feared the strain of a full Spanish season would tell on the Brazilian's slight frame 'The fitness trainers would like me to strengthen my muscles,' Robinho said. At the time the forward weighed just 60 kilos. 'With training, I'll improve.'

A string of disappointing results was not the ideal way of building up for 'el clasico' at the Bernabeu against Barcelona, but for the Spanish media, the game was built up to be a mega clash of the titans, with Robinho and Barcelona's Argentinean trickster, Lionel Messi, the centrepieces of the battle.

'The new Pelé vs the new Maradona' the papers dubbed the duel, which was reminiscent of the showdown between Carlos Tevez and Robinho the previous season, when the Brazilian inspired Santos to a famous victory over their rivals and his Argentinean counterpart. However, this time, it was Argentina who won the battle on 19 November. Barcelona battered their arch-rivals on their own ground, emerging 3-0 victors and humiliating Los Blancos in the process. 'The Catalans cruelly exposed Real Madrid's galacticos in front of their own fans and proved that it is they who are the true exponents of the "beautiful game"', reported Spanish sports paper *Marca*.

Barça were led by the brilliant Ronaldinho, who hit a double before Samuel Eto'o capped the win. Ronaldinho's performance was so impressive he was given a standing ovation by the Bernabeu crowd after netting his second goal, an unprecedented act by the Madrid support, as much in mockery of their own team as acknowledging the talents of Barça's star player.

As autumn turned to winter Robinho, posted up front as the point of Real's attack in the absence of the injured Ronaldo, was desperately struggling for form. He was failing to live up to his price tag and, with his goals drying up, he had hit the back of the net just twice in 18 domestic and Champions League games since his move. In the meantime, Real were six points off the pace set by their impressive rivals Barcelona and by the start of December had dropped to sixth spot in the league.

'It's difficult because Ronaldo is injured. Playing at the front of everybody isn't usual for me, but I'm trying to adapt. It's a bit tricky,' conceded the youngster, who was now drawing criticism from the press. However, the

Brazilian refused to concede defeat in his battle to prove his doubters wrong. 'Pressure is normal at Real Madrid. It's my first year. I have to work and perform on the pitch. The team has injured players and it's more difficult. I don't have problems of adapting. All I have to do is put in the work,' he told the club's official website. 'There is always pressure wherever you go. I'm used to it because I was in the Brazil team very young and that means having to perform in every game. The people expect the spectacular and it's the same at Real Madrid.'

It seemed odd that Luxemburgo, who had drawn the best performances from Robinho in his early career at Santos, had now placed him all alone up front, where the long balls sailed over his head and he bounced off the burly centre-halves. However, he stood by the Under-fire manager who had helped him realise his dream of playing in Spain. 'It's difficult as we know that we have to improve. The coach is experienced and he's used to this type of pressure. They have to be patient with me and with everyone else. We are not worried about Barcelona, but about ourselves.'

However, his pleas fell on deaf ears and within days of Robinho's comments Luxemburgo was fired by Real Madrid. It seemed the humiliation by Barcelona was the final nail in his coffin after just six months at Real, proving the short-term lives of managers in Spain were no different to the high-pressure placements in Brazil.

'It's what happens in football,' a disappointed Robinho told press after Luxemburgo's dismissal. 'He is a great coach, as he has proved in Brazil, winning the league so many times. But Real Madrid is a club where you have to win always. And when that doesn't happen it's normal that they change the coach.'

Replacing Luxemburgo was the relatively inexperienced Spaniard Juan Ramon Lopez Caro, who had been in charge of the Real Madrid B team.

If there was any threat to his position at the club following the departure of Luxemburgo, Robinho responded superbly, his masterful display inspiring Real Madrid to their first win under their new coach in a 2-0 triumph at Malaga. Sergio Ramos rose to head home a Zidane corner to open the scoring, and then Robinho sidestepped a defender before cracking a shot into the roof of the net to cap a fine display. Robinho had been moved out to the wing by Lopez, where he could receive the ball in space, cut inside and run at the heart of defences. 'I am more content on the wing,' he said. 'That is where I played for Santos. It's where I feel I'm better suited.' Ironically, despite Luxemburgo's familiarity with Robinho, it was Lopez who had turned the Brazilian back into being a threat.

Despite the decent start, rumours continued to surface in the Spanish press that Lopez was merely a stop-gap at Madrid before Real could persuade Arsenal's Arsène Wenger to join the club. Matters weren't helped when Real failed to capitalise against 10-man, top-of-the-table Osasuna.

Although the display was disappointing, there appeared to be little option for Real other than to stick with Lopez. With most of their world-class targets tied into contracts, Real opted to avoid mid-season negotiations, which might disrupt the squad, and stand by Lopez until the end of the season, when they would re-focus on hiring a big-name boss. 'The news fills me with satisfaction. I'm excited and aware of the responsibility upon me. Real Madrid is a great club and I have a team of great players who are very keen to develop and improve the team's level,' Lopez Caro was quoted as saying by sports daily *Marca*.

As is sometimes the case, despite Lopez not being of the usual calibre of Real coaches, the stability he brought to the side in the wake of Luxemburgo's departure allowed Madrid to develop and the Spaniard began to engineer a turnaround in the side's fortunes.

Real progressed to the last eight of the Copa del Rey with a 4-0 hammering of Athletic Bilbão at the Bernabeu. A double from Robinho set up the victory while Sergio Ramos and reserve team striker Roberto Soldado secured the 5-0 aggregate win over their Primera Liga opponents.

That return to form crossed over into the league where Real put together a run of six straight wins. The sixth, a 2-1 win over Celta Vigo on 29 January, saw Robinho hit the net once again for Real, sliding a low shot past the Celta keeper after good work from Julio Baptista. The victory lifted Real back into third spot in the league, though the galacticos still trailed their Catalan rivals, Barcelona, who were now back ahead of Osasuna and 12 points clear of Madrid.

It was a tall mountain to climb, but a more likely target for silverware in 2005/06 was the Copa del Rey. Madrid had reached the semi-finals of the contest and now faced Real Zaragoza in the final four showdown. Their opponents had experienced a mixed campaign that left them free from the trials and tribulations of relegation, but too far behind the league's front runners to aim for the European qualification spots, so their sights were firmly set on progress in the domestic knockout competition. And with the scalps of Atletico Madrid and Barcelona already in their locker, the club from the north-east of Spain, who many expected Real to overcome, could not be taken lightly.

Whether Real Madrid did underestimate their opponents is unclear, but the result in the first leg of the semi-final on 8

February was a humiliation for the Spanish giants. The nine-times European champions crumbled at Zaragoza's La Romareda stadium. Argentine striker Diego Milito fired four past the helpless Iker Casillas as Zaragoza routed the Spanish giants 6-1, seemingly putting the tie beyond doubt. The Argentine notched his hat-trick in less than 20 minutes and Ewerthon, his Brazilian strike partner, completed the demolition, with Baptista's goal the only cheer for Madrid. If it were not for the woodwork and some fine stops from Casillas the result could have been even more of an embarrassment for Lopez and his side.

'We played a brilliant game and the players were extraordinary in every respect', the Zaragoza boss Victor Munoz reflected after the match. 'Our performance bordered on perfection.' However, he was cautious of a Madrid backlash in the return leg at the Bernabeu, a week later: 'I honestly don't believe the tie is over. Madrid are a great team and deserve all the respect in the world. We are optimistic, of course, but the tie hasn't been decided yet.'

Real coach Juan Ramon Lopez Caro, however, was looking forward to the challenge of the second leg. 'Zaragoza played an exceptional game, they were phenomenal and were much better than us. For the cowards the tie is over but in my view we have a team with enough pride, guts and talent to believe that we can turn it round. Just as Zaragoza had a wonderful night, I believe we can have one too. This team has proved they can fight back after difficult situations and I have great confidence in my players.'

But the confidence in his side seemed misplaced: after all, Real were hardly a side riding high on confidence and the galacticos assembled at the club were not exactly familiar with being crushed 6-1 away from home by a mid-table team.

Fortunately, three days later they came up against a struggling Athletic Bilbão side in the league and goals from Robinho and Raul Bravo saw Real Madrid record a spirit-lifting 2-0 win to keep their league title dreams alive. Robinho's finish, a powerful left-foot drive after being played in perfectly by Zidane, was the mark of a player returning to form and the young Brazilian seemed, finally, to be settling in at Madrid.

Remarkably, Robinho's return to form nearly inspired Real to a comeback in their second leg against Zaragoza on 14 February. Madrid steamed into a 3-0 lead inside the first 10 minutes of the match, scaring the life out of their opponents, who had seen their comfortable first-leg lead suddenly stripped down to a mere two-goal advantage with 80 minutes to play. With 70,000 fans packed into the Bernabeu, delightedly cheering on the Real renaissance, the visitors were suddenly, and unexpectedly, rocking.

Brazilian full-back Cicinho started the fanfare with a 25-yard thunderbolt in the very first minute of the game. Just minutes later, Robinho steered in at the back-post after Ronaldo clipped the ball across the area before Ronaldo got on the scoresheet himself, stabbing home an inch-perfect cross from Beckham.

Zaragoza were stunned by Real's whirlwind start and nerves appeared to get the better of them as they made a series of errors in midfield and looked uncharacteristically shaky in defence. Roberto Carlos made it 4-0 just after the hour with a trademark rocket shot to set up a grandstand finish, with Madrid needing just one goal to seal a remarkable away-goals victory. However, despite a nervous and desperate final half-hour, Madrid were unable to find the final goal and Zaragoza scraped through with a nail-biting 6-

5 aggregate victory. It would be their third Copa del Rey final in six seasons, but surely the most thrilling semi-final encounter they had played in all those years.

With their marvellous cup performance behind them Real looked forward to the Champions League first knockout round, where they faced Arsenal on 21 February. The English club had comfortably won their group, conceding just two goals in their six games, and none in their last four. However, in the league, Jose Mourinho's Chelsea was pulling away from Arsène Wenger's side and Thierry Henry, the club's captain and star player, told reporters the club were now, like Real, pinning their season on progress in the European tournament: 'If we perform as badly away in that competition as we have in the Premiership, we will be out – it's as simple as that. We came through our group well and because we finished top, we play the first leg away from home. But we mustn't get carried away by what we did in the group stages. That is totally different from what we face now. If we have a bad 25 minutes away, that could be that.'

Unlike their opponents, Real were coming into the tie with a spring in their step from their improved league form, and had fired three past Alaves the previous weekend. Robinho was also hopeful of making a mark in the competition, after coming through the bad patch of form that had dogged the start of his Real career. 'I've never played in England before,' he told *The Times* ahead of the Round of 16 knockout game. 'I want to show everyone what I can do. The truth is, we didn't start the season very well in the Champions League or in our own league, but we are playing much better now and we are still going strong in both competitions.'

However, preparation for the game was hit by a bombshell from their striker, Ronaldo. The Brazilian marksman was whistled and jeered by some Real supporters after failing to score in the drubbing of Alaves and the abuse had clearly affected the forward. 'I've never felt at home at the Bernabeu, the fans have never treated me with affection,' the three-times World Player of the Year revealed. 'The fans have never accepted me. The reaction of the fans is something to take into account when thinking about my future. I've always said that I don't want to be where I'm not loved. I will make a decision at the end of the season. After all the effort I made to come to this club I don't understand why I'm treated like this. I will decide after the World Cup.'

Whether or not the threats of Real's striker to quit the club affected his team-mates, Madrid's players failed to perform in their first leg tie at the Bernabeu. Arsène Wenger's side sealed a 1-0 win on enemy territory – the first home league defeat for Real in 19 ties and the first time they had lost to an English club in the competition. Arsenal's clean sheet also took them within two shutouts of equalling AC Milan's seven-game record without conceding a goal. 'It's a long time since I have seen an Arsenal team play like that. We were brilliant defensively and the most important thing is that we were not scared to play. And when we are not scared, we can get results,' Thierry Henry proudly said of his team after the game.

In the other corner Real were not so content and Beckham exemplified Madrid's frustrations, uncharacteristically losing his cool with his team-mates. 'That is what happens when you don't work hard and tackle back,' said the disgruntled England captain. 'I am bitterly disappointed. I knew after five minutes we were going to lose, but we have got away with it, we could have lost by more.' It was even reported, in the *Mirror*, that Ronaldo and Guti broke out in a fight in the

Real dressing room after the defeat. Spanish international midfielder Guti missed his country's 3-2 win over Ivory Coast a week after the Arsenal clash because of a leg injury – rumoured to be sustained by a kick from Ronaldo after the Champions League first leg defeat. The pair, who were close friends, signified how high tensions were running in the Real Madrid camp, with the side desperate to avoid a third season without winning a trophy.

Real Madrid's problems, though, went from bad to worse. On 26 February the club lost 2-1 to Real Mallorca and then president Florentino Perez resigned a week ahead of their second leg with Arsenal at Highbury. The president admitted there were divisions in the dressing-room. Perez's policy of making big-name signings for vast sums of money and then insisting these players be 'undroppable' had caused problems at the club and upset home-grown stars, but he always answered criticism by pointing to Real's strength on the pitch and in the marketplace – where they had recently been named the richest club in the world.

Perez said that Sergio Ramos, the teenage defender, had been correct when he suggested that all was not well between the club's players and added that 'some players seem to be confused and perhaps I am responsible for that and that is why I am going'. Ramos scored in that Sunday's defeat by Real Mallorca and said afterwards, regarding the lacklustre celebrations from his team-mates, that it was 'as if Mallorca and not Madrid had scored.'

The construction magnate called to a close a six-year reign after his worst week since he took over at the Bernabeu. Eight days earlier, Ronaldo had spouted his intentions to leave due to poor treatment from fans. The next day, Real were defeated by Arsenal. In their first training session back after the loss, it was Raul's turn to add to the unrest. He criticised Ronaldo for his ill-timed comments, accusing him of destroying the magic of a Champions League night by thinking of himself instead of the team. The next day, Lopez, the coach, criticised both players for their public spat and Real went into the fixture against Mallorca, the relegation strugglers, lacking team spirit and togetherness. Mallorca took full advantage by winning 2-1 and leaving Real 10 points behind Barcelona, the La Liga leaders.

The defeat appeared to remove any hope of Real catching their Catalan rivals and, after the first-leg reverse against Arsenal and a Copa Del Rey semi-final exit, the president faced a third season in a row without a trophy: 'I decided after the defeat to Real Mallorca to resign', said Perez, adding that he thought it would have a positive effect on Real's season.

A disjointed, but determined Real arrived at Highbury two weeks after their home defeat to try and salvage something from the 2005/06 season. However, despite throwing everything at Arsenal, Real simply could not find a way through the London club's stubborn defence. Despite the best efforts of Raul, Robinho and Beckham they could not unlock the Arsenal back line and the home side held on for a superb 0-0 draw, which earned them a quarter-final tie with Juventus.

For Real, there was no option but to return to the Spanish league and hope a slip-up from leaders Barcelona could give them the opportunity to salvage something from their season. The Barça boys, though, were 9 points clear with 11 games remaining, and looked set to retain their title. However, a week after the Arsenal match, the league leaders went down 2-1 to Osasuna, giving their closest pursuers, Valencia and Real Madrid, a glimmer of hope.

'We have to be optimistic. If Barcelona lost against Osasuna they can also lose other games before the end of the season. Anything can happen,' Madrid goalkeeper Iker Casillas told sports daily *AS*.

With this new-found belief and hope Real set about making sure that if the title favourites did slip up they would be there to capitalise. Their football became more attacking, more determined, and as a result, more successful. Real emphatically crushed Deportivo la Coruna, a perfect example of their new attitude. Their coach, Lopez Caro, described his side's performance at the Bernabeu as 'spectacular', and the improvement was in large part due to the recall of David Beckham, who had sparked controversy when he was left on the substitutes' bench the previous week. It was his free kick that brought the breakthrough on 9 minutes, Deportivo defender Hector Berenguel turning the whipped cross past his own keeper. Robinho tricked his way to the by-line, and continued to torment his markers. He then opened up the Deportivo defence for Real's second, cleverly back-heeling for Roberto Carlos, who crossed for Ronaldo to score. In the second period Robinho spurned three good opportunities, all created by Beckham, but Sergio Ramos and Julio Baptista completed the scoring to seal a comfortable win for Real.

However, the victory merely kept Barcelona in sight on the horizon, the Catalan club continued to win, and when the sides met for the second time in the league on 2 April, Real were in need of a miracle to rein in the league leaders. However, it was not to be for Los Blancos. Roberto Carlos brought down Mark van Bommell in the box to concede a penalty, which was duly converted by Ronaldinho before the Brazilian full-back picked up his second yellow card, leaving Real an hour to play with 10 men, desperate to avoid the humiliation of the 3-0 drubbing they suffered at the Bernabeu earlier in the season. Robinho was sacrificed for the more defensive Mejia and Real saved face and secured a respectable 1-1 draw after Ronaldo fired an equaliser and some desperate defending kept Barcelona's forwards at bay.

The result effectively sealed the title for Barcelona with only one match of note left for Real in their disastrous 2005/06, season which had seen them close a three-year period without any silverware, their worst run since the 1950s. Zinedine Zidane played his final match at the Bernabeu in a 3-3 draw against Villarreal in May; the midfield magician who had orchestrated Madrid was retiring. The Frenchman put in an impressive display in his final game and when he nodded in a Beckham cross the 82,000 fans erupted with applause. This may not have been his most spectacular strike but it was fitting for the one-time Player of the Year, considered by many to be one of the best players ever.

Real finished the season 12 points behind their rivals, Barcelona, but their end-of-season recovery secured them second spot and an automatic berth into the Champions League, a point ahead of Valencia and two clear of Osasuna, both of whom would have to play in the preliminary rounds of the 2006/07 European tournament to make the financially rewarding group stages. Despite a turbulent season, Ronaldo finished as the league's fifth-best scorer, with 14 goals.

For Robinho 2005/06 had been a steep learning curve. He had hit the net 14 times in all competitions, but perhaps playing throughout the summer with Santos and Brazil and then straight into the autumn with Real had taken its toll on the forward. However, he had displayed glimpses of what he could do to the expectant Real support, and also shown resilience to adversity and an ability to bounce back when heavily criticised by the Spanish press. He had been unable to inspire Real, unlike Santos, to silverware but now he had an opportunity to prove his worth on the world stage: at the 2006 World Cup in Germany. Brazil were favourites to retain their crown from Japan and Korea. This would be his first major tournament for Brazil and one he would remember for the rest of his life.

CHAPTER 7
THE WEIGHT OF THE WORLD

On a calm morning on 22 May 2006, a plane took off from Rio de Janeiro without any fanfare or ceremony. Painted on one side of it were five large gold stars, symbols of Brazil's five World Cup wins – in 1958, 1962, 1970, 1994 and 2002. Inside sat the World Champions, en route to Germany, where they were fully expected to retain their title and claim an unprecedented sixth World Cup.

It was the first time the champions had flown out for a World Cup without any official leaving ceremony, though it would be wrong to suggest this was because the Brazilian population were not interested in their team's exploits. On the contrary, every four years Brazil turns into a sea of yellow and green national flags. Bars and clubs are packed with supporters watching the national team on TV. Every day of the tournament there is excitement, celebration and anticipation on the streets and beaches throughout the country. The progress of the national team takes over the back and front sheets of the country's newspapers and dominates television coverage. If football is a religion in

Brazil, then the World Cup is like Christmas Day for the avid supporters in South America.

Among the 23-man squad of players, Real Madrid's Robinho, competing in his first World Cup, proudly sat, eagerly anticipating his first major tournament representing his homeland. 'Ever since I was a kid I've dreamt of playing for the national side and I'm very happy,' he said at the time.

Brazil's initial base was in the Swiss town of Weggis. The squad and staff would remain in Switzerland until 3 June, when they would move to Germany and their base for the 9 June–9 July finals – Königstein im Taunus, near Frankfurt.

Unlike many other sides Brazil only had two friendly matches scheduled ahead of the tournament, coach Carlos Alberto Parreira preferring to focus on training sessions and tactical meetings rather than match-practice. In fact, only one of the friendlies was against a national side. They would meet Swiss club side FC Lucerne on 30 May before tackling New Zealand, who failed to reach the finals, on 4 June. The pre-tournament schedule seemed light, but the squad and staff were confident they were well-prepared to defend their crown. 'The core of the team has already been decided a long time ago and Parreira knows all the players,' young forward Fred, who was not expected to be a first-team starter, told reporters when the team touched down in Switzerland. 'The time spent in Weggis will simply serve to iron out some details.'

The day after the 12-hour flight from Brazil to Switzerland, the team began a series of physical tests at a top European clinic in preparation for the following month's tournament. While Robinho joined the first batch of players to undergo medical check-ups to ensure the squad was in fine fettle ahead of the World Cup, Brazil boss Parreira addressed the media with an air of confidence in his players. Despite the tournament being three weeks away, the coach was happy to reveal his starting line-up to the world's press. 'The national team hasn't played together in a long time,' he told reporters. 'So it's important we maintain the same team that played [in the last matches]. It might not be the set-up we finish the World Cup with, but we will start with it.'

Parreira's plan to begin the tournament with the side that defeated Venezuela 3-0 in their final World Cup qualifying match was not good news for Robinho. The Real Madrid forward had been used as a second-half substitute in the game, meaning he was likely to start his first World Cup on the bench as well. However, this didn't seem to affect the twenty-one-year old, who saw the bigger picture and a team's need for a strong squad at a long tournament like the World Cup. 'In the national team, not always the eleven who begin the competition are the eleven who finish it,' he said. 'I'm getting ready to play. In a World Cup several things may happen and I need to be prepared if an opportunity comes up. We have excellent group of players and I respect everybody, but I'll be working hard to get my spot.'

Robinho, though, was a favourite of Parreira's and likely to get some game time eventually. 'I think he's already become one of Real Madrid's most important players and will be one of the most exciting stars of the World Cup,' the Brazil boss told reporters before the contest. Mentally, Robinho also had the exact attitude Parreira wanted from his players. After winning the title in 2002 and making the final in 1998, Parreira needed to ensure the desire to win again in Germany was burning strong in the Brazilian players. 'That's the challenge, to make them hungry again,' he said. 'I'm not worried about our system or our tactics. And of course I'm not worried about the technique of the players. But if we are going to win, it's going to be with our heads. It will be a mental victory. If we are mentally strong, we will be very difficult to beat.

'We in Brazil have always had the best players by far, but even with the best players we went 24 years without winning the World Cup. Quality and talent are not enough to be world champions.

'In that sense, it's not fair; it doesn't tell you who the best team in the competition is. In a league you can lose games and still win if you are the best. In the World Cup, you can't have a bad day. I suppose that is why football is the No. 1 sport in the world. More than any other sport, the smaller team can beat the bigger team. You don't see it in basketball or volleyball or rugby. The small teams always have a chance. There might be a refereeing mistake or an individual mistake, or they can stop the better from playing or maybe it is just luck.

'You saw it in 2002. Look at what South Korea did to Spain and Italy, they almost reached the final. The US were much better than Germany on the day, they should have knocked them out. And yet we attach so much importance to this competition, to these seven games. I remember Holland '74 and Hungary '54, but today it is all changed,' he said, mentioning the two sides that failed to win the tournament but were widely considered the best teams at the World Cup for their fantastic forward play. 'Winning is more important than anything else. If you don't win, nobody remembers you. Brazil is considered the favourite because of the success it has had in the past, and that is natural. But the Cup is treacherous. It's seven games, and from the fourth match onward, it's single elimination. So being the favourite off the field doesn't count for much, because on the pitch, everyone is equal and we have to be very attentive so that we don't get taken by surprise.'

The 32 nations, out of the initial 198 that had begun qualifying, which had made it to the finals in Germany were split into groups of four, based on their qualification performance and world ranking. Brazil had been drawn in Group F with Australia, Croatia and Japan. For Parreira Croatia – who had won a qualification group including Sweden, Hungary and Bulgaria – held the greatest threat to Brazil's chances of winning the group, but he was positive his side were capable of beating anybody and dealing with the pressure of reigning champions. 'Croatia did very well in the qualifying round and beat Argentina [in a friendly],' he said. 'Germany, Argentina, England and Italy also have this "obligation" to win the title, just like Brazil. It's true that we have great chances to win the World Cup but that doesn't mean it's a done deal. We still need to play the matches and win them. And we know that's not going to be easy. All teams will be trying their best to beat the defending champions.'

Brazil had every reason to be confident, though. As well as current holders, their team seemed to be miles ahead of their nearest rivals in terms of technical ability, even their squad players were a match for a number of the big nations at the World Cup. They also had history on their side, as their record at World Cups is unmatchable. Prior to World Cup 2006, Brazil had reached the semi-finals in 10 of the past 17 World Cups since the competition started in 1930, and were the only team to have played in every tournament. As well as the five tournament wins the country had finished runner-up twice.

Confidence was also high in the camp. Striker Ronaldo, a Real Madrid team-mate of Robinho, told the press: 'We have a very strong team, very technical and experienced.' Ronaldo was the hero of the 2002 tournament for Brazil, and going into the 2006 competition was just three goals away from breaking Gerd Muller's record of most career World Cup goals, which stood at 14 and had not been beaten since the 1970 tournament.

World Cup football is high stakes sport. Clearly Parreira, in the back of his mind, knew that once Brazil navigated the reasonably simple group stage, as they should, a slip-up or moment of lost concentration could cost them dearly in the nail-biting knockout rounds. Parreira had an advantage over most coaches, though: he had been there and done it all before. He had won the World Cup with Brazil in 1994 and also guided smaller nations such as Saudi Arabia and the United Arab Emirates to the biggest stage in the world. His proudest moment, he told reporters, was not winning the World Cup for his country in 1994, but guiding Kuwait to the finals in 1982. 'Qualifying for the World Cup with Kuwait was much better than winning it with Brazil. I worked there for eight years, we built everything from zero. It was fantastic. I've been in football for 38 years, this is going to be my seventh World Cup,' he said. 'I was part of two winning World Cups, I've achieved a lot. My professional life is fulfilled, I didn't miss anything not working in other European leagues.'

However, despite his achievements, Parreira was surely aware that a failure to deliver with this hugely talented side, including the best player in the world, Ronaldinho, would take the shine off his glittering career as a coach.

On 28 May Brazil rattled up a 13-1 victory over Fluminense's junior side in a training session. It may have been good shooting practice for the Brazil forwards, and

Robinho in particular who netted four times, but the press questioned the sensibility of practising against such inferior sides ahead of the World Cup. Parreira was unfazed by the concerns. 'It doesn't worry me that we may not start the tournament playing at 100 per cent of our ability,' he said. 'If you start off at 100 per cent then you've got no room for improvement. My objective is to improve game by game so that by the end of the tournament we are at our peak.'

Two days later Brazil faced a moderately tougher test against FC Lucerne, but once again the strikers had a field day, Adriano and Ronaldo netting a brace each in a one-sided 8-0 win. Kaka, Lucio, Juninho and Robinho also got in on the act in front of nearly 30,000 fans, who had packed St. Jakob-Park to see little more than an extended training session.

After the match Parreira was happy with his team's display. 'Our adversary wasn't technically very strong, but for the beginning of the preparation [the result] was from regular to good. We still need to improve for the World Cup. The point of the match was to give the first team a chance to take to the field of play because these players have not played together since October last year. Today was only our eighth day of preparation, it's a short period of time to expect perfection.'

The only criticism of Brazil in the match was that Ronaldo, despite his two goals, seemed sluggish and not as sharp as Brazil's supporters would have hoped, two weeks before the World Cup. Parreira, though, was happy with the condition of his key marksman. 'Ronaldo played a match tonight for the first time in 52 days and he scored two goals. Ronaldo's aim is exactly that, scoring goals, and that's why he is in the Brazilian team.

'I'm sure Ronaldo will have a great World Cup, because he's a player for special moments. He enjoys great personal challenges. It would be a big let-down if he did not have a great World Cup. Ronaldo has to lead and has to be our reference point. He has to take this responsibility. In the World Cup, it's fundamental to have players with experience. If you just take a group of youngsters you are not going to get anywhere. But he is not going to be fresh at the start of the World Cup.'

Goal-scoring certainly wouldn't be a problem for the Brazilians. Arsenal's Gilberto was well aware of that. 'Look at our forwards – they are the best in the world. We have Robinho, Adriano, Ronaldo and Ronaldinho – who else can boast talent like that? The coach's problem is, of course, that it is not possible to play them all. But I believe Parreira knows what he wants. He is a strong coach. Whoever plays we will have quality out there.'

However, Brazil's preparations seemed to be shaken up when Swiss newspaper *Blick* reported seven players from the Brazil squad, including Robinho, Ronaldo and Adriano, had spent the night after the Lucerne victory in a bar until 3.30am the following morning. When Parreira was questioned about this, though, he was unconcerned about the incident, stating he would not punish the players. 'I have no comments concerning the players' free time. People are free to do whatever they want,' he stated. The players too were untroubled by the tabloid revelation. Their calm response to press questions, coupled with Parreira's placidity, proved the 'exposé' from Blick was nothing more than a storm in a teacup. 'We had a free day and went to a bar. It's no big deal,' shrugged Ronaldo.

Clearly, the night out had little effect on the players, who a few days later comfortably defeated New Zealand 4-0 in their final World Cup warm-up game at the Stade de Geneve, again in front of a packed crowd. Ronaldo, Adriano and Kaka were again on the scoresheet, while substitute Juninho also found the back of the net. 'You cannot expect the willingness, the mental toughness in this friendly game, but I was happy and satisfied with what I saw,' Parreira reflected after the game. 'When we were offered the opportunity to play New Zealand I liked the idea because they look like our group opponents, Australia. It suited us well. We haven't had many games in our preparation because we preferred training to playing.' Parreira was also pleased with the performances of his 'magic quartet' of Ronaldo, Ronaldinho, Adriano and Kaka, as well as Robinho. 'I don't need to tell you anything about Adriano, Ronaldo, Robinho and Ronaldinho. They are world-class players – everybody knows them and everybody knows their potential. We are going to see after the first game of the World Cup whether they are 100 per cent.'

With preparations nearly complete, the countdown to their first World Cup clash with Croatia was on for Brazil. However, the side were hit with the news that Ronaldo would be a doubt for the first game of the tournament. The forward, who despite criticism in the press about his condition had been scoring freely in the practice matches, was suffering with severe blisters on his feet. Ronaldo had been replaced at half-time in the New Zealand clash by Robinho and the star striker revealed he had been in extreme pain during the first 45 minutes. 'It's not just one blister, it's several on both feet,' he said. 'One is from an open wound and I am using ointment to accelerate healing. During the game with New Zealand I tried to put padding on the heel area, but it did not help. I have to treat myself well so that the blisters do not interfere with my World Cup preparations. Maybe there is a need to change the boots.'

Roberto Carlos, the Brazil and Real Madrid full-back also admitted that the squad were bound to feel some nerves ahead of their match with Croatia. 'Our biggest worry for the first match will be the anxiety,' he said. 'We'll need to find ways to control it.' Defender Lucio agreed: 'We've been waiting four years for this. There is a lot of anxiety, I'm sure everyone here is feeling it.' Even Brazil's veteran coach admitted he wasn't immune to first-match jitters. 'I would be lying if I said I'm not anxious,' Parreira said. 'We sleep a little less, eat a little less... but it's part of it, and I think it's good.' Robinho, one of nine players in Brazil's squad participating in a World Cup for the first time, was equally keen to get the initial match underway. 'We want the tournament to start, we want to begin playing,' the twenty-two-year-old said. 'I can't wait to get on the field.'

As Brazil's opening game of the tournament approached and the side's anticipation grew, so too did the excitement surrounding the squad. With a week to go until their Tuesday night opener, 22,000 fans, nearly all dressed in the team's green-and-yellow kit, turned out to watch Brazil's only public practice ahead of the World Cup. Fans packed Offenbach's Bieberer Berg stadium waving flags and chanting for Brazil, who underwent a light training session. Each player received a roar of appreciation as they were called out, one by one, by the stadium announcer ahead of the training session. The only player missing from the show was striker Ronaldo, who, as well as his blister problem, was also suffering with an illness. 'It's just an infection of his upper airways, with fever,' Brazil doctor Serafim Borges said. 'He's been treated and is recovering well, without any problems.' Fortunately the star managed to return to training the next day, back behind closed doors at the team's headquarters.

The Brazil squad, possibly the most expensive team ever at a World Cup, had an estimated net worth of £400 million on the transfer market and were hailed by former winner Pelé as not only having a superb starting eleven, but also a fantastic squad. He said: 'Brazil has two teams. If they have to change a player, it makes no difference.' Parreira, in praising his squad players, stoked some fires ahead of the Croatia clash, claiming even his second string could beat the European outfit. 'I think they are at the same level, not inferior,' he said when asked to compare the Brazil reserves to the Croats. 'They are better than a lot of the teams who made it to the World Cup. Maybe as good as the majority of the teams.' What sounded like boasting was in fact probably true. Looking at the players set for bench-warming duties in the first game, it would be hard to argue with the coach: Robinho, Cicinho, Lyon's Juninho and Fred, Arsenal's Gilberto Silva and Emerson of Juventus. 'That's the good thing about the Brazilian national team. We are not only 11 players, we can replace any player at a good level.'

Despite many talented players missing out on a starting berth, morale in the squad was excellent. On the eve of the Croatia game, the squad split into two to play a small-sided match at the Olympiastadion, the venue for the next day's clash with Croatia. Wearing orange bibs, Robinho and Ronaldo's team were victorious and shouts of 'E campeão!' – Portuguese for 'We are the champions!' – rang out around the empty ground. They had just beaten the team in blue, with Ronaldinho and Kaka. To celebrate their victory, the oranges huddled in a large embrace, jumped up and chanted in jest: 'Kaka's a load of rubbish!' With huge grins, the orange side spontaneously lined up for a team photograph.

DATE: TUESDAY, 13 JUNE 2006
TIME: 8.00PM
VENUE: BERLIN
OPPONENT: CROATIA
PHASE: GROUP STAGE

Following Australia's late, late show against the Japanese, where the Oceanic qualifiers scored three times in the last 10 minutes to overcome their Asian opponents 3-1, the Olympiastadion stadium in Berlin was sold out ahead of the World Champions' first match, where they took on Group F European qualifiers Croatia. Robinho, as Parreira had promised in the press three weeks before kick-off, had to start on the subs' bench with 12 colleagues as the Brazilian coach went with the same line-up that cruised past Venezuela nearly a year ago in their final qualifying match for this tournament. It was, though, a far from convincing display from the first-choice players. Kaka, the ever-reliable AC Milan maestro, fired the Brazilians ahead on 44 minutes but the first half was hardly a thrilling affair and the reigning champions nearly gave away that lead as Croatia showed little fear in the face of the tournament favourites.

Ronaldo also failed to impress, looking slow, sluggish and overweight during the 1-0 win. The forward barely touched the ball in his 69-minute run-out, and when he did so, the ball often bounced off him and straight to an opposition player. He had one decent scoring opportunity in the second-half but blazed his shot over the crossbar and was eventually substituted for Robinho in the 69th minute, allowing the former Santos star his first taste of World Cup action.

'Ronaldo hadn't been playing for two months... it's natural, on a hot day like today, that he felt the lack of rhythm,' Parreira conceded after the game. 'Certainly, from now on he will get in form little by little.'

Once on the field, Robinho was in complete contrast to his Real Madrid team-mate. A bundle of energy, he darted around the pitch, tackling hard, careful and productive in possession and able to angle some efforts at the Croatian goal. 'I'm always working to be ready to start,' he said after the match. 'Parreira is giving me opportunities and I'm trying to take advantage of them. If I get to be the starter, great.' Robinho's cameo clearly pleased Parreira: 'Robinho came in well... he helped on defence and performed well in his function.' He was less pleased, though, with the team's performance but was hopeful the side would hit their stride soon. 'The team's performance, evidently, needs to improve and it will improve in the next matches. In World Cups it's fundamental to win the first match.'

DATE: SUNDAY, 18 JUNE 2006
TIME: 5.00PM
VENUE: MUNICH
OPPONENT: AUSTRALIA
PHASE: GROUP STAGE

The victory over Croatia, although not convincing, had given Brazil an ideal start and the perfect opportunity to qualify for the knockout stage as group winners. With the perceived two weaker sides in the group still to play, the champions were almost certain to progress to the next phase. That theory was confirmed when the five-times champions sealed a spot in the next round by defeating Australia. However, the World Cup holders again failed to look like tournament favourites and had to wait until the 49th-minute before taking the lead against an impressive Australian side. It was Adriano who broke the deadlock with a well-placed strike from the edge of the box to unlock the Australian defence. Robinho once again replaced Ronaldo, this time in the 72nd minute, and he provided a spark to the Brazilians, adding speed, inventiveness and firepower to the attack. He fired just over the goal in the 76th minute after a flowing move, shimmied on several occasions past defenders, and in the 90th minute hit a vicious low drive to the right of goalkeeper Mark Schwarzer and onto the inside of the post. The rebound spun out across the face of the goal and Fred, who had just come on as a substitute for Adriano, tapped the ball over the line.

Despite calls from the press and supporters to drop Ronaldo for the inspirational Robinho, Parreira continued to stand by the striker and stated after the victory that Ronaldo would start against Japan in the final group game. 'Robinho is a different player to Ronaldo. It's also much different coming on for the last 20 minutes, compared to playing for the first 70. The game was opening up more and there was a lot more space. Robinho can help us and I am using him in a way where he can help the team.'

The coach was also impressed with an improved, if not convincing, display against the Socceroos. 'We are happy to have qualified, and it is a deserved victory,' he said. 'We imposed both our style of playing, passing the ball around, and also imposed ourselves physically. It is true that with three Australian forwards in our half it was more complicated, and we struggled at times but overall I think there are more positives than negatives.'

THE WEIGHT OF THE WORLD

DATE: THURSDAY, 22 JUNE 2006
TIME: 8.00PM
VENUE: DORTMUND
OPPONENT: JAPAN
PHASE: GROUP STAGE

Already assured of a spot in the knockout rounds, Brazil were able to rest several players for their clash with Japan. Adriano, Ze Roberto, Cafu and Emerson moved to the bench while Robinho did, in fact, get a start. However, he was paired with Ronaldo, rather than selected in place of him.

Managed by Brazilian legend Zico, Japan were no match for the Samba Boys, though, and Parreira's side dumped their Asian opponents out of the tournament with a 4-1 win. The Japanese needed to win by two clear goals to progress after drawing 0-0 with Croatia, and their need to push forward left spaces in behind for the Brazilian forwards to utilise. Brazil, however, were handed an early scare when Keiji Tamada fired Japan into a shock lead. With Robinho, Gilberto and Ronaldinho creating magic for Brazil, there was never any doubt about the outcome, though. Ronaldo began to show glimpses that he was hitting form and silenced his critics with a double that equalled Muller's goal-scoring record in World Cups. The goals kicked Brazil into life: Juninho Pernambucano hit a thunderbolt and Gilberto slipped in past the Japanese keeper to add to the scoresheet as Brazil ran riot in Dortmund. 'I'm really pleased I have improved so much physically and technically during the competition and am happy with my two goals and the win,' a delighted Ronaldo told reporters after the game. 'Patience was the key and I was able to stay calm and patient in all the difficult moments,' added the Real Madrid star.

The result ensured Brazil topped the group with a maximum of 9 points – a feat matched by only three other teams in the eight groups – 5 points ahead of Australia, with just the one goal conceded. The Australians were the surprise team of the group, their victory over Japan and 2-2 draw in the group decider with Croatia enough to see Guus Hiddink's side through to the last 16, and knock out hotly-tipped Croatia.

DATE: TUESDAY, 27 JUNE 2006
TIME: 5.00PM
VENUE: DORTMUND
OPPONENT: GHANA
PHASE: SECOND ROUND

As a reward for topping the group Brazil were drawn with the runners-up in Group E, Ghana, the only African side left in the competition. Tunisia, Angola and the Ivory Coast had been expected to do well in the competition but it was only Ghana, with impressive wins over USA and the Czech Republic, who progressed.

However, there was bad news for Robinho, who had lit up the match against Japan. The Real Madrid star had been fantastic in his first World Cup start, his jinking runs and flicks teeing-up Ronaldo on numerous occasions. However, he was to miss the Second Round tie with Ghana due to a thigh injury. The twenty-two-year-old, whose speed and trickery added a new dimension to the Brazilian attack in the 4-1 win in their previous game, pulled up in training three days before the match and his absence was confirmed by a Brazil physio. 'Robinho is ruled out and will continue his physiotherapy. We did an MRI scan today, there's no rupturing of the tendons, there is an oedema but the outlook is very good,' said team doctor Jose Luis Runco. There was, though, some good news – the injury wouldn't end Robinho's tournament: 'We've ruled out any possibility of Robinho being forced out of the tournament. This idea is to prepare him for Saturday if we get a good result against Ghana. I believe that on Wednesday, he can start working on the training field again.'

Robinho did not travel to Dortmund for the match and remained at the team hotel to continue physiotherapy. The youngster, though, was philosophical about the injury. 'I'm a bit sad and a bit upset to get injured, but fortunately it was nothing worse,' he said, adding that he had never suffered a muscular injury before. 'Having to stay behind at the hotel was a bit different, I'm used to going out and training. It was a small problem. I'll continue treatment and, God willing, I will be available for next Saturday's match if Brazil gets past Ghana.

'I spoke with my dad and my mum. They were a bit worried because they know it's rare for me to get injured. I told them it was nothing serious, that I couldn't play for this game but that in the next few days I'd be able to play. But it's normal for parents to worry.'

Parreira was clearly disappointed by the news, the injury coming just days after the forward had proven what an asset he could be to the national team in Germany. 'Robinho is a player who gives us a lot of options,' the coach said. 'It's a pity. He was very motivated.'

Despite missing Robinho, Brazil were still comfortable favourites to overcome Ghana, and there was little fear of their African opponents within the squad ahead of the game. 'If Brazil plays what it knows, it shouldn't have any problems getting past them,' Roberto Carlos confidently stated to reporters ahead of the knockout clash. 'How many world titles has Ghana won? None. How many has Brazil won? It makes a difference.'

Ronaldo was also in good spirits ahead of the match, having netted twice against Japan in the final group game to edge closer to taking the all-time World Cup scoring record. 'Brazil is prepared to face anybody. There's no reason to fear any opponent,' he said.

Indeed, Ghana held no surprises for Brazil. The defending champions cruised past their opposition with a comfortable 3-0 win which saw them through to the quarter-final stages of the 2006 World Cup. The real talking point of the match, though, was Ronaldo's record-breaking strike which was his 15th goal in World Cup competitions.

In fitting style Ronaldo scored the historic goal with panache. The forward timed his run perfectly to race clear of the Ghanaian defence and latch onto a beautifully-weighted through-ball from Kaka on 5 minutes. A trademark step-over deceived Ghana goalkeeper Richard Kingson and Ronaldo was left with a simple finish to break the record.

'I'm very happy with the result, and with breaking the record – but we win as a team. I get goals and on we go,' he proudly said after the game. 'The record had stood for seven World Cups so I am naturally very pleased to beat it. I want more and more and more!'

Adriano tapped in a Cafu cross from close-range in first-half injury time to virtually assure the South Americans victory, before Ze Roberto broke free to flick a Ronaldinho pass past the Ghana keeper and seal the win with a third goal in the 84th minute.

THE WEIGHT OF THE WORLD

DATE: SATURDAY, 1 JULY 2006
TIME: 8.00PM
VENUE: FRANKFURT
OPPONENT: FRANCE
PHASE: QUARTER-FINALS

Following their victory over the Black Stars, Brazil faced a rejuvenated French squad in the quarter-finals.

After a dismal defence of their 1998 World Cup in South Korea and Japan, where the holders crashed out in the group stages, France were recapturing their best form and were being driven forward by the masterful Zinedine Zidane. The midfield maestro had announced he would retire from football after the World Cup, and with each game potentially his last, he was rolling back the years, conducting, orchestrating and inspiring his French team-mates – most notably in their Second Round victory over highly-favoured Spain. Les Blues had fallen behind to a David Villa penalty on the half-hour mark, but bounced back with goals from Franck Ribery, Patrick Vieira and Zidane to spring a shock defeat on the Spaniards. Their next trick, though, would be much tougher – their ageing stars (Vieira, Zidane, Willy Sagnol, Lilian Thuram, Claude Makelele) would have to find a way past a fluid, fast-paced Brazil side, who were beginning to hit full-stride in this tournament.

The Samba Boys also welcomed Robinho back into the fold for the clash with the French. While the likes of Cafu, Ronaldo and Roberto Carlos experienced a painful defeat to France in the 1998 World Cup final at the Stade de France and were out for revenge, Robinho was one of several players in the Brazil squad who was too young to be involved in that tournament, but he still harboured hopes of avenging the 3-0 defeat his country suffered in Paris. 'I was really little, but it's a sad memory,' he recalled. 'I hope the story will be different this time. We know France is going to be a difficult opponent. But we hope Zidane will have to end his career against us.'

History did not bode well for the Brazilians, though. The boys in yellow and green had only overcome the French once in World Cup history, when Pelé scored three times in a 5-2 win in Sweden in 1958. As well as the World Cup final win in 1998, Brazil also fell to the French in 1986 – losing in the quarter-finals on penalty kicks after a 1-1 draw. Twenty years on from that Michel Platini-inspired victory would Zidane be the Frenchman to defeat the Brazilians?

Whether the history of the fixture played a part in Parreira's team selection, or if the team's first 2006 World Cup meeting with a 'major' side forced his hand, the Brazil boss opted to alter his winning formula. Parreira unexpectedly ended Brazil's 'magic quartet' scheme. Initial pre-tournament criticism of the Fab Four of Adriano, Ronaldo, Ronaldinho and Kaka's ability to work together had been swept aside by Brazil's ever-improving displays. Many thought the system was too attack-minded; however, the quartet had worked well up until this stage. Parreira, though, was unconvinced the system would hold up against France and swapped striker Adriano for midfielder Juninho, with Ronaldinho pushed higher up the pitch to support Ronaldo. Parreira had boldly announced his system for the World Cup eight months ahead of the tournament. Indeed, Brazil had been playing with the 'magic quartet' for over a year and a half before their arrival in Germany. It was a real risk to dismantle this tactic at the quarter-final stage of the World Cup.

'We all agreed we needed to crowd the midfield a little bit better,' Parreira said, defending his decision. However, the idea of stalling the French forward play by flooding the midfield did not have the desired effect. Instead of repelling the French attacks, the system simply invited the French forward. Time and time again, Brazil's backline were tested by France, who looked particularly dangerous from set plays. Curling the ball into the area, Zidane found Florent Malouda and Thierry Henry either side of the half-time interval, but both forwards missed the target with their headers. The continued pressure finally cost Brazil in the 57th minute. Another perfectly placed Zidane free kick, this time from wide on the left, sailed over all of the Brazil defenders and was met by a completely unmarked Henry, who tapped in at the back post.

With no momentum to build on, Brazil struggled to get back into the match and Juan nearly ended any hope of a comeback by putting the ball in his own net, miscuing his clearance of a Ribery cross narrowly past the far post. With little option, Parreira reverted to the 'magic quartet' system, introducing Adriano. Brazilian media and fans later criticised the Brazil boss for being too slow in making the change. Robinho was then called upon as Brazil became more desperate, replacing Kaka in the 79th minute. The Real Madrid forward was determined to drive his side back into the contest and within 2 minutes of his introduction, Robinho had a half-chance to level the scores. Ronaldinho nodded the ball into his path, but under pressure from two French defenders, Robinho skewed his left-foot shot well wide of the target. He continued to add spark to Brazil's attack, but his 11 minutes on the field were not enough for him to conjure up an equaliser and when Ronaldinho's last-minute free kick sailed over the crossbar, Brazil's hopes of retaining the World Cup were over.

'We made all the right choices,' Parreira insisted after the game. 'We are frustrated with the result, but our effort was good. We lost one match and have to go home. That's how things work in the World Cup. It's a difficult moment to be eliminated when we were so close to the semi-finals and final. I did not prepare for this and no one in our delegation prepared for this.'

Ronaldinho reiterated his disappointment: 'It's always sad when a team used to winning suffers a fall like this. Now it's time to put our feet on the ground and start thinking about what's next and Brazil's future.'

For Robinho, his first taste of World Cup football had been bitter-sweet. As a substitute in the group stages, he had injected life into the national side and as a starter against Japan, he had demonstrated his ability to give Brazil a more dynamic, agile and fast-paced forward line. The frustration of injury against Ghana was mitigated by his team-mate's comfortable passage past the African outfit, but the unexpected quarter-final defeat to an ageing French side, when he had hoped to avenge the 1998 World Cup final defeat, was a huge disappointment for the twenty-two-year-old. His reputation had been enhanced, the world's media now recognised his talent, but he had been unable to achieve what he had dreamed of as a child – replicating his mentor Pelé, and winning the World Cup for his country.

CHAPTER 8
VICTORY – AT ANY COST

U nsurprisingly, the untimely exit from the World Cup
signalled the end of Carlos Alberto Parreira's reign as
Brazil boss. Days later the manager resigned, admitting his
position had become untenable after failing to defend the
World Cup in Germany. 'It was impossible to stay. Brazil is a
power in world football and as a result the demands are very
intensive here', he said.

With his vast international managerial experience, Parreira
was quickly snapped up by the South Africa Football
Association to manage their side ahead of the next World
Cup in 2010. Brazil were not slow in appointing a successor
either. Former captain Carlos Caetano Bledorn Verri, better
known as Dunga, was appointed as the five-times World Cup
winners' new coach, despite not having any professional
coaching experience. The forty-two-year-old was entrusted
with leading Brazil to the 2010 World Cup and possibly
beyond, said CBF President Ricardo Teixeira. 'The
appointment of Dunga satisfies the desire of Brazilian fans
who want to see a vibrant coach', he announced.

It was also all-change at Real Madrid, where newly-appointed president Ramon Calderon carried out his pledge to appoint Juventus boss Fabio Capello as coach. The Italian had guided Madrid to the league title in the 1996/97 season, pipping Barcelona to the crown by 2 points, and it was hoped Capello could recreate that success once again at Madrid, who were suffering one of their longest spells without winning a trophy in their history. Capello's reign at Juventus had been a hugely successful one – claiming back-to-back Italian league titles for the Old Lady. His achievements at the club were tarnished, though, by a match-fixing scandal that resulted in one of the country's most famous clubs being demoted to the second tier of Italian football. There was no indication that Capello was involved in the scandal, but with the club relegated and stripped of its place in the Champions League, the Italian manager took the opportunity to return to Madrid.

With him came Italian national captain Fabio Cannavaro and Brazil midfielder Emerson. Cannavaro, considered by many to be one of the best defenders of the modern era, and Emerson, for so long Brazil's lynchpin that shored up the defence as the nation's more flamboyant players excelled, along with the signing of combative Mali midfielder Mahamadou Diarra from Lyon, signalled that, typically, Capello was planning to develop a side at Madrid that was strong, solid and mean in defence. His mission was to claim the La Liga title. Pretty football and flamboyant forward play would take second place to results under the manager the Spanish press dubbed 'Don Fabio'.

The team began their preparations for the 2006/07 season at a training camp in Austria in early August. However, the pre-season get-together turned into a media frenzy when Robinho became entangled in a fight with a team-mate. What was supposed to be a light training session turned into a brawl between Robinho and Danish midfielder Thomas Gravesen when the midfielder, renowned for his fierce tackling and aggressive, competitive attitude, allegedly caught Robinho with a late tackle. The pair squared up to each other and threw punches before team-mates rushed over to separate them. Both were sent from the training field by Capello. In fact, the altercation was Gravesen's third with a team-mate at the camp and within days of the bust-up, it seemed the Dane was heading for the exit door at Madrid. With the signing of Emerson his place had come under threat, and Gravesen told reporters he was unhappy with Capello, who had made it clear he was not in his long-term plans for the club. Within two weeks of the fight Gravesen signed for Celtic, while Robinho, seemingly the innocent party in the incident, remained at the camp and travelled with the rest of the squad to the USA where Real continued their pre-season programme.

The revitalisation of Madrid under Capello, however, did not start as well as hoped. Madrid met Villarreal in its first match of the 2006/07 season at the Bernabeu Stadium on 28 August, but the home side were held by their visitors to an uninspiring 0-0 draw. Despite the inclusion of all four of Capello's new acquisitions – Cannavaro, Emerson, Diarra and Manchester United's Ruud van Nistelrooy – Los Blancos could not find a way past their opponents and left the field to a chorus of whistles from their hard-to-please supporters.

It was also a disappointing start to the campaign for Robinho. After his impressive stint at the World Cup, and with Ronaldo undergoing knee surgery immediately after the tournament, it seemed the young Brazilian would be able to establish himself in the Real Madrid frontline under Capello and enjoy a far more prosperous season than his debut year in Spain. However, Robinho was confined to the bench for much of the game. Eventually he got on the field when he replaced David Beckham on 75 minutes but was unable, like his team-mates, to break down the stubborn Villarreal defence. Characteristically, Capello was unmoved by the performance and jeering. 'I'm not worried,' he said after the game. 'They were a strong team physically and played well.' Barcelona, meanwhile, got off to the ideal start, sneaking past Celta Vigo with a 3-2 win.

Fears for Real, though, were short-lived. Two weeks after that stalemate with Villarreal, Capello's side bounced back in style, demolishing Levante 4-1 away from home. New signing van Nistelrooy hit a hat-trick and Antonio Cassano completed the rout. It was a morale-boosting win for the team ahead of their first Champions League game of the season.

The nine-times European champions had been grouped with Lyon, Steaua Bucharest and Dynamo Kiev in the initial phase of the 2006/07 contest and travelled to France for their opening encounter with French champions Lyon.

A year earlier, Lyon had inflicted a 3-0 defeat on Real in the opening match of the 2005/06 contest. Real were determined not to let the same embarrassment befall them again. This time, they went down 2-0. Two goals for the French outfit inside the first half-hour of the match sealed the points for Lyon, Brazilian forward Fred and Portuguese midfielder Tiago doing the damage for the French outfit. Robinho, again, struggled to get any game time, eventually replacing the ineffective Raul on 69 minutes. Madrid, though, created little – not hitting the target until the second half – and never looked like recouping the early deficit suffered.

Fortunately, on returning to League action Madrid re-discovered the form that saw them thrash Levante. A 2-0 win over Real Sociedad at home was followed by a win on the road at Betis on 23 September which, with the whistles and jeers of the opening day seemingly long forgotten, moved Real up into second spot in the League, level on points with leaders Barcelona.

The opening round of the Champions League was also quickly forgotten by Real fans when Madrid destroyed Dynamo Kiev at the Bernabeu on 26 September. Raul, ending a year-long goal drought caused by a severe injury in the previous season, netted a brace as Real fired five past the stunned Ukraine side. Van Nistelrooy also weighed in with two more strikes before Jose Antonio Reyes finished off the goal-scoring showpiece. Once again, Robinho was left out of the starting line-up. Capello finally introduced the Brazilian with 7 minutes to play and the match effectively over.

Atletico Madrid proved a sterner test than Dynamo, holding Real to a 1-1 home draw the following weekend before Getafe handed Real Madrid its first defeat of the Spanish league season in the sixth round of La Liga. It was a poor display from Real, who went down to an Alexis Ruano header in the 59th minute. To add to Capello's frustrations, the returning Ronaldo was sent off for a second yellow card. Robinho nearly took advantage of his second-half opportunity, creating Madrid's best chance of the game before shooting just wide after he replaced David Beckham after 68 minutes, but he was still nothing more than a bit-part player.

A return to European competition on 17 October against Steaua Bucharest got Madrid back on track and finally gave Robinho a chance to show Capello what he could offer the Spanish giants. Starting his first game of the season in place of Cassano, Robinho came out all guns blazing, determined to shine. The young Brazilian didn't disappoint, hitting Real's third in a 4-1 away win against the Romanian side and producing an impressive display. Goian, the Steaua defender, who had had the dubious pleasure of marking the Brazilian was left in no doubt about Robinho's talents. 'Real proved that it is a great team,' he said. 'Robinho played a great match.' Real boss Capello was also pleased with his side's display, following their 1-0 defeat to Getafe: 'That was a good Real Madrid tonight. This match helped us forget the last one.'

A far sweeter victory, though, came five days later at the Bernabeu stadium when Real defeated their great rivals, and league leaders, Barcelona. Raul and Ruud van Nistelrooy scored a goal each in the 2-0 win, ending the defending champions' unbeaten start to the Spanish league season. Robinho, starting his first league game of the season for Los Blancos after his impressive display in Romania, was also a thorn in the side of the Catalan club and nearly netted his second in two games when he forced a fine stop from Barça keeper Victor Valdes midway through the first half. Robinho then teed van Nistelrooy up for the decisive second goal on 51 minutes, finding the Dutch striker in space to volley home his fourth of the season. Robinho picked up the Man of the Match award and finally, Capello seemed satisfied with his players. 'This team is now playing like a team, it has both spirit and quality,' Capello said. 'We had a serious talk following the Getafe defeat and after that there was a complete change in the team. I'm sure the turning point came after that discussion. These are three important points, bringing us closer to Barcelona, and are a major psychological boost for the players.'

Real Madrid continued their winning streak with a 3-1 win over Gimnastic before securing their place in the second round of the Champions League with a 1-0 win at home to Steaua Bucharest, courtesy of an own goal. Robinho once again took home a bottle of champagne after collecting his second Man of the Match award in two Champions League outings against the Romanians.

A run of five wins in eight matches kept Real in touch with Barcelona, who continued to lead the way in the league, as La Liga disbanded for its winter break. Real also secured two 2-2 draws against Lyon and Dynamo Kiev to finish runners-up in Group E of the Champions League, though their qualification to the next round had been long assured. Their final game before the winter break was a 3-0 defeat at home to Recreativo. It was not the ideal way to close the first half of the season, but with 16 of the 38 league matches played, Real were well-placed in the table. They held third spot, trailing Barcelona, who had dropped to second and new leaders Sevilla, who had enjoyed an impressive start to their campaign.

Robinho had experienced a mixed first term under Capello. After the exile and struggle to get into the team early in the season, his superb display in Romania had clearly lifted him in Capello's estimations. However, as Real struck up a decent run of form in the weeks before the winter break, Robinho once again found himself reduced to second-half cameo appearances from the bench on a number of occasions, having failed to tie down a starting spot on a permanent basis.

As he had made a habit of doing throughout his time in Europe, Robinho took the opportunity of the winter break to return home to Brazil to visit his friends and family in South America. On 27 December the Real Madrid forward returned to his former club, Santos, and stepped out onto the turf of the Vila Belmiro, where he had made his name.

Robinho had brought together a team of Brazilian soccer greats to play a charity match at the Stadium. Among the stars on show were his former team-mates, and still good friends – Diego, Elano, Renato, Leo and Deivid. Corinthians' Carlos Alberto led the rival team, which included Barcelona's Brazilian-born Portuguese midfielder Deco, Vagner Love, Romario and Falcão, the famous Brazilian *Futsal* star.

'It is a great joy to return to the Santos stadium, my second home, and to help Brazil's charities at the same time,' Robinho said. He had asked fans who wanted to watch the match to donate at least one kilogram of non-perishable food at the entrance to the stadium. 'We will play in white, the colour of peace, friendship and union between people,' Robinho added.

The season and spirit of goodwill, though, was short-lived for the Brazilian in the winter of 2006/07. Returning to Real, Robinho reportedly demanded showdown talks with Capello. He had been left in the stands for Real's first game back, a 2-0 defeat at Deportivo La Coruna, and *AS* reported a member of Real's coaching staff had informed Robinho that he had been dropped because Capello believed he had returned from the winter break out of condition. Capello was also seemingly of the opinion that Robinho had not given his all in at least two training sessions in the previous week.

A disgruntled Robinho returned to the squad for the club's home tie with Zaragoza on 14 January and when Raul went down injured in the 14th minute, the Brazilian took to the field. He played a key role in the approach play for van Nistelrooy's game-deciding strike but was dissatisfied afterwards with his treatment by Capello. 'I'm not happy. Capello doesn't have confidence in my football,' he told the press conference. The Brazil international said that Capello had not given him any explanations for his recent non-selection. Robinho's comments sparked transfer links with AC Milan and Juventus and his cause was not helped as he went in and out of the side for the next league games before, in an away game with Real Sociedad, was completely omitted from the squad. 'Right now I'm not happy because I'm not playing but I'm going to keep working to change that,' the Brazilian told reporters. 'I know that he [Capello] doesn't have confidence in my football because I'm not playing and I have to make him change his mind.' Asked whether he would consider leaving the club at the end of the season, he replied: 'I don't know. All I know is that with Capello I've been on the bench and if things carry on like that I will have to see what's best for me.'

As well as his infrequent starts for Real, Robinho had also seen his good friend Ronaldo depart from the club after falling out of favour with Capello. However, Robinho refused to attribute his unhappiness to the absence of his Brazil team-mate. 'Ronaldo is the best striker in the world but he wasn't happy because the coach didn't want him to stay here. I'm younger, I've still got a lot to learn and I've got a future.'

Robinho's relations with Real had been stretched earlier in the season when the club's sporting director, Predrag Mijatovic, had apparently claimed that the Brazilian had turned up for training smelling of alcohol. 'It wasn't true,' Robinho testified. 'I look after myself off the pitch. Mijatovic hasn't apologised to me or said anything. I don't like what was said, but it's in the past now.'

These comments drew further speculation Robinho's time at the Bernabeu could be up at the end of the season, with rumours of a senior Madrid official stating the player could well be sold in the summer.

Robinho was finally recalled to first-team action for the Champions League First Round knockout game with German champions Bayern Munich. The German side had topped a tricky group, including Inter Milan, Spartak Moscow and Sporting Lisbon, without losing a single match in the process. The first leg took place at the Bernabeu which, typically for a Champions League night, was swamped in a noisy, excited and energised atmosphere. Real had endured a difficult run of form since returning from their winter break. They had won just three times in seven games since their return to action on 7 January, and been knocked out of the Copa del Rey on away goals by Real Betis. However, with Real's reputation in Europe behind them they are always a daunting team for any side to play against.

The atmosphere, the occasion – whatever it was about visiting the Bernabeu – seemed to nullify Bayern Munich, who were pulled apart by Real in the first half. Raul scored twice and van Nistelrooy hit another as the Spanish club established a commanding first half lead, with Lucio's strike for Bayern the only blotch on an impressive opening 45 minutes from Real. In need of a good result, Capello began the game with an unusually attacking mindset with Raul, van Nistelrooy and nineteen-year-old forward Gonzalo Higuain forming a front three.

Beckham nearly made it 4-1 for the hosts with a trademark free kick, but he was denied by an acrobatic stop from Munich stopper Oliver Kahn. Robinho was then introduced to the action, replacing Higuain. Unfortunately for the Brazilian his arrival came just as the tide was turning and the German side were finally waking from their slumber. Much of Robinho's work was spent defending as Bayern pushed forward. When it seemed Real had held onto a valuable two-

Robinho squares up to France's Claude Makelele during the 2006 World Cup in Germany.

Above: Robinho celebrating with his Brazil team-mates after their orange-bibbed 'team' won a match in training. The exuberant players chanted '*E campeao!*' ('We are the champions!).

Below: Celebrating with England star David Beckham during the duo's time together at Real Madrid.

Above left: Robinho holds the Player of the Tournament award after Brazil's win over Argentina in the 2007 Copa America final.

Above right: The victorious Brazil players celebrate with the Copa America trophy.

Below left: Robinho eludes a defender during a league match for Real Madrid.

Below right: His famous thumb-sucking goal celebration – a tribute to his unborn child.

Above: Robinho celebrates a goal with another tribute to his son, Robson Junior, who was born in December 2007.

Below: In action for Manchester City. Robinho's move to the club was a sensation, as City swooped on the final day of the transfer window to sign the player for £32.5 million.

Robinho speaking at a press conference the day before the 2008 transfer window shut. At the time, he was eager to play for Chelsea, but the following 24 hours would see a rollercoaster of activity culminating in Manchester City securing his services.

Above left: Showing his appreciation to the City fans. The supporters have made Robinho a club favourite, with his arrival marking the start of a new era for the team.

Above right: Celebrating a UEFA Cup goal with Elano.

Below left: Back in action for Brazil in a qualifying match for the 2010 World Cup.

Below right: Wearing the No.10 shirt for City is important to Robinho – in Brazil, it is a sacred squad number that symbolises flair and creativity.

Above: Robinho makes his first appearance in England in a Brazil shirt, playing in a friendly against Italy at the Emirates Stadium in January 2009.

Below: Playing for City against Aalborg of Denmark, in the UEFA Cup Fourth Round.

Looking happy and relaxed, Robinho arrives in South Africa with Brazil for the 2009 Confederations Cup. Brazil won the tournament to cap an exhilarating year for the young star.

goal cushion, van Bommel popped up on the edge of the box to fire past Iker Casillias in the Madrid goal with just 2 minutes to play. It was a costly goal to concede. Real still had their one goal advantage but Bayern now had the all-important two away goals.

Real returned to league action with two local derby matches. First, they played away to Atletico Madrid – a side who always perform far better when they meet their bigger brothers from the Bernabeu. The sides drew 1-1, and Real then turned their attentions to another Madrid club, Getafe, who they faced three days ahead of their Champions League second leg on 4 March. In this game, Robinho was finally handed a proper second chance by Capello and he made full use of this starting spot to produce a convincing performance up front alongside van Nistelrooy. He was brought down in the box in the second half and his strike partner converted the spot-kick to seal another 1-1 draw for Los Blancos, which saw them slip to fourth in the table. Robinho, though, was satisfied with his performance and the reception he received from the Bernabeu crowd. 'I always try to do the things that Capello asks of me,' he said after the game. 'I played well and the team did also. I believe the fans want me to stay and are supporting me. It was very difficult to score and we lacked a little luck also. Now the two most important games for us are coming against Bayern Munich in the Champions League and Barcelona in La Liga, and for our future, we hope to be able to play as well.'

The decisive double-header came within three days of each other, with the Bayern Munich clash in the Allianz Arena on 7 March and 'el clasico' taking place on 10 March at the Nou Camp.

Robinho was relegated back to the bench for the

Champions League clash, as Capello opted for a more defensive-minded approach in the second leg with Bayern Munich. The midfield duo of Emerson and Diarra came into the side in place of the injured Beckham and the creative Guti to give the Spanish outfit more bite in their midfield. However, they were greeted by the same intensity as they and their fans had produced at the Bernabeu two weeks earlier and their hard-fought first-leg advantage was wiped out inside 11 seconds. Moments after kick-off Hasan Salihamidzic stole the ball from Roberto Carlos, ran down the right wing and crossed into the box where Roy Makaay volleyed past Iker Casillas to net the fastest goal in Champions League history.

It was not long before Capello realised he must act: Guti replaced Emerson just 30 minutes into the game and Cassano was introduced for Higuain at half-time, the Italian boss knowing that as things stood, his side were out of the competition on away goals. Bayern then struck again, Lucio, who had netted in the first leg, popped up once more to give Bayern a seemingly unassailable 4-3 lead, with Real needing to net twice in the last 20 minutes to progress.

A final roll of the dice from Capello saw Robinho introduced for Argentine midfielder Gago. The Brazilian had an immediate impact, and within 7 minutes of his introduction Lucio clumsily tumbled him in the box. Just as he had done against Getafe, Robinho earned Real a vital way back into the match. The penalty kick was expertly converted by van Nistelrooy and Real bombed forward in search of the crucial winner. With seconds left on the clock, Sergio Ramos headed in at the back post and the Real players wheeled away in jubilation. However, their joy turned to despair when they saw the goal had been cruelly ruled out for handball. It was not to be the Spanish club's night. Bayern stubbornly held firm and celebrated their progression to the quarter-finals of the Champions League, where they would meet eventual winners AC Milan.

Real's focus was forced to return to domestic duties, where, just three days after the drama in Munich, they would play arguably the most important match of their season.

Both clubs had been knocked out of the Champions League days earlier – Barcelona had crashed out on away goals to eventual finalists Liverpool – and for both sides the league was now the saving grace for their season. With neither team particularly setting the world alight in 2006/07, 'el clasico' was far from the most anticipated encounter between the two giants of Spanish football. Although it was likely to prove decisive, few predicted the superb display of football that greeted the fans packed into the Nou Camp.

It started with three goals in less than a quarter of an hour. Ruud van Nistelrooy scored twice, either side of a strike from Argentina wonder kid Lionel Messi to give Real the advantage before the game ebbed and flowed to a dramatic 3-3 finish. Both sides could easily have netted six goals each and Messi took the match ball home with a marvellous hat-trick and Man of the Match display – his final goal a point-rescuing 90th-minute effort that cancelled out Sergio Ramos' strike which, for so long, had looked like the winner for Los Blancos.

After the thrilling match with Barcelona, many expected Real to kick-on and swamp bottom-of-the-league Gimnastic at the Bernabeu. When the visitors went down to 10 men with just 7 minutes on the clock, the result seemed inevitable. However, Real struggled and stumbled through the first half, enduring boos and jeers from the 75,000 supporters in attendance. With the scores level at the break, Robinho was introduced for Cassano and the Brazilian once again took his opportunity.

He picked up a pass from Raul, stole in at the back post and fired past the Gimnastic keeper from close range. Four minutes later, he was denied a second by the post, when his fine right-foot shot rattled the woodwork with the keeper stranded. Real eventually got the second when David Garcia diverted Ramos' cross into his own net to give his side an unconvincing home win. Capello had promised results ahead of flair, and that was all Real were producing. The Italian boss admitted his players were struggling to perform in front of their home crowd – where they had won fewer than half of their home games. 'To play in the Bernabeu is a bit of an uphill battle. We are not playing with the same speed and calm that we do away from home,' admitted Capello at the post-match press conference. 'The Real Madrid fans are the Real Madrid fans. We can't change them. That's the way it is. We love them and they love us but this is their manner,' added the Italian with barely disguised sarcasm. 'After the first half I didn't believe we can still win the league but after the second half I saw another team with another dream. This was two different teams but we can't play for just 45 minutes,' he reflected.

Two weeks later, Robinho once again came to the rescue for Real. Confined to the bench for the first half, Robinho sat and watched Celta Vigo level the scores just before the break, cancelling out van Nistelrooy's opener from the penalty spot. His team-mates were again below-par and laboured in their efforts to break down their hosts. Robinho was finally introduced after 63 minutes for Real's misfiring captain Raul. Just as in the Gimnastic game, Robinho injected life and energy into his flagging team-mates and with just 7 minutes left to play, Robinho headed the winning goal for Madrid.

Finally, it seemed, Capello was happy with his Brazilian

forward. 'He's back to being a deciding factor in games,' he said. 'Robinho had a great game. I hope we can carry on like this in the following games.'

The win pushed Real into third spot and they followed it up with another victory, this time at home to Osasuna on 8 April. Robinho also continued his good run of form. Back in the starting line-up, the Brazilian pounced in the 80th minute to seal the win for Real after Raul had netted his first since November to put the hosts ahead.

Robinho's recent run of form had clearly impressed Capello – the Brazilian started the next four games, of which Real won three. In the fourth game, Real came up against second-placed Sevilla. They were level on points with Madrid and the fixture at the Bernabeu was to be a crucial one in deciding the destination of the title. It seemed, though, that Real were to be undone by the impressive visitors when a superb volley from Enzo Maresca gave the visitors the edge 4 minutes before half-time. However, Real were not giving up and van Nistelrooy levelled the scores in the 63rd minute. The Dutchman had picked up a superb pass from substitute Guti before firing home, and Guti was again the supplier 15 minutes later when he angled a pass through the legs of Aitor Ocio to find Robinho. The Brazilian calmly slotted home and wheeled away in celebration towards the Madrid fans. However, his delight was short-lived. His punishment for whipping off his shirt in celebration was a second yellow card. Robinho was stunned. With his head in his hands, he trudged off the pitch. But he needn't have worried: Real were rolling. Ocio saw red himself and Beckham finished off another fine Madrid move to seal the vital points for Real. Sevilla's Ernesto Chevanton netted a consolation for the visitors deep into injury time, but it was too little, too late.

The Bernabeu was rocking, the chanting and singing of the fans a clear indication that belief had been restored in Los Blancos. They were now just 2 points behind Barcelona, 2 clear of Sevilla, with five matches to play.

'We're at a stage where everything is working out. We're confident, team spirit has improved and we have the belief we can play well and win,' said Madrid left-back Roberto Carlos after the game.

Meanwhile, in the Barcelona camp nerves were jangling. 'We have no margin of error. We can't afford to draw or lose a match if Madrid wins all its games,' said Barça midfielder Xavi.

Next up for Real was Espanyol on 12 May. The Catalan club had spent much of the season loitering in mid-table and were just four days away from a UEFA Cup final in Glasgow when they visited the Bernabeu. However, with Robinho and Beckham suspended for the fixture, Real had to be on guard against their visitors. If anyone thought Espanyol's mind was focused on their cup final they were swiftly corrected inside 34 minutes. Espanyol striker Pandiani netted a quick-fire hat-trick and Real were in trouble and 3-1 down at half-time. Their title hopes were in tatters. They had targeted five wins from their final five games to peg Barça back and now, in the first of their five 'cup finals', they were seemingly set for defeat. However, a miraculous comeback saved the day for Real – Raul, Reyes and Higuain took advantage of a crumbling Espanyol, who had taken their eye off the ball in the second half. The thrilling 4-3 win, coupled with Barcelona's shock 1-1 draw with Real Betis, had propelled Real into top spot on head-to-head results. Within 45 minutes the Spanish giants had gone from seeing their title ambitions evaporate to moving into pole position.

Intent on atoning for their slip-up at Betis, Barcelona took out their frustrations on Atletico Madrid, thrashing Real's rivals 6-0 a week later. Los Blancos, though, continued to make hard work of their title challenge. Following their second-half renaissance against Espanyol, the returning duo of Robinho and Beckham combined as the Brazilian headed Real into the lead after just 9 minutes at Recreativo Huelva. A van Nistelrooy penalty in the second half seemed to wrap things up for Real. But typically another capitulation was just around the corner. Jesus Vasquez and Ikechukwu Uche fired a double salvo for the home side and with just 6 minutes to play, Real had been pulled back to 2-2. Los Blancos piled forward, but it seemed they had blown their chance. At least that was until, in the dying seconds, Roberto Carlos burst forward from left-back to slip the ball under the diving arms of Recreativo keeper Bertrand Laquait. The Brazilian full-back was mobbed by his team-mates as relief rang out from the travelling fans.

A more comfortable 3-1 win at home to Deportivo on 26 May followed for Real as Barça snatched a 1-0 win at home to Getafe. Sensationally, both sides drew their penultimate game 2-2 – Real with a last-minute equaliser from van Nistelrooy, Barça against a spirited Espanyol. This left both sides level on points; Real simply had to match Barça's result in the final game of the season to take their first La Liga title for four years.

However, a sideshow to this climatic end-of-season finale was Robinho's availability. The Real Madrid striker was at the centre of a struggle between the Spanish club and the Brazilian soccer confederation. Brazilian national team manager Dunga had summoned Robinho for the Copa America, the South American nations' championship that began on 26 June in Venezuela. The team was to assemble on 19 June at its training camp in Teresopolis, near Rio de Janeiro, to prepare for its 27 June opener against Mexico. FIFA regulations required clubs to release players 14 days prior to the start of a major tournament, such as the Copa America, meaning Madrid were supposed to have returned Robinho on 12 June. The Spanish side, though, wanted its striker for the season's decisive finale against Real Mallorca. Various reports in Spanish media suggested FIFA could strip Real Madrid of the points it could earn from its match against Real Mallorca if they insisted on playing Robinho despite Brazil's objection.

Ironically the likes of Kaka and Ronaldinho had been excused participation in the Copa America to recover from their exertions in the European leagues.

The debate continued to rage on for days, disrupting and distracting from the build-up to Real Madrid's do-or-die clash with Mallorca. Robinho's stance was that he wished to play for Madrid, his agent Wagner Ribeiro revealing that the player considered the match 'the game of his life.'

Finally the Brazilian football association yielded to Real's and Robinho's requests. 'In view of Real Madrid's recognition that the player legally could not be allowed to play, and the promise of the Spanish club's directory that such an event won't happen again, the CBF released Robinho and Marcelo... to report after Real Madrid's game on 17 June,' said the CBF in a statement.

Come match day there were few who doubted Real's ability to pull off the victory needed to seal the title. However, in the typical style that had made the season such hard work, they made their final must-win match tough on themselves. With just 17 minutes on the clock Fernando

Varela ripped up the script and put the visitors ahead. The goal silenced the 83,000 Real fans in the Bernabeu.

Real rallied and battled their way back into the game, but continued to struggle. As news came through of Barcelona's dominant display away to Gimnastic, the pressure grew on Capello and Madrid. The Italian pulled Beckham out of the action in the 66th minute, replacing him with former Arsenal winger Jose Antonio Reyes. It was Beckham's final game in the white shirt of Real before making his big-money move to LA Galaxy, but Capello had no time for sentimentality. Fortunately, the change was instantly successful.

Just 45 seconds into his arrival, Reyes sent the Real fans into a frenzy. The Spaniard, who had struggled to pin down a spot in the starting eleven since his move from England, levelled the scores and then, with 10 minutes to play, Diarra, who himself had received special permission to skip international duty for Mali, headed in the decisive second goal for Real. Reyes rounded off the scoring in the 83rd minute and that goal signalled the start of thousands of parties across the Spanish capital.

Barcelona had won 5-1 against Gimnastic, but it was inconsequential. Real Madrid's 3-1 comeback victory over Mallorca had won them a record 30th Spanish league title, their first in four years. It had been a hard-fought, difficult season, but, at last, the Galacticos era which had proved so fruitless and expensive in its twilight, had finally produced a trophy. 'This championship is not so much a difficult one, it was almost a miraculous one,' a relieved Capello said after the match. 'We came from so far behind Barcelona to win. We suffered and fought to recover the spirit of this team. Tonight, we saw this.'

Robinho, who had endured much suffering that season,

was also delighted with the outcome – his third league title in five seasons as a professional. 'We suffered but we have won. It is a great joy. It's my first title in the shirt of Real, but I hope there's more to come! We had to work very hard throughout the game. Most importantly, we did not throw in the towel.'

At times, it had not been an enjoyable season for Robinho, with his place in the side under Capello seemingly always in question, and his exploits from the bench seemingly never enough to convince the coach of his true worth until the final run-in. Capello, though, finally placed his trust in Robinho, and the Brazilian had produced for the Italian. Following the title win, Capello's tenure at Real came to an end. Ramon Calderon, the Real president, having ended the barren run, now looked to re-build the flamboyant and fast-flowing attacking football for which Real were renowned and decided to look elsewhere for that manager. One player who would not be suffering as a result of this reversion to old methods of flair would be Robinho, who had not always fitted into Capello's stern, stubborn, defensive line-ups.

A more recognisable environment awaited Robinho in the summer of 2007 – when he joined up with his Brazil team-mates as they took on the best in South America for the prestigious Copa America trophy.

CHAPTER 9
THE BRILLIANCE OF BRAZIL

The Copa America is the South American equivalent of the European Championships. First contested in 1916, it is the world's oldest surviving international tournament and, as a result, desperately sought after by the 10 South American nations.

To complete the tournament, two teams from other confederations are invited to compete. Since 1993, Mexico has been a popular invitee, regularly making it to the latter stages of the tournament and finishing runners-up on two occasions and third three other times. Other nations that have received invitations to the Copa include Costa Rica, Honduras and Japan. The USA had been invited every year since 1997, but regularly pulled out due to clashes with their domestic Major League Soccer season; however, in 2007, like Mexico, they agreed to participate in the prestigious event.

The 2007 tournament, the 42nd edition of the contest, took place for the first time in Venezuela. Courtesy of an alphabetical rotation system established in 1984, Venezuela had finally earned their chance to host the Copa, which was to be staged in the northern cities of the country.

Brazil came into the tournament as reigning champions, having defeated rivals Argentina 4-2 on penalties, following a thrilling 2-2 draw in the final of the 2004 tournament in Peru. Adriano had been the jewel in Brazil's crown that year, scoring seven goals, more than twice as many as his closest rival. Robinho was now hoping to emulate Adriano's achievements and, with the 2007 hero missing from the squad, and world stars Kaka and Ronaldinho also being rested after tough European seasons, Real Madrid's young forward would be the shining light of the national team.

On 1 June, in preparation for the tournament Brazil visited London to play England in the curtain-raiser of the new Wembley stadium. After nearly five years in construction, and at a cost of £798 million, the new Wembley became the largest stadium in the world with every seat undercover. After five years of touring the country, the England v Brazil match was the perfect homecoming for the English national team.

For many English supporters who had missed Robinho's display against Arsenal in the Champions League two seasons before, this was their first chance to see the Brazilian in the flesh and the Madrid magician didn't disappoint, treating the England fans to more than their fair share of step-overs, trickery and ambitious shots from the edge of the box. Robinho was finally taken out of the action on 74 minutes, but he had made his mark on the English supporters and revelled in the experience of playing in front of the renowned English fans.

After the exciting 1-1 draw at Wembley, where the home side had been leading through captain John Terry's header until the final minute of the game, Brazil's final European friendly before the Copa was in sharp contrast. With a lacklustre display in front of just 26,700 fans in Borussia Dortmund's 80,000-seat stadium, Brazil played out a dull 0-0 draw with Turkey. The starting eleven was greatly changed from the England game, with Brazil boss Dunga keen to take a look at the emerging talent available to him. However, the combinations didn't click and eventually he resorted to introducing Kaka and Ronaldinho to the action to inject some life into the contest. 'I expected more today. I didn't like the game,' Dunga admitted. 'But some people said I wouldn't dare sit down Ronaldinho and Kaka, but I don't do anything to please people, I do what I think is best for the team.'

The performance had left the sparse crowd somewhat dissatisfied, but despite the pressures and demand for the Brazil team to produce flamboyant entertaining football every time they crossed the white line, Robinho was enjoying his spell with the national team far more than his time with Real Madrid. 'I have more freedom with Brazil because manager Dunga allows me to play. The climate with the yellows is different from what I experience with my club, Real. It's different because there is little jealousy about the fact that one is Brazilian and has fame from being a good player,' he said. With the Brazil squad Robinho was not treated like any other player, he obviously had the respect of his Brazil team-mates and the support of his manager. 'Kaka is the best player at the moment, Ronaldinho has the capability to return to the top and Robinho could be up there,' Dunga told reporters, a clear message of his belief in the former Santos star.

Brazil's squad for the Copa America in Venezuela mainly included inexperienced rising stars of the game, with only seven of the squad present at the 2006 World Cup. Alongside Robinho in the 'experienced' bracket were AS Roma goalkeeper Doni, Werder Bremen playmaker Diego, Arsenal midfielder Gilberto Silva and Santos midfielder Ze Roberto. 'The new players arriving now can play at a high level too,' Dunga told the Brazilian media after the 22-man squad announcement in Germany. 'They are having opportunities and going through the same situations that Ronaldinho and Kaka already have gone through.'

After the disappointment of the previous year's World Cup, both Argentina – who crashed out of Germany in the quarter-finals after looking impressive in the initial group stage – and Brazil were aiming to lay the groundwork for their 2010 World Cup qualifying campaigns. For Argentina this was also an opportunity to put an end to their 14-year drought in the Copa America, in which time Brazil had shared the trophy with only Colombia and Uruguay.

Despite taking the trophy in four out of the five previous editions of the tournament, Arsenal's Gilberto Silva was fully aware that the pressure was still on the Samba Boys to produce the goods in Venezuela. 'Playing for Brazil we are always under a lot of pressure,' he said. 'Coming a year after getting knocked out of the World Cup there is that little bit more because we didn't perform well in Germany. Everyone was expecting us to lift that title. But against us everyone else plays the game of their lives.'

However, Robinho, billed as the crown jewel of the side, was confident his inexperienced team-mates could live up to the expectations placed on them by their demanding supporters and impatient national press. 'I know there will be very great pressure on this Brazilian national team, but our will is very great too. I hope this new generation can come out as the winner,' he said. 'The Copa America is important for any player and my goal here is to play well.'

THE BRILLIANCE OF BRAZIL

The twelve teams were split into three groups of four, with the reigning champions drawn alongside 2001 runners-up Mexico, and two un-fancied sides, Chile and Ecuador.

DATE: WEDNESDAY, 27 JUNE 2007
TIME: 8.50PM
VENUE: PUERTO ORDAZ
OPPONENT: MEXICO
PHASE: GROUP STAGE

The first game of the 2007 contest was an open affair between Brazil and Mexico. Both sides had numerous chances to hit the net, but it was the Mexicans who prospered, winning the match 2-0 with goals from Nery Castillo, who scored a spectacular solo effort, and Ramon Morales, who netted a 25-yard free kick.

Both strikes from the invitees came within the half-hour mark, leading to Brazil rampantly pressing forward for the rest of the encounter, forcing Mexican goalkeeper Guillermo Ochoa into a number of excellent saves to preserve his side's lead. Robinho, who was supporting Vagner Love in attack, looked particularly determined to wipe-out the deficit. The Real Madrid man saw his first-half bicycle-kick tipped onto the crossbar before testing Ochoa again in the second period with two angled drives. However, there was no way past the Mexican stopper and Brazil boss Dunga was left with little choice but to hold his hands up after the game and describe the keeper's performance as 'brilliant'. 'We created a number of chances, but their goalkeeper had an inspirational evening. Our team is on the right path, we just have to sort out a few details,' he said.

Robinho, though, was disgruntled he could not inspire his team-mates to victory and accepted that the team would be judged by their results. 'It's the time for our generation. I know that if Brazil doesn't do well, the criticism will rain down upon me. There's no point in playing well and losing. I don't want to be the best of the worst.' However, he was still confident of his team's chances in the competition. 'Of course we can qualify. That's our aim,' he said.

DATE: SUNDAY, 1 JULY 2007
TIME: 4.05P.M.
VENUE: MATURIN
OPPONENT: CHILE
PHASE: GROUP STAGE

It was almost as though Robinho had single-handedly taken on the responsibility of guiding Brazil to the knockout phases. Perhaps blaming himself for the missed chances against Mexico, or possibly just because he felt, as one of the more experienced stars in the team, that it was his duty to inspire the side, Robinho turned in a stunning display for Brazil in the next group game against Chile. In an otherwise poor performance from his national team, Robinho carried Brazil to victory with a fantastic hat-trick against Chile, a side harbouring qualification hopes themselves after defeating Ecuador. 'Robinho 3-0 Chile' read a headline in Brazilian newspaper *O Globo* the day after the Real Madrid star dazzled his opponents.

The Brazilian opened the scoring by converting a penalty after being brought down in the box. It was Robinho's first international goal since he scored in a 5-0 World Cup qualifier win over Chile in 2005, but the strike did not kick-start his Brazilian team-mates and Dunga's side endured a tense second half as Chile looked to find a way back into the match against their Under-performing opponents. However, Robinho put Brazilian fans' minds to rest in the 84th minute when Ze Roberto teed him up for a cheeky chip over the advancing Chilean goalkeeper. Robinho completed his first international hat-trick with just 3 minutes left to play; breaking from his own half he beat two defenders before firing a left-foot drive into the bottom corner to send the Brazil support into rapture, as a relieved Dunga embraced his coaching staff.

'I am playing well and am happy with the three goals,' Robinho told the press after the game. 'But I expect to achieve even more with this team and to keep moving forward in this competition. I feel strong, physically good, and I think that I am at a good level. To score goals is important and to score three is not something that happens every day, so I am pleased. I am also pleased with the win as now we have a good chance of qualifying for the next stage.'

Alongside his unerring self-belief Robinho has always been thankful for his team-mates and well aware that single-handedly he can't win the major trophies that he ambitiously aims for in every competition he enters. 'I played well but so did the other players,' he said. 'I haven't come here to be the star, but to help out. If that means a performance like today's, then that's fine. But if they want me to mark and tackle, I'm going to do that as well.'

The hat-trick was perfectly timed as, back in Madrid, Los Blancos had just appointed German Bernd Schuster as Capello's successor. 'Schuster is a great manager. And I think that he showed that when he was in charge of Getafe and they caused Real so many problems,' Robinho remarked on hearing news of the appointment after the Chile match. 'I hope we can become champions together.'

DATE: WEDNESDAY, 4 JULY 2007
TIME: 8.50PM
VENUE: PUERTO LA CRUZ
OPPONENT: ECUADOR
PHASE: GROUP STAGE

Robinho continued his one-man show for Brazil in the final group game against Venezuela. With Brazil needing at least a draw to qualify for the next round and avoid the third-placed play-off group, Robinho's penalty kick early in the second half secured them a spot in the Copa America quarter-finals. The Real Madrid striker had been hauled down in the box and then picked himself up, as he had against Chile, to score past Ecuadorian keeper Marcelo Elizaga.

It was another impressive display from Robinho, who had netted all four of Brazil's goals in the competition thus far. 'I will try to continue playing well for the team. But we are a team which is not just Robinho,' the twenty-three-year-old reminded reporters after the game. 'Brazil has brilliant players and can play much better. We have a lot of individual talent, but we are also strong on team spirit. We now need to improve as we are in the quarter-finals.'

He was also hopeful his scoring exploits would continue throughout the tournament. 'I'm only thinking about winning the tournament, but if I can be the top scorer then that would make it even better.' Manager Dunga also paid tribute to the Real Madrid star and praised his side's perseverance in overcoming the dogged Ecuadorians despite them again not producing a vintage performance. 'Robinho is a great player with fantastic individual skill,' he commented. 'But he also created a lot of chances for his team-mates. That's important.'

DATE: SATURDAY, 7 JULY 2007
TIME: 8.50PM
VENUE: PUERTO LA CRUZ
OPPONENT: CHILE
PHASE: QUARTER-FINALS

Chile, who finished third in the group stage behind Brazil and winners Mexico, progressed to the quarter-final stage along with Uruguay as their results were better than the other third-placed side, Colombia. Strangely both Uruguay and Chile were both paired with their group opponents in the quarter-finals, meaning Chile had the chance of revenge against Brazil.

However, Dunga was under no illusions that the second match-up with Chile would be far tougher than their first meeting, when Robinho's hat-trick gave Brazil a flattering 3-0 win. 'It will be harder than the first game. All play-off games are harder,' he said.

Those words, though, seemed just polite rhetoric after the game, when the defending Copa America champions thumped their opponents 6-1. Juan, the Brazilian defender, kicked off the scoring for the Samba Boys with a back-post header from Julio Baptista's corner. Six minutes later, Baptista converted a counter-attack move himself by rifling a left-foot strike in off the far post, as Brazil's talented squad finally emerged from Robinho's shadow. However, the Real

Madrid star was not to be left out of the onslaught. With just 27 minutes on the clock, Robinho added Brazil's third with a perfectly placed drive from the edge of the box. The game was already over before half-time, but Brazil continued to press forward in the second period and Robinho latched on to a deep cross to tap in at the back post for his sixth of the tournament. That strike left him two goals shy of Pelé's all-time Copa America record of eight goals in a single tournament, which had stood since 1959. However, it was Josue and Vagner Love who added the next two goals for Brazil, while Humberto Suazo failed to even raise a smile after scoring Chile's lone goal in the 75th minute.

Robinho was head and shoulders above the other strikers on display at the tournament; his nearest rivals in the goal rankings were Salvador Cabanas and Roque Santa Cruz of Paraguay and Argentina's Hernan Crespo, all of whom were well behind the Brazilian with just three goals from four games.

DATE: TUESDAY, 10 JULY 2007
TIME: 8.50PM
VENUE: MARACAIBO
OPPONENT: URUGUAY
PHASE: SEMI-FINALS

The semi-final encounter with Uruguay, however, was not so easy. After Maicon and Baptista had twice put Brazil in the lead, Diego Forlan and Sebastian Abreu twice pulled Uruguay back into the match, which eventually went to penalty kicks. Robinho, who had been a marked man in this contest, calmly slotted home the first strike for Brazil, which set the reigning champions on their way. Eventually, they prevailed 5-4, setting up a repeat of the 2004 final against Argentina.

'My footballers showed love for the jersey, they love the national team. I am very happy with them. These players have given up their holidays to come play the Copa America,' said Dunga after the dramatic win. Robinho, though, was more philosophical. 'The game was very balanced and very difficult,' he said. 'However, if we do not win the tournament, this triumph will be worth nothing.'

Dunga was resolute that the tough test and the good workout provided by Uruguay would stand Brazil's players in good stead for the future. 'To be a winning team, you have to know how to suffer,' said Dunga, who bounced back from failure at the 1990 World Cup to captain the team to victory four years later. 'In the most difficult moment, you have to have posture, courage and fight until the end.'

DATE: SUNDAY, 15 JULY 2007
TIME: 5.05PM
VENUE: MARACAIBO
OPPONENT: ARGENTINA
PHASE: FINAL

Argentina had routed Mexico, the only team to beat Brazil at the tournament, 3-0 to set up the organisers' dream final. The two most successful South American nations would meet each other in a Copa America final for the 10th time, with Brazil's victory in a penalty shootout three years earlier in Peru, the single time the Samba Boys had overcome the Argentines in a Copa final.

Argentina were intent on winning the prestigious title for a record 15th time, which would end their barren run in the competition. However, despite fielding a full-strength side they fell behind to a Kaka- and Ronaldinho-less Brazil in just the fourth minute of the final when Julio Baptista thundered a strike into the top corner, giving Argentina keeper Roberto Abbondanzieri absolutely no chance. An Ayala own goal on 40 minutes, when the defender inadvertently diverted a Daniel Alves cross into his own net, left the Argentina players with their heads in their hands, realising their chance of glory might have gone. Daniel Alves confirmed the Brazil win in the second half, netting the team's third by expertly finishing off a rapid counter-attack initiated by a long pass from the hard-working Robinho, who had tracked back to keep the Argentineans at bay.

Despite all the accusations of the Brazil squad not being good enough, or worthy of representing the country at the Copa America, Dunga had turned his second-string side into worthy South American champions. 'Lots of people criticised our team, but we are the champions,' said Brazilian striker Robinho, who finished as the tournament's top scorer with 6 goals. 'Despite the fact I could not score in the final I'm delighted because we clinched the title. I could not score a goal and bring joy to fans but I had to help out defensively.'

Dunga was equally delighted with his team's performance. 'The country is happy because we have recovered the self-esteem of Brazilian football,' he said in a press conference after the final. 'What we did was to play football, to know how to defend, to attack and to value the talent which our players had, which was more than many thought. Before the game, I told my players not to worry, that they were champions just by having got to the final. The winning formula was not so complicated. You have to have the ball, and when you do not have it you have to keep your balance. Everything has to be very simple.'

The impressive, if somewhat unexpected, retention of the Copa America propelled Brazil from third place back to top spot in the FIFA World Rankings, trading places with World Cup champions Italy. The Brazilians had been ranked the world's best side for 55 consecutive months before Italy's World Cup win in Germany, and the victory in the Copa America demonstrated that, even with different faces in the team, Brazil were still capable of matching the best sides in the world.

Robinho's sensational performance at the tournament, where he became Brazil's leading light, was a remarkable achievement considering the improved, yet still difficult second season he had had at Real Madrid. Clearly, the freedom and enjoyment he had playing for the national team brought out the best in him. Could Bernd Schuster unlock his talents for Real Madrid? If he could then there was every reason to believe that Real could retain their title in the 2007/08 season.

CHAPTER 10

MADRID DANCE TO ROBINHO'S BEAT

Forty-seven-year-old Bernd Schuster had spent the previous two seasons in charge of Getafe before joining Real Madrid in the summer of 2007. Replacing the departed manager Fabio Capello, who was fired in June despite guiding Madrid to its first league title in four years, the German was seen by the Madrid board as the best option to build on the success of Capello's season and introduce Madrid's more traditional values to the side – flair, adventure, attack. 'Today we begin down a new road and during this second year we intend for Real Madrid to be a team that we can all be proud of,' said club president Ramon Calderon at a news conference. 'We have faith that he will build a team that reaches excellence in the way it plays.'

The Real Madrid job had seen a regular turnover in recent seasons; the German becoming the eighth head coach in the past four years at Madrid. Following the league title win the previous year, however, there was an air of optimism at the club. At last, after the disastrous galacticos era, Real Madrid could regain its reputation as the best side in the world.

Schuster was no stranger either to the demands placed upon the Real Madrid managers. As a midfielder, Schuster played at Real Madrid, Atletico Madrid and Barcelona and saw first-hand the dismissal of several Madrid managers as he guided little Getafe to a ninth-placed finish in 2006/07.

The Real Madrid job, treacherous as it is for even successful coaches such as Capello, was too tempting for Schuster, who bought himself out of his contract at Getafe for £300,000. It was a small price to pay, he believed, for the opportunity to coach at such an elite club. 'From the day you begin thinking about coaching, you dream about triumphing with a great club, and there are three or four of them in the world, Real Madrid being one of them,' he said.

Although the German would inherit a team that was losing ageing stars such as Roberto Carlos to Fenerbahce and David Beckham to LA Galaxy, the squad still boasted the young talents of Robinho, Fernando Gago and Sergio Ramos. There would be a number of additions to the squad, too. Javier Saviola, Gabriel Heinze, Wesley Sneijder and Arjen Robben were among the eight new signings to join Los Blancos that summer. Schuster was also pleased that Real, while buying quality players, were moving away from the galacticos policy. 'The club is swarming with world-class players. Nevertheless the galacticos like David Beckham, Zinedine Zidane, Ronaldo have gone – thank God. I have felt in conversations with key people that the side's high-profile reputation hindered them, so I am glad a sense of normality has returned, as well it should be.'

The new era for Real under Schuster, following defeat in the Spanish Super Cup to Sevilla, began at the Bernabeu against rivals Atletico Madrid on 25 August. It was a game that saw the introduction of a new star for the Real Madrid fans – Wesley Sneijder, who scored the winner on his debut to give Schuster a victorious start – and showed the spirit within the camp was good, the team battling back from 2-1 down to win over their local rivals. Indeed, the ease with which the new signings had slipped into the Real Madrid fold pleased Schuster and suggested a good season lay ahead for Madrid. Speaking of new left-back Royston Drenthe, Schuster told *AS*: 'Drenthe is Dutch, but he seems Caribbean. And being so happy all the time helps him get along well with Robinho. They both generate a good atmosphere in the dressing room.'

With strong team spirit often comes good results and that's exactly what Madrid produced in their next game, away to Villarreal at the El Madrigal on 2 September. Villarreal had finished the previous season in sublime form and their 3-0 win on the opening day of the season against Valencia not only confirmed their position as title contenders, but also maintained their excellent unbeaten run of 18 matches in La Liga. The encounter between the two sides would set an early benchmark from which the clubs and supporters could judge the realities of their side's title challenge after the hype and enthusiasm of pre-season. For the first 38 minutes it seemed the talk of Villarreal as a major contender was fair. A solid back line, disciplined midfield and dangerous forward play made it easy to see how Villarreal had established such a fine run without defeat over the end of the previous season – form they were clearly taking into the new campaign.

Warning signs were there, however, that Real had not come to El Madrigal to become another name on the list of sides unable to defeat Villarreal. Robinho hit the post on a Madrid counter-attack after 15 minutes and van Nistelrooy had a shy at goal from distance. The deadlock was eventually broken when Sneijder found Raul with a long diagonal ball and the

Spanish forward made no mistake with his finish. With the start of the second half, Villarreal sought a way back into the game but Sneijder dealt them a vital blow, scoring Madrid's second goal of the evening with a perfectly executed free kick. The goal opened the floodgates for Madrid, and just 2 minutes later, a sweeping counter-attack fuelled by the running of Robinho ended with a Sergio Ramos pass to Van Nistelrooy, who, with his customary clinical finish stretched Madrid's lead further. Villarreal capitulated as Sneijder and Guti rounded off the second-half rout to seal an impressive 5-0 win for the visitors and reigning champions.

The victory made a huge statement in confirming that Schuster's Madrid not only had the ability to overcome formidable title challengers but also the capability to crush them in the way Madrid's fans craved. The second straight win of the new season lifted Madrid into top spot, authoritatively looking down on the likes of Barcelona, whose opening-day stumble at Racing Santander had left them in Madrid's wake. Barça's position was compounded on match day three when Madrid took full advantage of their disappointing 0-0 draw away to Osasuna by cruising past Almeira 3-1.

Madrid's perfect start in La Liga continued into the Champions League group stage, where the Spanish giants defeated Werder Bremen 2-1 to kick off their European adventure for the new seasons in ideal fashion on 18 September. The Spanish champions were dealt a far better hand in the 2007/08 Champions League draw than they had endured the previous season. They were grouped with far weaker opposition than in 2006/07 – Greek outfit Olympia, Lazio from Italy and German side Werder Bremen were the teams standing in Madrid's way of qualifying for the knockout phases. With the opening-day win at the Bernabeu secured, confidence was high at Madrid and they believed that they could easily escape their group and perhaps, finally, press-on in the knockout stages. For Robinho, 2007/08 could finally be the year he would couple his runners-up medal in the Copa Libertadores with a place in the final stages of the Champions League.

Dreaming of a tenth European title was put on hold though when Madrid returned to league action. Los Blancos were rescued from defeat by new-signing Javier Saviola, whose 87th-minute equaliser ensured Real didn't leave Valladolid empty-handed.

At the Bernabeu Real were still hugely dominant. Despite a slow first half against Real Betis, the introduction of Robben and Robinho in the second period saw Real spring to life. Robinho appeared to have broken the deadlock on 67 minutes, slotting the ball into the net, but his celebrations were cut short by the referee, who had blown for a foul on Raul in the penalty area before the goal. Raul stepped up to convert the kick and put Madrid ahead. Julio Baptista sealed the win with an overhead kick late on as Madrid strengthened their hold on first place. 'The changes proved pretty important,' Schuster said after the game. 'The team had a lot more pace and life with the entry of Robben and Robinho. It's nice to have these options. Thanks to them, we were able to win the game.' Real Madrid rounded off a great week in their title race by defeating Schuster's former club Getafe with a Sergio Ramos goal.

Robinho had begun the game against Getafe as part of a deadly threesome up front for Real, which included the Brazilian, Robben and van Nistelrooy. However, if Schuster had been hoping to implement the same tactic against Lazio, in their second Champions League game, he was to be disappointed. Two days later Robinho limped out of training with a bruised ankle, forcing him to miss the clash with the Italian giants. Madrid secured a 2-2 draw in Italy but Robinho was also forced to miss out on Real's win over Recreativo the following weekend.

The young Brazilian was, however, fit enough to travel to Colombia a week later, where Brazil were kicking off their marathon qualification campaign for the World Cup in South Africa 2010. Despite the tournament still being three years away, the South American nations began their 10-team league contest to determine the five qualifiers and one play-off qualifier for the tournament. It was a tough 0-0 draw between Brazil and Colombia, with Robinho managing to play an hour of the game before being replaced by his Real Madrid team-mate Baptista.

For Dunga's men it was a solid point away from home, and the team satisfied their supporters' demand for victory with a thumping 5-0 win over Ecuador three days later in Rio de Janeiro. Robinho kicked off the thrashing, looping the ball into the path of Maicon who, bursting in the box, squared the ball for a simple finish from Vagner Love. Ronaldinho then redirected an off-target Kaka drive into the bottom corner for Brazil's second before Kaka curled in a long-range effort himself. Sensational footwork and trickery from Robinho then led to Elano hitting Brazil's fourth before Robinho released Kaka to hit the fifth. The performance was superb and the crowd, a sea of blue and yellow, bounced like waves in jubilation at the display. On the pitch, the players danced with joy as each goal flew into the net. Their dancing later in the night, though, was followed by sterner faces the next morning.

Robinho and Ronaldinho had led the Samba Boys on a celebratory night out in Rio's Catwalk Club. Some of the partying players got carried away, however, and the Real duo, Robinho and Julio Baptista, were left stranded in Brazil after missing their scheduled planes back to Madrid the next morning.

The initial frustration at Real Madrid that two of their key players had missed their flights back from Brazil and as a result would not be able to play against Espanyol, turned to anger when reports in O Globo, a Brazilian newspaper, revealed the reason for this was because of their partying late into the night. It was even alleged in the newspaper that Robinho had asked a bouncer in the club to procure 40 condoms for himself and his friends. Robinho, though, strenuously denied the claims – reminding reporters that his fiancée Vivian Guglielmetti was pregnant with their first child. The couple had been together since before Robinho signed for Santos and Robson Junior was due to be born in 2007.

The controversy was made worse when Real Madrid suffered their first loss of the season to Espanyol. Robinho, who was reportedly set for a 4000-euro fine from the club on his return, was, however, reintroduced to the squad for the Champions League clash with Olympia on 24 October.

'Robinho is a player who needs to be happy, with neither pressure nor responsibilities,' Schuster said ahead of the tie. 'I also think we are yet to see the real Robinho, we need to give him this peaceful platform so he can express himself and succeed.'

In typical fashion Robinho burst back onto the scene and picked up where he had left off for Brazil. A left-footed pass from the twenty-three-year-old forward released van

Nistelrooy, and when the Dutchman's effort was blocked at close range by the Olympia keeper, Raul was on hand to slot into the empty net. However, the Greek side struck back through Galletti, and despite the sending-off of Olympia defender Torosidis, the home side took the lead early in the second half, when Julio César flicked in a deep free kick.

Robinho, though, was not finished. The small forward was left all alone at the back post when Sergio Ramos chipped in a cross and the Brazilian nodded in the equaliser for Real. Robinho then took the game to the Greek side and dazzled defender Paraskevas Antzas with a series of stepovers. Like so many defenders before him, Antzas could do little but fell Robinho in the box. The penalty-kick, though, was missed by the usually reliable van Nistelrooy and Robinho had to conjure up more magic to rifle Madrid's third into the roof of the net on 83 minutes. With all of the Olympia players pushed forward for a corner-kick in the final minute of the game, Robinho was left free up front. The Brazilian picked up Real's defensive clearance and dashed at the one Olympia defender still in his own half. Darting past his marker, Robinho slid the ball across the box for Balboa, who had also burst forward, to complete the 4-2 comeback win.

'I'm really happy to have helped the team to 3 points. We needed a little patience to win the match,' Robinho said after the game. 'I dedicate my goals to the boss because he backed me all the way. Now I want to continue at this level in the coming games and help the team to carry on winning, that's the most important thing. We started playing well but when they got an equaliser we lost a little of our patience and that's normally one of our best virtues when we are playing at home. At least in the second-half, we played better and finally deserved to win.'

MADRID DANCE TO ROBINHO'S BEAT

Pressed on the bigger issue of him failing to return on time from international duty, Robinho was happy to explain the confusion. 'I don't have to apologise for going out after the Brazil match. I was with the Brazilian team and when we lose we go straight back home, but if we win we choose to go out,' he said. 'What I do have to apologise for is returning late because I have an obligation to the club. I have talked with the boss who was very unhappy that I came back to Madrid late. In Brazil there were a lot of problems with the planes and I also thought that Real's game was on the Sunday not Saturday, but the responsibility for this is also mine. I hope I don't make the same mistake again. It was a complicated week but in the end it finished well. There were a lot of things said which were not true but in the end I gave my answer on the field,' he added. 'I'm grateful for the confidence that Schuster has shown in me.'

Schuster was also happy to forget the whole affair. 'I'm not going to go back to the other subject,' he said after the Olympia game. 'He's a player who knows how to win games. He started hesitantly but after he got his first goal he was outstanding, playing with much more confidence. Robinho responded, we worked well with him. What happened, happened but he's still a Real Madrid player and that's how I treat him.' 'Robinho carries on the party' was Spanish sports daily *Marca*'s cheeky view on his return.

Four days later on 28 October Robinho was back on the scoresheet, netting Real Madrid's third in a 3-1 win over Deportivo La Coruna to keep Los Blancos top of the standings in La Liga. Raul and van Nistelrooy had hit back for Real after Xisco put the visitors ahead after just 2 minutes. Robinho rattled the woodwork from long range in the 71st minute before eventually tapping in with a minute to play. With a new sense of freedom and joy at playing for Madrid, Robinho was finally delivering the sort of performances for Real that had caught the eye of so many scouts when he was at Santos. 'Capello used to ask me to track back and defend when we lost the ball,' he explained. 'Schuster doesn't ask me to do that, so I've got more energy and I'm not so tired when I get forward.'

Robinho's purple patch continued and he hit his fourth in three games, completing the 5-1 demolition of Valencia at the Mestalla stadium on 31 October. 'We were very superior from the first minute,' smiled Schuster after Madrid had swept aside yet another big Spanish club with ease. 'There were moments when I don't think we could play any better and that was reflected in the scoreline. But I'm not going to get carried away. We've got a difficult series of games coming up.' Robinho had once again been the centrepiece of the Real attack, dancing around four defenders before setting up Raul for the 45-second opener and, after van Nistelrooy had scored two more and Ramos got in on the act, the Brazilian fired home a strike of his own. The frustration and difficulty he was causing the Valencia backline was summed up when, 9 minutes from time, Raul Albiol was sent off for a blatant obstruction of Robinho as he tried to finish off another attack.

The tough games Schuster was referring to did cause a Real slip-up – first, a 2-0 defeat in Sevilla before a frustrating evening in Greece on 6 November, failing to break down Olympia. However, Real and Robinho were back on track at the start of November, kicking off their run-in to the winter break with a thrilling 4-3 win over Real Mallorca. Robinho grabbed his third and fourth league goals of the season within the first 15 minutes of the game, the first a header, the second a superb finish from a Raul pass. Van Nistelrooy eventually hit the winner after a see-saw match as Real remained top of La Liga. 'Robinho is in great form at the moment and he has maintained a very high level for several matches now,' beamed Real coach Bernd Schuster, before adding: 'That is what we expect of him. At Real Madrid we need players such as Robinho, Raul, Ruud and Sneijder to create problems for the opposition.'

Robinho's displays were now also attracting praise from Pedrag Mijatovic, the club's Director of Football. 'Last season, Robinho had problems because Fabio Capello's style of play does not allow freedom and he could not play when he felt ill at ease. This season, Robinho's playing very well,' Mijatovic told Radio Marca. 'I reminded him of the confidence the club has in him and he has responded. Schuster has given him the freedom he needs.'

Robinho's superb run of form had not gone unnoticed outside of Spain, either. The *Guardian* newspaper published a feature on the forward in November with the headline: 'Suddenly Robinho looks like the New Pelé, again.' At the heart of the piece was Robinho's resounding respect for Schuster and the German's ability to get the best out of him. 'The coach understands me,' he was quoted as saying. 'He speaks candidly with me because he's been through these situations. He always gives me good advice. Schuster allows me to play with more liberties on the pitch, and that's how I can develop my football.'

Robinho also stated his ambition of doing the double with Madrid – winning the domestic league and also the European Cup with the Spanish giants. 'We have to take it slow. We're in good form, leaders of the League, and first in our Champions League group,' said Robinho. 'I would love to win the Champions League. Every player here is excited about our chances. We're going to work hard in order to achieve great things.'

Following a 1-1 draw against Murcia, in which Robinho continued his fine scoring run by heading in the opener for Real, Madrid returned to their quest of Champions League success with their penultimate group game against Werder Bremen on 28 November. Real's qualification to the next round had been virtually assured with their draw against Olympia, but, gunning for top spot in the table, they fielded a strong side in Germany.

After Markus Rosenborg had put Bremen ahead, Real Madrid struck back, again through Robinho, this time the Brazilian cutting in from the left-flank to curl a fine shot into the far corner. The goal was Robinho's tenth for the club in his last eight games since returning to the squad after missing the Espanyol match. It was the best phase of his career to date. He had pinned down a certain spot in the starting line-up for the Spanish champions and was scoring freely, inspiring Real Madrid's stars as he had once been the centrepiece of Santos in Brazil. Madrid eventually lost a see-saw game against Werder 3-2 but returned to the Spanish league with two straight wins over Racing Santander and Athletic Bilbão before playing the final game of the Champions League group stages against Lazio on 11 December 2007.

Robinho, who had twice hit the post against Bilbão, got back to scoring ways against the Italians at the Bernabeu, poking a right-foot shot past Marco Ballotta, the Lazio keeper, on 36 minutes after playing a fine through ball for Julio Baptista to open the scoring and crossing for Raul to head Los Blanco's second. 'I'm not surprised by Robinho's

performance,' said Madrid coach Bernd Schuster after the
Brazilian had inspired Real to a 3-1 win and victory in Group
C. 'He's a great player and the truth is between his time with
Brazil and with us he is having a great season. At the start of
the season I thought Robinho had space for improvement
and he's proved it, especially in European games, where he's
been very impressive.'

Another victory in the league, a 2-0 win over Osasuna,
again highlighted Robinho's fine form – the forward jinxing
past three defenders to set up Sneijder for the decisive second
and put Real four points clear of Barcelona – who they faced
in their final game before the winter break the following
week on 23 December.

On the pitch, it seemed, Robinho could do no wrong.
Every time he played for the Spanish giants he seemed to
further extend his reputation as one of the most explosive,
thrilling and exciting players in world football. Off the field
his life was going equally well. Following the Osasuna victory
Brazilian website *Globoesporte* revealed his fiancée, Vivian
Guglielmetti, had given birth to their first child, a boy named
Robson Junior, in São Paulo, Brazil.

The couple had been together since before Robinho signed
for Santos as an eighteen-year-old and had known each other
since the age of twelve. Since May 2007 Robinho had been
celebrating every goal by sucking his thumb – a tribute to his
unborn child. 'My thumb-sucking celebration is for him,' he
revealed in 2008. 'But my wife [the couple actually married
in the summer of 2009] is a bit jealous now because I used to
celebrate for her.' Now, with both mother and baby healthy,
Robinho was immensely happy and eager to return to Brazil
to see his childhood sweetheart and baby son. However, there
was one more thing for him to do before he could join his

family – he would play in '*el clasico*' on 23 December.

Undefeated in their past six games in La Liga, Real edged a vital win over a patchy Barcelona side at the Nou Camp, securing a 7-point lead at the half-time interval of the season. With the first part of the job done, Robinho flew back to Brazil to meet his new son and rejoin Vivian.

Real and Robinho returned to La Liga on 6 January 2008 and picked up where they had left off. Robinho provided a deft chipped cross for van Nistelrooy to head home in the second half against struggling Zaragoza before the new father added the second and decisive goal himself. Two more 2-0 victories and a 3-2 win over title-chasing third-placed Villarreal extended Madrid's lead over Barcelona to 9 points. Barcelona's 1-1 draw at Athletic Bilbão had given Real the perfect chance to extend their advantage and they took it with both hands courtesy of a brace from Robinho, who had celebrated his twenty-fourth birthday two days earlier. 'This has been a great birthday for me,' Robinho beamed after the game. 'The title race is not over yet because there are lots of games left, but we have taken an important step for sure.'

Their quest for the title took a blow away to Almeria, when the reigning champions were defeated 2-0 by Juan Gutierrez and Alvaro Negredo goals, which put an end to the Spanish league leader's eight-game winning streak. However, in typical fashion, Madrid bounced back at the Bernabeu on 10 February. Raul and Guti each scored a brace in a 7-0 drubbing of Valladolid. Baptista, Robben and substitute Royston Drenthe also netted for Madrid, but for Robinho it was not such a pleasant evening. The forward fell to the ground unchallenged shortly after the half-time break and, after being immediately substituted, was found to have torn muscles in his stomach. The injury, a painful one for

Robinho, kept him out of action for Real's next two league games and the first leg of their Champions League knockout round with Roma. It was perhaps no coincidence that Los Blancos lost all three.

The defeats to Betis and Getafe in the league resulted in Barcelona narrowing Real's advantage to just 2 points, while a 2-1 defeat in Roma after Raul had put the visitors ahead was a serious blow to their hopes of progressing to the next round.

Real fans were, however, heartened by the news of Robinho's return to fitness and Madrid centre-back Fabio Cannavaro summed up his team-mates' attitude towards the Brazilian. 'Robinho is a spectacular player, he has a lot of quality,' said the Italian. 'When he has the desire, when he wants to score a goal, he does it. He is the guy who can decide a game. The blackest moment for Madrid has been when Robinho has been injured. He is a key player for the team.' As if to reiterate his point, Robinho, in his first game back from injury against Recreativo, scored twice and took the Man of the Match award, inspiring Madrid to a 3-2 win.

Robinho had entered the fray in the 71st minute, shortly after Recreativo had been reduced to nine men. Real were already down to ten after Sergio Ramos's dismissal, and the game was balanced at 1-1. However, within seconds of arriving on the pitch Robinho had fired Madrid ahead, squeezing his shot between Recreativo keeper Stefano Sorrentino and the post. In the final minute of the game, Robinho put the win beyond doubt – the Brazilian beat the offside trap and produced an exquisite chip over the advancing goalkeeper to cap his impressive return to action.

With Robinho in the side, Real were a different proposition for Roma in the return leg at the Bernabeu on 4 March. As well as having to deal with the 80,000 roaring Real supporters at Madrid's famous stadium, Roma coach Luciano Spalletti was fully aware Real's main weapon was back in the fold and raring to reverse the first-leg result. 'Robinho is football,' stated the Italian manager to Spanish sports daily *AS* ahead of the tie. 'He has the quality and the senses. There are players that can invent but can't score, but he does both.' Robinho had harboured Champions League hopes since his arrival at Madrid. Missing the first leg was a bitter blow for the Brazilian, but now he was fired up to make his mark on the match. 'The minutes I played against Recreativo have made me ready to face Roma,' he said. 'I'm crazy to play.' Robinho's importance was heightened when striker van Nistelrooy was ruled out of the game with an ankle injury. 'Robinho is a really important player for us and we need him,' midfielder Guti said. 'When he's playing we can rest at ease. He can turn matches and score goals. He's a phenomenon.'

However, even Robinho could not reverse the fact that for the past four years Real had failed to progress beyond the first knockout round. From the first whistle, the forward set about orchestrating Madrid attacks but Los Blancos' mission to overturn the first-leg deficit was made all the more difficult when centre-half Pepe saw red midway through the second half as he picked up his second booking of the match. A minute later, Roma midfielder Rodrigo Taddei scored the vital away goal for Roma, and, although Raul converted Robinho's cross 2 minutes later, Real's fightback was ended by Mirko Vuãiniç in the dying seconds. Once again Madrid, and Robinho, had seen their dreams of a Champions League win dashed. 'To me, it's not a loss,' Bernd Schuster told the press after the match. 'The ball just didn't want to go in.'

With no European distractions and their run in the Copa

del Rey ended at the round of 16 stage by Mallorca, Real's eyes were focused simply on fending off the challenge of Barcelona and Villarreal in La Liga.

The team immediately bounced back from their Champions League heartache with a 2-1 win over Espanyol on 8 March but an own goal by Pepe gave Deportivo La Coruna a 1-0 win over Real Madrid a week later. That defeat was compounded when Copa del Rey finalists Valencia netted a late goal to secure a sensational 3-2 win over Madrid at the Bernabeu the following Sunday. Angel Arizmendi's strike, coupled with Barcelona's 4-1 win over Valladolid at the Nou Camp, had dragged Real's advantage down to just 4 points.

It was nothing more than a blip, though. Real took 7 points from their next three games and, as Barcelona struggled to juggle Champions League matches – where they had progressed to the semi-finals – with La Liga commitments, Real Madrid extended their advantage to an almost unassailable 10 points with a 2-0 win over Racing Santander. Wins over Athletic Bilbão and Osasuna all but sealed the title for Madrid and Schuster, and their retention of the Spanish crown was confirmed in style at the Nou Camp when Madrid humiliated their arch rivals 4-1 at their own ground on 7 May.

A 2-2 draw with Zaragoza and a 5-2 celebration win over Levante at the Bernabeu capped off the season, but it was the 4-1 win over Barça that summed up Real Madrid's dominance. They had more wins than any other side in the league, fewest defeats, most goals scored, fewest goals conceded and the best goal difference by 25 goals. Real Madrid, the dominators of La Liga 2007/08 had won their 31st league title at a canter.

Real's league win had been established with a sensational

display in the first half of the season. With Robinho firing on all cylinders with the approach of Christmas, Real wrapped up 53 points in the first 21 games of the season. Despite a slump in February and March the champions finished strongly, taking 19 points from the last seven games in sharp contrast to Barça, who took just one win in their last eight games of the season.

It had been a monumental season, too, for Robinho. Off the field, he was having the time of his life, revelling in his new role as a father. On the field, he was finally playing as well for Real as he was for Santos when he caught the Spanish giant's eye. For Brazil he had become a key component and was recognised throughout the world game as a major star. Surely now he would be able to consolidate his position at Madrid and go on to become a legend at the Bernabeu?

CHAPTER 11
THE UNWANTED HERO

On the pitch Robinho was the hero of the Real Madrid fans. He had just secured his second La Liga title in two years and his fourth league win in six seasons as a professional. In addition, he was certain of a starting spot among the most talented names in world football at the biggest club in the world, where he had netted 15 goals in his 35 games and 7 substitute appearances in 2007/08. He was also key to the fortunes of his nation, having guided Brazil to Copa America success in 2007. Off the field he had settled down with long-time girlfriend Vivian Guglielmetti, whom he married in the summer of 2009, and was enjoying his role as father to six-month-old Robson Junior.

However, Real Madrid's aggressive and rampant pursuit of Manchester United's Cristiano Ronaldo at the end of the 2007/08 season would massively affect the Brazilian.

On 24 May 2008 *The Times*, as well as a number of other British newspapers, reported that Real Madrid were willing to include Robinho in a £64 million part-exchange deal with Manchester United to bring Ronaldo to the Bernabeu. The

United winger had enjoyed a record-breaking year with the English champions, winning the Premier League, Champions League and netting 42 goals in all competitions. He would later take every Player of the Year award on offer and was one of the most sought-after players on the planet. When the Portuguese winger failed to confirm or deny his future lay at United, Ronaldo had escalated speculation that he would be heading to Madrid in the summer of 2008 – sparking the apparent offer from Real of Robinho, plus money to obtain his services.

The idea of a move from Madrid left Robinho deeply disappointed. The Brazilian had dreamed of playing for the European giants in Spain and was hugely excited when a deal was agreed between Real and Santos to allow him the opportunity of playing for the Madrid club. Despite a patchy first season, in which he struggled to find the form which had lit up the Villa Belmiro, Robinho, in his second season at the club, had forced Fabio Capello to re-think his perception of him as a 'luxury player'. In his third year with Real, under the guidance of Schuster, Robinho had enjoyed the freedom to express himself – producing some of the best football of his career. Now, it seemed, he was not the 'new Pelé', or Madrid's catalyst: he was nothing more than a pawn for Madrid, to entice a so-called bigger, better player to the club. Perhaps the biggest insult of all was that it wasn't even alleged to be a straight swap. Madrid were willing to hand him over *and* pay United a record-breaking £64 million for the Portuguese winger. Robinho's agent, Wagner Ribeiro, who masterminded the move to Madrid, announced that his player felt undervalued by Madrid and was seeking a way out of the club to somewhere his talents would be more appreciated.

With news of Robinho's intentions made public, Chelsea re-ignited their interest in the forward. The Blues had missed out on Robinho when he left Santos, trumped by Real Madrid, but hoped they would finally be able to get their man in 2008, three years after their initial interest in the Brazilian. On 2 June Robinho – who had also been told by Madrid that he would not be allowed to join up with the Brazilian Olympic team as one of their over-age players – confirmed the rumours of his departure. 'There are proposals, yes,' he said. 'One is from Manchester United, which would be in exchange for Cristiano Ronaldo, and the other is from Chelsea. I have never hidden my desire to remain at Real Madrid. But if the negotiations materialise into something I will have no problem in leaving.'

Later that month *Marca*, the Spanish sports paper, claimed Real Madrid were planning an 85-million-euro raid for Ronaldo, financed by the sale of Robinho to Chelsea. It was not just Robinho who was upset by the talk of his exit, though. Wesley Sneijder, his fellow midfielder at Madrid, could see no reason why Real would want to sell Robinho to get Ronaldo. 'I want Robinho to stay with Madrid because I think he's almost the same as Ronaldo,' the Dutch playmaker said. Bernd Schuster was also adamant the decision to sell Robinho was not his – on the contrary, the German was hopeful the Brazilian would stay at the club and admitted he was desperately trying to convince him to do so. 'I don't see Robinho out of this team because it doesn't make any sense,' he told Spanish newspaper *AS*. 'He has to be with us. He's a player in our project. We've shown him his goals from last year and we all realised that he is one of the most important players in this squad and we need him for the next few years.'

On 27 July the *Daily Telegraph* reported that the Real

Madrid forward had agreed personal terms with Chelsea, and that the club had made a first offer of £31.5 million for the Brazilian. The paper also claimed Real were simply lining up a replacement for Robinho before accepting the London club's offer. Chelsea had already brought Portuguese-speaking players Jose Bosingwa and Deco to the club, and with Luiz Felipe Scolari in charge – the Brazilian, reported the *Guardian*, had made Robinho his principal transfer target for the summer. It seemed Robinho would be more than at home in West London.

The speculation was met by a twist in Madrid's thinking. Three days later the Press Association reported Schuster had claimed Robinho and Ronaldo would now form a partnership at Real. 'The coaches believe they are compatible and Madrid don't need to raise funds to buy. To sign Cristiano we don't need to sell anyone and even less so Robinho. It's not like that at all. I don't have any reason to think that Robinho is unhappy. Schuster adores him, his team-mates want him and last year he was very happy at the Bernabeu,' insisted the German coach.

However, Chelsea's determination to secure the signing of Robinho stepped up a gear when their Ivory Coast talisman Didier Drogba was injured in pre-season training and would miss the start of the new campaign. Chelsea's new-signing Deco was also an admirer of Robinho's talents, and made no secret of his ambitions to play alongside the Brazilian wizard at Stamford Bridge. 'He's a spectacular player,' said the Brazilian-born Portuguese playmaker. 'He's got incredible skill. He has magic and is capable of anything on a football pitch. His quality is amazing. It would be great if he joined us and he'd be made very welcome here.'

All speculation of a move for Robinho, though, appeared to

come to an abrupt end on 8 August. Despite rumours of him being touted in a part-exchange deal for Ronaldo earlier in the summer, Ramon Calderon, speaking to BBC Radio Five Live, announced any transfer deal for Robinho was off. 'Definitely he's going to stay with us,' the Spaniard said. 'The coach has said he wants him in our team. We don't see any possibility of him leaving Real Madrid. We know Chelsea have been interested in signing him. He's one of the best players we have got in our team – we need him for the next season.'

A week later Robinho was included in the Real Madrid squad to face Valencia in the first leg of the Spanish Super Cup. The move seemed to confirm Calderon's statement that Robinho wasn't leaving the Madrid club that year. 'I am certain he is going to stay at the club and I don't have to drive myself crazy because he is going to remain as our player. It is not a problem,' Schuster stated in his pre-game press conference.

Robinho started the game for the Spanish champions and played for 64 minutes before being substituted with Real 2-1 down to their hosts. Madrid eventually lost 3-2, but the main story surrounding the match was about Robinho's future. 'Robinho has looked very happy in the hotel, he is going to play this season with us, I am absolutely sure. He has looked lively, very happy and full of desire. And the coach Bernd Schuster has told me that he is training very well,' Calderon revealed the next day.

However, just five days later Robinho finally broke the silence to state his intentions. 'I want to play in the Premier League,' the Brazil forward said. 'Chelsea have a great squad, a great team and their offer is good for me and for the team. It isn't because of money, it is simply because I want to leave. My personal aim is to be the best player in the world and that isn't going to be possible at Real Madrid.

'I've finished my cycle. I've played three seasons at Real Madrid and have given everything. I have scored goals, won two leagues and that isn't easy. I think my period at Real Madrid has come to an end. I hope the directors reach an agreement with Chelsea to resolve my situation as quickly as possible.'

Calderon reacted sternly to the comments. He told Spanish radio station Cadena SER: 'He would terminate his contract and the courts would decide what he has to pay to Madrid. We want Robinho to stay at Madrid, but this situation leaves us unable to do anything.'

Schuster's faith in the forward, though, remained unshaken. Despite the statement, the German surprised everyone by naming Robinho in his 18-man squad to take on Valencia in the return leg of the Spanish Super Cup. 'Robinho has not told me to leave him out tomorrow, he is an important player for us and we have let him see that very clearly,' he told the official Real Madrid website. 'He is in the squad because he is in perfect condition to play. I want to win the trophy tomorrow.'

This time, though, Robinho was an unused substitute and forced to watch from the sidelines as his side scored four second-half goals to shock Valencia, turn over the first-leg deficit and win the Spanish Super Cup at the Bernabeu. During his time on the bench, Robinho would have certainly noticed the flags and banners draped around the stadium. While some banners criticised him for wanting to leave Madrid, many implored him to stay. The begging banners, though, would not be enough to keep him at the club. The next day *Marca* reported that Chelsea chief executive Peter Kenyon had flown to Madrid to hold negotiations with Real officials to agree a fee for the player. The rumoured offer from Chelsea was 40 million euros, while the offer for Robinho was said to have been a large increase on his current reported 2.1-million-euro annual salary.

Following the meetings the *Daily Mirror* led with a story claiming the deal was done. The clubs had reportedly agreed a £31 million deal, while the forward would sign a contract worth £120,000 a week – the contrast with his early days at Santos was stark and Robinho's agent, Wagner Ribeiro, confirmed the speculation. 'The deal is about to be reached,' he said. 'Robinho's cycle in Spain has come to an end and he is looking forward to a new project.'

However, on 29 August, just two days after the deal was reportedly sealed, the *Daily Star* broke the news that Real Madrid were sensationally set to pull the plug on the transfer. Chelsea, seemingly assured of the new signing, had begun selling replica shirts with Robinho's name on the back on the club website. The move had apparently insulted Real Madrid, who were now considering forcing their player to stay at the club rather than sell to Chelsea. The club issued the following statement two days later: 'Real Madrid profoundly regret the conduct of the Chelsea directors, who despite knowing perfectly well the decision not to transfer the player, have continued making declarations and have gone as far as to sell shirts of the player through their official website. All this has done nothing but cloud the situation and confuse public opinion.'

Robinho, however, had had enough of the transfer saga and called his own press conference in Madrid to issue a short, sharp and concise statement of his intentions. 'I have a contract with Real Madrid now, but we are still negotiating with Chelsea,' he said. 'We are working to seal my future, nothing else. I don't want to stay at Real Madrid. I've already told the president, the coach, management and the media: my head is there [at Chelsea], I want to play over there. The club showed little interest in keeping me until they did not manage to recruit Ronaldo.'

Meanwhile, away from the bickering of Chelsea and Madrid, the newspaper speculation and official press conferences, in the north of England significant events were unfolding that would turn the Robinho situation on its head.

Manchester City had enjoyed a much improved season in 2007/08 under the guidance of Sven-Göran Eriksson, who had transformed a team of journeyman players with the money of former Thailand Primer Minister Thaskin Shinawatra, bringing players such as Elano to the club and guiding the side to a top-ten finish. However, Shinawatra was caught up in political corruption charges in Thailand and seemed set to sell the club. This led to the emergence of the Abu Dhabi United Group as leading contenders to buy Manchester City. Owned by Sheikh Mansour bin Zayed Al Nahyan, a member of the Abu Dhabi Royal Family and Minister of Presidential Affairs for the UAE, the private equity company struck a deal with the former Thai PM to purchase the club on 1 September. As a statement of their intent to transform the club into a major team, the new owners released large sums of money for Manchester City to rapidly pursue big-name targets in the final hours of the transfer window. Sensationally, they had stepped in while Chelsea and Madrid were squabbling, to gazump the London club.

'Real Madrid has finally decided tonight to transfer player Robson de Souza to Manchester City,' Madrid revealed on their website late on 1 September. The deal had an air of mystery around it – not only had Manchester City suddenly become a player in the transfer deal, but with Robinho in Brazil for World Cup qualifiers and unavailable for comment, it wasn't until the following day that the deal was confirmed to the media. The *Guardian* revealed that City had smashed the British transfer record to secure his services – buying the player from Madrid for £32.5 million, dwarfing the £30 million outlay Chelsea had spent on Premier League flop Andriy Shevchenko two years earlier – and handed Robinho a contract worth £160,000 per week, £40,000 more than the initial estimation in the *Daily Star*, making him the best-paid player in the country.

'I am absolutely delighted to get the opportunity to work with such an incredible talent like Robinho,' City manager Mark Hughes told the club's official website. 'I have said that in order to compete with the best teams in the Premier League we have to be in the market for players of this calibre, and Robinho is undoubtedly one of the best players in the world. I am really looking forward to introducing him to the rest of the squad, and to the City fans at the earliest opportunity. This is a real statement of intent as to the ambitions of Manchester City Football Club.'

Calderon confirmed the deal, though soured Robinho's exit with some spiteful words about the Brazilian. 'We have agreed to sell the player for human reasons, for footballing reasons and for an important quantity of money,' said the Real president. 'Every time I have spoken with him he was very sad, crying and asking to leave Spain. He's a great kid, but badly advised.' Robinho later laughed off the accusation in his first interview as a City player. 'At the end he made things even worse for me to leave, but I didn't cry.

I only told him the truth, that was, if the club didn't want me to stay there, then I didn't want to stay at Real either. I wanted him to let me go, through the front door, without any fight.'

The Abu Dhabi United Group had also launched a last-minute attempt to prize Dimitar Berbatov away from the clutches of rivals Manchester United. According to the owners, this was a statement of their intent to transform the club into Premier League and Champions League winners. 'The owners are going to challenge the top teams, not just in this country but in Europe over the next few years,' Mark Bowen, City's assistant boss, told BBC Radio 5 Live shortly after the takeover.

It was the club's ambition to bring the best players in the world to City and build a new superpower that inspired Robinho to join the club. The Brazilian also credited manager Mark Hughes with playing a big role in his move: 'I met with the manager and it went very well. I know that he was a great player and I think that will be a big help to me. I want to help the manager and the team to win the Premier League, that's my ambition here. I knew that Manchester City is a very big club, there's a great team there already and this is an exciting project. I liked the project, and when City made the offer to Real Madrid, I decided to come here. I liked the plans that Manchester City have and I want to succeed with them. I want to repay this excitement by performing on the pitch, and scoring a lot of goals for the fans.' Robinho also joined up with fellow Brazil internationals Jo and Elano, who would be key to helping the new star settle in at Eastlands, or as the supporters had now dubbed their stadium, Middle-Eastlands. 'Jo and Elano are my friends and I know them very well,' Robinho said.

'Having such great players already at City was one of the reasons why I decided to come here.'

Not everyone, though, was impressed by Robinho's move to City. Many people in the game criticised the forward for moving to a 'small' club, claiming he had followed the pound signs rather than targeting more silverware.

Vanderli Luxemburgo, his former coach at Santos and Real, commented: 'I was quite shocked by the news. The media was talking about moving to Chelsea but he finally moved to Manchester City. If you want to become the best, you need a team with possibilities to shine and I don't think City will achieve that this season. I don't know if his football or his career will go back at Manchester City. It depends on the plan the club set. If they build a big team, that's fine. The problem is they don't seem to be building a big team.'

Santos president Marcelo Teixeira stormed: 'This is one of the most disgraceful episodes in Brazilian football. He is a player who is an idol to children, an example. But he has not acted like one.' Meanwhile, Pelé also had strong words for Robinho: 'Chelsea are lucky. This boy needs some serious counselling. In my view he has been badly advised,' said the former Brazil star.

However, Robinho responded by saying that if people understood the position he was in at Madrid, they would see why he made the move. 'Look, I accept Pelé's criticism. He is the king of football. But, maybe, if he were in my shoes he would have done the same thing. I think that only someone who suffered as I suffered in Real Madrid may have something to say on this. For people from outside, judging this situation is easy.'

Criticism of Robinho's decision to move to City was also compounded by the player's slip-up at a meeting with members of the press shortly after the deal was completed. 'On the last day, Chelsea made a great proposal and I accepted,' he told the reporters, one of whom replied: 'You mean Manchester, right?' 'Yeah, Manchester, sorry!' answered Robinho, bashfully.

However, when given the opportunity to speak with the English press for the first time, Robinho gave City fans all the reassurance they needed. Asked about his proposed move to Chelsea, he said: 'Chelsea? This question belongs to the past. I'm a City player and I only think about making the club successful. I don't regret the choice I've made – I'm very happy at the club.' Chelsea's manner of pursuing him, though, had surprised and disappointed the forward. 'It was Chelsea's fault,' he said. 'Everything would probably have been OK, but Chelsea put that picture of me on their website [advertising replica shirts bearing the name of their new 'signing'] and Madrid were upset about that. They also didn't want to sell to Chelsea because they are in the Champions League and, with me, would have been even stronger. Then, on the last day of the transfer window, Manchester City made an offer that was very good for myself and my family, so I accepted.'

He refuted, though, the comments from the likes of Pelé that he was only at City for the money. 'That is not nice to hear,' he said. 'When Brazilian footballers leave Brazil, it is to improve their lives. But the reason I came to Manchester City was not only for the money. If it was for the money, I would have gone elsewhere, Saudi Arabia or Japan.'

He also seemed content for his future to be at City, as the project of making them the best club in the world got underway. 'It's not in my mind to leave this club at all,' he said. 'The only thing in my mind is to stay here for many years. Next year we will try our best to reach the Champions League. The project here is very ambitious and Manchester City will grow very quickly over the next few years. In football, nothing is impossible. Manchester City might be classed as a small club today, but in two or three years' time, who knows? Three or four years ago, Chelsea were considered a small club, but now they are a big club. Anything can happen.'

CHAPTER 12
A NEW DAWN

After all the rumour, speculation and controversy of the summer of 2008, the atmosphere at City's Eastlands stadium reached fever pitch as Chelsea and Manchester City began to emerge from the tunnel. As if keeping his new fans in suspense, Robinho eventually came out into the September sunshine, ten seconds after the rest of his team-mates had run onto the field. The Brazilian sauntered onto the pitch, crossed himself and jogged into the fray as an eruption of cheers rang out around the City of Manchester stadium. Robinho had gone straight into City's starting XI after returning from his goal-scoring trip to Chile with Brazil and now one of the most eagerly awaited debuts in Premier League history was about to begin.

Wearing the No. 10 shirt – 'that shirt means that I have a duty to entertain' – it was not long before Robinho gave the City fans what they had come to see. From his first touch, he played up to his role of superstar signing, teasing the Chelsea defence and amazing City fans with cheeky stepovers and flicks. When Ricardo Carvalho brought down Jo on the edge of the box the whole stadium seemed to hold their breath as Robinho stepped up to take the dangerously-positioned free kick. The whistle blew and he paused. Off-putting jeers from the Chelsea support sounded towards their would-be hero, but they were silenced when, stepping up to the plate, Robinho clipped the ball into the top corner, thanks to a slight deflection off the wall. The City supporters exploded into life, spontaneously bursting into a chant of 'Robinho, Robinho, Robinho!'. It had taken their new signing just 13 minutes to confirm his quality and seemingly assure the City faithful that, yes, the Abu Dhabi dream would come true.

A pinch of reality came for City as the rest of the match unfolded. Three minutes after Robinho's strike Carvalho levelled and Frank Lampard and Nicolas Anelka capped a 3-1 victory for Chelsea, which had highlighted the gulf in class between the two sides. City were, after all, still very much a side in transition.

City manager Mark Hughes was sure the introduction of Robinho to the squad would see City become a far better team, though. 'In any situation he will make the right decisions more times than a lesser player would. That's why they are great players. When you get a player as talented as Robinho coming in, the level of the others rises automatically,' he said. 'That's always happened and it's a football thing. With a player of his quality around, it raises the bar for everybody else. It makes my job easier because every player has an ego and wants to judge themselves against the best players. With Robinho coming into the club, the training will be of the highest quality simply because of the players I have brought in.'

Robinho's second game for the club was perhaps a taste of reality for what he had signed up for. The day after Real

Madrid had just kicked off their Champions League campaign for the new season Robinho was battling with the rest of his Manchester City team-mates to come back from a goal down against Omonia Nicosia in Cyprus in the First Round of the UEFA Cup. Jo eventually got City out of jail with two second-half strikes, but the exact current position of City in the world order must have hit home with Robinho in that game.

Returning to the Premier League, though, and to Eastlands, City were flying once again. On 21 September they thrashed Portsmouth 6-0 in Manchester to maintain fifth spot in the league. Robinho and fellow Brazilian Jo combined sensationally well as both got on the scoresheet. For the first time, Robinho truly showed the City fans what he was capable of. He had a hand in all the goals as captain Richard Dunne, Shaun Wright-Phillips, Ched Evans and Gelson Fernandes completed the rout. With the club to formally move into Arab hands the next day, City chairman Khaldoon Al Mubarak could hardly believe what he was watching as his new club ripped their opponents apart.

However, a difficult-to-explain inconsistency was to be the hallmark of Manchester City's first season with Arab wealth. Robinho flew back to Brazil after the Portsmouth win to sort out passports for his fiancée and son, fortunately missing the embarrassing penalty shoot-out defeat in the Carling Cup to Brighton, but he could not escape the tough and bruising encounter City faced against Wigan. Once again, Hughes's charges struggled away from Eastlands and City went down 2-1 to Steve Bruce's side.

A 2-1 home win over Omonia Nicosia on 2 October saw City safely through to the group stages of the UEFA Cup before Robinho faced his second big test in English football. Liverpool came to Manchester City undefeated in the league but Robinho was relishing his early experiences of the English game. 'The tempo in English football is different from anything I've experienced so far. The rhythm is high speed and the quality is excellent – better than I expected. It's the best league in the world,' he told the *Sun*.

He also insisted he was having no trouble adapting to the Premier League. 'The difference between England and Spain is smaller than the one I experienced when I moved from Brazil to Spain. The pitch is wet, just like in Spain, which makes the game faster. I think the big differences are the referees, who let the game flow without conceding many fouls, and the supporters. They are much more involved in the game than in Spain – they shout a lot and push us more.'

Robinho was also enjoying his star status at City after being just another big name at the Bernabeu. 'People recognise me all the time in the city,' he said. 'They are very kind to me. They tell me great things and this kind of motivation is very important for a football player. I am already a god and I didn't do a thing! But my desire is to pay it back, to show the supporters my gratitude with goals, great play and victories.' City fans warmed to the striker even more when it was claimed he had been spotted taking the bus to the Trafford Centre. Alas, the rumours turned out to be false, but Robinho's status as fan favourite remained untarnished.

Hughes, the City manager, had spoken about the importance Robinho had in raising his team's ability but he had also, in the new signing's first few games for the club, shown a willingness to build the team around the talented Brazilian – something Robinho was pleased about and determined to make the most of. 'What makes me most happy is that I am finally playing in my real position and it never happened in Spain. I am playing as a second striker, with total freedom to move and get involved in every play – not just restricted to the left wing.'

Of course Manchester did have its drawbacks: 'There is no beach and no sun. But I am enjoying Manchester so far. Elano took me for a city tour and I loved it. After what people had been telling me, I feared the worst. I thought I would arrive here and find nothing but wasteland. But it's not like that. There are fine restaurants and entertainment places, the city is beautiful. I have no problem with the food. There is a great Brazilian restaurant in the city centre and I'll become a regular customer.' A particular favourite of Robinho's was Bem Brasil. Robinho and his fellow Brazil internationals created a home from home at the £1m Manchester city centre restaurant – lured in by the exceptional food and dance floor. Since his arrival stars from Manchester United, Liverpool and Everton have followed him there with United's Portuguese duo Cristiano Ronaldo and Nani regular customers.

Bem Brasil host Alan Clemence said: 'There is an element of homesickness for some players. They are only young kids and miss their mums and their home cooking. So they love it here.'

City served up a treat for their fans in the first half against title-chasing Liverpool on 5 October. Stephen Ireland scored from Wright-Phillips's cross on 20 minutes and just before the break Javier Garrido's exquisite free kick left Jose Pepe Reina with no chance. It seemed the City express was on its way to a significant and impressive victory over one of the four giants of the English game. However, Fernando Torres, Liverpool's key forward, began the fightback in the 55th minute and when Pablo Zabaleta saw red for a reckless challenge on Xabi Alonso, City struggled to contend with the Reds. Torres headed in the equaliser before Dirk Kuyt dramatically slotted in at the back post deep into injury time to break City fans' hearts.

The following week it was City profiting from a late goal, Ireland equalising at Newcastle after Robinho's early penalty kick had been cancelled out by strikes from Shola Ameobi and an own goal from Dunne. There was to be no denying Robinho, though, against Stoke City on 26 October. A superb display from the Brazilian, who grabbed a fine hat-trick in the game, inspired Manchester City to their first Premier League win in four games and lifted them up to seventh spot. Evans and Daniel Sturridge had teed Robinho up for his first two strikes and, after Stoke keeper Thomas Sorenson denied the Brazilian with two fine stops, Robinho finally hit his hat-trick, angling the ball into the bottom corner after more good work from Sturridge. City could have had more, had Ireland and Jo converted good passes from Robinho. After the game, Robinho delighted City fans by revealing his ambitions for the season. 'The main objective is for the team to do well but personally, I want to score more than 30 goals,' said the hat-trick hero. 'I am very happy but not completely happy because I still have a lot to learn. I will be truly happy at the end when we finish what I hope will be a good season. The Champions League is our goal. The Premier League is very competitive and it'll be very difficult to get into the top four. But I believe in the team and I think we can get there.'

Mark Hughes was equally ambitious for the forward after the superb display. 'Robinho is key to what we are trying to do here,' he said. 'Maybe in the past he has not had that feeling. He is responding in a really positive way. The crowd adore what he is producing and rightly so. He has a really close relationship with everyone here, which shows what an impact he has made here in a very short space of time. Maybe there will come a point when his form will dip, but we have to make sure we have enough information at hand to ensure it is not too detrimental and his performances don't tail off markedly. I don't think that will happen. Given the way he approaches training and the work we put into him, I can see him having a great season from start to finish.'

Despite their new-found wealth, City could not rid themselves of the inconsistency that had so long been associated with the club. The comfortable win over Stoke was followed by two 2-0 away defeats with the team simply unable to produce the form they showed at the City of Manchester Stadium in their away fixtures with Middlesbrough and Bolton.

A better performance came in the UEFA Cup first group game on 6 November. City faced Steve McClaren's FC Twente at home and delivered a 3-2 victory. Robinho smashed the goal of the game into the top corner from the edge of the box, capping another impressive performance with his first European goal for the club. Hughes was delighted with his contribution. 'Robinho could have had a hat-trick. But we were grateful for the strike for the second goal. He has fantastic ability in those areas. He is one of the best players I have seen in that position to be able to manipulate the ball and create things inside the box. Overall, we are delighted. We have got a positive result and that is what we need to achieve at home to progress.' The club would have to negotiate three more matches in the group phase, but the home win had given them the perfect start to their UEFA Cup campaign.

Robinho added to that strike in the Premier League the following Sunday, reacting quickest to fire Darius Vassell's parried shot back past the stranded Heurelho Gomes against

Tottenham Hotspur. Harry Redknapp was now in charge of Spurs and it seemed that, after beating his Portsmouth side 6-0 earlier in the season, Robinho and co would now dismantle the Tottenham side as well. However, since Redknapp had taken charge of struggling Spurs they had been unbeaten in their last four and two strikes from Darren Bent either side of the half-time break silenced the City support.

City's struggles on the road continued at newly-promoted Hull City on 16 November when Hughes's side could only take a point after going 2-1 ahead in the second half, but the Blues delivered in emphatic style when they returned to Eastlands a week later. Arsenal, reeling from an outburst by skipper William Gallas who had been dropped for the match, were hammered by the home side. Stephen Ireland gave City the advantage in first-half injury time after an even first period, clipping in the opener. The goal gave City new belief and confidence, and Robinho was the driving force behind a more vigorous and vibrant second-half display from the home side. The Brazilian raced onto a Wright-Phillips pass to cheekily chip Manuel Almunia for City's second before seeing an even more exuberant back-heel beat the Arsenal keeper, but his effort was ruled out for offside. Only the desperate lunge of Johan Djourou denied Robinho a second strike, clearing the forward's effort off the line after he had taken the ball around Almunia. Robinho injured himself in the process and had to be substituted, but City did eventually hit the net again, Daniel Sturridge converting a penalty after Djourou brought him down. The victory was City's first over one of England's 'Big Four' under Arab ownership and was a significant scalp for Hughes's side.

The injury Robinho sustained kept him out of City's 2-0 away win at Schalke on 27 November, which confirmed their place in the last 32 of the UEFA Cup. The Brazilian, though, was determined to return for City's next league game, against bitter rivals Manchester United.

'United are a club known all around the world,' he told the *Sun* ahead of the famous Manchester derby on 30 November. 'No matter where you grow up, if you love football then you'll know about Manchester United. I saw United matches on TV as a kid in São Paulo. I loved watching Ruud van Nistelrooy. He was a hero for me because of the way he scored goals in all competitions. He's such an intelligent striker and I have tried to copy his technique to improve my game even though we are not similar players. When I signed for Real Madrid, it was like a dream. I walked into the changing room and there was one of my football heroes. I feel very lucky that I got to play with a guy who I worshipped from far away and I am very proud to call him my friend. We still stay in touch and speak on the phone very often.'

Now, though, Robinho was the one being worshipped. The striker had netted nine goals for his new club in fourteen games, was the hero of the City support and even drew compliments from Sir Alex Ferguson, the United boss, ahead of the Manchester derby. 'You say "Well, £32 million, is it worth it?"' commented Ferguson. 'But you have to say "yes" because he is producing something others can't do.'

However, Robinho could not provide the cutting edge for City against United; instead it was the visitors' Wayne Rooney who hit the decisive goal, following up a Michael Carrick effort. Meanwhile, City struggled to impose themselves on their neighbours and once again the difference in class between City and the major sides in the league told.

City endured a disappointing run-in to Christmas, drawing at Fulham before losing against both Everton and West Brom to injury-time winners. The dismal run of form had seen City sink to 18th place in the league, and it seemed Hughes's side would be spending the New Year celebrations in the relegation zone. However, City's supporters got the perfect present for Christmas, a thumping Boxing Day victory over Hull to end their four-game winless run. The Blues made relegation talk seem laughable when Robinho's exquisitely-flighted pass to Ireland was squared across goal for Felipe Caicedo to tap in.

A carbon copy of that move saw Caicedo notch a second before Robinho rifled a low shot into the bottom corner. When Wright-Phillips crossed for the Brazilian to blast home a fourth on 36 minutes, City's humiliation of Hull was all but complete. Phil Brown conducted his half-time team talk on the pitch but it did little good: Elano and Robinho combined to release Ireland for the fifth after Craig Fagan had pulled one back for the visitors to propel City back up to 15th spot.

Robinho then salvaged a 2-2 draw for City against Blackburn when he slotted past Paul Robinson in the 94th minute before a 1-0 win over Wigan moved the club into a more comfortable 11th place on 17 January.

When Robinho arrived at the club there were many who believed he would not last long in Manchester. However, City fans, delighted with the Brazilian's start to the season were given a further fillip when it was reported in the press that the record-breaking star had invested in a home in the area – suggesting he was planning a long stay at Eastlands. Robinho's new pad was a £2.5m luxury converted barn, which he had been renting since his arrival at City. The stunning five-bedroom property featured every mod con and state-of-the-art gadget he could wish for. A source told the *Daily Mail*: 'He has been renting it but he is now in the process of buying it outright and it is currently under offer. He loves the place and it has every conceivable luxury that he requires including a gym and swimming pool. It has got loads of land, which he likes – there is so much that there has been talk he is going to build his own football pitch on it. He is really delighted with the house and is happy with the price. He sees this as a big commitment and a sign that he is at City for the long-term.'

However, Robinho's commitment was again thrown into doubt just two weeks later. The team took advantage of their exit to Nottingham Forest in the FA Cup by flying out to Tenerife for some warm weather training during the weekend of the Second Round of the Cup, but Robinho disappeared from the squad after a day on the Spanish island. As rumours circulated, it was revealed the midfielder had taken a flight back to Brazil for 'family reasons', presumed to be the celebration of his 25th birthday with his family. The forward had been used to the long winter breaks in Spain and it was thought that he had seen the gap in the fixture list as his only opportunity to get back to Brazil. There were also rumours he had lost faith in the City project after the club failed in its audacious bid to land AC Milan's Kaka for a reported £100 million.

Hughes, though, was relaxed about the situation and dismissed the rumour-mongers for trying to upset his City squad. 'Robby left without permission and obviously felt that he had personal things to address,' he told the *Manchester Evening News*. 'He made the decision to leave the camp and go back to Brazil and that wasn't with my permission. Once he is back I will sit down and explain my feelings on the situation and then decisions will be made after that. I have already spoken to him. He rang me and we had a brief chat which was obviously difficult given the language constraints but he understands that we need to address this and we will but then we will move on. He felt he had permission to go, that wasn't the case.'

Hughes also refuted suggestions Robinho had left because of the failure of the Kaka deal. 'Robby has come out and said he was on a plane to Brazil before the Kaka deal was dead and buried. People who are trying to link the two events are just trying to cause a little bit of mischief,' said the City boss.

Thanks to flight times Robinho was unable to rejoin the squad in Tenerife and flew straight back to Manchester ahead of his side's return to action against Newcastle United on 28 November. On his return, Robinho received a warning from Hughes about his future conduct and was reportedly handed a fine of two weeks' wages – a colossal £300,000, according to *The Times*. Robinho, though, did not seem too upset by the fiasco. Pictures of him smiling, laughing and enjoying being back on the training field with his team-mates were broadcast on television and the matter appeared to be laid to rest.

However, Robinho's reasons for flying to Brazil were further called in to question when, on 28 January 2009, the *Sun* revealed the Brazilian had been arrested by Yorkshire Police 'in relation to allegations that an 18-year-old woman was raped in a nightclub.' A university student told police she had been attacked in the VIP area of the Space club in Leeds in the early hours of 14 January. Chris Nathaniel, Robinho's spokesman, told the *Sun*: 'He strenuously denies any allegation of wrongdoing or criminality and is happy to co-operate with the police if required further.'

Manchester City also offered their full support to the player. They issued the following statement: 'The club have been liaising with and assisting both the player in question and the authorities in relation to the West Yorkshire Police investigation. Both parties have been given the full support of the football club. No charges of any nature have been brought against the player and no further statement will be made while the investigation is continuing.'

For three months the allegations hung over Robinho and, although he refused to blame the stress of that situation on his form, many suspected the claims took their toll on the player. His performances on the field, which had thrilled fans in the first half of the season, were below par and the Brazilian's scoring touch had deserted him.

However, on 8 April it was announced that the charges had been dropped. 'A file was submitted to the Crown Prosecution Service who decided that no further action should be taken,' announced a police statement. Robinho had strenuously denied the allegations from day one and the 25-year-old's advisor said: 'I am pleased to announce that Robson de Souza [Robinho] has been cleared of all allegations of rape. He has maintained his innocence throughout the police interview process and I am delighted that all charges have been dropped. Robinho is a hard-working family man, who is extremely passionate about football. He now wishes to focus his attention on Manchester City and to pass on his sincere thanks to all his family, friends, fans and Manchester City colleagues who have supported him through this terrible ordeal.'

City club captain Richard Dunne was sympathetic towards his team mate and told newspapers that it had been a terrible ordeal for the young forward to endure. 'It was an awful thing to be accused of and it would affect any man in that situation,' Dunne said. 'He's got a young family and they are his main concern, so hopefully that has lifted a bit of weight off his shoulders and he can start playing with a smile on his face again and showing what he can do.'

Dunne also insisted Robinho would need the continued support of the City fans to return to his pre-Christmas form and hoped some pressure will be relieved from the talented star's shoulders. 'It's easy for people outside the club because nobody seems to want him to do well. So it's important for us here and the fans to be 100% behind him. Every stadium we go to, people are expecting him to do amazing things. It's not going to happen all the time. He's probably feeling the pressure of having to keep proving himself. Once he relaxes he will be fine. The players see how good he is every day in training. We all firmly believe in him and that he will return to his earlier form. That will be a real boost for us.'

Robinho, whilst on bail, seemingly left his off-field concerns behind against Newcastle United on 28 January when two deft touches from the Brazilian on the edge of the box played in Wright-Phillips to score the opener against the relegation-threatened Magpies. New signing Craig Bellamy fired in the decisive second to seal the points for City and make Andy Carroll's late strike nothing more than a consolation. The victory nudged City up into ninth place and Mark Hughes revealed he had no concerns about fielding Robinho for the match: 'I spoke to him this morning and it was clear he was preparing for the game. I know the events of the last week have not changed his focus and I had no qualms about playing him tonight.'

The Brazilian was far short of his best though in a dismal defeat to 10-man Stoke City the following week, which once again highlighted City's inadequacies.

Craig Bellamy was on hand a week later to seal a 1-0 win at home to Middlesbrough but while the match at the City of

Manchester stadium went down in the record books as a 1-0 win to the home side, it was really the Shay Given show. City's new stopper had to be at his best to keep Boro's Afonso Alves at bay on four separate occasions as the home side squeezed past the relegation-bound Boro.

City's troubles on the road continued the following week on Valentines Day 2009. Earlier in the season City had drubbed Portsmouth 6-0 but, as the distracted Robinho's form tailed off, Pompey secured a comfortable 2-0 win at Fratton Park. The defeat summed up City's fluctuations in form and enraged the Citizens' striker Craig Bellamy who launched into a dressing-room tirade at his City team mates after the game, with Robinho bearing the brunt of much of his verbal attack.

The Welsh international reportedly criticised Robinho for being 'lazy' and failing to show enough commitment and desire away from home. What may have simply been a post-match, heat-of-the-moment release of tension appeared to be a deeper rift in the squad's morale when, the following day at the City training ground, it was claimed the pair were no longer on speaking terms. It also seemed City manager, Mark Hughes, along with Bellamy, was growing tired of Robinho's struggles away from the City of Manchester Stadium. Only two of the Brazilian's 12 goals up to February 14 had come away from home, one being a penalty at Newcastle, and Hughes told reporters he was hoping to inspire Robinho to produce consistent performances away from Manchester, especially with the club's crucial UEFA Cup Round of 32 clash against FC Copenhagen in Denmark on 19 February looming. 'We have had a brief word with Robinho and we will have another opportunity now that we are away,' said Hughes after being asked about the Brazilian's poor display at Fratton Park.

'We will speak in depth – not only to Robinho but to everyone. It wasn't just about Robinho's performance, it was about our collective performance. I know he took a lot of criticism but other players should have come into focus as well. He hasn't had a great deal of Premier League football away from home and I think that's the key to it. The setbacks we are having now will stand him in good stead because away from home you have to adopt a different mentality.'

Hughes also noted that City's best away results had come on the European stage and called for an improved display in Denmark. That is exactly what he got from his side, with only Martin Vingaard's late goal denying City victory in the Danish capital. A 2-2 draw, though, stood City, with their strong home record, in good stead and Hughes's men followed up that good result with an impressive display at Anfield, matching Liverpool over the course of 90 minutes and coming away from the title challengers with a 1-1 draw. There were still question marks over the relationship of Robinho and Bellamy off the pitch but on it the duo were combining well – the Brazilian teeing up Bellamy to score the opener against the high-flying Reds.

After the game, Bellamy moved to dispel any suggestions the pair had seriously fallen out, no doubt to the delight of City fans. 'What I said in the dressing room at Portsmouth was very mild, I can assure everyone of that,' he said. 'I'm not going to shy away from challenges here, though, and if people don't play well – or I don't play well – then we must expect others to have a go at them. At this level you need to work hard and show fire in your belly to get results and that is exactly what we did at Anfield. It was a well deserved point and a hard-earned one against a team who are formidable at home. Now we need to show this kind of attitude everywhere we go. There's no doubt whatsoever we have the ability. We're now at the stage where we will be a target for rumours and stories that are not necessarily true and it might go on for a few seasons yet. We're the richest club in the world and we're aiming to be the biggest club in the world and that creates its own interest. Other clubs have had to put up with this kind of thing for years.

'I'm a massive admirer of Robinho,' he added. 'I adore him as a player. How could you not? He is an exceptional talent. Robinho is our talisman and when people think of Manchester City at the moment it is Robinho they think of and that is a worldwide thing. He is our biggest player by a mile and our best player – and for us, he is a man who needs to be performing at his best every week. A lot of teams know how good he is, too, and set out to stop him. But people could see in the second half against Liverpool that when he plays well, we play well, and we need him on top of his game. I know it's a lot to ask but he is so important to us. When he plays well he makes us such a better team.'

After the verbal insistence from Bellamy that the pair were on good terms, their performance in the second leg of their UEFA Cup tie with Copenhagen demonstrated the duo were working in perfect tandem as, on 26 February, City became the only English side to make the last 16. Robinho and Bellamy combined brilliantly throughout the clash with FC Copenhagen and could have had half-a-dozen goals between them. Bellamy rattled the post before Robinho somehow missed from four yards. The Welshman eventually made the breakthrough on 77 minutes before Robinho pulled the ball back from the touchline for his strike partner to net his second, rendering Vingaard's second injury-time strike in two games meaningless, and sealing City's place in the next round of the competition, a tie with another Danish side, Champions League drop-outs Aalborg.

Following another away-day defeat at West Ham (stretching the club's winless run in the Premier League away from home to 14 matches) Robinho missed City's impressive 2-0 win over Champions League-chasing Aston Villa in the more comfortable surrounds of the City of Manchester stadium. The Brazilian had been struggling with a recurrence of a thigh injury he suffered against Portsmouth the previous month and flew to São Paulo where he was treated by Brazil national team physio, and former Santos physio, Luiz Rosan.

The Brazilian was back, though, for the first leg contest with Aalborg, but played a smaller part in the 2-0 success than his new team mate Shaun Wright-Phillips who ran the Danish champions ragged with his pacy dribbling on 12 March.

Three days later Robinho found himself at Stamford Bridge in London, the home of Chelsea. He could have been playing for the title-chasing Blues but, instead, he was with the visitors who were still scrambling to ensure their Premier League safety. No doubt it seemed a long time ago for City fans, and Robinho himself, that the Brazilian had ignited hopes and dreams in the Man City fans' hearts with his free-kick past Chelsea's Petr Cech on the opening day of the season. However, in the build up to the fixture the Brazilian insisted he had no regrets about heading north, telling the *Daily Telegraph* on 13 March: 'Manchester City made me a great offer and the opportunity to be involved in a huge project. I'm very pleased the way things have gone so far. One day we can rival clubs like Chelsea. We are a very ambitious club and we are underestimated. Manchester City are after big things and with the wealthy owners, anything is possible. We want to be up there and maybe win the Champions

League one day. All I want to do is help the club, to repay the trust of the supporters and the team. I'm very pleased with the way things have gone so far and I'm hoping that one day we can rival clubs like Chelsea, and we will. Chelsea came in with a good offer and they are a huge club. They also had a coach in Luiz Felipe Scolari at the time who I have a lot of respect for. But Manchester City made me a great offer and the chance to be part of a huge project.'

However, despite his assurances to the City support, 'mischievous' journalists (as Mark Hughes branded them) suggested Robinho could still be Chelsea-bound, in the summer of 2009, as a part-exchange deal for Chelsea and England captain John Terry. These rumours weren't helped when Guus Hiddink, the caretaker Chelsea manager, confessed he had long admired the Brazilian, and had even tried to sign him from Santos before his big-money move to Real Madrid. 'Robinho is a very attractive player,' Hiddink said. 'I had the plan when I was at PSV to sign him. I met him in Brazil and we were close. We had this plan like we had with Romario and Ronaldo before at PSV. Before going at that age to the big leagues it is good to go to another league where they can get used to European football on a different level. We were close to having him sign for PSV. At the last moment in came Real Madrid – and then you are outplayed, of course.'

Robinho's quiet display before being substituted at Stamford Bridge in a 1-0 defeat showed little of the magic which had Hiddink purring and vying for his signature several years earlier. The performance sparked more criticism from the press, and City boss Mark Hughes was once again required to defend his front man, who had now failed to score in eight league games while City had slumped to just six points clear of the relegation zone following their run of one win in five games. 'We have other players who have to stand up and be counted. Robinho's general performances have been good. He has scored 11 league goals and has had a real impact. It has been more difficult for us to get him in the right areas to score, but he has created a number of goals for us and is helping the team. All our attackers struggled against Chelsea so it's unfair to pinpoint him.'

The Brazilian had perhaps been hampered by the injury that had kept him out of the Aston Villa game, or perhaps the occasion and expectation surrounding his first game at Stamford Bridge got the better of him – either way Robinho was back in full flight four days later on 19 March as City took on Aalborg in the second leg of their UEFA Cup Round of 16 tie.

Arriving in Denmark with a two-goal advantage from the first leg, City were expected to comfortably see off their opponents and, with Robinho teeing up Shaun Wright-Phillips early on and jinking past defenders before testing the keeper it seemed City, inspired by their resurgent star, would see off Aalborg in style. However, ask any Manchester City fan about their club and they will tell you the Citizens do things the hard way – and that is exactly what happened in Aalborg. Having wasted several good scoring opportunities in the first half City came under immense pressure from the home side in the second period, with referee Stephane Lannoy waving away three decent penalty appeals from the Aalborg players. Shay Given was in top form pushing away shot after shot, but even then City were still wasting chances. Ched Evans, the young Welsh international, blasted over from 10 yards out while Robinho thundered a shot off the crossbar.

With six minutes remaining Aalborg finally made the

breakthrough – Luton Shelton blasting home from close range. The strike set up a tense finale and, to Mark Hughes's horror Evans handled in the City penalty box, with just a minute left on the clock, and finally Lannoy had little choice but to point to the spot. Michael Jakobsen made no mistake and, remarkably, City were facing extra-time.

Typically, extra-time proved to be even more tense and nail-biting for the City support that had travelled to Denmark, but, as is often the way, with no side wanting to make the costly error that would seal their exit from Europe, few chances were created – penalty shoot-outs would decide matters.

Robinho had been replaced in extra-time as Hughes looked to sure-up his back line so the Brazilian could only look on as Jakobsen coolly put the home side ahead. However, his team mates were not so calm and Given saved strikes from Thomas Augustinussen and then, decisively, the former Sheffield United striker Shelton.

'We don't do things easily,' mused Hughes after the game. 'We were in control for an hour but Aalborg played very well in the second half and put some dangerous balls into our box. When Aalborg equalised I did start to scratch my head and wonder how it had happened. But knowing Shay was between the sticks gave me and the lads confidence. Shay's made crucial saves for us.' Despite their best efforts to squander a comfortable two-goal advantage, City had made it through to the quarter-finals of the UEFA Cup.

Returning to league action, Robinho endured another difficult afternoon at home to Sunderland. Looking more timid and less determined to get involved than usual Robinho found himself on the fringes of the action for most of the game. However, when City won a penalty mid-way through the first half the Brazilian sensed the opportunity to end his

ROBINHO – KING OF THE CITY

barren run of 13 games without a goal. His limp effort, though, was saved by keeper Martin Fulop. Robinho put his head in his hands; so did the City support and so did Mark Hughes. City were poor, unable to break down the 10-man Sunderland who had lost George McCartney early on and only a late Micah Richards header saved the day, and Robinho's blushes. However, after the game, Hughes was quick to defend his under-fire forward. 'Robinho was confident enough to take the ball and try to score,' said Hughes. 'He wants to make a positive impact and he was disappointed not to put that one away.'

Despite Hughes's defence of Robinho after the visit of Sunderland, the Welshman's commitment to retaining Robinho was again questioned when rumours surfaced that Hughes would be prepared to sell the Brazilian to make room in his squad for French forward Franck Ribery of Bayern Munich – a similar player to Robinho. Hughes again moved to silence reports him and Robinho had fallen out. 'There's a perception that there are issues between me and Robinho, and Robinho and his team-mates, and that everything is doom and gloom and the dressing room is fractured,' said Hughes. 'We have all the predictable stories emanating from outside parties, but it's calmer than people would imagine. Robinho is in my plans long term. People who say otherwise are just being mischievous. He is an outstanding player who wants to be part of what we are doing but he is also a professional football player and he doesn't enjoy getting beaten.'"

However, there were even more problems for Robinho laying just ahead. As a young, up-and-coming star at Santos, Robinho's greatest admirer had been Pelé. However, Robinho's decision to quit the Brazilian leagues and test

260

himself on the European stage had disappointed the Brazil legend. But Robinho had signed for Real Madrid and few people, Pelé included, could criticise the youngster for wanting to pull on the famous white shirt of Real. When Robinho signed for City, however, Pelé was again critical of the player he once dubbed 'the next Pelé'. He accused Robinho of a lack of ambition, of chasing the money and even suggested he should seek psychiatric help. In 2009 Pelé and Robinho's paths would again cross when, speaking in court in defence of his son who was accused of drug-related crime, Pelé said: 'It is unfair to talk about drugs in football because of just one or two cases, like Ronaldo and Robinho, who had that problem.'

The accusation apparently originated from a rumour that Robinho and Brazil team-mate Ronaldo had used recreational drugs at a private party in São Paulo. Robinho, understandably, was outraged.

The City star immediately demanded a retraction from Pelé – whose comments had caused a huge stir in Brazil, where he is a figure of authority – or, if an apology was not forthcoming, Robinho would take his idol to court. 'A formal retraction from Pelé will be requested, if what he said was not misinterpreted by the media,' a statement on Robinho's website said. 'And if Pelé does not come forward, he will have to deal with his very unfortunate comment in court.

'Robinho is upset and disappointed at Pelé, who seems to have forgotten the great idol he was. It appears Pelé must be reading sensationalist [media] to come up with such a wrongful statement.'

Within 24 hours Pelé had come out to apologise to the young player and insisted that what he had said had been misquoted in the press. Robinho was quick to accept the retraction and told reporters: 'This issue is over.' Although finished before it really got started, the accusation of drug-use was another unfortunate, hurtful and worrying incident – the kind which seem to have haunted Robinho throughout his career, from his mother's kidnapping, to the accusations of infidelity, and rumours of him falling out with players, managers and chairmen.

Now, during another run of bad form for the Brazilian forward, his commitment to the City cause was again being called into question. It was hard for journalists, City fans, and, indeed, Mark Hughes, to fathom why the mercurial talent who on 10 February, playing for Brazil against Italy in a showpiece friendly at the Emirates, had wowed the carnival crowd with his trickery before a sublime piece of skill saw him cut inside his Italian marker and bury the ball into the corner of the net, scoring one of his most memorable goals, could then play so poorly against Portsmouth four days later and go on to stutter for City for the next two months. Robinho told reporters it was through no want of trying that his form for Brazil had rarely been seen, since Christmas at least, by the City supporters. 'I truly dedicate myself to my club. Sometimes I am questioned as to why I play better for the national squad than my club Manchester City. I have the same will at both places, but Manchester City is one team and the national squad at Brazil is another. No disrespect to the players at Manchester City, who are very good, but here I play with Kaka, Ronaldinho, and it is totally different. But I believe I am playing well at City and have scored 11 goals in the league.'

Indeed, Brazil have the likes of Kaka, Adriano and Dani Alves feeding Robinho the ball while City, as the former player demonstrated in January, still have trouble attracting that quality of player to the club.

If flying to Brazil to play in his country's 3-0 World Cup qualifier win over Peru had helped Robinho forget his City troubles he found on his return that little had changed – except now his manager Mark Hughes was considering 'resting' him for the clash with Arsenal on 4 April. Two months earlier for Brazil Robinho had lit up the Emirates, now his powers were being questioned ahead of his return to the London stadium.

'He's never knocked on the door and said, "I'm tired", but there have been times when you look at him and there has maybe been a bit of flatness in his play,' Hughes told the press. 'It's understandable because it's his first season in one of the strongest and most physical leagues in the world. He's playing week in week out and he hasn't done that for a long time.

'He's come into a new league, a new team, a new club, and initially had a great impact, but he's not used to playing every week. There's been a reaction to that and he has not been able to have the impact he had in the first half of the season. He has great qualities but we have to find a way of getting the best out of him because it's obvious we're not doing that right now.'

Hughes also suggested that Robinho was being targeted by opposition defenders as the 'key man' and, as a result was being marked out of games. 'They know now what he is capable of doing if he is allowed to play,' he said. 'They know he can win a game on his own. We're at a point where people understand what he wants to do, and they will try to stop him. That's a learning process for him.'

Eventually, due to an injury to Stephen Ireland, Robinho started against Arsenal but it was another disappointing display in another disappointing defeat and kicked off a terrible 12 days for the club.

Five days later, despite a neat interchange between Robinho and Ireland putting City one up, the Citizens crumbled to a 3-1 defeat in Hamburg, leaving them with a huge uphill task to qualify for the semi finals of the UEFA Cup. That defeat put their hopes of European glory on the line, while City's defeat to Fulham the following weekend (minus Robinho who was left on the bench throughout) virtually ended their hopes of qualifying for the 2009/10 Europa League (the new name for the UEFA Cup) via the Premier League. Their only hope of sealing European football for the next season would be to win the UEFA Cup, and that meant producing a stunning result at Eastlands against a Hamburg side that, despite conceding an early goal, had dominated proceedings in Germany in the first leg.

'Robinho has had a great first season but he has been among those responsible for carrying the vast majority of the workload, and it was my first opportunity to give him a break,' Hughes had said after the Fulham game. He would be hoping that the break would refresh and revitalise his key player when he needed him most.

However, just 11 minutes into the crucial game, City failed to deal with a routine cross from Jonathan Pitroipa and Paolo Guerrero took full advantage to score from close range for Hamburg. Elano and Caicedo fired City to a victory on the night but the club's hopes of a semi final spot were ended with that first goal. Robinho's performance was better than in recent weeks and, but for a few defensive interventions and a couple of fine stops from the Hamburg keeper, he may have handed City a lifeline.

That, though, was effectively the end of City's season. They were out of Europe and unable to qualify for European competition via the League, but at least they were safe from relegation and heading for a mid-table finish in the first season of their new era. Ironically, and perhaps sadly for Robinho, it was then he found his shooting boots.

'Red boots, sunny spring Sunday afternoon and West Brom, the team who cannot defend, as your opposition. What a perfect occasion for the boy from Brazil to score his first goal of the year,' wrote one journalist. For the first time since 28 December Robinho hit the back of the net, his well-taken left-foot volley from 10 yards left Scott Carson with no chance.

'We are pleased he has got back on the goal trail,' said Hughes. 'It's important because with Robinho not having scored this year people would keep highlighting that. But, hopefully, that will now set him on a run again.'

Indeed it did. Against Everton at Goodison Park on 25 April Robinho was back to his superb best, opening the scoring before teeing up Ireland for City's second in a 2-1 win. The *Telegraph* described Robinho's display as a 'revelation' and, in the spring sunshine, Robinho looked like he had never had so much fun. After a winter of discontent now was his spring of hope.

He made it three goals in three games against Blackburn on 2 May. It was a remarkable return to form for the Brazilian who had spent months enduring criticism from all quarters but now, with renewed confidence he was rewarding Hughes's faith in him. 'When he's in the mood, Robinho embodies the dictionary definition of the word genius,' wrote the *Sun*.

With his improved form going forward Robinho's hard-working displays had also returned with Ireland commenting in the *News of the World*: You can see how everyone has adapted to what the gaffer wants. Elano and Robinho's work-rate is phenomenal now. At the end of the season they were running past me to help defend and I was thinking "Wow". I was really impressed with them.'

City took three points from their last three games, losing to Manchester United and Tottenham before beating Bolton on the final day of the season in front of their own fans to finish in tenth spot, just three points off the European places. Following the hype and excitement at the start of the season it had been a turbulent year for City and their fans, and the team had fallen short of the high expectations the new owners had brought to the club. No player at the club, though, had endured a tougher year than Robinho – perhaps the hardest of his professional life. After a blistering start to the campaign he had struggled at the start of 2009 on the field whilst off it he had been linked with moves away from the club, charged with sexual assault, rumoured to have fallen out with everyone at the club, accused of taking drugs and had his desire and commitment to Manchester City repeatedly questioned by everyone from the press to former players. However, he had shown a glimmer of what he is capable of doing at the end of the season and, like City, with the foundation season of the new era under his belt he will come back stronger, better prepared and fully aware of the challenge that awaits him as City, and their owners, get serious about winning titles.

CHAPTER 13
A BRIGHT FUTURE

A year ahead of the 2010 World Cup in South Africa, just as before the Germany tournament in 2006, Robinho was selected for Brazil's Confederations Cup team, which was seeking a record-breaking third straight win in the contest.

After helping Brazil to two more victories in their 2010 World Cup qualifying campaign – including a superbly well taken back-post strike against Paraguay – to keep the South American giants top of the CONMEBOL table Robinho was considered one of the 'senior' players in the Brazil squad for the tournament in South Africa.

Running from 14 June to 28 June 2009 the World Cup warm-up tournament, used to test out stadia, infrastructure and South Africa's ability to host the world's second biggest sporting event after the Olympics, brought eight of the world's best national sides together. World Cup winners Italy, Gold Cup winners USA, Copa America champions Brazil, Asian Cup winners Iraq, African Cup of Nations winners Egypt, European Cup winners Spain and the Oceanic Nations Cup winners New Zealand joined hosts South Africa.

Ahead of the tournament, which grouped Brazil with USA, Italy and Egypt in the first round, Robinho was eagerly anticipating the contest. There were only four players younger than Robinho named in the squad but the City star had been representing his country since 2003 and was one of the more experienced players, along with Kaka and Lucio.

It was a role Robinho relished: 'On the field, everybody has to be a leader but I'm much more mature now, more experienced. With time, you start getting a feel for what it is like to be playing for the national team. My responsibility is greater now, there is no doubt. Each year you become more experienced, but the pressure also increases. My goal is to win the World Cup, and for this dream to come true I need to take advantage of my opportunity here and secure my spot for next year. Hopefully with more practice time here in South Africa I can get in shape faster and do well in the Confederations Cup too.'

Brazil's campaign kicked off against Egypt and within five minutes classy Kaka, who had just joined the Real Madrid renaissance for £56m, showed the Spanish club what they were buying by slaloming past three defenders before neatly finishing to put Brazil ahead. Egypt responded swiftly, with Mohamed Aboutrika's right-wing cross being headed in by Mohamed Zidan but Brazil went into the half-time break two goals to the good thanks to Luis Fabiano and Juan headers, both from Elano set-pieces.

Despite four first half goals, the real drama was still yet to unfold, though. Egypt fought back and scored twice in two minutes to pull level. First Mohamed Shawky hit a firm, low drive from the edge of the box before Zidan struck again on 55 minutes. Egypt thought they had a draw sewn up until the last kick of the game when a Brazil effort on goal was cleared off the line – referee Howard Webb initially appeared to give a free-kick to Egypt but, after consulting his assistant, awarded Brazil a penalty which Kaka despatched to secure victory for the reigning champions.

A more routine win came three days later on 18 June when Brazil swept aside the challenge of USA with a 3-0 win. Robinho also notched up his first goal of the tournament, finishing off a superb counter-attack move started by Kaka, with a cool finish. Goals either side of that move from Maicon and Felipe Melo secured a comfortable victory and booked Brazil's place in the knockout rounds.

However, when the Samba Boys hit top form a dead-rubber doesn't slow them down and Brazil used their group game with World Cup winners Italy to demonstrate their strength, smashing the world champions 3-0 in Pretoria. A Luis Fabiano double put Brazil in control and when Andrea Dossena bundled Robinho's cross into his own goal Italy were out of the contest before the teams had even played 45 minutes.

While Brazil had stuttered at the start of the tournament against Egypt they had revved up into top gear by the time they faced Italy and Robinho, who was linking up with Kaka to devastating effect, was enjoying his time in South Africa. However, his ambitions about winning the tournament were very serious. 'Brazil's main objective is to win,' the Manchester City striker said. 'Of course we want to play well, too. Sometimes you can do both, but sometimes you have to play ugly to win. The priority is always to win.

'When we play bad, it's not always as bad as people say. When we play well, it's also not always as well as they say, either. We may be going through a good moment right now, but if we lose everything changes.'

Brazil fulfilled their main objective of winning against South Africa in the semi-final, but it was only thanks to an 88th-minute free-kick from Barcelona's Daniel Alves. The host nation, backed by superb support, had squeezed through the group stage thanks to a win over New Zealand and draw with Iraq but put on a fine display against the tournament favourites. After the game the Brazil players admitted they were shocked by the performance of the hosts. 'They surprised us,' midfielder Ramires said. 'We knew they were going to defend well and mark well from the beginning, but we didn't expect the kind of intensity they had.' Luis Fabiano, meanwhile, the eventual tournament top scorer was virtually invisible throughout the game and the few times the ball got to him he had his back to the goal and was marked by at least two defenders. 'There was no space anywhere,' he said. 'Everywhere we went there was someone right there with us.' Brazil's few opportunities came with long-range shots by midfielder Ramires and a couple of individual runs by Kaka and Robinho. They were eventually rescued by Alves's heroics, but knew they would face a far sterner test against USA in the final, who had ended Spain's 35-game unbeaten run with an unlikely 2-0 win.

In the final in Johannesburg on 28 June it seemed USA were set to pull off an even greater shock when they raced into a 2-0 half-time lead against Brazil, the team that had dismantled them with such ease in the group stages a week earlier. Clint Dempsey and Landon Donovan had fired the Eagles ahead to the shock of the crowd, the Brazil squad and, perhaps, even the Americans themselves.

It wasn't all one way traffic, though. At 1-0 Robinho curled an effort from outside the box into Tim Howard's arms before Felipe Melo and Maicon were also denied by the stopper. However, USA, reminiscent of Brazil's second against them earlier in the tournament, raced down field on the counter attack and Donovan seemingly put the game beyond Brazil's reach.

Brazil emerged from their dressing room well before USA after the half-time interval, eager to set about the task of rescuing the game. That intent didn't take long to transform into an end product as, just seconds into the half Sevilla's Fabiano swivelled brilliantly and smashed a shot through USA defender Jay Demerit's legs and past Howard to half the deficit.

The goal inspired Brazil and sent a tremor of nerves through the Eagles side. Minutes later Kaka's header from close range flew up off the ground and bounced off the post and crossbar before Howard eventually smothered the ball.

The equaliser eventually came on 74 minutes when Kaka crossed for Robinho. The City star fired into the underside of the bar, but fortunately for Brazil, Fabiano was on hand to tuck the ball away and seal his position as tournament top scorer with five strikes. American hearts were broken when Lucio nodded in Elano's corner with just six minutes to play.

The Brazilians had retained the Confederations Cup for a record third time and, although their early-tournament style was missing in the closing stages, they hadn't lost the knack of winning which, as Robinho said, was their main objective.

The Confederations Cup victory was a good way for Robinho to end a difficult year and was the start of a good summer for the Brazilian. After the tournament he returned to Brazil where, after 11 years together, he married his childhood sweetheart, and mother of his son Robson Junior, Vivian Guglielmetti.

The couple had met in Santos long before Robinho had

found wealth and fame on the football field – a sharp contrast to the WAG culture of modern footballer's partners – and the couple stayed together throughout his rise and transformation into one of the most talented, exciting and talked about players on the planet.

Their marriage on 9 June 2009 took place at the Casa Grande hotel in Guaruja. The beautiful wedding ceremony, although not flamboyant like many footballer weddings, was attended by a number of familiar faces with Kaka, former Real Madrid midfielder Julio Baptista, national team boss Dunga, and of course, Elano, among the guests as Robinho's national team mates joined him in the celebration. All the guests were asked, instead of buying presents for the couple, to donate money or send food packages to the couple's listed charities.

'I am very excited. The party was exactly as we dreamed. Now it's time to drink and celebrate with my friends!' Robinho said after the marriage. Unsurprisingly for a Brazilian wedding, the partying went on late into the night with dancing, food and singing until the early hours.

One of Robinho's best men at the wedding was Marcelo Teixeira, the president of Santos, a sign that, despite leaving the club under a cloud Robinho and the club that signed him as a 17-year-old had settled their differences. Teixeira even holds onto the hope Robinho will one day return to the club. 'Now that he is married and calm, it will be easier for him to return to play at Santos,' he said. 'It is a plan that both he and I have. I wish he could return to the club as soon as possible.'

While Robinho embarked on a new chapter in his life with Vivian, there were exciting changes happening at his club as well. When the new owner Sheikh Mansour bin Zayed Al Nahyan joined the club at the very end of the 2008 summer transfer window there was only time for City to snap up Robinho before the window shut. As a result the Brazilian was the only star name to arrive at the club for the first five months of the season. The January transfer window was lit up by City's dramatic and ambitious pursuit of Kaka but, as with all big deals, the mid-season interval was not the best time to sign big names.

However, come the summer of 2009, with a longer period to negotiate and plan their purchases City began making waves in the transfer market. Carlos Tevez, Gareth Barry, Roque Santa Cruz and Emmanuel Adebayor all joined the club in big-money moves. None of the players would have considered City as their first choice before the investment of Sheikh Mansour – a signal that they, like Robinho, have bought into the project of building City into one of the giants of European football.

Robinho was reportedly disappointed and disillusioned with the club when they failed in their bid for Kaka but, as the top-class players started heading towards Eastlands in summer 2009, the Brazilian's passion to remain with City and lead the team to new heights was renewed. Interviewed during pre-season the Brazilian was genuinely excited about the prospect of a season with City challenging for honours.

Asked about the arrivals of the new forwards he said: 'We need four top-quality forwards because the season is so tough in England. I hope the club keep signing players with that quality. A player like Santa Cruz is more than welcome and I've heard a deal for Carlos will be sorted very soon. That would be great because I know Tevez is a world-class talent, one of the best in the world and I'd be happy to play alongside him. It is very good to know my club is going for top-quality players like these. I hope the club keeps signing players with that quality. If so, we will be almost unbeatable.

I'm really excited and I can't wait to start working with my new team-mates.'

When Robinho arrived at City, many accused him of simply chasing the pound signs but, despite a tough first season where he had experienced the highs and lows of the English game, the Brazilian is still desperate to prove himself and ensure he doesn't leave these shores without adding to his pile of medals and trophies.

'When I play football it has nothing to do with money and everything to do with the fact that I am in love with the game. Of course, I understand that I am in an extremely privileged situation at this club, but the only aim I had when I joined City was to win cups and titles.

'I came here because I thought Manchester City had a very good project – and I still believe that. I think my team-mates will tell you I am always smiling – because I am happy here. I am doing what I love to do best. My family is happy here and I am playing football for people who love me. I believe I can achieve great things at City – we will become champions over the next two years.

'I was told when I signed for City that the aim was to do that very quickly. I would have loved to have won a title this season, but it was not to be because the team is developing. We will be aiming to do it next year. But on an individual basis, I think my first season has been very, very good. I am scoring lots of goals, which I love doing, and the players at this club have excellent quality.

'I would tell anyone thinking about joining City to do it. This is an excellent club and the supporters are fantastic. Despite what some people have claimed it has not been difficult for me to settle here at all, apart from a certain period of the year when it became very cold.

'But that doesn't mean I don't love City. I want the fans to know it is just the opposite: I do love City. And now I just want to look to the future – my dream is to be seen as the best player in the world – and I want to be No.1 while I am with City.'

Whether Robinho's City dreams are realised in the coming seasons or not, one thing is for certain – the mercurial forward's skill, pace and ambition are sure to delight fans worldwide for many years to come.

Amy pointed at the screen as the nurse, Lynn, resumed her checks. 'I know him.'

Lynn's eyes darted over to the television, taking in the hunk currently filling the screen. Amy bristled. She could almost hear her thoughts.

Lynn gave a small smile. 'Well, you're a lucky lady, then. I imagine he's one of the best neonatologists in the world if he's looking after the President's baby.'

'He is. I tried to get hold of him yesterday but he didn't answer the text I sent him. I guess he was busy.' The message *I need your help* had been direct and to the point without revealing anything. Her voice was quiet, thoughtful. Her hands rubbed up and down her stomach. 'How is it?' she asked as Lynn unwound the blood pressure cuff. She knew the answer before Lynn spoke, but her head was currently in another place. There was only one person in the world she trusted right now to take care of her baby. 'I can't let anything happen to this baby,' she whispered. 'He's my only chance.'

Lynn wrapped her hand around Amy's. 'I know that.' She hesitated, glancing towards the television. 'Maybe it's time to ask a friend for help?' Her eyes were fixed on the television screen. 'If I knew my baby was going to come early I'd want the finest neonatologist in the world to be at the delivery.' Her voice was firm and strong. 'Wouldn't you?'

Amy's phone beeped and she reached into her pocket. It was a reply from Linc. Three words. *Anything. Any time.*

Their eyes met. Amy bit her lip and took a deep breath. The shine of unshed tears was visible in her eyes. 'Exactly how far away is Pelican Cove?'

Dear Reader

This is my second story in the fictional setting of Pelican Cove based around the White House medical staff.

Picking a setting for a story is always difficult. When I started to write these stories I could see Pelican Cove very clearly in my head. A small town, sort of based on *Murder She Wrote*'s Cabot Cove, but set on the Californian coast. I also found a picture of a beautiful studio flat in San Francisco and used that as the setting for Lincoln's apartment. I almost wish I could have stayed there myself!

Part of this story is about a young woman who has had breast cancer. I took this part of the book very seriously, and spoke to a number of women who have beaten this disease. I hope I've captured realistically everything that they told me. The most poignant part for me is the scene in front of the mirror with Amy and Lincoln. I just hope I've done it justice.

I love to hear from readers, so please come and visit me at: www.scarlet-wilson.com

Many thanks

Scarlet

WEST WING TO MATERNITY WING!

BY
SCARLET WILSON

First published in Great Britain 2012
by Mills & Boon, an imprint of Harlequin (UK) Limited.
Large Print edition 2012
Harlequin (UK) Limited, Eton House,
18-24 Paradise Road, Richmond, Surrey TW9 1SR

© Scarlet Wilson 2012

ISBN: 978 0 263 22483 2

Harlequin (UK) policy is to use papers that are
natural, renewable and recyclable products and made
from wood grown in sustainable forests. The logging
and manufacturing process conform to the legal
environmental regulations of the country of origin.

Printed and bound in Great Britain
by CPI Antony Rowe, Chippenham, Wiltshire

Scarlet Wilson wrote her first story aged eight and has never stopped. Her family have fond memories of 'Shirley and the Magic Purse', with its army of mice, all with names beginning with the letter 'M'. An avid reader, Scarlet started with every Enid Blyton book, moved on to the *Chalet School* series, and many years later found Mills and Boon®.

She trained and worked as a nurse and health visitor, and currently works in public health. For her, finding Medical Romances was a match made in heaven. She is delighted to find herself among the authors she has read for many years.

Scarlet lives on the West Coast of Scotland with her fiancé and their two sons.

Recent titles by the same author:

THE BOY WHO MADE THEM LOVE AGAIN
IT STARTED WITH A PREGNANCY

These books are also available in eBook format from www.millsandboon.co.uk

Praise for
Scarlet Wilson:

'Stirring, emotional and wonderfully absorbing, IT STARTED WITH A PREGNANCY is an impressive debut novel from a fabulous new voice in category romance: Scarlet Wilson!'

This book is dedicated to my aunt—
Margaret Wilson. Not everyone is as lucky
as I am to have such a fabulous auntie.
One who offers unfailing support to her three
nieces and many great-nieces and nephews.
And brings us wonderful holiday stories of
'exploding' strawberries and cream!

And to my editor, Sally Williamson, thank you
for bringing me into the Mills and Boon family
and looking after me so well.
It's been a pleasure working with you.

And to women the world over who've suffered
from breast cancer. This one is for you.

PROLOGUE

LINCOLN ADAMS stuck his fingers into the collar around his neck and pulled—hard. The collar was at least an inch too small for him. It didn't matter that the whole ensemble was Italian made from the finest materials. The suit trousers were an inch too short and the waist was an uncomfortably snug fit. He kept his arms firmly by his sides, his hands clenched in his lap, because if he leaned forward onto the table in front of him, the jacket would stretch across his back, restricting his movements. It was bad enough having to borrow someone else's clothes, but when they were a size too small… The sooner he was out of here the better.

The White House press secretary swept across the room in a flurry of eye-catching blue silk with a tailored black jacket on top. Every pore of her skin emanated professionalism and efficiency, and she knew how to work a crowd. This was all her fault.

He gave a forced smile at David Fairgreaves, who sat down next to him. The old man didn't look in the least fazed by the pandemonium surrounding him. In fact, he looked as if he might actually be enjoying it. Was he mad? Then again, for an international-award-winning doctor, this would be all in a day's work.

Diane Green stood behind the podium next to him. Almost instantaneously the cameras started snapping around them and the noise level increased frenetically. She raised her hand and the press pack heeded. She had the information they'd all been waiting for.

'Thank you for joining us here today at Pelican Cove for our happy announcement. You will all be aware that President Taylor and his wife, Jennifer, were expecting their first baby on seventeenth October. However, today, on the twenty-third of August, Charles and Jennifer Taylor are delighted to announce the arrival of…' she paused for effect '…the First Daughter, Esther Rose Taylor, weighing four pounds ten ounces.'

The room around her erupted, questions being

shouted from every angle. 'Isn't the baby too early?'

'What was the First Lady doing in Pelican Cove?'

'Where is her own obstetrician, Dr Blair?'

'Was the President here?'

'Where did the name come from?'

But Diane Green was the epitome of calm. Continuing with her carefully prepared statement, she lifted her hand again until the room was silent. 'Esther Rose Taylor was born at thirty-two weeks gestation. The First Lady had been ordered to rest in the last few weeks of her pregnancy and had come to Pelican Cove to do exactly that. She was accompanied by her obstetrician, Dr Blair, who unfortunately had a myocardial infarction in the last few days. As a result of that the First Lady was looked after by...' Diane Green gestured towards the seats to her right '...Dr David Fairgreaves, one of the foremost leading obstetricians in America, and Dr Lincoln Adams, one of our finest neonatologists.' She gave a little nod towards the reporters. 'I am pleased to report that the President was here for the arrival of his daughter and she is named after Jennifer

Taylor's beloved and much-missed grandmother. Any questions regarding the health of the First Lady and the First Daughter—' a genuine smile swept across Diane Green's lips, as if she was still to get used to saying that '—can be answered by our two highly qualified doctors here.'

Once again the room erupted and Lincoln Adams took a deep breath as this time the barrage of questions was directed at him. *Let me out of here!*

Amy Carson sat on the cold, clinical hospital bed, usually occupied by a patient, her hands fixed firmly on her swollen stomach. The plaster was falling off the ceiling above her and the wall hadn't seen a coat of paint in— How long? What did the patients who usually ended up in this room think? The role reversal of staff member to potential patient wasn't lost on her. Everything about this place was bland. Did she really want to end up delivering her baby in a place like this?

She gulped. How had she ended up here? The door opened and the nurse appeared again, wheeling the trolley that held the foetal monitor and sphygmomanometer. Amy felt herself tense.

She knew it was going to be the same again—borderline.

She loved her colleagues here, but none of them had the specialist skills and expertise that this baby would need. More than that—nowhere in the surrounding area had facilities to deal with a premature baby. Everything about this made her uncomfortable. If only Lincoln would answer his phone…

Movement on the television in the corner of the room caught her eye. She leaned forward. 'Can you turn that up, please, Lynn?'

Her colleague nodded and automatically twisted the knob on the antiquated television set. 'Delighted to announce the arrival of…'

Amy listened to the announcement. Another baby born too early. But probably the most famous baby in the world. A baby that would have the most prestigious, experienced medical care that money could buy.

No! Surely not? Amy's chin dropped to her chest. Lincoln Adams. *Her Lincoln Adams* was shifting uncomfortably on the screen in front of her. He tugged at his shirt and answered question after question about the baby's condition.

His voice was rich, smooth. If she couldn't see his image on the television in front of her, she'd imagine he was the calmest man in the world. But he wasn't. And she could tell he hated every moment of this.

Delivering the President's baby. Wow. So that's where he'd been.

Her heart constricted in her chest. Six years and he still had the same effect on her—even in her current state. She watched as he took a question from a blonde journalist, dazzling her with his twinkling blue eyes and easy smile. He was still a flirt. It was so ingrained in him that he didn't even realise he was doing it. One smile from Linc and the journalist, covering the biggest story of her life, was a babbling mess.

She pointed at the screen as the nurse, Lynn, resumed her checks. 'I know him.'

Lynn's eyes darted over to the screen, taking in the hunk currently filling the screen. Amy bristled. She could almost hear her thoughts.

Lynn gave a small smile. 'Well, you're a lucky lady, then. I imagine he's one of the best neonatologists in the world if he's looking after the President's baby.'

'He is. I tried to get hold of him yesterday but he didn't answer the text I sent him. I guess he was busy.' The message "*I need your help*" had been direct and to the point without revealing anything. Her voice was quiet, thoughtful. Her hands rubbing up and down her stomach. 'How is it?' she asked as Lynn unwound the blood-pressure cuff. She knew the answer before Lynn spoke but her head was currently in another place. There was only one person in the world she trusted right now to take care of her baby.

Lynn frowned. 'Actually, it's a little higher. I'm sorry, Amy, but as a fellow professional I'm not going to beat around the bush. With your other symptoms, it's definitely looking like borderline pre-eclampsia. The good thing is we've caught it early. It's time to see your obstetrician. And from one colleague to another, I definitely think it's time to stop work.'

Amy nodded her head, tears prickling at the sides of her eyes as she swallowed the lump in her throat. 'I can't let anything happen to this baby,' she whispered. 'He's my only chance.'

Lynn wrapped her hand around Amy's. 'I know that.' She hesitated, glancing towards the television. 'Maybe it's time to ask a friend for help?' Lynn's eyes fixed on the television screen. 'If I knew my baby was going to come early I'd want the finest neonatologist in the world to be at the delivery.' Her voice was firm and strong. 'Wouldn't you?'

Her phone beeped and she reached into her pocket. Two words. Anything. Any time.

Their eyes met. Amy bit her lip and took a deep breath, the shine of unshed tears visible in her eyes. 'Exactly how far away is Pelican Cove?'

CHAPTER ONE

LINCOLN burst through the doors to the adjoining office and wrenched the scarlet tie from his throat. The force popped the button on his shirt and sent it flying across the floor.

David Fairgreaves strolled in behind him and lifted one grey eyebrow. He took off his suit jacket, hanging it on the chair behind him. 'Problem, Lincoln?' He looked vaguely amused, another irritation to add to Lincoln's list.

Lincoln stalked over to a nearby shelf and pulled down a pair of green scrubs—he wasn't wearing this damn too-tight suit a second longer.

Washington's finest shirt lay in a crumpled heap at his feet as he pulled the scrub top over his head and turned to face David. 'How can they ask questions like that?'

David gave a little shrug of his shoulders, picked up an apple from the nearby table and crunched into it, putting his feet up on the desk. 'They're animals.'

Lincoln shook his head. 'How can you stand it? How can you sit there and smile at those idiots?'

'You've got to give it some perspective. I've just looked after the First Lady. It's news that they'll report all around the world. And they'll all be looking for their own spin—their own edge to make them stand out from the pack. Truth be known—I really don't care what any of them think. The only thing I care about is my patient.'

Lincoln stared at him. David was the only reason he'd come here in the first place. The chance to work with the man who'd been the first to retrieve stem cells was too good an opportunity to miss. The irony of it was—he looked like a bumbling old fool but was probably the most forward-thinking clinician Lincoln had ever met.

David caught him with his sharp gaze. 'What's with you anyway? You've been like a bear with a sore head all afternoon.'

Linc sighed. The man missed nothing. 'I got a strange text message last night from someone I haven't seen in years—at least, I think that's who it was from. I've texted back but I can't seem to get a signal right now, so I don't know if she's re- plied.' He held his cellphone up near the window and turned in various directions. Still no signal.

David gave him a knowing look. 'I take it this was a female someone?'

Linc nodded and smiled. 'Let's just say it was an unexpected blast from the past.'

'A good one?'

'She certainly wasn't that easy to forget so I hope so. But with everything that's happened in the last two days I've just not had a minute.' He ran his fingers through his dark brown hair. 'I can't remember the last time I actually slept.'

David nodded. 'Having the head of White House Security turn up at your door at three in the morning and tell you to pack up to deliver the President's baby would flatten most men.' He frowned. 'Your text. Was it from a real friend? Or a fair-weather friend? I've experienced lots of those—people who the minute you appear in the media have apparently been your "best friend" or "closest colleague" for years—even though they don't know when your birthday is or what car you drive. Fame does funny things to folks—

you need to be careful, Lincoln. This is a whole new ball game for you.'

Lincoln looked thoughtful. He gestured towards the door. 'Well, that was my first official television appearance, so she can't have known anything about it. She sounded—I don't know—in trouble.'

'Just what every man loves—a damsel in distress.' David flashed him a smile. 'Come on, Lincoln, let's go and look after our girls.' He tossed his apple core into a trash can on the other side of the room.

'I told you to stop calling me that. It's Linc. My friends call me Linc.'

David looked aghast. 'Linc? Certainly not. You, my friend, are named after the finest President we've ever had and you should wear that name with pride.' He put his hand on the doorhandle as a frown puckered his forehead. 'Just don't tell Charlie Taylor I said that.'

Lincoln laughed. 'I may well use that as blackmail material.'

Amy glanced at her watch as the cab seemed to meander up the coastal road. The traffic was almost at a standstill and she watched as only a few vehicles got through the cordon in front of them. The rest were directed to turn and head back down the hill. Her stomach churned. This had to be the worst idea she'd ever had.

A uniformed officer approached the cab and rapped sharply on the window. He glanced in the back seat towards Amy. 'Where are you headed?'

The taxi driver gestured behind him. 'Got a pregnant lady to drop at the hospital.'

The cop gave a little start. He looked like a man who had heard every line in the book today but he leaned forward a little to get a better look. He obviously hadn't heard this one yet. 'Can you step out the car please, ma'am?'

Amy fumbled for the doorhandle and stepped out into the warm sea air. She pulled some money from her purse and handed it to the driver. 'Thanks very much.'

The cop ran his eyes up and down the length of her body. It was almost as if he was checking she actually *was* pregnant. Her white tunic and expanding trousers flapped in the wind, exposing every part of her body, including the currently out-turned umbilicus. She pressed her hands self-consciously over her stomach.

'Your name, ma'am?'

'Excuse me?'

'You have to give me your name—and the name of the doctor you have an appointment to see.'

Amy hesitated. 'I don't exactly have an appointment, but I'm here to see Dr Lincoln Adams.'

The cop looked down at the list in his hand and stared at her. 'This isn't exactly the time for social calls.' His eyes narrowed suspiciously, 'Dr Adams, he's a neonatologist, isn't he?' He nodded towards her stomach. 'What do you want to see him for? You haven't had your baby yet—shouldn't you be seeing an obstetrician?'

Amy sighed. The sun in Mendocino Valley was strong. She could feel it beating down on the pale skin at the parting in her red hair. A parting she usually always kept covered—too bad she'd forgotten her sunhat. She swallowed nervously. Trust her to get the cop who was smarter than the average bear.

She fumbled around her bag, looking for the bottle of water she had been drinking in the cab.

Two hours in a cab with no air-conditioning with the heat so strong you could practically see it rising from the ground. Four hours in a train beforehand that had been packed with tourists. This trip had been a nightmare. There was no way she wasn't getting to see Lincoln.

She pulled her tunic from her sweating back. At least the sea winds around her were giving some relief.

'Ma'am?'

The cop was getting annoyed. She could sense that good cop had retreated and bad cop was hovering near the door.

'Here.' She pulled out a battered envelope from her bag containing her medical notes. 'Give these to Lincoln Adams, he'll see me.'

The cop rolled his eyes. 'Dr Adams is currently looking after the First Daughter. He won't see you or anyone else.' He pointed in the direction of a cluster of reporters as he handed the notes back to her. 'Nice try, though.'

Amy felt a wave of panic wash over her as her baby gave a few anxious kicks. This heat was really starting to get to her. What if Lincoln wouldn't see her? What if he refused to look after her baby when it was born? What if didn't even *remember* her?

The blood rushed to her cheeks. Surely he hadn't forgotten her? How could he possibly forget those six months spent on the Amazon aid boat? She couldn't forget a single minute. The hours they hadn't spent working, they'd spent in his bed—and neither of them had been sleeping.

Trouble was, even though she remembered every minute of their time together, did he? She'd heard sneaky rumours that Lincoln had had a long line of female friends on his Amazon trips. Was it possible she had been just another pretty face to him? Had she just been a summer-long fling?

Six months with the most gorgeous man on earth. A man who hadn't cared about appearances. He hadn't been looking for a designer-clothed, styled woman, piled with make-up. Which was just as well since her luggage had gone astray at Iquitos airport in Peru and hadn't arrived until two weeks later. She'd spent the first two weeks with her hair pulled back in her solitary hair bobble, wearing pale blue or green surgical scrubs and paper knickers. Just as well her breasts hadn't been big enough to really need the support of a bra.

She looked downwards. Things had certainly changed in the last six years. In more ways than one. Her extended stomach was definitely evidence of that.

Her hands went back to guarding her stomach. Her precious bundle. Her one and only chance of motherhood. Was it so wrong to want the best man in the land to look after her baby? More than that, someone she trusted. Someone she'd seen battle the odds to help a baby survive. Someone who refused to take no for an answer.

She wanted that. She wanted that for her baby— her son. Lincoln was the best neonatologist she'd ever worked with. If anyone could help her with an early delivery, it was him.

Her eyes drifted upwards. The cop was dealing with someone else now and looking more and more agitated by the minute. The sun was obviously getting to him too.

She looked around her. Security was everywhere. And no wonder. If reports were to be believed, the President, the First Lady and the First

Daughter were currently in the hospital at the top of the hill. So how was she going to get in there?

Amy took a deep breath. 'Officer, officer!'

The cop scowled at her and walked back along the cordon. 'You again. What do you want?'

'You never let me finish,' she panted as she pushed her stomach out as far as she could. 'Lincoln Adams—he's my husband. So you have to let me in to see him.'

Where had that come from?

Amy was starting to feel light-headed. She really needed a seat. Oh, boy. She was definitely going to be caught out now. The cop squinted at her, 'You do know I'll radio up and check, don't you?' It was almost as if he could read her panicking mind and was giving her a last-minute opportunity to give up the madness, admit that she'd lied and retreat—never to be seen again.

But Amy was determined. She would see Lincoln, no matter what. She would get him to look after her son, no matter what. She drew herself up to her whole five feet five inches and stared him straight in the eye. 'Can you tell Dr Adams that his wife, Amy Carson, is here?'

'Different names, huh?' The cop eyed her suspiciously as he lifted his shoulder to speak into the radio attached to the front of his protective vest.

Amy's hands rested on the steel grating in front of her. Her eyes drifted across the nearby ocean. It was beautiful here. But the Californian heat seemed to be suffocating her. She could feel the sun beating down, making her itchy and scratchy. In fact, her whole body felt itchy. She pulled her smock top away from her body in an attempt to get some air circulating.

She blinked. A wave of nausea swept over her. Her head was beginning to spin. Suddenly watching the boats bobbing up and down in the cove didn't seem like such a good idea. The momentum of the waves was making her feel worse, her legs turning to jelly, and little patches of black had appeared at the edge of her vision...

'Ma'am! Ma'am, are you okay? Quick! Someone get me an ambulance!

'Dr Adams!'

The voice cut across the emergency department like a siren. Lincoln spluttered his coffee all down the front of his scrubs and onto his open white coat. He glanced at the cup of lukewarm coffee. His first since yesterday and he wasn't going to get to drink it. He tossed the cup in the trash and turned towards the voice.

James Turner. Head of the President's security detail. Not again. This man was beginning to haunt his dreams—both at night and during the day.

But something was wrong. He had someone— a woman—in his arms. Linc strode towards him as James Turner unceremoniously dumped the woman on top of a gurney behind one of the sets of curtains. Beads of sweat dripped down his forehead and nose. Linc wondered if he'd managed to change out of his obligatory black suit at all since he'd arrived in Pelican Cove.

'I think I found something belonging to you, Dr Adams.'

'To me? I don't think so.' Lincoln shook his head and moved over to the gurney.

'Really?' James Turner raised an eyebrow. 'You mean you don't recognise your own wife?'

'My what?'

'I knew it. Another scam artist. It's ridiculous

the lengths some of these reporters will go to. Don't worry, I'll get rid of her.'

Linc moved nearer the woman on the gurney. Her head and body were turned away from him but from the back the curly red hair looked like someone else's. Someone he'd known five years ago. Only then she'd spent most of the time with it tied up in a ponytail, not spread across her shoulders and back, like it was now.

He leaned closer, then started. Yip. That definitely was a very pregnant abdomen. At least six months. His eyes flickered to her face. Pale skin, flawless, almost translucent, with a faint sprinkling of freckles across her nose. And she was out cold. And James Turner was trying to pull her upwards, obviously thinking she was faking.

'Stop!'

This time his voice was every bit as loud as James's had been.

The cold, hard stare he was getting used to met him again.

'Get your hands off her.' Lincoln walked around to the other side of the gurney. He had to be sure. He had to be sure his eyes were not deceiving him.

No. They weren't. This was Amy Carson. This was *his* Amy Carson. The one he'd spent six hot, sweaty months with on the Amazon aid boat. Spending the days looking after a range of new-born ailments and spending the nights lost in the sea of her red hair. And he could absolutely authenticate it was her natural colour. This was definitely Amy Carson. The same one that had asked for help only forty-eight hours ago.

A very pregnant Amy Carson.

'What happened?' he asked James, as he spotted the crumpled envelope at the top of her bag. No one usually carried an envelope that size— not unless they were carrying their hospital notes.

'I got radioed from the checkpoint. She was apparently making a scene, saying she had to see you. The cop on duty had her sussed the moment he saw her. The paparazzi have been trying every angle to get up here. Never thought they would resort to this, though. It's really taking it a bit too far. She collapsed down at the checkpoint a few minutes ago.'

Lincoln stuck his head from behind the curtain. 'Nancy, I need some help in here. Can you get me a foetal monitor, please?' he shouted to one of the E.R. nurses. He turned back angrily to James, 'And you? Go and get David Fairgreaves and tell him I need him to see a patient.' He yanked the cardiac monitor leads and BP cuff from the wall. 'Not every person you meet is trying to get to the President, Mr Turner.' He touched the pale face lying on the gurney. 'She—' his voice lowered automatically '—was trying to get to me.'

He waited for James to depart and pulled the curtain tightly closed.

Amy Carson.

The girl he'd searched for. The only girl to ever get under his guard. He'd almost resigned himself to the fact he wasn't going to see her again. But here she was, in the flesh, right before his eyes again. Except her flesh had expanded considerably, creating a nice neat bump under her breasts. Nothing like how she'd looked the last night he'd seen her as she'd danced about their cabin in her underwear, laughing and teasing him. This time she wasn't laughing at all, she was out cold. And she'd been looking for him. What on earth was going on?

Nancy came in, clutching the Doppler scanner, and grabbed a nearby patient gown. She pushed

Lincoln aside as he struggled with Amy's long white smock top. 'Here, let me,' she said, as she deftly manoeuvred the top out of place, replacing it with a Velcro-fastened green gown. Her hand slid underneath the gown as she attached the leads from the cardiac monitor and pressed the button to switch the machine on. Lincoln fixed the cuff on Amy's arm and watched for a few seconds as it inflated. Without saying a word, he already knew what it would say.

Nancy pulled a white plastic patient clothing bag from the locker and folded Amy's white smock. Her eyes fell on the patient notes, still in their battered envelope, currently lying at the bottom of the bed. 'Have you read those yet?'

'No. I haven't had a chance. Why?'

'Do you know her?'

He hesitated. But Nancy was as sharp as a tack. 'Do you want me to get someone else to see her?'

Linc shook his head. 'I asked James Turner to go find David Fairgreaves for me.' He waved his hand over Amy's stomach. 'I'm not an obstetrician.'

Nancy picked up the notes beside the bed and

started to write down her heart rate and BP. 'I need a name, Linc.'

Lincoln picked up the Doppler scanner and put a little gel on Amy's stomach. He pulled her maternity trousers down slightly, adjusting them to reach the area that he needed to. He slid the transducer across her abdomen and after a few seconds he heard it. There. Thump, thump, thump. Like a little butterfly beating its wings. The baby's heartbeat. Whatever had happened to Amy, her baby was safe. A smile broke out across his face.

'Linc, I need a name—for the admission notes?'

'It's Amy. Amy Carson.'

'Do you know her date of birth?'

He blinked. 'August 14.'

Then he realised something. He picked up the buff-coloured folder from the bottom of the gurney. 'You could have got all that from the notes she brought with her.'

Nancy smiled. 'Yes, I could have. But the fact you know it makes it all the more interesting why this young lady ran the gauntlet today to see you. Pelican Cove just got a whole lot more interesting. Something you want to tell me, Dr Adams?'

Her eyes were fixed expectantly on Amy's stomach—as if Lincoln had a closely guarded secret to tell. She leaned over and stuck the tympanic thermometer in Amy's ear.

He shook his head firmly and let out an almost forced laugh. 'You can't possibly think...'

Nancy rolled her eyes. 'I never said a word.' She picked up the notes. 'I'll go and get Ms Carson logged into the system...' her eyes swept over the nearby locker '...and bring her some water. I think she'll need it. This girl's overheated. I wonder how long she was standing out in the sun.'

Lincoln watched as she swept out of the cubicle. His eyes drifted back to the monitor.

Amy's heart rate was slow and steady but her BP...? It was way too high. He glanced at the chart. Her temperature was above normal too. He pulled up a nearby chair and sat down next to her. The noise of the E.R. seemed to fade away.

It was the first time he'd seen her in six years. His Amazonian fling. One of the best things that had ever happened to him. Six months of hard work and great sex. She'd left to go back to the US for a holiday but had told him she would be coming back in a few weeks to rejoin the boat.

Next thing he knew, two weeks had passed and she'd quit. With no reason. And no forwarding address.

So what had happened to her? What had she been doing for the last six years? And why had she texted him two days ago, asking for help? Was it about this? About being pregnant?

Because this was last thing he'd been expecting.

Over the last few years he'd tried to push Amy completely from his mind. And if thoughts of her ever did creep in, they certainly didn't look like this! He'd always imagined he might meet her again on another aid boat or working in a different hospital. He certainly hadn't expected her to seek him out as a patient. And it made him almost resentful. A sensation he hadn't expected.

He reached out and touched her skin again. She was hot. She hadn't had a chance to cool back down in the air-conditioned E.R. One of her red curls was stuck to her forehead and his fingers swept across her skin to pull it back.

She murmured. Or groaned. He wasn't sure which. His hand cupped her cheek for a second. Just like he used to. And her head flinched.

Moved closer. As if his hand and her cheek were a good fit. As if they were where they were supposed to be.

Something stirred inside him. And he shifted uncomfortably. They hadn't made each other any promises. He'd been surprised that she hadn't come back—had been surprised that she hadn't got in touch. She'd had his mobile number, scribbled on a bit of paper, but he hadn't had hers. She hadn't brought her phone to the Amazon with her, thinking it would never work there. And she couldn't remember her number. But it hadn't mattered, because he'd thought he would be seeing her again in two weeks.

Only he hadn't. Not until now.

That was the trouble of having a reputation as a playboy—sooner or later you started believing your own press. Everyone had expected him just to take up with the next pretty nurse that crossed his path—so had he. But something had been wrong. That pale-skinned redhead hadn't been so easy to forget. Amy Carson had got under his skin.

Even two years later, when he'd found himself swept along into an engagement with an elegant brunette, something just hadn't felt right. The first whiff of wedding plans had made him run for the hills. And he hadn't stopped. Until now.

His eyes darted to her notes and he picked them up, flicking them between his fingers. He wasn't her obstetrician, he shouldn't really read them. But he had acted as an E.R. admitting doctor, so surely that meant he should find out about his patient's history?

But he couldn't. He couldn't do that. There was a boundary here. David Fairgreaves was much more qualified to look after her and he would be here in a matter of minutes. There were some ethical lines that he wasn't sure he wanted to cross.

He looked at her overstuffed black shoulder bag. Maybe he should look in there? Maybe she might have her mobile and there could be someone he could contact for her? Or what about a next of kin? She was pregnant, so there was probably a husband.

The thought stopped him dead. He stared at her left hand. It was bare. Did that mean there was no husband? So who was the baby's father?

He pulled the bag up onto his lap. For some reason it felt wrong. Awkward. To go searching through an almost stranger's bag. Years ago, as an attending doctor he would have had no qualms about this. Lots of patients came into the E.R. in an unconscious state and had their pockets or bags searched. This was something he'd done a hundred times before. So why didn't he want to do it now?

And then it happened. Her dark green eyes flickered open. And a smile spread across her face. 'Linc,' she whispered huskily, her lips dry and her throat obviously parched. 'Do you always search through your wife's handbag?'

CHAPTER TWO

HE STARTED. For a second he'd been lost in his own thoughts. He should have known better. That was what you always got from Amy. *Miss Unpredictable*. That was the nickname the staff on the aid boat had given her. She'd never said what you expected her to say. Maybe that was what made her so unforgettable.

Everything about her was the same. And yet, everything about her was different. She gave a little smile as she tried to sit up on the gurney and he moved swiftly to her side to help adjust the backrest and pillows, automatically pressing the button for the electronic BP monitor again. Her smile was disarming him. It reminded him of a hundred things that weren't appropriate for an E.R. It reminded him of a hundred things that probably weren't appropriate for a pregnant lady. He felt his breath leave his body—had he been holding it? And felt the tension leave his shoulder muscles. He could stop worrying. She was awake.

'So what's the problem, *Mrs Adams*?'

Amy's heart was fluttering in her chest and she didn't know if it was to do with her medical condition or from the effect of seeing Lincoln in the flesh again. Thank goodness she was currently lying down, because she was sure her legs had just turned to mush. Old blue eyes was back. All six feet, broad shoulders and dark curly hair of him. Hair you could just run your fingers through...

Her grin spread wider, then she laid her hand on his arm. 'I'm sorry about that, Linc. But it's like Fort Knox out there and I really needed to see you.' Her mind was spinning. Could he hear her heart beating frantically in her chest? Could he know the effect that he still had on her, six years on? She hadn't expected this. She'd expected to get in here and persuade him to look after her baby if she delivered early. Instead, she found herself being pulled into his deep blue eyes. Deeper and deeper.

'Amy, I'm happy to see you. Doubtless, I would

have been happier if it was six years ago, but you didn't need to lie to get in here.'

She sat back against the pillows. 'Wow. You don't beat about the bush.'

'Neither do you apparently.' His eyes were resting on her abdomen but his voice had reverted back to teasing.

She took a deep breath. It didn't matter that something was currently doing flip-flops in her stomach. She needed to focus. To let him know how important he was to her right now. 'I did need to tell lies to get in here, Linc. It was really important that I see you and the cop had already told me to go away.'

'So you decided to faint?' He raised his eyebrow at her.

She gave a little laugh. 'Nah, the heat decided that for me.' Her eyes fixed on his and she hesitated a little. 'I did try to text you—but you weren't answering—and then I saw you on the television this morning and realised where you'd been.'

He pulled the chair back over and sat next to her again. 'Yeah, I've been kind of busy. And I should warn you—I haven't slept in two days.'

She rolled her eyes. 'Oh, no! You're like a bear with sore head when you don't sleep. I pity the poor nursing staff working with you.'

A lazy smile crept across his face. 'You're the second person to say that to me today.'

She felt something wrench at her. It was so easy to fall back into their way of teasing each other. It was so easy to forget the most obvious reason she was here. Six years felt like nothing. It was almost as if the last time they'd spoken had been yesterday. She knew him so well. But who else knew the same things about him that she did?

She bit her lip. There was every chance that Lincoln was happily married. But she wasn't here looking for romance. She wasn't here because he was the best lover she'd ever had. This was even more personal than that. He had no idea how much life had changed for her in the last six years. She was only half the woman he used to know… She gave herself a shake. She was here to find someone she trusted to look after her baby. The most precious thing in the world to her.

He shook his head. 'Enough about me. Let's get back to the matter at hand.' His voice dipped.

'Why are you here, Amy? What do you want from me?'

The professional head was gone again. This time, the hundred questions that were spinning around his head in frustration came bubbling to the surface. He hadn't seen her in six years. She'd appeared out of the blue, pregnant and asking for him. What on earth was going on?

She touched her abdomen. 'I have signs of pre-eclampsia and this baby means more to me than anything in this world. If my baby is born prematurely I want him to have the best chance in the world.' She hesitated for a second, before looking into his eyes. 'And I knew the best chance for my baby would be you.'

Lincoln shook his head and his brow furrowed. He waved his arm. 'You must know a dozen doctors who could take care of your baby. Why me, Amy?'

Her answer was immediate and straight to the point and he could see tears glistening in her eyes. 'I might know a dozen doctors, Linc, but none of them are like you. You're the best. The best neonatologist I've ever known. You did things on that boat that TV movies are made out of—with virtually no equipment and only the most unskilled staff.' She gestured towards herself.

He shook his head. 'You're not unskilled, Amy. You're a damn fine nurse and you know it.'

'I'm a damn fine *theatre* nurse, Linc. I had no experience at all with neonates. I went there as a specialist nurse in eye theatre, and that was fine for all the cataract, squint and glaucoma surgeries. I even managed to struggle through with cleft-palate surgeries and emergency appendectomies. But I'd never really worked as a general, medical or paediatric nurse before—I'd never looked after pregnant women before. I was seriously out of my depth and you helped me—you know you did.'

Lincoln leaned over and took her hand again. 'But we were a team, Amy, we helped each other. Everyone was selected because of their individual skills and level of expertise. But at the end of the day we treated what came through the door.'

She shook her head. 'No one was as dedicated to those babies as you were, Linc. You were the one who would stay up half the night, watching over them.' His brow furrowed. 'Why was that, Linc? I asked before, but you wouldn't tell me.'

He shrugged his shoulders and she could see him searching for the words. His eyes looked darker than normal, heavier from fatigue. He sat down next to her. 'My sister had a premature baby around twenty years ago. There weren't any facilities near where we stayed and her daughter—my niece—died.'

Amy took a sharp breath and rested her hand on his shoulder.

He gave a rueful smile. 'My sister was ten years older than me at the time. I watched my little niece struggle for breath, turn blue and die. Our family didn't really talk about it after that. It was too painful. I hadn't really been interested in school before then. I was just coasting along. But everything changed after that. I knew if I wanted to be a doctor to help babies like my niece, I had to knuckle down and get the grades—so I did. Medicine for neonates has come a long way in the last twenty years. If my niece had been born now, she would have survived.'

'You never said anything. Why didn't you tell me this on the boat?'

Lincoln met her with a pointed stare. 'Some things are easier not to talk about—don't you think?'

The heavy air hung between them. Amy held her breath, waiting to see if he would say anything else.

'Dr Adams?'

A nurse appeared at the curtains, with David standing behind her. 'They need you in NICU.'

NICU. The neonatal intensive care unit. A place that normally didn't exist in Pelican Cove—there had never been a need for it. A place that currently held the First Daughter. In the last two days more personnel and supplies had been transferred down from San Francisco Children's Hospital than he'd thought possible. Didn't there have to be more than one baby for it to be termed an NICU? He pushed the thoughts from his mind.

'What can I do for you folks?' David strode through the curtains with his normal joie de vivre. Lincoln's eyes met his and he lifted the battered envelope from the bottom of the gurney and handed it to him. 'I need you to see a friend of mine, please, David.'

David's face changed, his eyes taking in the patient on the bed. The pregnant patient on the bed. He pulled the notes from the envelope, glancing to see which hospital they had come from, then gave Lincoln an inquisitive stare.

'My patient now, Dr Adams.' David's manner was brisk and to the point. 'I'll let you know if I need you.' His tone was almost dismissive. Whilst at times he gave the impression of being a bumbling fool, as a clinician he was second to none. And Lincoln knew it—it was why he'd asked for David's help. Amy couldn't be in safer hands. But there was no mistaking who would be in charge here.

Linc took a deep breath and stepped away from the gurney. 'I'll be back,' he muttered, his eyes not meeting hers, and he stepped through the curtains.

David's hand caught his shoulder. 'Dr Adams?'

The professional title. He must be annoyed. 'Yes?'

'Just remember your first and *only* priority is the First Daughter. Don't let other things get in the way. Don't get distracted.'

'You think I am?' The words came out automatically, snappier than he expected.

David's voice was quiet. The voice of years of learning and experience, both academically and human. 'I think you could be. Let me handle this.' He turned and ducked behind the curtains, pulling them tightly shut behind him.

Linc walked the few hundred yards along the corridor. Pelican Cove was a small community hospital, not a sprawling metropolis with new technology sprouting from every corner. That was why, when the First Lady had gone into labour here, he'd had to transfer staff and equipment from San Francisco Children's Hospital to ensure the safe delivery of the thirty-two-weeker.

As usual, the black-suited security detail was at the door—it was getting to the point they just blended into the background. He pushed open the door to the newly kitted-out NICU. The heat encompassed him immediately, the temperature warmer in here to compensate for the early arrival's rapid heat loss.

He walked over to the incubator. Two of his best nurses were on duty.

'What's up?'

For a premature baby, the First Daughter had an air of determination about her, obviously a chip off the old block. She'd come out scream-ing, breathing on her own and continued to do so.

He glanced at the nearby monitor. Her O2 lev-els were good and there was no nasal flaring.

'She's not feeding well. In fact, we can't get her to latch on at all.'

Lincoln frowned. A common complaint in pre-mature babies who hadn't yet learned how to suck. 'What about kangaroo care?'

Ruth, the nurse, nodded and stared down at her charge, 'The only reason Esther is back in here is because Jennifer Taylor is currently sleeping. She's exhausted. Up until now it's been skin-to-skin contact the whole time. Six hours since de-livery and we've not managed to get her to feed yet.' She leaned over the incubator. 'And little missy is getting cranky.'

Lincoln scrubbed his hands at the nearby sink. He'd already examined Esther just after delivery, but there was no harm in rechecking. He pulled on some sterile gloves and slid his hands into the incubator. He ran his hand around and inside her mouth, ensuring her palate was correctly formed. Checked her skin tone, colour and fontanel for clinical signs of dehydration. Sounded her chest

to check her heart and lungs and gently prob-
ing her small abdomen. Once he was finished
he stripped off his gloves, washed and dried his
hands again and checked her charts.

'Okay, there are no immediate problems, except
her blood glucose has dropped slightly since delivery. Once Jennifer Taylor wakes up, can you
give me a shout and I'll go and have a chat with
her? I'm really reluctant to start any kind of sup-
plementary or tube-feeding. At thirty-two weeks
I think she's more than capable of breastfeeding and I don't want to do anything that will
jeopardise that. We might have to suggest that
Jennifer expresses some milk in the meantime
to try and get some fluid into her.'

Ruth gave a nod. 'I'm sure she'll be awake
shortly. I'll give you a shout.'

Lincoln entered some notes in the electronic
record and went back outside, glancing at his
watch. Half an hour. Would David Fairgreaves
be finished with Amy yet?

He walked over to the nurses' station, glancing
around him before picking up Amy's notes. They
were thicker than he would have expected for a
healthy woman her age and he started to flick

through them to read over her obstetric care. If he was going to look after her baby he needed to know what he was dealing with. *IVF pregnancy.* The words caught his attention instantly.

Why had Amy needed IVF? His fingers went backwards through the notes—away from the area of his expertise—and froze at the long clinical letter near the end. His eyes scanned it quickly, his breath catching in his throat. The diagnosis was in bold type at the head of the letter. Breast cancer. Amy had breast cancer.

No. She was too young. She didn't smoke, rarely drank alcohol, and lived a relatively healthy lifestyle. How on earth could she be a candidate for breast cancer? It seemed unreal. Even though the words and clinical evidence were there in front of him. He couldn't believe it. It was almost as if he were reading about someone else.

His eyes raked the letter for a date. And his brain did rapid calculations. He felt himself sag into a nearby chair.

Six years ago. Her diagnosis had been made six years ago when she'd left the Amazon boat. Had she known she was sick? Why on earth hadn't she told him?

His hands skipped over her treatment plans, test results—some good, some bad. He turned to the inside cover of the notes, searching for her next of kin.

Nothing. No one listed. He'd known that her mother and father had died a few years before she'd joined the boat. She'd gone through all this herself?

Something twisted in his gut. Surprise. Anger. Hurt.

She hadn't told him—and he was hurt. Six months he'd spent with her. They might not have confessed undying love to each other, but surely she'd known he would have supported her? Wasn't that what friends did?

After all, that was why she was here now. She needed help—or her baby did. She obviously felt she could ask him for help now, so why not then?

He could feel the tension in his neck and jaw. Irrational anger built inside him. His fingers brushed the notes again. He had to push this stuff aside. He had to deal with her in a professional capacity.

He edged back along the corridor, approaching

the curtains quietly. Two seconds later he heard a peal of laughter.

Not girly. Not tinkling. Deep, hearty, genuine laughter. David had obviously turned on his natural charm again. The man could have people eating out of his hand within two minutes of meeting them. Something about the ease and instant familiarity between the two of them bothered him. Made him want to march into the cubicle and stand between them. How crazy was that?

Linc cleared his throat loudly and edged his way between the curtains. 'How's things?'

David turned to face him, his head flicking back towards her. 'Amy? Are you happy for Dr Adams to know about your condition?'

Amy blinked. They obviously hadn't had that part of the conversation yet. 'Actually, Dr Fairgreaves, Lincoln's the reason I'm here. If this baby is coming early, I'm hoping that Lincoln will look after him for me.'

Lincoln cast his eyes over the monitor again, noting her rising blood pressure. 'And is it, David? Is this baby coming early?' Did he really want to have two premature babies in a community hospital not designed for the task?

David's face remained static, expressionless to the underlying current of tension between the two of them. He nodded briefly and handed the notes to Lincoln.

'Ms Adams in twenty-eight weeks pregnant. For the last few days Amy has shown some mild signs of pre-eclampsia. A slight rise in blood pressure, a trace of protein in her urine and some oedema. However, on today's examination things appear to have progressed.'

He pressed a finger lightly into the swollen skin around Amy's ankle, leaving a little dimple in the pale flesh that remained there once he removed the pressure.

'Pitting oedema is now evident, her BP, both systolic and diastolic, has gone up by another 10mmg and the amount of protein in her urine has increased.' He gave Amy a wry smile. 'I'm giving Ms Adams the benefit of the doubt that she didn't have the easiest job getting here today and that could account for the rise in blood pressure. She also assures me that, as of yesterday, she is now officially on maternity leave from her full-time job.' His eyes went carefully from one to the other.

'For the next twenty-four hours I've agreed with Ms Adams that she requires some careful monitoring. We're going to monitor her blood pressure, her fluid intake and output and do a twenty-four-hour urine collection. So...' he looked directly at Lincoln '...your services aren't required in the immediate future but...' he gave a little nod to Amy '...I'm not ruling it out.'

David took a measured breath, his cool grey eyes resting on Lincoln. 'I'm sure you realise the importance of ensuring Ms Adams has a calm environment. I trust there will be no problems?'

Linc shifted uncomfortably. So David definitely had heard the earlier exchange. And even though his words were phrased as a question, this was a direct instruction.

Linc fixed a smile on his face. 'Absolutely, Dr Fairgreaves. Thanks very much for agreeing to monitor Amy.'

His point made, David's face relaxed and he gave a nonchalant shrug of his shoulders. 'Hey, what else am I doing?' Then he slid out between the curtains.

The silence screamed in Lincoln's ears. She was watching him again, waiting to see what he would say. His hand automatically ran through his dishevelled hair—what he wouldn't give for a shower and a comfortable bed right now. What he really needed was twelve hours' solid sleep, with some serious blackout blinds. But the way his brain was currently spinning, there was no chance of that.

He pulled the chair over again and sagged down into it. 'Okay, Amy. Let's get to it. What's going on here? Where do you normally stay? And what did David mean about maternity leave? Where do you normally work?'

She crossed her hands in her lap. 'Wow, an interrogation. Or is it an interview? Is this how you talk to all your potential patients, Dr Adams? Do I have to pass muster before you'll take my son on as your patient?'

He shook his head. Sleep deprivation was making him ratty. It didn't matter what he'd read in her notes. He wasn't going to make this easy for her. She was going to have to tell him herself. 'This is how I talk to the girl who walked away six years ago without a backward glance, and then turns up when she sees me on television.'

Amy felt her bottom lip tremble. This wasn't

going well. She could see he was tired. She knew he would be under extra stress looking after the First Daughter, but perfect timing was the one thing she didn't have here. And she needed the assurance of Lincoln's help now.

'That's not fair and you know it.'

He shook his head in frustration. His voice was quiet but even. 'I know.'

She switched into professional mode. 'Okay, Dr Adams. I normally live in Santa Maria in Butte County—around four hours from here. I work in one of the free clinics there. And my maternity leave started...' she glanced at her watch '...officially around twelve hours ago.'

Her notes were still in his hands. But he wasn't looking at them. It looked as though he hadn't read them. It would be so much easier if he did, then at least he might understand why she'd left.

'Why me, Amy, and why now?'

A loud burr came from the monitor beside her and the electronic blood-pressure cuff started to inflate again. Amy winced as the cuff over-inflated on her arm. Linc watched with alarm as the reading on the monitor climbed higher and higher. One-eighty…one-ninety…two hundred. *Please don't let her blood pressure be that high.*

Amy's voice cut through his thoughts. 'There are a lot of kids currently alive in the Amazon because of you, Linc, and you know it. Kids who would have died if you hadn't been on that boat.'

She saw him bite his bottom lip. Linc was a team player, not a glory hunter. She knew how uncomfortable he'd been in that press interview. He must have said the words 'I have a fantastic team' at least five times. She knew he wouldn't be interested in the chat-show interviews or celebrity magazine spreads that would materialise in the near future.

A black-suited figure crossed the gap in the curtains. She waved her arm. 'Look at all this, Linc. When the First Lady went into premature labour, who did they call? You. They must have been able to get almost any doctor in the world, but they chose you to look after the First Daughter. The first presidential baby in nearly fifty years. What does that tell you?'

'It tells me I was in the wrong place at the wrong time, Amy, nothing else.' He shook his head, 'You make it sound grander that it actually was. Abby Tyler was the admitting physician here in Pelican Cove. She works with me at San Francisco Children's Hospital. They asked her for a neonatologist and she recommended me.'

Amy waved her arms, 'And you're telling me that the whole secret-service brigade out there didn't check your credentials? To make sure that only the absolute best of the best was looking after the President's baby? I seriously doubt that. Hell, the other doctor is an award-winner.'

He smiled at her. 'You'll find it hard to believe, but that was sheer coincidence. David Fairgreaves has a boat moored in Pelican Cove, the man is an old sea dog. Whenever he's here, Abby has an arrangement to call him for any obstetric emergencies. He apparently likes to keep his hand in.'

Amy folded her hands across her chest. 'Oh, come on. You're telling me the secret service didn't check on him too? Especially that old stony-faced one. Does he ever smile?'

Linc laughed at her description of James Turner, the head of the presidential security detail, the original man-in-black. 'I think I've only seen him smile once in the last three days—and that's when he told Luke Storm, one of the other docs, that he couldn't leave. Somehow I think his job must drain all sense of humour from his body. He spends his life looking over his shoulder for potential threats to the Presidential family.'

The blood-pressure cuff stopped abruptly. The hiss of air seeping out from it. Linc glanced at the screen again—150/96. A bit higher than before, but not yet dangerous. Still worth keeping an eye on. His eyes fell to his watch. There were a million things he wanted to say right now. A million things he wanted to know. Six years to catch up on. But David had been right. He had other duties—other priorities—that he couldn't get distracted from.

'I'm sorry, Amy, but I seriously need some shut-eye and I've a neonate to deal with who doesn't want to feed.'

Her eyes fell to the notes, still clutched in his hands. She couldn't hide the slight tremor in her voice. 'Will you read my notes and tell me if you'll agree to be my baby's doctor?' Her hands were back at her stomach, protectively rubbing her extended abdomen.

The notes. She knew exactly what he would read in there. But for some reason he didn't want to give her an easy way out. Why couldn't she just find the words to tell him? She had no idea he'd already read them. And he was beginning to feel too tired to care.

'In the interests of professionalism I'll read your notes, not now—later—but I want to hear everything—straight from the horse's mouth, so to speak. There's nothing in these notes that you won't be able to tell me yourself. I'll come back later. We'll talk then—and I'll decide if I can be your baby's doctor or not. I can't do it if there's going to be a conflict of interest for me, and...' his eyes rolled towards the outside corridor as he gave her a crooked little grin '...your timing could have been better.'

Amy watched as he exited through the curtains, her throat tight.

She needed him. She needed him to be there for her baby—and for her. He was the best in the world. No one else would do. She couldn't lose this baby.

It had all seemed so simple in her head. As soon as she'd known she was at risk of pre-eclampsia, she'd known she had to find Linc.

She'd seen him bring neonates that should have died back to life. And that was normal for him.

The long line of mothers who'd queued up on the banks of the Amazon to show them their healthy, growing children—children he had saved in previous years—was testament to that.

There had been no doubt in her mind. This was all about her baby. All about the little boy currently growing in her stomach.

So why was she feeling like a teenager with a schoolgirl crush? She hadn't thought about Lincoln for the last five years.

No. That wasn't strictly true. He'd crept into her dreams on a few occasions—all of them X-rated. But dreams you couldn't control. Truth be told, she hadn't let herself think about playboy Linc for the last five years. Too much potential for heartache. She'd had to concentrate all her energy on beating the cancer.

And now she was only here because she needed him for her son. Really.

When she'd had her detailed scan she almost hadn't asked what sex her baby was. But at the last moment she'd changed her mind. She'd wanted to prepare for her son or daughter. She'd wanted to pick his pram, his bedclothes and the paper for his nursery wall. She'd even picked his name. Zachary. Zachary John Carson.

She whispered the name as her hands ran over her stomach. 'Stay inside just a little longer, Zachary. I need you to be as healthy as can be when you come out. Momma needs to know that you're going to do just fine.' A tear slid down her cheek and the anger started to rise in her chest.

Why should the First Lady's baby be any more important than hers? And why did she, after everything she'd been through, have to develop a condition that could threaten her baby?

But this was it. Cancer had crept through her body tissues and the chemotherapy had ravaged them. She'd lost her ability to have a baby naturally and this embryo was her last chance. Her only chance.

So how come she couldn't just focus on her baby?

From the first second she'd opened her eyes and seen Lincoln again, her heart had gone into overdrive. There were so many things about him she'd forgotten. His intense gaze. His lazy smile.

His flirting. The way he could comfort her with the touch of his hand and the stroke of his finger.

And the camouflage he kept around himself.

She'd seen how he jumped from being really comfortable around her one minute, like it had only been a few days since they'd seen each other, since they'd slept together and been wrapped in each other's arms, to shifting into the professional role, the possibility of being her baby's doctor and all the lines that blurred in between.

But she wasn't asking him to be *her* doctor, so surely that simplified things?

So why did her heart keep beating rapidly in her chest every time he was next to her? Why did her hairs stand on end when he touched her and make her feel as if an electrical charge had run up her arm?

Amy squeezed her eyes shut tightly. She couldn't allow herself to feel like this. Lincoln wasn't interested in her. She was a six years past girlfriend who'd had a mastectomy and was carrying a child that wasn't his. Why would he even give her a second glance?

He was only being kind. He was only being a

friend. He couldn't possibly want anything else from her, could he?

This was Lincoln Adams. And yesterday this gorgeous blue-eyed, brown-haired doc had been announced on television as looking after the First Daughter. He was world news. Women would be throwing themselves at his feet.

She had to concentrate on the most important thing right now—a safe delivery and outcome for her baby. She'd come here to find Lincoln Adams because he was the best doctor to care for her baby. Nothing else. No matter how he currently made her feel.

CHAPTER THREE

'LINC? Linc?'

The voice was quiet, softly spoken, but the hand pressing down on his shoulder was firm, stirring him from the first hour's sleep he'd had in two days.

'What…what is it?' His hands automatically went to his sleep-filled eyes and he rubbed hard. He looked around him. He'd sat down for just a minute in the NICU, waiting for the First Lady to awaken and try to feed her baby again, but the heat from the unit had enveloped him and before he'd known it…

Val, one of his nurses, was standing next to him smiling. 'Wake up, sleeping beauty, you're needed.'

'Is Jennifer Taylor awake?'

Val nodded. 'She's been awake for the last half-hour. Both Ruth and I have tried to assist her with breastfeeding, but the truth is we just can't get this baby to latch on.' She glanced down at her watch. 'And if we're going to follow the protocols we normally use at San Fran then we're at our time limit for getting some fluids into this baby. You're going to have to come and talk to her.'

Linc gave a nod, stood up and tried to flatten his rumpled scrubs. He walked over to the nearby sink and splashed some cold water on his face and hands.

Neonates could be hard work. Esther, who had been born at thirty-two weeks, hadn't yet developed her natural mechanism to suck and feed. It was a common complaint in premature babies and one he was used to dealing with. The last thing in the world he wanted to do was to put a tube into the baby's stomach and feed it artificially. The First Lady wanted to breastfeed and he would make sure that he and his staff did everything they could to make that happen.

He pulled some paper towels from the nearby dispenser and dried his face.

'Have you had any success expressing some breast milk?'

Val nodded. 'Ruth's in there with her now—we knew that would be the next step.'

Lincoln took a deep breath and pushed open the door into the adjoining room. Charles Taylor, the President of the United States, was perched on the edge of the bed one arm wrapped around his wife's shoulders, the other cradling daughter Esther. By neonatal standards Esther was a healthy weight at just under five pounds. Would Amy's baby be so lucky? Where had that come from? Lincoln felt a little shudder drift down his spine. He had a job to do. He couldn't allow himself to be distracted.

Jennifer's brow was furrowed, her eyes fixed on the pump that the nurse Ruth was using to help her express some milk from her breasts. She looked exasperated as the smallest trickle of creamy breast milk started to collect in the receptacle.

'What's wrong with me?' she gasped. 'Is that it? No wonder my baby can't feed.'

Lincoln crossed the room in a few steps and sat down at the bottom of the bed. This was no time for pomp and ceremony. The last thing he wanted was for Jennifer to think she was failing at feeding her child.

'Give it a few minutes, Jennifer. Ruth is an expert at this and it takes a bit of time for your milk to come in. Remember, Esther is a tiny baby and she won't need a huge amount to start with.' He pointed at the small amount already collected. 'That is called colostrum. And it's like gold dust for babies. It contains antibodies and is rich in protein and carbohydrates—exactly what your baby needs.'

The tears were already starting to form in Jennifer's eyes. 'But she won't feed. I can't get her to take anything.'

Lincoln nodded. 'And that's entirely normal for a thirty-two-weeker. Her natural instincts to suck and feed haven't kicked in yet. Sometimes it can take a few weeks. In the meantime, we have to look at how to get some fluids into her. The last thing we want is for your baby to dehydrate.'

Jennifer sagged back against the pillows behind her. The effect of the relaxation had an immediate impact on the flow from her breasts. 'Look, there's some more. Once we have a few more mils we'll start to look at an alternative method for getting some breast milk into Esther. Any extra milk we can refrigerate or freeze.'

'But I want to breastfeed. I told everyone I want to breastfeed.'

Lincoln could see the stress on Jennifer's face. He reached out and automatically touched her hand. 'And you will. In the meantime, in order to keep your daughter from screaming the house down, we'll give her your breast milk another way.'

'How?'

'There's two possibilities and it all depends on the baby. We can try cup feeding or finger feeding. What we definitely won't do is put your breast milk into a bottle.'

'I've never heard of these. How on earth can a baby drink from a cup?' She turned to face her husband. 'Have you ever heard of these?'

Charles lifted his eyes from his daughter, still caught in the rosy glow of new parenthood, smitten with his daughter's face. 'Nope, you've got me. Never heard of them.'

Lincoln smiled. 'The word cup might not be strictly true. We don't use a regular cup—we use a medicine cup and, to be honest, this type of feeding isn't anything new, it's been around for a long time. We place the edge of the cup at the baby's mouth and bring the liquid up to baby's lower lip, so she can lap it up—a bit like a pussycat. It can get a little messy.' He smiled at Charlie, who still had his suit on. 'We can you give something to change into.' He nodded at Val, who had just detached the breast pump. 'One of us will take some time and teach you how to do it. It can take a little bit of practice to get it right. It does mean, though, that you can both help with Esther's feeding.'

Charlie gave a broad smile. There was no mistaking the joy in his eyes as he looked at his daughter. 'Whatever she needs,' he murmured.

Lincoln watched Jennifer's face. She looked a little easier. 'This is only a temporary measure to help get some fluids into Esther. We'll still try putting Esther to the breast and encouraging her to latch on.'

'Wouldn't it just be easier to put a tube down?'

'In theory it might be. But if we feed Esther by tube and she has the sensation of feeling full, she won't have any motivation to suck. That's what we really need to work on. Feeding by tube would be the last resort and I don't think we'll need to do that.'

Jennifer nodded slowly. 'So how do you know if she's getting enough?'

'We'll monitor her diapers and check the tone and elasticity of her skin.' His eyes caught sight of Val, transferring some of the breast milk into one of the medicine cups. He stretched his hands out towards Charlie. 'Do you mind if I take her for a minute? We want to be sure and have her wrapped up securely before we start—little hands can make a terrible mess when we're cup feeding.' He smiled at the President's suit. 'Wanna play doctor for the day and change into a set of scrubs?'

Charlie nodded. 'Come with me,' Ruth, the other nurse, said as she headed towards the door. 'I'm sure we can find something for you.'

Lincoln tried hard to focus on the task at hand. Getting the First Daughter to feed should be his first and only priority. So why were his thoughts filled with pale skin and red, curly hair?

The buzz from the monitor and the tightening cuff on her arm woke Amy from her daze. Damn cuff. How was anyone supposed to sleep with this stupid thing going off every thirty minutes?

No wonder her blood pressure was rising—she couldn't get any peace and quiet.

A smile crossed her face. Things were different from a patient perspective. She'd never really given much thought before to the electronic monitoring devices that she used as a nurse. Cardiac monitors that beeped incessantly, IV fluid pumps that alarmed when they needed changing and syringe drivers that required hourly monitoring. It was no wonder patients complained.

She turned her head and glanced at the screen beside her. Damn! Her blood pressure hadn't gone down at all. The curtains surrounding her had been pulled tightly and lights around her had been dimmed. What time was it? Was it night-time? It must be—she'd just been about to slip into another X-rated, Lincoln-filled dream. Definitely not suitable for a hospital stay.

She swung her legs from the trolley and reached for her bag. Somewhere in the depths of this giant tote bag should be her watch—she'd slipped it off earlier when her wrist had felt uncomfortable. She rummaged around inside the bag—lipstick, phone, receipts, purse, umbrella, spare undies, fold-up flat shoes, pens, pens and more pens.

Ten minutes later she gave up. She pulled the cuff from her arm, the ripping Velcro echoing around the quiet emergency department. Where had everyone gone?

As her bare feet hit the cold linoleum floor her head swam a little. How long had it been since she'd eaten? Judging from how her stomach felt, it must have been hours. A little gust of cold air struck her back. Blast! She still had on her hospital gown. It fastened down her back and currently felt like fresh-air fortnight back there; thank goodness she had respectable undies on. She grasped the back of her gown in her hands and stuck her head out between the curtains, glancing one way, then the other, out into the eerie silence, before heading towards the nurses' station. It was deserted and according to the white board on the wall she was the only patient currently in the E.R. No wonder it was so quiet around here.

Then the thought struck her. Of course there were no other patients—the President and the First Family were in this hospital. She'd only got in here by default. Fainting at the police cordon could do that for you.

A packet of half-eaten cookies sat on the desk. She looked around again. Still no people. Well, if someone wanted to leave an open packet of cookies unguarded they could take the consequences. She flopped down into one of the nearby chairs and grabbed a cookie, oblivious to the crumbs falling down the front of her hospital gown, and closed her eyes. Bliss.

'Do you always steal the staff food?'

Amy's eyes shot open and she spluttered, which turned into a cough as part of a cookie lodged in her throat.

Lincoln looked amused as he went around behind her and gave her two hard slaps on the back.

She coughed the piece of cookie back up, catching it in her hand before depositing it in the trash can. She held her hands up. 'Guilty.'

She looked around the darkened corridors. 'Where did you spring from? I never even heard you. This place is like a scene from a bad slasher movie.'

Lincoln laughed, looking at the deserted corridors. He pointed to a door down the hallway. 'I came from the staffroom, where the current E.R. staff are watching reruns of the baby announcement. Don't think they've ever had it so quiet. And you...' he pointed at her '...are apparently resting peacefully with a still-borderline blood pressure and signs of pre-eclampsia.'

Amy rolled her eyes. She lifted her leg and stuck it on the nearby chair, prodding around her ankle and then further up her shin. 'I think the oedema is getting worse.'

Lincoln bent his head towards her leg under the dimmed lights. He was so close she could feel his breath on her skin. He ran his hand up and down her leg.

Wow! A physical examination wasn't supposed to feel like that. It wasn't supposed to make your skin prickle and your blood heat. Thank goodness she'd shaved her legs, or the hairs would currently be standing on end!

But what about him? How was he feeling right now? Did he know the effect he was having on her? Lincoln had always had a wicked sense of humour—was he teasing her? Knowing that her insides had currently turned to mush?

'Any oedema around your abdomen?'

His voice broke through her thoughts. So much for illicit daydreams. She bit her lip and shrugged her shoulders. 'To be honest, I didn't really look when I woke up. I was too busy in the hunt for food.'

'Do you want me to get you something to eat?'

'Can you? This place looks as if it's closed down for the night.'

'Aha.' He put a finger to his lips. 'I might only have been here for two days but I prioritised. I made sure I'm best friends with the canteen staff. What do you want?'

Pictures of barbecue chicken breasts, fresh green salads and French fries swam in front of her eyes. Closely followed by images of scrambled eggs and sausages. It was amazing the weird cravings that pregnancy gave you—even in the middle of the night. She sighed. 'To be honest, Linc, I'll take whatever I can get.'

He stretched out his hand towards her in the dim light. She hesitated, just for a second. Was this a doctor-patient thing? No. It wasn't. David Fairgreaves was her doctor. Linc was her friend. Her good friend. A friend she was going to have to persuade to take care of her baby.

She reached up towards his hand. 'You're going

to have to heave, Linc, I don't think I can get out this chair.'

He enclosed her hand with both of his and gave her a gentle tug from the low-seated chair. The momentum caught her unawares and she took a few steps forward, her hands coming automatically upwards and resting on his hard chest.

And she stopped.

Both hands were resting on his firm muscle, his face just a few inches from hers. In the dim light she could see his dark-blue-rimmed eyes pulling her in. See his perfect skin, with a light stubble on his chin. Before she knew it, her fingers had moved upwards and touched his shadowed jaw. *This was how her dream started.* A smile broke across his face, his hand moved across her back and she felt two fingers resting lightly at the base of her spine, between the gap in her patient gown. Would he kiss her?

When was the last time she'd felt like this? When was the last time she'd wanted a man to kiss her? To feel his touch on her skin? Her lips tingled, aching to feel his pressing against them. Her tongue ran along them, desperate to give them some moisture and invite him in.

'I don't know if I'm dressed appropriately for the staff canteen,' she whispered.

He looked downwards. His eyes following the gentle swell on one side of her breast. Her breath caught in her throat. Would he look to the other side? Would his face register disgust or displeasure?

Neither. His eyes stayed fixed on one side. As if there was nothing wrong. As if the gap on the other side was the most natural thing in the world. Something lurched inside her and she almost jerked in recognition of what it was. Acceptance. This was her. This was her body shape now. And there was no need to feel ashamed or embarrassed. Her skin flushed. For the first time in a long time she felt like a woman again. His lips brushed against her ear, his voice husky. 'From where I'm standing, you look just fine.'

I'm dreaming. This isn't really happening. I'm still lying on that hospital gurney, waiting for the BP cuff to go off again.

Light spilled across them. The door from the staffroom opened. A person still facing inside and laughing at the jokes stood with their foot jammed in the door, sending bright white light spilling down the corridor towards them.

Lincoln stepped backwards. For a second he looked like the proverbial deer caught in the headlights, before he regained his composure and cleared his throat.

'The canteen,' he said. 'I was going to take you to the canteen.' It was almost as if he was saying the words out loud to remind himself what he was supposed to be doing.

His hands fell back to his waist and he gave her a nod in the other direction. 'The canteen's this way, Goldilocks. Let's see what we can get you to eat.'

He took a few long strides ahead of her, making short work of the corridor and pushing open the swing door at the other end and holding it open for her.

'I think Goldilocks was a blonde, not a redhead,' she murmured as she followed him, still grasping self-consciously at her gown.

'But look how much trouble she got into for the search for food,' he replied promptly, sending another smile across her face. The easy banter between them was returning as quickly as it had left. Linc was obviously relaxing again. And she was glad. That was when she liked him best.

They stepped into the canteen, which was bathed in the usual bright hospital lights. Amy squirmed, looking around at the deserted tables and chairs. 'Are you sure we can get something to eat?'

Lincoln nodded, smiling at her again as though his moment of discomfort had passed. 'Sure we can. They've got to feed the nightshift, remember?' He ducked behind the counter and into the kitchen beyond. Amy could hear the happy chattering inside and looked at the empty canteen around her. Even this was strange. She was used to sitting in hospital canteens in her uniform, not in a patient gown. On past occasions when she'd had her surgery and treatments she'd never even made it down to the hospital canteens. At that point food had been the last thing on her mind. A few minutes later Lincoln came out, clutching a tray with a teapot and cups.

'Food will be out in a minute,' he said as he set the tray down on the nearest table. Amy gave him a smile. 'I didn't know you were a tea drinker.' She lifted the cups from the tray.

He wrinkled his forehead. 'Generally I'm not. But I didn't want to come out here with a double-shot coffee when you probably aren't drinking it right now.'

His eyes rested on her extended abdomen and she nodded knowingly. 'It's been a slow, hard fight to stop the addiction to the double shots we used to drink.'

His face broke into that easy grin again. The grin he'd given her when it had just been the two of them, standing in the dim E.R. He lifted the lid of the teapot and gave the water a little stir.

The door clanged open behind them and a little grey-haired lady appeared with a plate in either hand. The delicious aroma of food swept around them and Amy's stomach responded by rumbling loudly.

'Oh, wow!' she said as the plate was set before her. 'Thank you so much.' She beamed. The steam was rising from the freshly made pancakes on the plate, with a pile of sausages and scrambled eggs on the side. 'You must have read my mind,' she said accusingly at Lincoln. 'I was dreaming about these earlier.' *Better than telling him what else she'd dreamed about.* She picked up the pepper pot and sprinkled pepper over her scrambled eggs. 'I am so-o-o hungry.'

He sat for a few seconds, watching her. The way her hair fell over her eyes, one delicious auburn curl just begging to be tucked behind her ear. Sitting like this, her extended abdomen was tucked under the table. For a few seconds he could actually forget she was pregnant. Forget she was here, looking for his help because she was afraid she was about to have a premature baby. He could forget the questions spinning in his head about the pregnancy, the conception, the father. All the things he wanted to ask her about. Right now, the clock was spinning backwards in his head. Back to those six precious months when she'd been *his* Amy. Back when they'd been in the first flush of heat and passion. When they hadn't been able to keep their hands off each other. When stifling hot long days had turned into even hotter and longer nights.

The pale green colour of the hospital gown reminded him of the scrubs they'd worn on the boat. A colour that seemed to reflect the darker green of her eyes, drawing his attention to them from the first second he'd seen her.

Damn! He could kick himself. Was there something else he could have done to find her? Why hadn't he insisted on getting her phone number?

The last six years could have been entirely different.

She leaned back in her chair with a contented and relaxed look on her face, her extended abdomen becoming visible again and jolting him back to the here and now. 'Oh, wow, Linc. I don't know who made those pancakes but we should wrap her up, steal her and take her home with us.'

Her eyes flew open and she sat bolt upright. Had she just said that out loud? Oh, no! 'I didn't mean... I mean I wasn't suggesting...' She couldn't find the words, her brain was scrambled at her ridiculous faux pas. Fatigue and irritability had definitely got the better of her. It didn't help that Linc was sitting staring at her with his fork poised frozen just outside his mouth. But he didn't look shocked. He didn't look upset. He looked...amused.

'Relax, Amy,' he said in a teasing tone. 'Don't get wound up. I know what you meant and we certainly don't want your blood pressure getting any higher.' The gleam in his eyes spoke a thousand words that he wasn't saying out loud.

And then he couldn't stay silent any longer. The frustration from earlier in the day came bubbling to the surface and he wanted to hear the words coming from her lips—not read them in her medical records. 'Why didn't you come back? You left for a two-week holiday and never came back. What happened?'

The question jolted her back to reality. No pleasantries. No niceties. What had happened to playboy, sexy Linc? This was right at the heart of the matter.

And she'd known at some point he'd ask her. And she'd practised what she would say in her head. Words that she'd rehearsed a hundred times in the cab on the way here. Words that just seemed to stick in her throat.

'Well?' He was still staring at her. With those big dark blue eyes. She'd seen eyes like that on a model advertising aftershave once. Everyone had commented on them. But that guy's eyes weren't a patch on Linc's. That guy didn't have a dark blue rim encircling his bright blue iris. Something that pulled you right in and didn't let go. Her hand ran down his arm and her fingers intertwined with his. She needed to do this. She needed something familiar. Something to give her strength right now. It didn't matter if he had a wife outside. They were friends. Or they *had* been friends. And right now she needed her friend's support.

She needed to make him understand why she hadn't come back to the boat. And she already knew how he'd respond—he'd want to know why she hadn't told him at the time. But those were all questions she could field. She needed his skills right now, and his expertise for her baby.

'I was sick, Linc. I couldn't come back.' The words were faint, almost whispered, and his head jerked upwards from its focus on their intertwined fingers.

This was where he could make it easy on her and tell her he'd read her notes. But he didn't want to, he wanted to hear her say the words. 'What do you mean, you were sick?'

She shook her head, a watery sheen across her eyes. She gave his hand a little squeeze. Why did she have to tell him here? In this hospital canteen in the middle of the night? Why couldn't they be sitting somewhere in private, looking out over that wonderful cove?

She took a deep breath. 'I had breast cancer.' There, she'd said it. The words that no one liked to say out loud. The words that people normally whispered around about her.

His face didn't change. And she almost wished she hadn't told him. But she had to. She had to make him understand why this baby was so important to her. Why this baby was her only chance.

Then he did it. The one thing he used to do all the time. He rubbed his thumb lightly along the palm of her hand. The softest of touches. The most delicate of touches. Like he'd used to do when they'd had a stressful day on the boat. When there had been too many patients and not enough staff. When they hadn't been able to treat everyone they'd wanted to. When patients had got really sick, and some had even died.

His face was serious now. And in amongst all this madness—the press pack outside, the security staff everywhere, him looking after the First Daughter—she knew she had made the right decision. Linc was one of the good guys. He would help her. She could feel it.

He cleared his throat. 'Why didn't you tell me?'

She sighed. 'How could I tell you that, Linc? I went home for a holiday. I had the first proper shower in months and felt a lump under my breast. And I'd no idea how long it had been there. Two days later I had a fine-needle biopsy that told me I had cancer.' Her finger reached up and twiddled one of her long red strands of hair, her other hand still intertwined with his. 'I'd only known you six months. You were on a boat on the Amazon, thousands of miles away. How could I phone and tell you I had cancer and needed treatment?' She flung her arms in the air in an act of exasperation. 'Let's face it, Linc, I was your yearly summer fling.'

He winced at the harshness of her words. So she *had* heard about his reputation. He'd always hoped no one had mentioned that fact that each year he'd had an affair with a colleague on the boat. He wanted to shout out, *Of course you should have told me!* But he understood the futility of the answer. Amy was right. They had only known each other a few months. And life on the Amazon was all-consuming—you lived in each other's pockets and had very little time off. Everything was about the work and the people. Lots of medics had relationships on the Amazon boats, but when they got back to normal life the relationships tended to fall apart as they found they had nothing in common any more. What would he have done if she'd told him? Left the boat? Gone to find her? Would she even have wanted him there?

His anger from earlier felt misplaced. If the shoe had been on the other foot and he was one who had been sick, would he have told Amy?

He wasn't sure and he hated to admit that. Would he really have wanted to put that responsibility onto her? He would have hated it if she'd felt obliged to help him out of an innate sense of duty, especially when he didn't know how she felt about him.

His lips tightened and he gave her hand another squeeze. 'So what happened, Amy?' Although he couldn't help it, his eyes went automatically to her breasts. The professional in him knew better than that. But the personal element kept distracting him. He'd had his hands all over those beautiful breasts. And as for the pink rosy nipples…

He saw her shift uncomfortably, her hands rising to her chest. 'I had a mastectomy on one side.' The words were simple, but they masked how they made her feel. What would Linc think of her body shape now if he could see it? The two of them had danced naked around his little cabin and the memories of that now could make her cry. She could never do that now. Never feel that confident in her body.

'Really?' Now he couldn't avert his eyes because, if she'd had a mastectomy, it wasn't apparent. And he'd only flicked over the treatment plan—he hadn't read it in detail. 'Did you have a reconstruction?'

Her hands self-consciously stayed where they were. And under them she could feel the long-term results of her disease—full, soft breast on one side and a gap on the other side, currently filled with a pale pink silicone breast enhancer. 'I meant to but, no, not yet,' she murmured.

His brow crinkled. 'So what stopped you?' She was a beautiful young woman. It seemed strange she hadn't completed her treatment and moved on to the next part of her life. Most young women he'd ever met, and it was only a few, who'd had breast cancer had had some kind of reconstruction done at a later date.

Amy ran her hands over her baby bulge. 'I haven't really had time to get around to it. But it's in my plans.'

Lincoln's eyes fell again to her stomach. His brain was working overtime, trying to remember dates. If she'd had a cancer diagnosis just after leaving the boat, then undergone surgery and treatment, could she have had five years cancer-free before falling pregnant?

No. It didn't add up. According to his calculations she just fell short. Lots of physicians were wary about the effect pregnancy hormones could have on cancer cells. Was it really wise for her to be pregnant? What age was Amy? Thirty-two? She could have waited another year before doing this. Had someone pushed her into it?

He remembered the empty next-of-kin box in her notes and tried to pull his professional head back into place. 'Do you have a husband? A boyfriend I can call for you?'

She shook her head. 'It's just me, Linc.'

The enormity of the words hit him. She was alone. And while one part of his heart wanted to suddenly break into song, he immediately felt angry. Who had left a woman like this, alone and pregnant, after she'd already been through breast cancer?

He stood up, his voice rising in pitch, 'What do you mean, you're alone? Where's the baby's father? Why isn't he here with you?'

'It's just me,' she repeated, the words almost whispered. Most days she was fine with this. Most days she was confident and sure of herself. Confident in her abilities to be a single parent and to stay on top of her previous diagnosis. But sometimes, just sometimes, particularly when someone made a comment around her, she realised the enormity of the task in front of her. If this baby was born prematurely then she might have to deal with a whole host of complications. How would she feel then? Would she still feel confident in her abilities?

Then there was Linc, standing in front of her and right now looking like her knight in shining armour. But what if he refused to help? What if, over the last six years, he'd met someone, fallen

in love and now had a whole host of other responsibilities that meant he wouldn't be comfortable
helping her?

She raised her eyes to meet his. 'What about
you, Linc? Are you on your own, or are you playing happy families somewhere with a wife and
a houseful of kids? Is there a real Mrs Adams?'

She held her breath. Why was this answer so
important?

Linc looked momentarily thrown by the question. A flickering parade of a variety of short-
term lovers passed in the blink of an eye, ending
with an image of an irate brunette. He hesitated
then answered, 'No. There's no Mrs Adams. It's
just me.'

Amy could almost feel the relief flush over her
body. Then curiosity got the better of her. 'So
what happened? Did the playboy never meet his
match? Haven't you met Miss Right?'

The words hung in the air. She saw a flash of
something in his eyes—was it annoyance? Linc
looked uncomfortable, as if he didn't know how
to answer that question.

'I thought I had. I was engaged a few years ago
to girl called Polly, a pharmaceutical rep. We

even had the wedding planned. But in the end it just didn't feel right. So I had to end it.' He gave a rueful smile. 'And it wasn't pretty.'

Amy sat back in her chair. 'What happened?' She was fighting the horrible sensation that was creeping across her skin. Lincoln had been engaged. It made her feel sick.

'I called it off just after we'd paid the deposit for the reception, the photographer and the cake. I came home to find my apartment cleared out and samples of wedding cake smeared into my suits.'

Amy's eyes widened. 'Wow. I guess you weren't popular, then. The playboy struck out.'

He paused, stopping his mouth from saying the first words that came into his brain.

Amy Carson had shaken him to the core. He'd been a fool, with a playboy reputation that he hadn't ever meant to earn. It had only been when she'd never come back that he'd realised how special she'd been.

She was joking, he could tell by her tone, but the playboy jibe had cut deeper than he liked, leaving him feeling distinctly ill at ease. It was too late at night for conversations like these. He looked at the half-eaten plate of food in front of her. 'Do you want anything else?'

She shook her head and rubbed her hands across her stomach. 'I don't think I've got room for any more. Junior takes up more space in here than you think.'

'Junior?' He raised his eyebrow at her. 'That's what you're calling your baby?'

She shrugged her shoulders. 'Well, I know I'm having a boy and I have picked a name, but I want to wait until he's here before I share it. So for the moment he's Junior.'

Lincoln's brow furrowed. 'I'm kind of surprised you found out what you were having. I would have taken you for a surprise kind of girl. We used to call you Miss Unpredictable on the boat.'

'You did?' Her eyes widened. She'd never heard the nickname before and, what's worse, it suited her—or at least it used to. She couldn't afford to be unpredictable any more. Amy's lips tightened. 'I wanted to plan ahead. Decorate the room for the baby coming, pick him some clothes, buy a stroller.' She stared off into the distance. 'I always thought I'd want it to be a surprise too, but when the time came I had to have a few detailed scans and because I work in a hospital where they do maternity care I'm used to looking at scans— it was kind of hard to hide the obvious.'

Lincoln's brow furrowed. 'Why did you need detailed scans? Did they suspect a problem?' He hadn't seen anything in her notes that would have made him think there was something wrong with the baby.

Amy lifted her eyes to meet his and for the first time tonight he noticed how heavy they were. She was exhausted. She leaned her chin on her hands. 'No. No problem. It's just that the clinic where I had my IVF wanted to keep a close eye on me. My embryos had been frozen for five years and then there was a problem…'

'What problem?'

She sighed. 'I had been planning on using the embryos but I was going to wait until I was five years clear of disease and I'd had my reconstruction surgery.'

'So what happened?'

'The storage facilities were compromised.' She lifted her hands. 'We live on the San Andreas fault. Earthquakes are an occupational hazard.'

'An earthquake? Surely any IVF storage facility made plans for that?'

'Even the best plans can be compromised. The DEWAR tank containing my embryos developed a slow liquid nitrogen leak. Some of my embryos perished in the thawing process but I was lucky. A few good-quality embryos survived and I had to make a decision quickly about what I wanted to do.'

He gestured towards her stomach. 'So you went ahead with implantation before you were ready?'

'I had to, Lincoln. This was my only chance to have a child of my own.' She leaned back in her chair again. Was it the conversation making her uncomfortable or was it something else? That was the third time she'd shifted position in as many minutes. She shrugged her shoulders, 'I'm not really that different from lots of other people who find themselves pregnant before they'd planned to be.'

He shook his head, 'But you are different, Amy. You've got a completely different set of circumstances. You had a disease that threatened your life. This baby didn't materialise out of thin air—or as the result of failed contraception.'

'I know that, Linc.' Her eyes clouded over. 'You can't possibly understand.' Her voice lowered. 'You can't possibly know how it feels to have the world whipped out from under your feet. One minute you think you have your whole life to plan a family, to choose when you have it and with whom. Then the next minute you're asked hard questions and you've got about two minutes to make up your mind—because they have to schedule surgery for you and a whole plan of chemotherapy. And in the meantime the clock is ticking because every second you delay could be the second that means your cancer grows and spreads somewhere it shouldn't. The second that could be the difference between life and death for you.'

Lincoln drew in a deep breath. She was tired, he knew she was tired. It was two o'clock in the morning and she was sitting in a strange place, with symptoms that could affect her baby, and with someone she hadn't seen in six years. So why did it feel as if someone had just fastened a thick fist around his heart and squeezed tightly? Why did the heart-wrenching words she'd just said make him feel as if his stomach had just turned inside out?

She fixed her green eyes on his. 'This was it for me, Linc. This was my only chance to have a baby of my own—and even then there was no guarantee that the embryo would take. But I had to try. I couldn't give up that one chance just because the timing wasn't perfect.'

'And the father?' It was a loaded question, and the one he was most interested in.

She gave a rueful smile. 'I didn't have a significant other when I was diagnosed with breast cancer and I was advised to freeze embryos instead of eggs. So I used a sperm donor. What else could I do?'

A sperm donor. An anonymous man who would never know he was the father of Amy's baby. Did that make him feel better or worse?

The words were echoing in his head. *She didn't have a significant other when she was diagnosed.* But she could have. She could have had him.

He looked down. The plate of pancakes and scrambled eggs that had seemed so appetising ten minutes ago now seemed to turn his stomach. The last time he'd felt like this he'd been out

on the town with his friends and had had no idea
how or when he'd got home.

Amy shivered. The hairs on her arms were
standing on end. How stupid of him. He was
sitting here in theatre scrubs and a white coat
and all she had on was a hospital gown. He was
an idiot. He pushed his chair back. 'Come on,'
he said as he walked around the table and put
his arm around her shoulders. 'You're cold. It's
time I tucked you into that extremely comfortable
hospital gurney and let you get some rest again.'

She rolled her eyes and nodded as she stood
up next to him, her small frame fitting perfectly
under his arm.

Then something struck him. Amy was wrong.
He did know how it felt to have the world whipped
out from under your feet.

It had happened to him six years before when
she'd gone on holiday and had never come back.

CHAPTER FOUR

LINCOLN glanced at his watch as he strode down the darkened corridor. Twenty-four hours later and he still hadn't left this place. Sleep was apparently for the faint-hearted. At least that's what Val, the nurse practitioner, had told him when she wakened him at 2:00 a.m. to come and help with baby Esther.

Jennifer Taylor was really struggling with breastfeeding. Esther, on the other hand, had taken to cup feeding like a duck to water. She was already sleeping for two-hour stretches, but still showed no interest in latching onto her tear-filled mother.

Lincoln knew that the next few days were crucial in helping establish the feeding and that mother-baby bond. There was also the small issue of the world's press. They had developed a persistent interest in how the premature First Baby was being fed. There was no way he was going to say that even though the First Lady had attempted to breastfeed, it had so far been unsuccessful. What kind of message was that to send? And more importantly how would that make Jennifer feel? If people knew that the First Lady had chosen to breastfeed her baby, it could encourage other expectant mothers to do the same. This was a chance to try and influence other people to give their baby the best start in life.

Then there was the matter of Amy. And how he felt about her being here.

In one way, he was relieved he'd finally seen her again. But circumstances for both him and her weren't great. Had she really just come looking for him again to be her baby's doctor? Or could there be something else?

There was no getting away from the fact she was pregnant, had pre-eclampsia, and in all likelihood would deliver this baby early. But deep down Lincoln really wanted to believe there was more to this. More than just the fact he was a good doctor.

He stopped at the door to the side-room and pushed it gently open. 3:00 a.m. and Amy was sleeping soundly on her side with the arm with the blood-pressure cuff attached lying above the covers. The soft hum of the cuff starting to inflate began and Amy started.

'Damn cuff,' she muttered under her breath.

Lincoln smiled and sat down on the chair next to her bed. She was definitely a restless sleeper. Her brow furrowed and her nose twitched as she lay against the pillows, her long red curls spilling over the covers.

He almost felt guilty watching her like this. But he hadn't had much of a chance to talk to her today and she'd been moved from the E.R. to one of the ward side-rooms for monitoring.

Her eyelids flickered open as the cuff tightened on her arm. 'Linc?' she whispered, peering at him through sleep-filled eyes.

He leaned forward and touched her arm. 'Hi, Amy.'

She didn't move, didn't seem surprised to see him. Instead, she seemed to snuggle even closer into the pillows, as if she was sinking into a dreamlike state. 'Hi, yourself,' she murmured as a smile danced across her lips. 'Did you bring food?'

He blinked and held up his empty hands remorsefully.

'No, sorry.' His eyes flickered around the room to the empty bed table and locker. Amy didn't know anyone here. She wouldn't have had any visitors today. No one to bring her grapes or magazines or the occasional bar of chocolate. Why hadn't he thought ahead? 'Do you want me to go and get you something?'

She grimaced as the cuff reached its tightest point, shifting onto her back. 'No, it's fine really. Just wishful thinking perhaps.'

He smiled and leaned forward. 'Wishful thinking about what?'

She ran her tongue along her bottom lip and shrugged her shoulders. 'That when the hero finally appears he usually brings the sleeping princess some gifts. I was kinda hoping for cookies.'

'So now I'm the hero?'

'You were in my dream…' Her voice trailed off, as if she hadn't really thought about what she was saying. Her eyes fixed on his, which were fixed on the monitor at her side. The thoughts of a medic were written all over his face. So much for dreaming.

'David started me on some anti-hypertensives today.'

He pulled his eyes from the monitor screen—conscious of the fact she'd been watching him. 'And how do you feel?'

He knew better than to rely on readings from instruments when a patient could tell you exactly what you needed to know.

Amy gave a sigh of relief as the cuff released then propped herself up in the bed. She pushed her hair out of her eyes, tucking it behind her ears.

Lincoln fisted his hands, resisting the urge to do it for her.

'Crabbit.'

'What?' That got his attention. *Miss Unpredictable.*

She gave him a wicked smile. 'Crabbit—that's how I feel. I could cheerfully take that blood-pressure monitor and lob it out the nearest window.'

He gave a rueful smile. 'It is kind of noisy.'

'It's not the noise—it's the discomfort. Every time I think I'm about to fall asleep the damn thing goes off again.' She narrowed her eyes. 'I thought hospitals were supposed to be places of rest, Dr Adams?'

'No chance,' he muttered, sagging back in the armchair, his legs and arms flopping in exhaustion.

She raised her eyebrow. 'No rest for the wicked?'

He shook his head. 'I don't know about the wicked but there's definitely no rest for me. I keep snatching a few hours here and there, but I feel as if I'm walking about this place in a trance.'

Amy nodded slowly. It was always like this for a doctor on call. As soon as their head rested on the pillow, their pager would go off again. By the end of their shift they looked like death warmed over.

Although still one of the best-looking men she'd ever laid eyes on, Lincoln looked tired. Bags hung under his eyes, and the little lines surrounding them seemed deeper—more ingrained.

She was angry with herself. Had she forgotten the amount of responsibility he had right now? He must be stressed up to his eyeballs, and her presence here couldn't be helping.

She felt a surge in her chest. Her heartbeat started to quicken. Lincoln was looking tired and vulnerable, but sexy as hell. He was watching her through half-shut lids and it was sending tingling sensations along her skin. Why had she come to find him? Was this only about safeguarding her baby? Or was this about something else?

In the whole six years since she'd left the boat she'd never met anyone else like him. No one else had had the same effect on her that he'd had. And it wasn't just the sexual attraction. It was the friendship, the conversation and the flirting. And she'd missed it. She'd missed it all.

There was no one else about. It was just the two of them. Maybe for five minutes she could forget about things. She could forget that she'd had breast cancer. She could forget about the problems with her pregnancy. She could just be Amy. And he could just be Linc.

She pulled the cuff from her arm.

Lincoln watched as she lifted the covers and slid her legs to the side of the bed, turning to face him. Long, slim, white legs with only the tiniest bit of oedema around her ankles. And red-painted toenails with tiny silver stars.

He'd forgotten about that. He'd forgotten that she loved nail art and although, as a nurse, she couldn't have it on her fingernails, he'd never seen her toenails without it.

'Nice stars,' he murmured, his eyes fixated on her toes. She slid forward to the edge of the bed, the loose T-shirt she was wearing hitching up around her hips and sliding down one of her shoulders. The movement gave him the tiniest glimpse of bright pink panties. The lights in the room were dimmed—to let her sleep whilst still being observed by the nursing staff. Her tangled red hair was loose around her shoulders, creating a perfect frame for her white skin and dark green eyes. Something had changed. Something was different.

His breath hitched in his throat. It was how she was looking at him. Her gaze was intent and he heard her take a deep breath and let the air out slowly through her pink lips. For the first time since he'd met her two days ago she didn't seem afraid. She didn't seem worried. She seemed strong and self-confident.

Her hand reached over and took his. 'So, Lincoln...' Her voice was low, husky. 'If you're so tired, what are you doing here in the middle of the night, visiting me?'

He heard the words, but was too captivated by the picture in front of him to answer. A smile appeared on her lips and she turned his hand over in hers, running her fingertips lightly across his knuckles then across his palm. Did she know what she was doing?

She moved his hand towards her body and rested it firmly on her hip. Yes, she knew exactly what she was doing. Amy lifted her hands to his head, running her fingers through his tousled hair. He let out a groan, his other hand automatically lifting to cradle her other hip. He closed his eyes as her fingers trailed over the top of his head and down towards his neck.

The sensations igniting within him were spurred by memories of the past. Six years he'd waited for this. Six years he'd waited to have her in his arms again. He ignored the tiny red flags in his brain. The ones that tried to make him think rationally. Right now he didn't care about professional boundaries. Amy wasn't his patient—and never would be. Her touch was like a drug. His sleep-deprived brain was addicted. His head and neck were on fire underneath her fingertips and he wanted more, he wanted to be closer.

It was instinct. Pure instinct. He heard her feet touch the floor in front of him and he pulled her towards him, lifting his head as she bent hers to meet his.

There was nothing unsure or unconfident about this kiss. Her lips met his, full and plump, kissing him as if her life depended on it. His lips parted as her tongue entered his mouth and he pulled her closer. He ignored the extended abdomen and pushed his hands up the length of her back and into her tangled hair.

Ringlets. Little spirals. That's what he felt. On a lazy day he would have lain next to her in the bed, pushing his fingers gently into her hair, teasing the curls. Tonight he just wanted to touch her hair. Mess it up. Feel it between his fingers again. Remember everything about what it felt like to touch.

And her skin. He wanted to feel her soft, smooth skin. His hand fell to her bare shoulder, running along the curve of her neck, across her delicate bones and back again to the base of her neck, where his fingers danced lightly across her skin again. She gasped, her legs wobbling, her lips releasing from his and her eyes catching his in the dim light. 'Oh, Linc,' she groaned, 'you *know* what that does to me.'

And he was there. Caught in this moment. Mesmerised by the woman before him. His hands curved around her back, sliding under her T-shirt, his fingertips dancing up and down her spine like butterfly wings. His lips touched her ear, his voice deep with desire. 'I remember *exactly* what this does for you.'

Amy tipped her head back, revealing the pale skin on her neck as he bent his head towards her. This was just like the dream she'd had. This was exactly what Lincoln had been doing to her. Only this time it wasn't in her imagination. It was real. She could feel him. She could smell him. She could *taste* him.

And nothing tasted as good as this.

Well, maybe almost nothing.

Her hands dipped lower. He was still wearing the hospital-issue scrubs. The lightest, flimsiest material in the world. She could feel him pressing against her. But it wasn't enough. She wanted to touch him.

Her hands slid beneath the thin material, to what she imagined was his trademark white jersey boxers underneath. A surge of pleasure swept through her as she felt his back stiffen and his breath catch as she touched him. Running her fingers up and down his length. When had the last time been she'd felt this much in control? When had the last time been she'd had any sort of sexual encounter? Had even thought of sex?

This was exactly how she remembered it. Every pleasurable second.

His hands swept around from her back towards her breasts. Towards her *breast*. And she stopped. Her heart beat furiously against her chest. Panic overtook her.

She'd been so busy thinking about other things, she'd forgotten about this. She'd forgotten about the fact she was no longer a whole woman. Her hands jerked back from where she'd been holding him. Back to her breasts. Back to her *breast*.

Lincoln froze, feeling her instant stiffening and her pull away from him. What was wrong? He didn't want this to stop. He didn't want this to stop at all.

'Amy?'

He lifted his head from her neck and pulled back, watching her in the dim light. She looked stricken and her cheeks were tinged with pink. She was embarrassed? Why on earth would she be…?

Then it hit him like a blow to the head as he realised how her hands were positioned. He lifted his finger to her pale cheek and stroked it gently as a slow, silent tear slipped down it.

He moved forward, this time to sit alongside her at the edge of the bed and put his arm around her shoulders. She was trembling.

'I'm sorry,' he whispered, 'I didn't think. I just acted on instinct.' He pulled her closer and dropped a kiss on her head as she rested it against his shoulder. 'But you should know, Amy, that it doesn't matter to me.'

He could hear her breathing, ragged and uneven. So he held her closer, wrapping both arms around her. His mind was whirling. Was this his fault? Had he taken advantage of her?

No. He didn't think so. She'd seemed sure. Confident about what she was doing.

Her hand reached over and squeezed his. 'I wasn't thinking either. I haven't been close to anyone since I had my surgery. I didn't know what to expect.'

Linc stepped in front of her, cupping her face with his hands. 'I wasn't trying to make you uncomfortable. I would never do that to you.'

She nodded. 'I know that, Linc, it's just that… I'm not comfortable with it yet. I don't feel right. I don't feel normal.' The tears were flowing freely down her cheeks now. She looked down her uneven frame. 'This just doesn't feel like me.'

Her voice was shaking as she struggled to get the words out. 'And now with everything else…'

He brushed one of the tears from her cheek. 'I know this is hard. But you're still Amy. You're still little Miss Unpredictable that I met six years ago on the Amazon.' He pointed a finger to the centre of her chest. 'I don't need to tell you this, but it's what's in here that counts—not what's outside. Look how many kids we worked with on the boat who had facial abnormalities, what did we tell them?'

She collapsed back against the bed, her head in her hands as the sobs racked her body. 'But that's just it, Linc, I feel like such a fraud. I said all those words to those kids. But now that it's me, I don't believe them, I don't believe them in here.' She prodded at her heart. 'I don't want to be like this. I want to have my body back. The one I'm comfortable in. I had my surgery planned— I even had a date set. Then this…' she pointed at her stomach '…other stuff happened and everything else had to go on hold.'

'Have you ever spoken to someone about this?' Linc's professional head was pulling into focus. This sounded like someone who hadn't really come to terms with what had happened yet.

And he was used to this. Used to dealing with patients and their families. Used to seeing women who had healthy pregnancies then, for unknown reasons, went into premature labour and often had to deal with very sick babies with a whole range of complications. The counsellor attached to his NICU in San Francisco was one of the most essential members of staff. His unit couldn't function without her.

He walked over to the bathroom and grabbed some toilet tissue, handing it to Amy and sitting back down on the bed beside her. 'I'm sure there is someone who you will be able to talk to about this.'

Amy pushed herself up on the bed and blew her nose. 'I've tried, Linc. I went to a local group.

It was all women who had breast cancer. But I just didn't fit in. There were some really strong personalities—some women were really against any type of reconstructive surgery. They thought you should embrace the fact you'd had a mastectomy and beaten the disease.' She shook her head. 'But that just wasn't me. It wasn't how I felt about things.'

Linc touched her arm. 'But there has to be more than one group. Maybe you could try another one, with different personalities?'

Her hands settled over her stomach and she raised her red-rimmed eyes to meet his. 'It's more than that. When you touched me...' Her voice faded out.

'What? When I touched you, what?' He didn't want to push, but right now it was clear that Amy needed to talk.

She buried her head in her hands again. 'It didn't feel right. When you used to touch me, I loved the feel of your hands on my breasts. This time your hands came round and I expected what I used to feel. Except this time I felt nothing. It was like a big blank. I wasn't ready for that.'

Lincoln bit his lip. 'Amy, the part of you that's

missing is important. You had a huge amount of nerve endings and fibres that just aren't there any more. So it will feel different when someone touches you.'

She lifted her hand and pressed it against her absent breast. 'But I didn't know it would feel like *this*.'

Linc lifted his hand. A loose curl was dangling in front of her face and he brushed it aside, tucking it behind her ear. He gave her a little smile. 'Maybe it's time to relearn things. Maybe you just have to take it slow.'

Amy's hands fell to her extended abdomen. 'I just feel as if there's so much going on right now.' Her hands stroked up and down her bump. 'I don't know if I can do all this at once. I'm so worried about the baby. My blood pressure isn't getting any better and I'm worried about an early delivery. David said he would review me again in the morning, but I can already tell that the symptoms aren't getting any better.'

Lincoln tucked his arm back around her shoulders. 'Don't focus on the bad, focus on the good. Your symptoms haven't got any worse, that's what's most important here.'

She nodded and leaned her head against his shoulder again. 'I know that, but I still can't help worrying.' She reached over and placed her palm on his chest. 'And it doesn't help that the best neonatologist in the world still hasn't told me if he'll look after my baby.'

Lincoln threaded his fingers through hers. 'Amy, of course I'll look after your baby. That was never in any doubt.'

'Promise?'

'Promise.' He stood up, straightening his scrubs and bent forward, lifting the covers and sweeping her legs back up onto the bed. He glanced at his watch. 'Now, Ms Carson, you should be getting some rest.' He picked up the discarded blood-pressure cuff and fastened it back onto her arm. He raised one eyebrow at her. 'Keep it on— doctor's orders. And I'll come back and see you in the morning while David is here.'

Then, just when it seemed he'd reverted back to doctor mode, he stopped and looked at her. She could see the dark blue rims around his eyes. He was watching her. And it seemed as if there were a million things going on his brain, a million things still unsaid. 'Just tell me what you want from me.'

She opened her mouth. She couldn't say what she wanted to. She couldn't say that she wished she could turn back the clock six years and pick up the phone to call him. She said the easiest thing that came to mind. 'I need you to be my friend right now, Linc.' The air deflated from her lungs. This was so *not* what she wanted to say. But anything else right now just seemed too hard.

His lips turned upwards, but the smile was almost...disappointed. The heat and passion that had been in his eyes earlier had vanished. Now his eyes seemed cool, resigned to their fate. He lifted his hand and his finger stroked the side of her cheek. 'Night-night, Amy.'

She turned on her side and snuggled under the covers. 'Night-night, Linc.'

He headed towards the door, pulling it gently shut behind him before taking a few strides down the corridor.

He stopped for a second and leaned against the concrete wall. The coolness spread through his thin scrubs to his heated skin. What was he doing? No—what had he just *done*? His brain

was spinning. Should he have professional boundaries with Amy if he was going to take care of
her baby?

Did that mean he should step away from her
completely? Let some other doctor take care her
and her imminent arrival?

He banged his head on the wall. Maybe that
would knock some sense into him. Ever since
he'd set eyes on her again, she had been all he
could think about. Every time he was in the same
room as her he just wanted to touch her.

Now he'd just agreed to look after her baby.

But how could he have said no? How could
anyone in his position have said no?

Right now Amy needed him. But not in the way
he wanted. She wanted to be friends. Friends?
Could he do that?

The blood was still coursing through his veins
from her earlier touches. The cool concrete wall
was doing nothing to soothe the heat emanating
from his skin.

He glanced at his watch again. The one thing
that Lincoln really needed right now was a good
night's sleep. A chance to clear his head and sort
out his thoughts. He glanced back towards the

dim light filtering out from under her door. But what were the chances of that?

Amy huddled under the covers as the damn cuff started to inflate again. Her body couldn't stop trembling.

She'd kissed him. She'd kissed Linc again. And it had been every bit as wonderful as she'd imagined it to be.

She'd touched him. She'd felt the strong muscular planes of his body under her fingertips.

The tears started to fall again on her already damp pillow. And he'd touched her. And said it didn't matter to him. He hadn't run screaming from the room because she'd had a mastectomy. He hadn't cared that she wasn't a whole woman any more. He didn't even seem to care that she was carrying an anonymous donor's baby.

But did he mean any of it? Because he might have touched her—brushed against her almost—but he hadn't *seen* her.

Lincoln had always been a gentleman. He'd always been a man with a good heart. Was he taking pity on her because of her current predicament?

Or could he really look at her as a real woman?

Amy pulled the covers up around her head. Maybe if she didn't think about this stuff right now it would go away. Maybe this was all just a bad dream and she would wake up in the morning, six years in the past, in her own apartment, ready to return from her holiday to the Amazon aid boat and her hot new doctor friend.

If only…

Lincoln had told her to focus on the good things. Not to think about the bad. She started to count them off in her head. So far, all her cancer check-ups had been clear. In a few months' time she'd reach the golden 'five years cancer-free'. She was being looked after by one of the best obstetricians in the country. There. Two already. This wasn't so difficult.

The finest neonatologist she knew had agreed to look after her baby. She'd just had the most erotic kiss she'd experienced in six years. She'd just felt like a woman again for the first time in six years.

Her mind drifted. Dark tousled hair. Electric blue eyes with a dark blue rim. Broad shoulders and firm, hard pecs.

Amy groaned and pulled the pillow over her head.

Linc. All about Linc. This clearly wasn't working.

'Dr Adams, a word, please.'

Lincoln glanced over his shoulder and heaved a huge sigh. James Turner was standing behind him with his arms folded tightly across his chest. He was quite possibly the last person Linc wanted to see right now. His temper was short and his nerves frayed. Not to mention there wasn't a single thought in his head that currently made sense.

'What word do you want, Mr Turner? How about "busy", "hungry" or "tired"? I'll let you pick.' He closed the notes he was writing in and stood up, sliding them back into the filing cabinet.

James's face remained fixed. 'She has to go.'

Lincoln turned to face him. 'Who has to go?' It was late, his brain was buzzing and he had about ten other things to do right now.

'Your friend Amy Carson. She fainted and now she's better. It's time for her to go home.'

'Really?' Lincoln raised his eyebrow as he tried

to control his temper at the sheer cheek of the man. 'And what makes you think that's your decision?'

'I'm in charge of the security for the First Lady. Everything around here is my decision. And I don't make compromises.'

Lincoln stepped forward until he was only inches from James's face. 'I don't like what you're inferring.'

'I don't care.'

'Well, in that case show me your medical degree, *Mr* Turner. Because unless you've got one, I think you'll find this is a medical decision—not a security decision.'

James scowled at him and shook his head. 'Don't make this into something it's not, Dr Adams. This isn't a medical decision, this is personal. Your lady friend turned up here to see you and blagged her way in. She shouldn't be here and she's compromising the safety of the First Lady and the First Daughter, so she has to go.'

Lincoln felt a red mist start to descend over his eyes. He jerked open the door of the filing cabinet and pulled Amy's notes back out. He didn't need to flick through them—by this point he knew them off by heart. 'Let's see. Ms Carson has protein in her urine, her blood pressure is above normal and pitting oedema is evident in her legs and abdomen. She is showing classic signs of preeclampsia.' He slammed the notes shut. 'She is at risk. Her baby is at risk. She didn't blag her way in here, Mr Turner, she's been admitted to this hospital because she's sick.'

'She can't be sick here, it's a security risk.'

'Don't be so ridiculous. Is there a pecking order here? Did I imagine it or did the doctors here tell me that you pulled up outside with the First Lady in labour, with no warning, no prior planning? Did you get turned away? Is the First Lady's baby more important than Ms Carson's? Is that the way things have become in the US?'

James pulled a stick of gum from his pocket and popped it in his mouth. 'So transfer her.'

'What?'

'Transfer her somewhere else. They can look after her.'

The man was inhumane. Linc wondered if he was actually a machine. James was immune to anger—he obviously enraged everyone he came into contact with. It was time for a new angle.

Lincoln took a deep breath and leaned against the filing cabinet. 'Fine. But if she goes, I go. I've agreed to be her neonatologist. I need to be there when she delivers. And to be frank, I don't care where that is. Make the arrangements, Mr Turner, let me know when we leave.' He turned away and started walking down the corridor. He got six strides before he heard the voice behind him.

'You can't be serious.'

Linc turned back towards the incredulous voice. James had followed him along the corridor. 'You're going to walk away from the First Lady? It's the best publicity you'll ever get,' he sneered.

Linc smiled. 'And if you've done your homework, Mr Turner, you'll know that I'm the doctor that doesn't like publicity and doesn't want it.' He tilted his chin. 'So what's it to be, Mr Turner? Because I'm too tired to fight with you about it. Do you want to arrange the transfer or not?'

James hesitated for a second. Lincoln could see a tiny muscle twitching under his eye. He was furious and Lincoln couldn't have cared less.

He let out a sigh. 'Okay, she can stay.'

'Finally, something we agree on.' And before he could answer Lincoln walked into the on-call room and slammed the door.

CHAPTER FIVE

DAVID stood at the bottom of the bed, his forehead puckered with a frown. 'Can you recheck her blood pressure manually, please?' He nodded to one of the nearby nurses.

He scribbled something in the notes before giving Amy a little smile. 'I'm a bit of a traditionalist.' He gestured towards the monitor. 'Some studies have shown that automated methods can underestimate systolic blood pressure, so I like it double-checked with a mercury sphygmomanometer. Trouble is, in the world of technology they can be hard to find these days.

He glanced back at Amy. 'Yesterday's blood results were fine, but I want to see what today's are like.' He lifted the bed covers and examined her legs and ankles, before unhooking the stethoscope from around his neck. 'Can I take a listen to your chest, please?'

Amy nodded and leaned forward as he lifted

her T-shirt, placing his cool stethoscope on her skin. 'Take a deep breath, please.'

Amy breathed in and out slowly as the stethoscope moved from under her breast to her back.

The nurse appeared back at the door with a manual sphygmomanometer in her hand. She took a few seconds to wind it around Amy's arm before inflating the cuff then placing the stethoscope inside her elbow. A few seconds passed before she released the valve and turned to David. 'Same as the machine. One hundred and fifty over one hundred.'

David gave a sigh and stood back.

Lincoln appeared at the door. 'Knock, knock.' He walked into the room, 'How are things, David?

'Your friend Ms Carson is proving quite an enigma.' He pointed at her chart. 'Her blood pressure is still borderline despite her being started on anti-hypertensives yesterday. There's still some protein in her urine. But her lungs are clear and her peripheral oedema seems to be improving.'

He turned back to Amy. 'Any other symptoms?'

She shook her head.

'Then we have a problem.'

'What?' Lincoln's head shot upwards. 'What do you mean, there's a problem?' He moved over to the side of the bed next to Amy.

David gave a little smile. 'In normal circumstances, at this stage, I would probably ask Amy to rest at home and come into the hospital every day to be monitored.'

Lincoln's brow wrinkled. 'I don't understand. What's the problem?'

David gave his shoulders a little shrug. 'It's my understanding that Amy doesn't stay around here. I can't exactly send her home and ask her to come in every day for monitoring if she lives four hours away.'

Amy nodded her head in relief. Thank goodness. For a second there her heart had been in her mouth—she'd wondered what David was about to say.

'But isn't it best she stays here if she's at risk of pre-eclampsia?' Lincoln looked agitated.

David shook his head. 'Not at this stage. Her symptoms aren't severe. Her blood pressure is still borderline and we've started her on some treatment.' He gave Amy a serious look. 'However, you still require careful assessment, daily blood and urine tests, and blood pressure monitoring. We also need to keep a close eye on you to ensure you don't develop any other symptoms.'

Amy gave him a smile. 'So what do you suggest, Dr Fairgreaves?'

'I suggest I give you a little more freedom.'

Amy's smile broadened. 'That sounds good.'

David gave a final glance at his chart. 'For the moment I'm going to recommend your blood pressure is monitored four-hourly. I'm still recommending rest for you. But I don't think a gentle walk outside in the fresh air will cause you any problems.' He gave Lincoln a little nod. 'Providing, of course, you have some supervision.'

Lincoln nodded his head in agreement. 'I think I can manage that.'

'I thought you might.' David touched Amy's shoulder. 'I'll come back and review things later once your blood test results are available. In the meantime, enjoy the sunshine.'

David turned and walked out the door, leaving Lincoln and Amy staring at each other.

'I don't know if I'm happy about this.'

'What's wrong, Linc, scared to take a girl to lunch?'

Linc folded his arms across his chest. 'You make that sound like a challenge.'

'It was. I know you won't be able to resist. You were always a sucker for a challenge.'

His eyes went over to the nearest window. In the last seventy-two hours all he'd seen of Pelican Cove had been the inside of this hospital. White walls and pale grey floors. The thought of getting out into the sunshine and down onto the nearby beach definitely appealed. Fresh air and the smell of the ocean, just like back home at Fisherman's Wharf. He couldn't think of anything better. Amy looked as if she could do with a change of scenery too. Being hospitalised was enough to send anyone crazy. He gave her a wink. 'I have a baby to check on. I'll be back for you in an hour.'

Lincoln picked up baby Esther from the crib in NICU. She opened her pale blue eyes and scowled at him, her tongue automatically coming out and lapping. He sat down in the nearby chair and picked up her chart. 'Hungry again, little lady? How about trying to latch onto your mom?'

Val appeared at his side. 'She's still being a little madam. We're trying to get her to latch on every time she's due a feed. But she's still not managing.'

Lincoln ran his fingers over the thick dark hair on her head, checking her fontanel, laughing as her tongue came out again. 'Let's take you to Momma and see how you do.'

He went into the room next door where Jennifer was lying on her bed, staring out the window. She sat up as soon as Lincoln came in carrying her daughter.

'Hi, Dr Adams. Is my girl looking for food again?' Jennifer swung her legs out of the bed and moved over into the nursing chair, settling a pillow on her lap and holding her arms out to take Esther. She arranged Esther comfortably and lowered her nursing bra to reveal her dark nipple, and spent the next few minutes trying to get Esther to latch on. Lincoln moved over to her side. 'Would you like to try another position?'

Jennifer rolled her eyes. 'What do you suggest? I've tried the cradle hold, the cross cradle hold, the football hold and the side-lying position. If you've got any others, feel free to tell me.'

Lincoln put his hand on her shoulder in reassurance. 'I know this is hard, Jennifer, but just persevere. Every time she's due to feed, put her to the breast and eventually her sucking reflex will kick in. Look at the way she's extending her tongue. She's doing really well with the cup feeding and she's almost regained her birth weight. She's only lost a few ounces—that's really good for a premature baby.'

He watched as Esther wrinkled her nose and started to wail in frustration, one little arm escaping from her blanket and pushing upwards. 'Here,' he said, taking her from Jennifer and wrapping her firmly in the pale pink blanket again. 'Let's try again for a few more minutes and if it doesn't work, I'll go and get you some of the milk you expressed earlier.'

Jennifer nodded and sat patiently while Lincoln tried to help her latch baby Esther onto her breast. After a few false starts Esther eventually tipped her head backwards and enclosed her mouth around her mother's nipple, but only for a few seconds.

Jennifer gave an exasperated sigh. 'No one tells you it's going to be this hard.'

Lincoln nodded. 'It is hard.' His eyes had a knowing glint in them. 'And although I've had no personal experience, from what I hear, when it does work nothing can compare.' He fixed her with one of his dazzling grins.

Jennifer shook her head. 'You're an incorrigible flirt, you do know that, don't you?'

Lincoln rolled his eyes. 'Me?' He pointed at his chest in mock horror. 'Never.'

She sighed. 'You are. There should be a licence against men like you. You're all big blue eyes and movie-star smiles. The nurses around here are practically falling on their feet around you. How many nurses' numbers have you got in your phone?'

Lincoln had the good grace to look embarrassed. 'None. Well—none from Pelican Cove,' he added. 'Anyway, Val and Ruth don't give me a second glance.'

She laughed. 'That's because they know you. They've obviously developed an immunity to you. It's all those other poor souls that haven't met you before I feel sorry for.'

She looked at him carefully. 'You don't even know you're doing it, do you?'

Lincoln gave a shrug and picked up one of her apples from the nearby fruit bowl, taking a big bite through the green skin. 'I don't know what you're talking about.'

He gave her a few seconds to think, as he looked around the room. Presents for the baby had been arriving from all around the world.

'Looks like you're going to need a room just for the presents soon.'

Jennifer looked embarrassed. 'Yes, I know. They've come from everywhere. There's no way in the world I'll be able to use all of this. If I'd been in Washington, one of my aides would have taken a note of them all, so we can send thank-you notes.' She bit her bottom lip. 'But I had a bit of temper tantrum and insisted all the aides leave. And I haven't had time to even look at most of them. I'm sure I can find a good home for some of these things.' She picked up the nearest parcel, with beautifully knitted matinee jackets in white and pink. 'What about the NICU? You work in there, Lincoln, could they use some of these?'

He gave her a smile. 'I'm sure we could. San Francisco has lots of families that need some support. Our unit often has to do fundraising so all donations are gratefully received.'

Jennifer eyes swept over the room. 'I've no idea what kind of thing would be best for your unit. Do you want to give me a list?' She pointed towards the door, where the latest pile of parcels had just been delivered. 'And I'm terrified in amongst all this stuff there's going to be a present from my Great-Auntie Bertie that I'll miss, or something from my third cousin twice removed.'

Lincoln laid a gentle hand on her arm. 'Maybe it's time to relent and tell James Turner you want one of your aides back. These presents look like a full-time job.'

Jennifer frowned. 'They do, don't they.' She bent her head as she adjusted her daughter in her arms. 'And to be honest, I want to spend my time concentrating on Esther.'

'That's the way it should be.'

Jennifer looked up again. 'If there's anything you want to take in the meantime—I mean, if there's anything you think the people in Pelican Cove might need—just take it.' She waved her arm, 'It's not like I'll miss it.'

Lincoln gave a wry grin. 'Actually, there is something, but it's not what you think.'

Jennifer raised her eyebrow in interest. 'Really? Now, that sounds fascinating. What is it?'

Lincoln bent over and picked up a battered sunhat from beside the bed. 'Can I borrow this? I'm taking a friend for lunch and I think she might be a little unprepared. A sunhat would be perfect.'

A knowing smile spread over Jennifer's face. 'Would that sunhat be for a pregnant pale-skinned redhead?'

Lincoln started. 'How on earth…?'

She tapped the side of her nose. 'I'm the First Lady, Linc. I know everything.' She laughed. 'Actually, does she need some maternity clothes? I've got a whole wardrobe full that I won't need. Help yourself.' She pointed to the wardrobe in the corner of the room.

Lincoln wrinkled his nose. He hadn't even thought about clothes. And truth be told, Amy probably needed more than a sunhat. Would she be offended if he took her some of the First Lady's maternity clothes? No. He didn't think so.

He gave a little nod. 'Actually, that might just be perfect. Now, let's see if we can get Esther latched on again.'

Amy was sitting on the edge of her bed, wearing the same white smock top and maternity jeans she'd had on three days ago when she'd been admitted. Her eyes widened in shock as Lincoln burst through the door, having changed into jeans and a T-shirt, his arms jammed with clothes, which he dumped on the bed next to her.

'What on earth…?'

'Sorry I'm a bit late,' he said breathlessly. 'I was checking on the First Baby and Jennifer asked if you'd like some of her maternity clothes. She says she won't be needing them any time soon. I hope you don't mind—I said yes on your behalf. I wasn't sure if you'd brought any more clothes with you.' Lincoln held his breath. Had he just committed a huge female faux pas?

Amy turned and looked at the pile of clothes next to her, fingering the expensive fabrics of the designer clothes. 'Wow!' she whispered, as she took in the wide range of styles and colours. Her dark green eyes turned to Lincoln, who breathed a huge sigh of relief. She wasn't angry. Instead, she looked like a child in a sweetie shop. 'She said I could have all these?'

Lincoln nodded and shrugged his shoulders. 'She wanted someone else to have the use of them. She thought you were probably the same size as she is.'

Amy nodded and picked up a summer dress embroidered with tiny flowers. She held it up next to her. 'What do you think Linc?'

'Will it go with this?' He held up the battered summer hat. 'This is what I originally asked for—thought you might need it out there.' He pointed out the window at the blistering sunshine. 'Looks like we're in for a scorcher.'

Amy was rummaging through the clothes on the bed and pulled out a pale green bolero cardigan to match the summer dress. 'Perfect!' she exclaimed, before heading off to the bathroom. 'Just give me a few minutes until I get changed.'

'Take all the time you need,' murmured Lincoln at her retreating back. This was the Amy he knew. Happy and bubbling with excitement. When had the last time been he'd seen her like that?

A vision from the night before flashed in front

of his eyes. Images of a beautiful redhead with seduction in her eyes. And he quickly shook it off. This was Amy Carson—friend. Not Amy Carson—former lover. He had to keep things amicable between them. More importantly, he had to keep his mind from wandering.

Amy pushed open the bathroom door, a broad smile across her face. 'Well, Linc, what do you think? Do I look like First Lady material to you?' She swished her flouncy dress, which came to just above her knees, from side to side.

Lincoln tried to stop his mouth from falling open. Pretty as a picture. The words danced around his mind. The dress fitted perfectly, with the cardigan over her shoulders to stop her fair skin from burning and her curly red hair framing her face. His eyes fell automatically to her legs. There was only the slightest amount of oedema around her ankles. A non-medic wouldn't even notice and that was a good sign. He tossed her the sunhat. 'Here you go, don't want you getting scorched out there in the sun.'

She laughed and stuck the hat on her head. 'Have you got any food?'

'Have I got any food?' Linc let out a hearty

laugh, 'Amy, when have you *ever* known me to go anywhere without food?' He pointed to the door, where a small picnic basket sat on the floor, with a picnic blanket tucked under the handle.

'Where on earth did you get that from?'

'The kitchen staff. They love me. No, no, you don't.' He whipped the basket back up as she attempted to open the cover and peer inside. 'You don't get to look until we are sitting comfortably on the beach. *Then* you get to look.'

'If you're going to make me wait it had better be good, mister.' She folded her arms across her chest. 'How far away is the beach anyway?'

Lincoln picked up another bag he'd left at the doorway. 'Apparently about two minutes down a path at the side of the hospital. Or we can take the path at the other side and head down to the harbour. Neither is too far and you should be fine, so take your pick.'

'The beach. Definitely the beach. I can't remember the last time I smelled the ocean.' She wrinkled her nose. 'I don't think I could take the smell from the fishing boats today.'

Linc gave her a smile and extended his arm towards her. 'Then let's go.'

* * *

Nope. She wasn't imagining it. There were definitely tingles shooting up and down her arm. Her hand was tightly enclosed in his as he led her down the stone path towards the beach. It wasn't particularly steep, or treacherous, but there was something nice about holding hands. Something familiar and yet intimate at the same time.

The beach already had a number of families set up for the day, with chairs and blankets spread out across the sand, and numerous little kids running around covered in white sunscreen, carting buckets filled with sea water across the sand. Linc pulled the blanket from the under the handle of the hamper and spread it on the sand. 'Is here okay with you?' he asked.

Amy nodded and settled down on the blanket. She slipped off her sandals and buried her toes in the sand. Bliss.

She shaded her eyes from the glare of the sun, already beating down on her pale legs. Thank God she'd thought to pack some factor fifty. It was a gorgeous day, but she didn't want to end up frying in the sun. Her fingers caught the fine cotton material of her dress—the First Lady's dress—and a little smile appeared on her face.

The pale green material, dotted with tiny pink, blue and cream flowers, was gorgeous, the style perfect for her extended abdomen. She couldn't have picked a more perfect dress if she'd tried.

With the hat firmly on her head and the cardigan protecting her shoulders, she leaned back on her hands and looked out over the ocean waves. Pelican Cove was apparently renowned for its surfing and today was no exception. There were numerous surfers out on the waves, their brightly coloured boards and shorts making them easy to pick out against the deep blue ocean.

Surfing. Another thing on the list of things she'd never tried. Maybe, once her baby was here, she would give it a go.

Lincoln pulled food from the basket and began setting it out on the blanket—chunky brown bread sandwiches, a pile of fruit and some sodas. He glanced around about them, acknowledging a few smiles and waves from people he recognised. People from the hospital at the beach with their families.

He'd only been here a few days and already people were recognising him. Was Pelican Cove really that small? Or was it just that friendly?

He watched as one of the nurses walked past, hand in hand with a chubby toddler. She gave him a small smile and joined her husband on a nearby blanket. Was that what they looked like? His head flicked from side to side. Did the other people on the beach assume that they were a family? He, Amy and the bump. Lincoln swallowed the lump currently fixed in his throat. That's what they must look like—walking down the coastal path hand in hand, like a husband and wife with a baby on the way. Lincoln felt uncomfortable.

What did he want people to think? Amy had already told people that she was his wife. No one had questioned her different surname. Did they know she'd been lying? Or were they just being polite, and not asking any questions? Even Val and Ruth, the two NICU nurses he'd brought with him from San Francisco's Children's Hospital—two nurses who had known him for the last five years—hadn't asked him about his *wife*. They knew he wasn't married. So why hadn't they asked any questions?

His eyes were drawn back to Amy. There was a smile on her face as she stared towards the ocean. Jennifer Taylor had been right about them being the same size. The outfit fitted perfectly, complementing her skin tone, even down to the wide-brimmed floppy hat.

The same question kept turning over and over in his mind. Why was Amy here? Was this just about her baby? Or had something else motivated her to come? Sure, he might be a good neonatologist, he might even be a great neonatologist, but there must have been someone else she worked with that she could have trusted—trusted with the life of her baby. Was it really just him? And was it really just his skills and expertise? Or was it something else, something deeper that had brought her here? And why, right now, was his stomach clenched in the hope that it was?

He blinked. Amy hadn't moved, her eyes still fixed on the horizon. 'What are you looking at?'

She smiled and turned towards him, leaning back on one of her elbows. 'The surfers. Something on my list.'

'Your list? What's that?'

She gave a little sigh. 'When I was sick I made myself a list of things I'd like to try once I was well again. It kind of helped me get through the bad days—the days when the chemo made me sick to my stomach and I thought I'd never get out of bed again.'

Lincoln felt a chill running down his spine. The thought she'd been *that* sick, *that* unwell really unnerved him. Why hadn't someone been there for her? Why hadn't *he* been there for her?

He forced a smile onto his face. 'So, surfing's on the list?' She nodded. 'What else?'

Amy leaned over and picked up one of the sandwiches he'd unpacked. She nibbled at a corner of it. 'There are lots of things. Lots of places I want to visit. Lots of things I want to experience that I haven't tried before.' Her hands ran over her stomach and her eyes met his. 'But there's one thing on the list that I've already got.'

He nodded. It was obvious that would be on the list. She'd had to undergo a cycle of fertility drugs to stimulate her ovaries before undergoing chemo so it kind of went without saying that having kids would be on the 'want to' list.

'Anything else I can help you with?'

She raised her eyebrow at him. 'You want to help with what's on the list?' She looked a little unsure.

Lincoln nodded. 'Why not?' Was it guilt that

was making him say that? Guilt, because he hadn't been there for her when she'd been sick—even though she hadn't asked?

Amy shifted uncomfortably. 'I've never actually shown anyone my list,' she murmured.

Lincoln sat backwards. 'You actually have it—a list—written down?'

She nodded slowly, looking slightly amused. 'That's what a list is, Linc.'

This time as she watched him his smile reached his eyes, right up to the corners. Not like a few minutes ago. His eyes were twinkling. 'I thought we were talking hypothetical, I didn't realise you'd actually written it down.'

Amy bent forward and rummaged around her bag, unzipping a pocket inside and pulling out a piece of red paper, which she carefully unfolded and placed in the middle of the blanket. Lincoln leaned forward, intrigued. 'Silver pen?' He raised his eyebrows at her. 'Red and silver…' he nodded towards her feet '…just like your toes.'

Amy looked surprised and wriggled her toes in the sand. 'I hadn't even thought of that, and I was planning on changing my toes.' She wiggled them again. 'I like the stars but thought maybe midnight blue with gold stars this time.' She gave a little smile. 'More dramatic.' She waved her hand at the list. 'That's why I picked the red paper and silver pen, I wanted it to look bold, strong and powerful. Make me feel confident that I would be here to complete it.' Her voice had faded away and she was staring out at the ocean again.

Almost on instinct Lincoln reached out his hand and intertwined his fingers with hers. It was comfort, that was all. He was comforting a friend, showing support. So why did he feel the need to tell himself that inside his head?

He looked down at the paper again and gave her fingers a squeeze. 'I think I would have to be a billionaire to help you with some of the things on this list.'

Amy looked embarrassed, pink tingeing her cheeks. 'Not all of them.' She leaned her head over next to his. 'Some of these were just wishful thinking.'

He quirked one eyebrow. 'That would be the two-carat diamond ring and the trip to Monte Carlo?'

She nodded. 'Exactly.' And took another bite

of her sandwich. 'The others are much more reasonable.'

He looked at the neat, deliberate writing in
front of him. Small script, carefully written.

1. Do whatever it takes to have a family.
2. Buy a gorgeous two-carat diamond ring.
3. Go on a trip to Monte Carlo and take a
photograph outside the Hotel de Paris.
4. Learn to surf.
5. Learn to salsa.
6. Go to a *Star Trek* convention.
7. Travel on the cable cars in San Francisco.
8. Go back on the Amazon Aid Boat.
9. Join one of the social networking sites and
find old friends.
10. Learn how to crochet and crochet a baby
blanket.

A higgledy-piggledy, jumbled-up list. No priorities, just everything down there on paper.

The list looked a little well worn—rough
around the edges—as if she'd pulled it from her
bag on many occasions to read it. The red paper

was still bright and the silver ink still glistened in the sun. It should be a happy, sunny list.

But it terrified him. Because for him it was evidence that at some point Amy had actually thought she was going to *die*. She'd actually put pen to paper and written a list of things she still wanted to do. She may have said the list was to make her feel better, but Linc was no fool. People didn't just write these lists to plan ahead—they wrote these lists as things to do before they *died*. And the thought made him feel physically sick. The sun was shining in the sky above him but the hairs on his arms were standing on end—as if he'd just walked through a chilly morgue.

He tried to push his thoughts away. He couldn't think about this. It was making him question everything about himself and his relationship with Amy. They'd been skirting around things. Playing at being friends—when they both knew there was a huge potential for more.

Did he want to have a relationship with Amy? Was it sensible? What if this pregnancy made her cancer come back? How would he feel then? And what about Amy's baby? Sure, he'd considered all the clinical aspects of a premature baby, but he hadn't considered the emotional aspects. The emotional aspects of having a relationship with a woman who had another man's baby. At least he had the satisfaction of knowing that the sperm donor would never appear. But that was little consolation if something happened to Amy. Would he be prepared to take on another man's child? Could he even consider bringing a baby up himself—one he had no genetic relationship with—if something happened to Amy?

Lincoln gave himself a shake. The sun was getting to him. He tried to focus on the list again and found his heart beating furiously in his chest. He looked at the items again. It couldn't be a coincidence—the boat and finding old friends. She'd produced a list when she'd been at her lowest ebb and two of the references on it could be about him.

Okay, so the list didn't say 'Find Lincoln Adams'. But why would she want to go back to the Amazon aid boat? And why would she decide to look up old friends? Was it really all just some strange coincidence, or was he making a mountain out of a molehill?

He cleared his throat, readying himself to ask

the obvious question. 'So how many of these have you actually done?'

Amy gave up on the sandwich and picked one of peaches he'd unpacked from the picnic basket, taking a big bite and letting the juice trickle down her chin. 'From the list?' He nodded. She was licking the juice from her fingers now. 'Just two.' Her voice sounded bright and breezy, as if she were discussing the latest episode of her favourite TV drama, instead of the 'try before you die' list.

He gave a little laugh. 'You're joking, right? Two? In five years?'

A wicked smile stole across her face. 'Let's just say I had a bit of a slow start,' she teased. Her hands rubbed her bump. 'And, anyway, this is a pretty big one. It's taken up a lot of my time.'

Lincoln leaned backwards. 'Okay, I'll give you that.' He watched as she discarded the half-eaten peach, wrapping it in a napkin and pulling out a lemon cupcake. 'Do you finish anything you eat these days?'

Amy peeled the case from the cupcake, tapping her stomach again. 'Not much room in here these days. I tend to eat little and often at the moment.

I only really finish anything if it's the middle of the night—for some reason I'm always starving then.'

'So what was number two?'

'What?' Amy was lost in the land of lemon cupcake.

'You said you'd done two things on your list. Number one is obvious so what's number two?'

Amy waved her hand. 'Oh, that was easy. I made myself a page on one of those social networking sites so I could track down some old friends.'

And with that wave of her hand Lincoln felt his insides plummet. She'd done the social networking, she'd tracked down 'old friends' and he obviously wasn't among them.

He shifted uncomfortably on the sand. 'Which one did you use?'

She named the most popular one around, one where he had a page posted.

He bit his bottom lip. 'So did you track down your old friends?'

Amy picked up a can of soda. 'Yeah, loads of them. All my old classmates from high school, old nursing friends from college, and people from some of the towns we stayed in as a kid—we moved about a lot.'

Lincoln asked the next question with a sinking feeling. 'So how many friends have you got, then?'

'Eight hundred and forty-two.' Eight hundred and forty-two. As if it were the easiest thing in the world. Pushing his paltry twenty-six 'friends' into oblivion. Amy changed position on the blanket. Moving up on to her knees and digging deep in the basket, she lifted her eyes, giving him an innocent smile. 'You know I reconnected with loads of people from the Amazon aid boat—Lily Carter, John Rhodes, Frank Kelly, Gene Hunt, Milly Johnson...' She finally found what she was looking for, a bunch of green grapes, and pulled them out from the basket. 'You know—you should join.'

For the first time in years Lincoln could feel the flush of colour in his cheeks. 'I've got a page,' he murmured.

'You have?' Her eyes were that bright, sparkly way again. 'You should send me a friend request, then—I'll accept.' A definite twinkle had appeared in her eye. She was teasing him again.

He rolled over on the blanket, groaning and putting his head in his hands. 'Okay, spill. How come you never sent me a friend request? You seem to have sent...' he waved his arms in front of him, out toward the ocean '...everyone else in the world one but me.'

Amy lay down next to him, resting her head in her hands, her hat flopping over her eyes. She was so close the length of her body was touching his, her bare legs next to his, the brim of her hat almost touching his head. She looked out toward the ocean, back at the surfers, and gave a little sigh.

'It just didn't feel right.'

His face was shadowed under her hat, his blue eyes even darker than normal. 'What do you mean, *it didn't feel right*?'

She looked downwards, towards the sand that was now trickling through her fingers. 'Some people knew that I'd been sick. They might have asked me how I was doing. I didn't want you to read it online.'

Lincoln opened his mouth and then stopped. It was time to use his head, not blurt out the first thing that came to mind. He pushed the thoughts of why she hadn't sent a private message to one side—along with the quip about whether it was more appropriate for her to turn up unannounced as his pregnant wife.

'I tried to find you, you know.' His fingers delved in the sand next to hers, pulling tiny pieces of a million years ago and rubbing them between his finger and thumb.

Her hand had stopped in mid-air. Her face turned to his. 'You did?' She looked shocked—surprised—as if it was the last thing she'd expected. Her green eyes were fixed on his, as if she was holding her breath, waiting for his response.

He moved his fingers from the sand and brushed them off, putting his hand over hers. 'Of course I did.' He was looking directly at her. Something he hadn't done much in the last few days. Last time he'd looked at her like this had been when they'd kissed.

His finger touched her cheek. 'I'd just had the best six months of my life—professionally and personally—and then poof!' He blew into his fingers. 'The best thing disappeared.'

Amy could hear thudding in her ears. Was that

the sound of her heart beating? Had he really just said that?

She felt a tingling sensation across her skin. Wasn't this what she'd really wanted to hear but he'd never said? She couldn't stop staring into those eyes. Those dark blue rims were really fascinating up close. Her throat felt dry, closed up, and she swallowed nervously. 'You never said anything,' she whispered. 'I thought I was just your summer fling.'

'I think six months qualifies as a little more than a summer fling.' He blinked, breaking off his gaze and staring back down at the sand. 'And, anyway, what was there to say?' His voice sounded rueful. 'I met a gorgeous girl and spent six fantastic months in bed with her, then she disappeared.' He never lifted his head, just kept staring at the sand, his hand scooping up big piles that he let run through his fingers again.

'I contacted a few people and tried to get your number, called Human Resources—who said that you'd quit. No one else on the boat seemed to have contact details for you. So that was it.'

So that was it. It sounded so final.

'You should have told me, Amy. You should

have told me you were sick.' The sand was trickling through his fingers again. 'I don't think I can forgive the fact you didn't tell me.'

The words spun around in her head. After all this time, and all her explanations, he was still angry with her. The tiny spark that had been ignited inside her was dying. Being described as someone he'd 'spent six fantastic months in bed with' didn't fill her with inspiration. It made her feel like a sex object. Not a living, breathing human soul.

Not someone who he'd connected with. And definitely not someone he might have loved.

CHAPTER SIX

LINCOLN laid baby Esther on the scales again. Four pounds twelve ounces. A slight increase on her birth weight and she was finally feeding well. He gave Jennifer a little smile. 'Well, I think I can officially give the First Daughter a clean bill of health. There's really no reason to keep her here any longer.'

'I can go home?' The relief in Jennifer's eyes was apparent. Her husband, Charlie, had had to leave again two days ago and she was anxious to be with him.

Lincoln gave a nod.

'Do you have a preferred paediatrician in Washington? I'd like to handover to him or her before you go home.'

Jennifer gave a little nod. 'David Fairgreaves recommended someone to me—Linda Hylton. Have you heard of her?'

Lincoln nodded. 'We were paediatric residents

together. She's great and she'll look after you. I know her number so I'll give her a call this afternoon.' He rolled his eyes at the black-suited figure visible through the glass in the door. 'I'll speak to your security detail. If you go home tomorrow, I'd expect you to see Linda in the next few days.' His nose wrinkled. 'I don't suppose you're going to be able to attend a regular appointment.' He shook his head, 'Obviously not. Once I've spoken to Linda, I'll give James Turner her information and let him sort the appointment details out. Are you happy with that?'

Jennifer gave a watery smile. 'I'll just be happy to get home,' she whispered, then looked up again. 'Wait a minute—is Linda Hylton one of your love victims? Should I be careful what I say about you?'

Lincoln rolled his eyes. 'I don't know where you get these crazy ideas. I don't go out with *every* woman I meet.'

Jennifer folded her arms. 'So what was wrong with Linda Hylton?'

Lincoln smiled. 'Okay, you got me. She was dating one of my friends. Satisfied?'

Jennifer nodded her head, stifling her laugh.

'What about some help with your breastfeeding? Do you want me to arrange some support for you?'

Jennifer breathed a sigh of relief. 'Thankfully that's the one thing that I arranged a few months ago. I've got a friend who's a specialist NICU nurse in Washington—she's taking a leave of absence from her work for a few weeks and she's going to be around.'

Lincoln sat in the chair next to her, scribbling a few notes in the chart. 'Let me try and sort out the logistics of this.' He glanced around her jam-packed room, where even more presents seemed to have materialised. 'You just worry about how you're going to fit all this stuff into Air Force One.'

Jennifer shook her head. 'Now, now, Lincoln. It's only Air Force One if the President is on board—I thought everyone knew that. It's just an ordinary plane without him.'

Lincoln shook his head. 'I wouldn't let you fly with a neonate this young on an *ordinary* plane, Jennifer. But I'll do a final check on Esther before you go. Everything looks fine, so I don't imagine there will be any problems.'

Jennifer paused. 'Just out of interest, Linc. What does your "friend" make of your flirting?'

He stopped. The question had thrown him. He shrugged, shuffling the notes in his lap. 'Funnily enough, she's not interested in this hot body, she's only interested in my clinical skills.'

Something about saying those words made his stomach clench. He'd said them in jest but the irony wasn't lost on him. Amy had been clear about why she was here. For his skills as a neo-natologist.

He went to stand up but Jennifer reached over and touched his arm. 'Did she like the maternity clothes?'

'Yes…yes, she did. Thank you. And you were right. They fitted perfectly.'

Jennifer gave a little nod, a little smile appearing on her face. 'I thought they might.' She waved her arms around the room. 'And your friend—does she need anything else? Anything for her baby?'

He shook his head. 'She's picked out most things and paid for them already. She just needs to pick them up.'

Then it struck him. Pick them up. From where?

Suddenly it all seemed so ridiculous to him. How on earth was she going to be able to pick up her baby things?

He'd seen the baby catalogues stuffed in her bag and she'd showed him the items that she'd chosen. A white wooden baby crib and chest of drawers, a bright red pram and stroller, a zebra-print baby seat and a polished wooden high chair.

All apparently paid for and waiting in a store in Santa Maria, Butte County. Four hours away from where he stayed in San Francisco and even further from Pelican Cove.

'Thanks for all your help, Lincoln...' The First Lady was talking to him but his mind had drifted off. He was just about to discharge baby Esther, which meant that he, and his whole entourage of staff and equipment, should pack up and leave. Leave to go back to NICU at San Francisco Children's Hospital. Something that deep down he knew they all wanted to do.

But that would mean leaving Amy with no facilities for her baby. No staff and no equipment for a premature delivery. Her blood pressure was still borderline, with no particular response to the anti-hypertensives. She should be reviewed on a daily basis. Who would do that if they all left?

'So I was wondering if you would mind?'

'Mind? Mind what?' Lincoln snapped out of his thoughts with the distinct impression he'd just missed something important.

Jennifer laughed, the amused expression on her face unhidden. 'You haven't listened to a single word I said—have you?'

Lincoln felt embarrassed.

'You're too busy thinking about a beautiful red-head, I imagine.'

'What? No? Of course not.' He was babbling and he knew it.

'Oh, don't make excuses, Linc, you've done everything you can for me...' she bent her head and kissed her baby on the forehead '...and Esther.' She waved her hand in the air. 'So go and see your lady friend.'

Lincoln's lips formed a tight smile and he left the room, stopping in the middle of the corridor. What on earth was he going to do? He'd promised to look after Amy's baby—how could he do that in San Francisco?

He strode quickly down the corridor. Right

now he needed someone to talk to. Someone who could give him some advice. But all his friends were in San Francisco, and the only other people he knew well were Val and Ruth. He couldn't discuss Amy with them, it just wasn't his style.

He walked out the front doors of the hospital into the Californian sunshine. It was another gorgeous day. Just like the one a few days ago when he'd taken Amy for the picnic on the beach.

The day that had left an awkward and uncomfortable silence between them. He'd obviously said something to offend her—but, for the life of him, he couldn't think what it was. She seemed almost…disappointed in him.

Lincoln walked over to one of the benches outside the hospital doors and sat down. He took a long, slow breath, in and out. He had to take some time to think about this—think about what to do.

If he discharged baby Esther tomorrow, he would have to tell Amy that it was time for his staff and equipment to leave Pelican Cove. So why did his stomach churn at the mere thought of that?

He stared out over the ocean, watching the crashing waves. It was time to stop skirting around the edges. It was time to face up to the facts. How did 'playboy Linc' really feel about Amy?

He could remember how much he'd missed her when she'd left the boat. But then he'd thought it was only a holiday and she'd be back before he knew it. Except she hadn't been.

When she'd gone on holiday it had hit him how much he missed her. He'd lain awake in his cabin at night, listening to the sounds of the Amazon rain forest, his thoughts filled with her, stealing his sleep away from him. He'd watched the calendar hanging in the galley, counting the days until she came back.

Except she hadn't.

And the feelings that had descended on him when she hadn't returned had been a first for him. He had been frustrated beyond belief by the fact that no one had been able to tell him where she was, or why she hadn't returned. Most of the other staff had just shrugged their shoulders and said it happened often—people went home to their nice, clean homes and calm lives, and decided not to return to the damp, humid conditions of the Amazon.

Everyone just seemed to accept it and carry on with their lives—whilst Lincoln had felt as if he was losing his mind.

So he'd pushed it all away. Put his mind on the job at hand, the fate of a thousand people living on the banks of the Amazon and coming for medical care and treatment. Then, six months later, his new position in the States at San Francisco's Children's Hospital and the chance to be part of a world-class team had arisen.

But he couldn't shake her from her his mind. He couldn't replace her in his thoughts with the next nurse that came along—the next woman who showed interest in him. Even his potential bride didn't push her from his thoughts. Poor Polly didn't deserve the cold way he had treated her, but in the end he just couldn't stop the visions of the long red curly hair and dark green eyes.

Even months later, in another world, another city, he would see a turn of a head, a flash in the corner of his eye and the feeling of his heart in his mouth when he'd thought he'd glimpsed her again, only to have it plummet seconds later at the realisation it wasn't her. It wasn't Amy.

And then, a few days ago, he'd seen her again and all those feelings came rushing back. His skin on fire, his heart pounding in his chest, and the sick feeling in his stomach when he realised she was unwell, and then again when he realised she was pregnant.

The horror when she told him she'd been ill. Breast cancer. Even now, the mere thought of it made him angry. Those tiny malicious cells growing around her body, filling her with disease. Filling her with fear for her future. Then the horror of her treatment—treatment that some people maintained was worse than the disease. How on earth had she managed that on her own?

He shook his head. How would he have coped if it had been him? Could he have been so brave? So sure? So steadfast? So determined? Then the list—the list she'd written to get her through. To give her focus and a way ahead.

Another sensation surrounded him and he sank his head into his hands. Because this feeling made him feel sick to the pit of his stomach. Guilt.

Guilt about the relief he'd felt when she'd revealed that there was no one in her life. No husband. No father for the baby.

Was that wrong of him? Was it wrong of him to feel that way? Was it wrong that those words had given him a small sliver of hope?

And what about the baby? If Amy's condition didn't improve, her baby could arrive in a matter of a few weeks, or even days. Would that change the way he felt about her? He was a playboy, no matter how much he detested the word. He'd never given children a second thought—well, not children of his own.

His stomach was churning. Any day now he was going to have to pack up and leave. But what would happen to Amy then?

She could stay here in Pelican Cove. David would continue to be her obstetrician. But there was no neonatologist if she had an early delivery. It was routine procedure that any woman at risk in Pelican Cove would be transferred to San Francisco. His home. Chances were, he would have ended up being her neonatologist by default if she'd turned up there.

This was so complicated. Should he offer her help? Support? What would he do if this was just another female friend? If this wasn't Amy—a woman who messed with his mind just by being there?

The most sensible solution was to invite her to stay with him in San Francisco and let her continue her obstetric care there until the baby arrived. That's what he would do for anyone else. Anyone he considered a friend.

The thoughts jumbled around in his head. But was that really sensible? She could deliver in two days or two weeks. How would it feel to have Amy in his apartment—under his roof?

Lincoln closed his eyes and took a deep breath. He was helping a friend. And maybe, just maybe, if he kept repeating that, he might actually believe it.

Lincoln stood at the nurses' station and looked over Amy's chart quickly. David had reviewed her again this morning, taken more blood samples and adjusted her blood-pressure meds.

The handwritten script in the case notes was precise. David felt she was teetering at the edge. She was still clearly at risk of her pre-eclampsia developing into the full blown disease. He wanted her treated with caution and monitored daily.

Lincoln understood. And strangely it filled him with confidence that he'd made the right decision and was about to take the right steps.

He leaned over to the nearest computer and checked his e-mail account. Because he was away from his normal hospital, all his e-mails were currently being diverted to his personal account. 'What the…?' He leaned in closer to his account. Three thousand e-mails. He squinted at the screen. A voice behind him laughed, leaning over his shoulders.

'Wow,' she said, 'that's a *lot* of friend requests.'

Lincoln shook his head, 'I don't get it,' he mumbled, the thoughts of his paltry list of twenty-six friends the day before bewildering him. 'Who on earth are all these people?' His eyes ran up and down the names on the list. 'I don't even recognise any of them.'

The nurse behind him patted him on the shoulder. 'That's what happens when you appear on the TV as the President's doctor, handsome.' She gave a little laugh as she walked away.

Lincoln sat for a few seconds. Instant fame. He

hadn't even given it much thought. One television appearance and suddenly half the world wanted to be his 'friend'.

A small hand positioned itself on the box on the counter next to him. 'Lincoln, we didn't know you cared.'

His hands shot out and grabbed the cake box and carton of coffee on the counter. 'I don't.' He gave the nurse a smile. 'Hands off. These are my bargaining tools and I think I'm going to need them.'

She shook her head. 'Just don't let her throw them off the wall—those cupcakes are too good to waste.'

Amy's door was slightly ajar and he could see her lying in the darkened room. Her blinds were drawn to block out the glaring sun and she lay on her side on the bed, her eyes closed, wearing a pale blue smock and drawstring linen trousers.

'Knock, knock.'

Her eyelids flickered open, a smile starting on her face before her brain switched into gear and she remembered she was angry with him.

She pushed herself up the bed. 'Hi, Lincoln, what do you want?'

He put his gifts on the bedside table, pushing it up towards her until it sat just before her extended abdomen.

Amy took a deep breath. Coffee. That was definitely coffee she could smell. She lifted the lid on the cup and inhaled. Even better, it was a caramel latte. She'd seriously thought about killing someone for one of these the other day.

She pulled the pink ribbon on the cake box, tugging it clear and lifting the lid on the box. Cupcakes. Strawberry, chocolate and lemon. And all of them had her name written on them. Literally.

Her taste buds started watering. Lincoln knew her well. The best way to her heart was through her stomach. What was he up to?

She picked up a pink cupcake, peeled the paper case and took a bite. 'Mmm. I know that there is probably an ulterior motive to these...' she raised her hand '...but I don't want you to tell me what it is until I've finished eating. I *don't* want you to spoil this.' She eyed the cup. 'I thought you weren't letting me drink coffee?'

'It's a special occasion.'

She took a sip of the caramel latte. Perfect. Her

taste buds exploded. Oh, how she'd missed this. Her eyes swept over the box of cakes. Could she eat another before he started speaking? Probably. They were tiny—two bites and they were gone. Her fingers hovered over a chocolate cupcake, the next in the box.

She lifted her eyes to look at him. Lincoln was sitting in the chair next to her bed, waiting patiently for her to finish. But he didn't look ill at ease or nervous. No, he looked cool, calm and confident. In short, he didn't look like a man who thought he'd have to bribe his way into the room. He looked like a man who'd already made whatever decision had to be made. And it made her feel distinctly uncomfortable.

She set down the chocolate cupcake, praying whatever he said wasn't about to ruin her appetite. 'What do you want, Linc?'

He nodded slowly, his eyes fixing on hers. 'We need to talk, Amy.'

She bit her lip. Where was this going to go? 'What about?'

He sat a little straighter. 'Baby Esther is ready to go home—to go back to the White House.

She's ready for discharge, and once I finish her paperwork, the plans will be in place.'

Amy nodded. What did this have to do with her?

Lincoln's face was serious. 'Once she's ready to go, *I* have to go. *W*e have to go.'

The penny dropped. Like a huge boulder throwing itself off the edge of a cliff. 'Oh.'

She should have known this was coming. At first, it hadn't even occurred to her—the fact that Lincoln wouldn't be staying here. She'd been so caught up in getting to where he was and making him agree to look after her baby that she'd had tunnel vision. But after a few days stuck as an inpatient in Pelican Cove she'd started to worry. The First Lady wasn't likely to stay here for long. What would happen then? The truth was, she'd more or less expected to have her baby in a matter of days. But Junior seemed to be making his own plans.

'So, it's time to make a decision.' Amy felt as if she could throw up. Once baby Esther left, there was no reason for any of the staff or facilities that had been spirited into Pelican Cove to stay.

What about her? What about her baby? And why did Lincoln look so calm?

'I need to pack up all the NICU equipment and arrange for my staff to return to San Francisco.'

Duh. She'd just realised that.

'I need to return to San Francisco, as I've got duties and commitments there...'

She nodded dumbly. Of course he did.

'So I thought it best to make some arrangements for you and the baby.' He picked up her chart. She hadn't even noticed him bringing it into the room. *Arrangements*. Did he know how clinical that sounded?

'David still has some concerns about your condition. You're coming up on twenty-nine weeks, but your blood pressure is still borderline—even with the anti-hypertensives—and you're still showing protein in your urine.'

His hand brushed against hers, his voice softening, becoming less businesslike and more friend-like. 'Chances are, this baby is still going to come early. You came to Pelican Cove because you wanted me to be the one to look after your baby. Is that still what you want, Amy?'

She nodded. Words escaped her right now. Her

mind was too full of jumbled thoughts to say anything coherent. Where was this going?

Lincoln nodded and gave her a little smile. 'In
that case, I think I might have found a solution
for us, then.'

'Solution?' The word gave her hope. Because,
right now, she needed some.

'You can come back to San Francisco with
me.' There. He'd said it. The words that had been
coiled up inside his chest since he'd came to the
conclusion a few hours ago. In his head, that
made perfect sense.

Right now he was leaving out the way he felt
drawn to her room in the hospital, day or night,
for no good reason. She was like a magnet to him
and he was instantly drawn.

And in his head that was perfect. She'd disappeared out of his life before and he'd no intention
of letting it happen again. But this time he'd be
more careful. Amy had searched him out. She'd
come to find him. She wanted his skills and expertise—and she could have them. And maybe
it could give him some time to work out how he
felt about her.

It took him a few seconds to realise she hadn't

spoken. She seemed frozen to the spot, or to the bed. Her mouth was hanging open, and her hands had the slightest tremor.

Time to fill in the blanks. Time to persuade her it was most reasonable and viable option for her.

'I know you've been looked after in Santa Maria—but you came here because you didn't have a physician there you could trust. And the most important thing is that you have someone you trust looking after your baby.

'David will be staying in Pelican Cove. He could continue to treat you, if that's what you prefer. But even he is worried about an early delivery. The normal protocol in Pelican Cove is that someone in your condition would be transferred to San Francisco Children and Maternity Hospital—where we have excellent facilities for neonates.' He let her take in the words, rationalise it in her brain.

'I can arrange for one of the obstetricians there to take over your care. There are two I would absolutely trust with my life. I wouldn't recommend them to you otherwise.' He ran his fingers through his tousled hair, a sign of his nerves. Was this going well?

'We could arrange to get there tomorrow. I'll get one of the obstetricians to review you immediately and decide on how to proceed. If there's any emergency, I'll be close by and available to be at the delivery.'

His words hung in the air. There. He'd said them. And whilst he knew every word he'd said was true, there was still that tiny little bit of him that knew there was an element of emotional blackmail in there. He was using her fear for her child to get her exactly where he wanted her.

He didn't like the word *manipulate*. It seemed like something from a bad-guy movie. Something that the villain did. But he'd never said he was perfect. He'd never said he didn't have flaws. He was just a man. Trying to get his girl.

Amy's hands were resting on the bedside table—probably to control a tremor. She thought of her empty apartment in Santa Maria, with the baby's things still flat-packed into boxes. She didn't have any family any more, but she had good friends there who were happy to help out and support her. She was lucky that she had regular hours at the clinic that meant she could plan her childcare hours in advance. So why did it feel as if all the plans she had made were crumbling around her?

'But where would I stay? I don't know anyone in San Francisco?' It looked as if it was just one of a million thoughts that were currently scurrying around in her brain.

'That's easy. You'll stay with me.'

Amy choked, then coughed and spluttered, her face turning redder and redder by the second. Lincoln jumped to his feet and leapt behind her, thumping his hand on her back until she stopped then grabbing a glass of water from the nearby locker and handing it to her. 'Here, take this.'

She took a little sip, taking in deep frantic breaths, trying to fill her lungs with the air that seemed to have been sucked from them when he'd said those words.

She blew the air out slowly through thick pursed lips, then turned to face him. 'How on earth can I come and stay with you, Lincoln? You haven't seen me in six years. You don't owe me anything. Yes, I want you to deliver my baby but I don't expect anything else from you, and I certainly don't expect *this*.'

Her voice was slow and steady, but he could

see the panic in her eyes. She was frantic, swimming in an ocean where she was out her depth and being pulled out with the current. Seemed she was as scared of the scenario as he was.

'Amy, the fact is you can stay anywhere you want to. But if you are going to come to San Francisco, it makes sense that you stay with a friend. There's no point in running up a hotel bill—you could deliver tomorrow, or in six weeks' time. And in your current condition it makes even more sense if that friend has some medical expertise.' The words were plain. Sensible, and he knew it. They sounded rational and reasonable.

They didn't tell her that his heart was suddenly thudding against his chest and his stomach was turning inside out at the thought of her not agreeing to this.

'I'd like to think that as soon as we get to San Francisco one of my colleagues will assess you. They might even want to admit you. But if, like Pelican Cove, they want to see you on a daily basis, it makes sense that you stay with me. I live five minutes away from the hospital in a two-bedroom apartment. I've got a housekeeper that comes in twice a week, so you won't feel obliged to do anything. Just relax with your feet up and wait for this baby to arrive.'

She was still silent. It looked as if she were trying to formulate words in her brain. Was she looking for an easy way to let him down? To tell him she couldn't possibly stay with him? He couldn't hear that.

It was time to play his trump card.

He kept his voice strong and confident. He wanted her to feel assured, safe. He also wanted to play to her fun side. 'Look at it this way, Amy, you'll get to do another thing on your list.'

'My list?' Her eyes were blank, as if the list was the last thing on her mind.

Lincoln nodded and touched her hand. 'I didn't mention where I stay, did I? I've got an apartment in Fisherman's Wharf in San Francisco. It's actually just where the cable cars turn to start their journey again. You'll have number seven on your list at your fingertips.'

Even as he said the words he questioned his wisdom. Doing something on her list was never going to be the deciding factor for her. But right now desperate times called for desperate measures. And he'd use whatever it took.

She looked a bit dazed, shocked.

'Amy?'

Her voice had the slightest tremor. 'It's a lot to think about.' She stood up and pushed the bedside table away, walking over to the window and looking out over Pelican Cove. Her hands were placed protectively over her stomach, as if she were cradling her baby inside.

Inside her brain was in turmoil. Why hadn't she planned ahead? Why hadn't she foreseen this? The safety of her baby was always going to be paramount, but what about the safety of her soul?

The last few days had brought a huge surge of emotions to the fore. Maybe they were pregnancy related? But right now every time she was in a room with Lincoln she couldn't think of anything else.

The thought of running up a hotel bill made her blood run cold. Her maternity salary was comfortable enough to cover her rent and outgoings, but not unexpected outgoings like these.

Stay in his apartment? He must be out of his mind! She had visions in her head of two lions stalking around their prey. That's what it would feel like. How could she possibly be relaxed around Lincoln when every second she would be waiting to see if he would touch her, look at her, take her in his arms and…

'I don't think it would work.' The words were out before she had a chance to think about them.

'Why?' Lincoln looked confused. He walked towards her and put his arms on either side of her shoulders. His face seemed so open, so honest. With no concerns, no worries. He really didn't know. He really didn't realise what he did to her.

But, then, how could he, if she'd never told him?

'I… I…' Her throat was dry, her tongue sticking to the top of her mouth.

'It's the perfect solution—surely you can see that?' Then he did it. He gave her that killer smile. The one that used to unnerve her from across the room and make her knees buckle. The smile that sent a thousand feather-like touches skittering across her skin. And something inside her heart lurched.

Hope. The feeling she'd felt when she'd seen him on television and had known she'd be able to find him and ask for help.

The sensations that had engulfed her when she'd first set eyes on him after six long years.

The heat and warmth that had swept through her body when he'd touched her, when he'd kissed her.

The look in his eyes on the beach when he'd told her that he'd searched for her and it had sent loose a thousand butterflies, beating their wings inside her chest.

Hope.

A sensation she only recognised now. The same sensation she'd steeled inside herself when she'd written the list.

He reached up, catching a curl of hair that had fallen in front of her eye, tucking it behind her ear. He was looking at her with those dark-rimmed eyes. She was mesmerised. And she wanted more.

Maybe this was the way to get it.

'You're right,' she breathed. 'It makes perfect sense. When do we leave?'

CHAPTER SEVEN

AMY looked out of the apartment window, across the rippling San Francisco bay to Alcatraz. What a view. It was strange how a piece of rock could seem so foreboding and enigmatic, rising up from the grey waves. Even from this distance she could see the ferry pulling in again, no doubt unloading its cargo of tourists all anxious to capture the moment on camera.

Everywhere she looked there were tourists. The iconic Powell-Hyde cable car turntable at Fisherman's Wharf was practically under her nose, with a constant stream of people lining up to get their photo snapped next to it. She looked back over her shoulder, into the spacious wooden-floored apartment. This really was a prime piece of real estate and she shuddered to think how much it had cost.

Amy glanced at her watch for the third time in ten minutes. 'Resting' wasn't easy for a girl who was used to being on her feet in a busy ward for twelve hours a day. Three long days she'd been looking out of this window into the wonderful world of bustling San Francisco beneath her. Currently just out of her reach.

Daily hospital monitoring and strict bed rest. It almost sounded like a prison sentence. The irony of the view of Alcatraz wasn't lost on her.

Her blood pressure hadn't improved, her urine still had protein in it, but thankfully her oedema was under control and she hadn't developed any other symptoms. It hadn't stopped her newest obstetrician, Cassidy Yates—a statuesque blonde who watched Lincoln out of the corner of her eye—from referring to the local protocols and administering some steroids to help develop the baby's lungs in case of early delivery. For the past three days Amy had travelled with him into work and he'd dropped her at the day unit for monitoring and assessment.

Twenty-nine weeks and three days. Right now her extended abdomen felt like a ticking time bomb. Then there was being *here*. In Lincoln's apartment, surrounded all day by little pieces of him.

The good thing was…he'd been the perfect gent. Welcoming, considerate and ever attentive. The frustrating thing was…he'd been the perfect gent. And it was driving her crazy.

Amy sighed and flopped down into the nearby red leather armchair, pushing until the seat tilted backwards and the leg rest sprang out. There was nothing to do—Lincoln had said he would take care of dinner, so all she could do right now was wait.

The trouble with waiting was that it left too much time to think. Too much time to look out at the busy life below and wonder when you could be part of it again. She felt a sharp kick under her ribs and drew a deep breath. She pulled up her smock top to reveal her baby bump.

She watched the squirms under her skin—if this were a movie, any minute now a twelve-armed alien would burst from her stomach. Baby Zachary had obviously decided to have a party in there, and he was certainly beginning to object to the reducing space. Her hands hovered just above her belly, wondering where the next punch would appear. It really was amazing to think that she would hold him in her arms soon. What would he look like? Would he have red hair and pale skin like her? Or the physical characteristics of his sperm donor father?

She could remember the details on the resume. Sperm Donor 867. Dark hair, green eyes (best to choose someone with the same eye colour you had), over six feet tall, college education. But did any of that really matter? Would genetics really decide the sum of her baby? Was it all nature or was it nurture?

She lifted her hands to her head, gently massaging her temples. Her head was starting to throb slightly, nothing to worry about—not enough to search the cupboards for paracetamol, just enough to annoy her thought processes.

What would her son's interests be? Her sperm donor had been a jock—no doubt about that. Every sport known to man had been on his list of interests. What did she know about football? But he'd also been academic, and had special-ised in education.

So would her son be like his father or more like her? Reckless at times, occasionally unpre-dictable? In future years would she have to sit up at night, worrying about what time he would come in?

Zachary squirmed again under her skin, as if sensing her breath was currently caught in her chest. Why did she feel so panicked? She'd started this process six years ago—more than enough time to think about the end product. She'd spent the last two weeks worrying about premature birth and safe delivery. So why now was she panicking about hair colour and little-boy interests?

'That's some sight.'

Amy let out a shriek, pulling down her smock top and leaping up from the chair. Lincoln stood leaning against the doorframe, his arms folded across his chest, a smile of amusement on his face.

'Lincoln! I didn't hear you.' She could feel the colour rushing into her face. 'Where did you spring from?'

He crossed the room in a couple of steps, his hands resting lightly on the tops of her arms. 'Where I always spring from—work. Sorry, didn't mean to scare you.'

'You didn't... Well, you did, but I think that I... I mean...'

'You're babbling.' His voice was calm, but there was a distinct twinkle in his eye that even she could notice in the dimming light.

She looked around her. When had it got so dark? 'What time is it?'

'Just after seven. Sorry I'm a bit late, we had an emergency in NICU.'

She gave a quiet nod—she could hardly object, conscious of the fact that in a few days' or weeks' time her baby could be the emergency in NICU.

'I guess I lost track of time,' she murmured looking back out over the bustling city. Last time she'd looked outside it had been late afternoon. Had she drifted off to sleep? Her stomach growled loudly, reminding her of why she'd been waiting for Linc. 'Did you bring dinner?'

'Ahh…about that…' His forehead puckered in a frown.

This time it was her turn to smile. 'You forgot—didn't you?'

'Not exactly.' He extended his arm towards her, trying to push aside the delicious thoughts of the scene he'd just witnessed, his brain swiftly improvising. 'I decided to take you out to dinner. You must be going crazy, stuck in my apartment.'

Amy pressed her palms against the window. 'I don't know if crazy is the right word, but I definitely feel as if I'm missing out on something. I've dreamed about exploring San Francisco for years, and now that I'm here I feel as if it's just outside my reach.' She turned to face him and flattened her back against his picture window. 'I want to ride on the cable cars—I don't want to watch them turn underneath me. I want to do the boat trip to Alcatraz and stand in the cells and feel the atmosphere of the place. I want to go down to Pier 39 and have my picture taken next to the Fisherman's Wharf sign. I want to go and explore Chinatown. I want to eat there, see the colours and smell all the wonderful food. I want to spend the day wandering around Fisherman's Wharf wondering what type of ice cream I want to eat next. I want to sit in some of the quayside restaurants and eat all the fish on the menu.'

Lincoln raised his eyebrow at her, folding his arms across his chest. 'You have been going crazy in here, haven't you? Why didn't you say something sooner?'

She sighed. 'You've been busy, Linc. The last

thing you need to do is try and entertain an un-invited house guest.'

He shook his head. 'Why do you keep saying stuff like that?'

'Stuff like what?'

His brow was puckered again. '*Uninvited* house guest.' He looked annoyed. 'You're not uninvited. I invited you.' He swung his arms wide, 'This is my home. I wanted you here.'

Amy licked her lips, as if she was preparing to say something. Her eyes were fixed on his again. And he could sense something. Something bubbling just underneath the surface, getting ready to erupt. The hairs stood up at the back of his neck, making him feel distinctly uncomfortable. All of sudden he felt as the though the walls of his spacious apartment were starting to close in around him.

'Come on.' He extended his arm towards her, anxious to break the tension between them. 'You can pick wherever you like. Let's eat.'

The street was packed. The early evening tour-ists were crammed onto the sidewalks, reading menus and deciding what restaurant to eat in.

Lincoln weaved seamlessly through the crowd and pushed open a heavy wooden door, holding it open until Amy was safely inside.

She blinked furiously, her eyes struggling to adjust to the gloomy interior, but Lincoln took her hand again and eased her through the dimly lit restaurant, pulling her into a wooden seated booth.

'I thought I was getting to pick?'

He rolled his eyes. 'If we'd waited for you to pick, we'd still be standing on the sidewalk at midnight, peering at menus.'

He handed her a plastic-coated menu. 'What do you want to eat?'

Amy looked around her. The gaudily decorated interior of fake wooden barrels and ship's wheels draped with Hawaiian garlands left her speechless. To say nothing of the life-size pirate standing the corner of the room.

'This looks like a bit of a tourist trap,' she mumbled, her eyes running over the menu in the hope it could redeem itself to her.

Lincoln leaned back in the booth, 'That's the beauty of this place,' he said, a smile plastered across his face. 'It looks dark and seedy. But it hides San Francisco's best-kept secret. My mate Johnny is the chef and he makes the best food in the world.' He leaned across the booth towards her. 'So what do you fancy?'

The English terminology made her blink, as did the double meaning. What she 'fancied' wasn't on the menu in front of her. But right now she couldn't even contemplate what she 'fancied'. Not while she currently felt like a beached whale.

Her tongue ran nervously along her lips, her eyes fixed on the plastic menu—because looking upwards would mean staring into those deep blue eyes and she couldn't face that right now. Junior gave another kick and she winced.

Lincoln's hand shot across the table and caught hers. 'Are you okay? Is something wrong?'

Yes, yes, something was wrong. Her brain couldn't focus. Her rational thoughts had left the building. She wanted to blurt out everything that was currently spinning around in her head. She wanted to tell him that she wished she'd called him six years ago when she'd got the cancer diagnosis. She wanted to tell him that she wished the baby she was currently carrying in her belly was his, instead of donor 867's. She wanted to tell him that she wished she'd had her surgery and her body looked normal again so she could finally stand and look at her naked reflection in the mirror again. She wanted to tell him that her back ached, her feet were sore and her headache was really starting to annoy her—but he'd just taken her out and the last thing she wanted to do right now was head back to the apartment. Because there it would just be the two of them. Alone.

Suddenly the grubby-looking restaurant didn't seem so bad. At least there were other people around.

A man appeared and slapped Lincoln on the shoulder. 'Who's the lovely lady, Linc? And why haven't you introduced me?'

Lincoln smiled. He seemed relaxed and easy in here and the tension that had been between them seemed to have left his tightened shoulders. He held his hand out towards Amy. 'This, Johnny, is my good friend Amy Carson. She's never sampled the delights of your cooking, so I hope you're going to impress her—otherwise she'll bend my ear all night for bringing her to such a dive.' He gave her a little wink across the table.

Johnny laughed. A deep, hearty laugh that seemed to come from all the way down at his toes. 'Impress? Me? Once I've fed this lady, she'll never look at you again, Linc.' He bent his head and picked up Amy's hand, kissing it with a flourish. 'So, beautiful, what can I get you?'

Amy looked back at Linc in panic. She hadn't even read the menu properly yet.

Lincoln pointed towards her. 'Why don't you decide for us, Johnny? Only be careful what you give my pregnant friend, we're hoping to avoid an early labour.'

Johnny's eyes turned to where Amy's extended abdomen was tucked neatly under the table in the darkened booth. He beamed. 'Congratulations, beautiful lady. I'm sure I can rustle something up that will delight your little bambino.'

He wandered back off to the kitchen and left the two of them sitting in the booth. Amy held her breath. Johnny was obviously a friend; would he assume the baby was Lincoln's? Or was her imagination just making wild leaps?

She could be a colleague from work, a neighbour, an old friend from school. There was no reason for Johnny to think anything else. So why was half of her hoping that he was?

Her stomach growled loudly. 'So what am I going to get to eat, Linc? With my current busy lifestyle, food is becoming a very important part of my day.'

Lincoln smiled at the lilt in her voice. This was the Amy he remembered. A bit cheeky, with a definite sarcastic edge. Not the nervous and up-tight woman he'd spent the last few days with.

'I think I can safely say you'll get a feast fit for a king.'

'Or a queen?' The teasing tone was apparent.

'Ouch. Yes, or a queen.' He rested his head on his hands. 'What did Cassidy say today?'

Amy could feel the smile drop from her face. Why was it the mere mention of that woman's name automatically put her hackles up? Cassidy had only ever been pleasant and professional to Amy, but Amy could see the way Cassidy looked at Lincoln—even if he couldn't. His easy flirta-tious manner was coming back to bite him on the…

'Nothing's changed. I've to go back tomorrow for more of the same.'

Lincoln leaned back and looked at her face. She looked vaguely irritated, as if she was annoyed. Surely, at this stage, no news was good news?

'So what's with the long face?'

Amy took a deep breath. This was where she should play the nice house guest. Happy, amenable and anxious to please.

Except these pregnancy hormones were driving her nuts. Her aching back was driving her nuts. Living under the same roof as Lincoln was driving her nuts. And seeing some gorgeous, statuesque blonde looking at Lincoln, *her Lincoln*, the way that woman did was driving her nuts.

She opened her mouth to speak just as Johnny reappeared and slid the biggest platter known to man onto their table. Grilled shrimp, Dungeness crab, scallops and crab cakes with rice and salad on the side. Then another plateful with grilled chicken, peppers, onion, a bowl of ratatouille and some garlic bread. Johnny folded his arms across his chest. 'Before you start, I know all of this is high in Omega 3 and can assure you it's all completely fresh and fully cooked. No tuna, no tilefish, no mackerel. All safe for a pregnant lady.' He shrugged his shoulders. 'But I also made you some chicken and garlic bread in case you were a little wary.'

Amy's face relaxed as the wonderful smell of freshly cooked fish wafted towards her. Her smile lit up her face. 'Johnny, how can a girl come to Fisherman's Wharf and not sample the Dungeness crab?'

She lifted her napkin from the table and spread it across her bump. 'Not the most glamorous, I know, but I'd hate to ruin these gorgeous clothes that you stole for me from the First Lady.'

Lincoln laughed as he pulled a plate towards him and started lifting some food from the platter. The maternity clothes had been a godsend. Today Amy was wearing a deep purple smock, which complemented her red hair and pale skin perfectly. In fact, every time he saw her she had a different outfit on. He had the distinct impression that the First Lady had known exactly the impact her 'cast-off' clothes would have. Brownie points. Big time. 'I didn't steal them. She wanted you to have them. And it's obvious you're making good use of them—that's what she wanted.'

Amy lifted a fork to her mouth. 'So are you going to tell me anything interesting about the First Lady?'

'And break patient confidentiality?' He'd raised one eyebrow at her, in mock indignation, then bent over and took a bite of his crab, shaking his head as he quickly swallowed. 'Nope. I'm not going to tell you a thing. Except she wanted you to use those clothes. Oh, and that she called me an incorrigible flirt—how dare she?'

Amy laughed. 'Well, she got that right.'

'I do not flirt, I'm just a friendly person,' Lincoln protested.

Amy rolled her eyes. 'Women fall at your feet everywhere, Linc.'

He paused for a second, as if lost in a thought, 'Mmm, not all women. It's only useful if it's the woman you want.'

The air seemed to go silent around them. Amy bit her lip. *What did that mean*? Did he mean her? Had she fallen at his feet on the Amazon boat and he hadn't wanted her to? Or was he talking about now, and how she was trying to keep her distance? She had no idea what was going on inside his head.

Amy took another bite of her shrimp, then broke the garlic bread in half, handing it to him across the table. A little twinge came across her back. Junior felt as if he was turning around inside her right now. She crossed then uncrossed her ankles, trying to find a more comfortable position.

'Everything okay?'

'That's twice you've asked in the last fifteen minutes.'

'And that's twice I've caught you looking at me as if you want to take a meat cleaver to my head.' Lincoln put his food back on the plate. 'So spill, Amy, what's eating you?'

'Nothing.'

Lincoln gave a sigh and lifted his glass of root beer, which had magically appeared at his side. 'So, if nothing's wrong, quit being snarky. I've had a crappy day at work and I just want to come home and relax.'

'Snarky? Is that even a word?' She couldn't help it. No matter how hard she tried, the words were practically a growl.

He lifted one eyebrow at her again. It was a

habit of his that was really beginning to annoy her. No matter how chilled she tried to be.

'Amy, I'm only going to ask this once more. What's wrong?'

All of a sudden the gorgeous platter of food didn't seem so appetising. It looked as if it could catch in her throat and choke her to death. Worse, she could feel tears start to form in her eyes. Why was she about to cry? What the hell was wrong with her?

She gulped as one tear escaped and slid down her cheek and she fumbled for her napkin. 'Nothing's wrong. And everything's wrong. That's just it, Linc. I don't know what's wrong—I just know something is.'

Within seconds he'd reached across the table and captured her hands in his. She could feel the warmth from his hands creeping up her arms. Her hands felt cold, like blocks of ice. Truth be told, her whole body felt like that.

Another tear slid down her face and she pulled her hand away, brushing the paper napkin against her face. 'Damn pregnancy hormones,' she muttered.

'Don't, Amy. Don't do that. Don't blame this

on the fact you're pregnant. We both know it's not that.' His voice cut through the dim light like a brilliant strobe, making her breath catch in her throat. He was looking directly at her, one hand now at the back of his head, pulling at his hair. His frustration was evident.

Silence. She didn't know what to say. She didn't know what she should say. She didn't know what she *could* say.

In her head it was easy. She was a princess in a pink satin dress, standing at the top of her tower, and he was Prince Charming on the white charger below. But she wasn't a child, and this wasn't a fairy-tale. This was real and in her head the princess wasn't pregnant with a sperm donor's baby and hadn't suffered from breast cancer and had a mastectomy. In her head the princess was the perfect healthy, whole, fertile partner that Prince Charming deserved.

Something she would never be.

'You do know she's got a crush on you—don't you?'

'What?' Lincoln looked confused at the change in subject. 'Who?'

'Cassidy Yates, that's who.'

Lincoln shook his head in bewilderment. 'No, she doesn't—that's ridiculous.'

Amy banged her hand on the table. 'Oh, yes, she does! I can see it every time she looks at you.'

Lincoln slammed down his glass, sloshing root beer all over the table. 'And why does it matter? Why does it matter if she does have a crush on me? Why does it matter to you?'

She could feel her lips trembling and her hands begin to shake. He was angry. She'd never seen Lincoln angry before.

And it knocked the wind clean out of her sails.

He pushed himself up. 'This isn't about Cassidy Yates. This could *never* be about Cassidy Yates. This is about you and me, Amy. Don't pretend it's anything else.'

She could see the fire in his eyes, the pent-up frustration so tangible she could almost reach out and touch it.

Something gripped around her heart, squeezing it tightly. Could she tell him that she loved him? Could she say that right now she couldn't bear to be in the same room as him because she ached for his touch? Could she tell him that she wished she could turn back the clock six years?

No. No, she couldn't. Because Lincoln didn't need half a woman. He needed a whole one. He didn't need a woman who was carrying someone else's baby—a woman who would never be able to have any more natural children. He needed someone else, he *deserved* someone else. Someone who could give him children of his own.

But being around him and knowing that hurt like hell.

She had to get of there.

'I can't do this, Linc.' She stood up and slid out from the booth. 'I can't do this right now.' Her shaky voice grew firm, determined. 'This isn't a good time.' Her hands rested on her belly. 'I need to concentrate on this. I need to concentrate on *him*. Nothing is more important than this baby. I can't let anything else confuse me.' Try as she may and no matter how steady her voice was, she couldn't meet his gaze. One look into those eyes right now and she could crumble.

Lincoln's voice was barely contained. 'So I "confuse" you now? That's rubbish and you know it.' He came around and stood directly in front of her, his hands touching her shoulders. 'Tell me, Amy. Tell me how you feel.'

Her resolve started to shatter underneath her. Tears started to spill down her cheeks again. 'I don't know. I don't know how I feel. I don't know if any of these feelings are real, or if they're just a huge rush of hormones and nostalgia.' She flung her arms out in frustration, then raised her hands to her temples. She winced as her fingers touched the sides of her forehead. 'I can't sort anything out in my head right now. I can't think. I can't concentrate.' She shook her head furiously. 'I can't get rid of this damn headache!'

Her eyes finally met his. 'I didn't come here for me, Lincoln. I didn't come here for you. I came here…' she pressed her hands to her belly again '…for my son.'

Lincoln threw his hands up in frustration. He couldn't stand this any longer. He'd spent the last few days tiptoeing around her. Keeping his distance—even though it was killing him. Giving her space, giving her time.

'So this is all about the baby? Nothing else?'

'I can't let it be.'

The heavy silence pressed in on them as they stared at each other in the dimly lit room.

Lincoln wanted to storm out. He didn't need this. Six years of wishing you could see someone again, talk to them. And this was it.

Someone who pretended things weren't happening. Someone who tried to put a cap on their emotions. Someone who wouldn't face up to the facts between them. Someone who wouldn't even give him a chance. Enough was enough.

The headache was pounding in her ears. The breath in her chest started to tighten. Zachary started kicking, as if he could feel it too. Her head was swimming and heat started to creep over her body. What was this?

Blackness crept into the edges of her eyes. She blinked twice. Had some lights just gone out? Then panic crept across her chest. Her legs starting to buckle underneath her. 'Lincoln…'

He looked upwards just as she crumpled to a heap on the floor—too late to save her from smacking her head on the thick wooden planks. *Johnny!'*

He turned her on her left hand side, making sure her airway was clear and checking her pulse.

'*Get me an ambulance!*' His hands fell to her abdomen, feeling the little life inside pushing against him.

He squeezed his eyes tightly shut as guilt engulfed him. This could be a dozen different things, but he knew right now which one it would be—eclampsia. The headache, she'd said she had a headache and he hadn't listened. She'd been checked that morning at the hospital, but this was new, this was a different complaint and one that could be a sign of eclampsia. One that should have made him take her straight back to hospital.

Instead he'd been too self-absorbed. Too worried about developing a relationship with her that would meet his own needs. Too worried that she wouldn't tell him how she felt. He'd been angry. Shouted at her, probably raised her blood pressure.

He'd promised to look after her baby. He'd promised her a safe delivery.

Her body started to twitch. The first signs of a seizure. What had he done? Lincoln watched as things started to slip through his fingers—like the grains of sand on the beach.

He lifted his head. *'Where the hell is that ambulance?'*

CHAPTER EIGHT

LINCOLN shifted his position, his aching limbs objecting to the firm hard-backed chair. Was it possible his body was getting used to no sleep?

A little grunt came from under his chin. Baby Carson wriggled in the strip of cloth currently cocooning him against Lincoln's bare chest. It was almost as if the baby could hear the steadying beat of Lincoln's heart and was trying to get closer to it. He could feel the heat from his body wrap around the little figure, currently nestled under his shirt. He, better than anyone, knew that kangaroo care offered a huge range of benefits for pre-term babies—normalising temperature, heart and respiratory rate, decreasing stress, reducing risks of infection and promoting earlier discharge for premature babies. As a neonatologist he was a huge advocate for the technique. But he'd never actually done it himself. He'd never actually been the one sitting in the dead of night with a three-pound baby strapped to his chest. He swallowed the lump in his throat. He had to do this. He had to do this for Amy.

Cassidy Yates touched his shoulder. 'How you doing, Linc?' She sat down in the chair next to him, her blonde hair pulled backwards in a bun, her eyes lined and tired.

He moved forward to speak, but a little squeak from the baby made him shift back to his original position. 'Is something wrong?' His voice was strained. *Please let Amy be okay.*

Cassidy shook her head. 'There's no change, Linc. She still hasn't woken up.' Cassidy gave a sigh. 'It's only been forty-eight hours.' A tight smile appeared on her face. 'She'll wake up today. I know she will.'

The words hung in the air between them. Both of them hoping they'd be true.

Lincoln brushed his hand against hers. 'This is my fault, Cassidy, not yours. I was the one who took her out to dinner. I was the one she got into a fight with. I didn't even realise she had any other symptoms.' He moved his hand back and ran it through his hair. 'If I'd been paying enough attention…'

'Stop it, Linc. I was her obstetrician. I should have admitted her.'

Lincoln shook his head. 'But why? You'd monitored her every day. There had been no change in her symptoms. What reason could you have for admitting her?'

Cassidy sighed. 'Good old-fashioned instinct. I knew this wasn't going to turn out well. I let Amy down.'

Lincoln looked at the little bundle under his chin. He reached up and stroked a gentle finger across the top of the baby's soft fontanel. The first few sprigs of dark hair were just starting to appear.

Cassidy leaned forward in her chair, staring at Linc with her weary eyes. 'I told her to phone me as soon as any other symptoms appeared. How long did she have that headache, Linc? Why didn't she phone me?'

Because of me. Guilt tightened across his chest. Cassidy hadn't slept in the last two days. She was worried sick. She felt guilty—as if she'd made a mistake. But she hadn't. *He had.*

Deep down he knew why Amy hadn't phoned. She hadn't been focusing on her symptoms.

She'd been fixated on the fact that she thought something was happening between Lincoln and Cassidy. *She'd been jealous.* And it had affected her relationship with her obstetrician.

Lincoln cringed. He couldn't believe it had come to this.

Seeing Amy lying on the floor of the restaurant, seizing, had been the single most terrifying moment of his life. Never had a five-minute ambulance journey seemed so long.

And the E.R. events that had followed had felt like an out-of-body experience. For once, he hadn't been in control. He'd watched as they'd put her on monitors, inserted IVs and catheters, and stabilised her. Once the seizure had been under control, a quick confab with Cassidy and the anaesthetist had resulted in a rapid trip to Theatre and an emergency Caesarean section.

Two hours after he'd brought her in her son had been screaming in his gloved hands in the operating room.

And then he'd made the biggest decision of his life. Because that's when it hit him. Like a lightning bolt. He loved her.

And he couldn't be the baby's doctor. No matter what he'd promised Amy, he couldn't be the neonatologist her child needed.

He'd too much emotional investment in this. And it would ruin his objectivity.

Yes, he could stand on the sidelines and discuss clinical decisions with the surrounding physicians but he had to step back. He had to take himself out of the equation. Because he didn't feel like a doctor around Amy's son. He felt like a parent.

But the one thing Amy had asked him to do was be her son's doctor. And chances were she would never forgive him.

Cassidy stood up again. 'I'm going back to ICU. She's going to wake up today. I want to be there.' Her voice was steady and determined, but Lincoln didn't know if she was trying to convince him or herself.

His hands cradled the little baby next to his chest. In most cases kangaroo care was carried out by the mother. But in this case, while Amy was unavailable, it seemed the most natural thing for him to be doing.

But he'd had no idea it would feel like this. The feel of the tiny translucent skin against his, the feeling of the little body warming against his, had swamped him. All this time he'd only really thought about Amy. He hadn't really brought her son into the equation. And now he was here, front and centre, and for the first time in his life Lincoln hadn't been able to distance himself into professional mode. He hadn't been able to sit on the sidelines and watch. He'd had to make sure he was in the middle of it all. No one else was allowed to carry out care for the baby.

And it would be easy right now to pretend this was all about guilt, and that he felt he owed it to Amy to look after her little boy. If that was how he felt, he could have stayed in doctor mode, in clinical mode, and done the best job that he could. But it wasn't how he felt. He could see Amy in this baby. And all the feelings he felt for her, whether he'd vocalised them or not, seemed to be intensified into this tiny body. Who could have known it could feel like this?

He'd often heard parents talk about being swamped by their feelings. But he'd never experienced it. Not like this. And he couldn't even begin to explain it. He had no genetic connection to this child. He had no parental rights.

Amy could wake up today and tell him she never wanted to see him again. And he knew all of that. But it didn't change how he felt.

He shifted the little feeding tube currently taped to the side of the baby's nose. Amy had wanted to breastfeed her baby, so they'd used some of the breast milk available in the NICU, but so far Junior hadn't responded to cup feeding or finger feeding and with a premature baby time was of the essence, so they'd had to resort to placing a small tube down into his stomach. So every few hours Lincoln got a small syringe and fed Amy's son tiny amounts of breast milk. Anything to help him.

'Okay, Junior, let's get you back inside your incubator for a while. I need to go and see your mommy.'

He glanced down at his rumpled clothes—the same shirt and jeans he'd been wearing when Amy had seized in the restaurant two days ago. He really needed to get changed.

Lincoln placed the baby carefully back inside the incubator, pulling a little blue hat over his head. He checked the chart hanging at the end of the crib. Baby Carson was actually doing quite well. His weight at three pounds eight ounces was good, and gave him a ninety-five per cent survival rate. The steroids had obviously done their job of maturing his lungs and he'd come out screaming and breathing on his own. There had only been a few incidences when he'd tried to feed that his oxygen saturation had dropped. And since he'd had the tube put down, there had been none.

The little guy had fighting spirit. Now, if only he had a name.

But Amy hadn't told him what she was going to name her son—she'd expected to be there to do that herself.

Lincoln felt the small hand wrap itself around his finger. *Please let her wake up soon.*

Amy felt weird. She was having a dream. But instead of a nice, pink, floaty dream, this was a strange, distant far-away dream. And her throat ached. Her mouth was dry and felt brittle and she couldn't even swallow. Her head was pounding and noises were disturbing her peaceful sleep. She couldn't concentrate. Maybe if she could just have a drink of water…

Her eyes felt heavy, crusted, and she struggled to pull her eyelids apart. White. That was all she could see. *What was that?*

She moved her hands. Something was hurting her wrist. Like a little pinch, a little squeeze. Her hands moved to her stomach, seeking the comfort of the rounded bump she'd spent the last few months embracing. The firmness was gone. In its place only soft sagging skin. Alarm bells started racing in her head. Something wasn't right. Where was she? What was happening?

She could feel something pressing on her face and she reached up to pull it aside. She started struggling to breathe, taking short, rapid breaths. A figure appeared in her line of vision. Blonde. Boobs. Was it Barbie?

The voice was talking, but she wasn't sure what it was saying. A strong, calm voice. 'Amy. Amy. Calm down. Everything's fine. It's Cassidy Yates. You're in hospital—in San Francisco Maternity. Here…let me put this mask back on your face for a few moments.' The figure moved around to the side. 'I'm going to raise your bed slightly, Amy.' There was a buzzing noise and Amy felt herself move upwards. The white view changed to a hospital scene.

A hospital scene she should be familiar with. A busy ICU. As a former theatre nurse she'd spent many hours transferring patients to and from Theatre to ICU and back again. But even the familiarity didn't help.

There was a sense that something was wrong. She didn't feel right. She felt…empty.

Then it struck her. Her brain shifted sharply into focus and a million panicked thoughts filling her mind. 'My baby? Where's my baby?' Although she felt as if she was shouting, her voice was quiet, barely a whisper.

Cassidy leaned forward, touching her hand and squeezing it tightly. 'Your son is fine, Amy. He's in NICU. Lincoln's with him—I don't think he's left his side in the last forty-eight hours.'

Amy blinked. This wasn't real. This couldn't be happening. What did she mean—the last forty-eight hours?

The confusion must have registered on her face. Cassidy kept hold of her hand. 'Amy, do you remember anything about what happened?'

Amy shook her head. Her mind was currently

mush. She couldn't take in where she was, let alone anything else.

Cassidy bent closer, reaching up and moving some loose strands of hair from her face. Why was this woman being so nice to her? Something turned inside her stomach. *She didn't like this woman*, but she couldn't remember why.

Her eyes went downwards. There was an IV in her hand. That's what the strange feeling was at her wrist. The tape surrounding it was catching the little hairs on her wrist. Tiny pieces of the jigsaw puzzle started slotting into place in her brain. Cassidy was talking again. 'You had a seizure, Amy. Two days ago. Lincoln brought you in, we stabilised you, then we had to take you to Theatre and deliver your baby. You've been in here ever since.'

Amy clung to the one part that registered in her brain. 'Zachary. How is Zachary?'

Cassidy's face broke into a smile. 'Zachary? That's what you're calling your son? What a beautiful name.' She glanced over her shoulder. 'Lincoln will be so pleased to hear it. He's been calling him Junior these last two days.'

Amy tried to pull her dry lips together again. 'Lincoln's looking after my son?'

Something registered on Cassidy's face. A fleeting glance, as if she shouldn't say something. But she pressed her lips together. 'Yes…and no.' It took her a few seconds to decide what to say. 'He's not your son's doctor. But he's been acting as a…surrogate parent for the last two days. He hasn't left Zachary's side. He's been doing all the kangaroo care for your son.'

Images flooded into Amy's mind. Her brain was still befuddled. Lincoln with her baby. Holding her baby, feeding her baby. She knew Zach would have been in safe hands. But hadn't he promised to be her baby's doctor?

'I don't understand…'

Cassidy stood upright, the relief on her face obvious. 'Oh, good, he's here. I'll let him speak to you himself.' She gave a final squeeze to Amy's hand. 'I'll come back later—to talk with you about your treatment.'

She walked towards Lincoln and gave his shoulder a little squeeze on the way past.

Amy watched as the green-suited figure appeared in the doorway. Her eyes were taking a little time to focus. Why was that?

Then she felt him engulf her in a hug, pulling her head and shoulders clear of the bed and into his chest. He held her so tightly she started to cough.

He released her quickly. 'Sorry. I'm just so pleased you've woken up. I've been so worried.' He clasped her hands, words tumbling from his mouth. 'The baby's doing well. He's breathing on his own—right from delivery—and he's a good weight for twenty-nine weeks: three pounds eight ounces. He's not feeding on his own yet, we've had to put a tube down, but I've made sure that he's getting breast milk. Oh, and you need to tell me his name, so I can put it in his records.'

Lincoln. It was definitely Lincoln. He was babbling. She didn't have any problem focusing up close. She could see his green theatre scrubs, his tousled dark hair and blue-rimmed, tired eyes. There was a definite shadow around his jaw—she'd felt it brush her cheek as he'd hugged her.

She blinked, focusing further—giving her brain time to make sense of it all in her head. She could see the deep lines etched into his forehead and filtering out from the corners of his eyes. Had they always been there? He looked exhausted.

She blinked. And in that instant there was something else. A fleeting picture of a darkened restaurant and a smell…a strong smell of fresh fish. The memory gave her a jolt, startling other little pieces of the jigsaw puzzle into place. An expression on Lincoln's face that she didn't recognise. He'd been angry with her. They'd been fighting.

That's why he looked like hell.

His fingers touched the inside of her palm. 'Amy, are you with me?' The anxiety was back.

She nodded, her dry tongue coming out and trying to lick her lips. He responded instantly, picking up a glass of iced water with a straw from her bedside table. Where had that come from?

He held the straw at her lips and she sucked deeply. 'Steady,' he said, pulling it away for a second then bringing it back to her again. He let her take some more sips. 'Better?'

She nodded and let out a sigh. 'Zachary. Zachary John Carson. That's my son's name.'

His eyes met hers and he nodded in recognition. 'It's a beautiful name.'

'I want to see him.' Now she'd found her voice again, it was steely and determined. A wave of emotions rode up inside her, like a crest of a wave. She'd missed the first two days of her son's life. She hadn't been the first person to hold him, to hear him cry or feed him. She'd missed so much already. 'I want to see him now.'

Lincoln hesitated. 'You've just woken up, Amy, I don't think you're stable enough to go to NICU. And I'm sorry, but I can't bring Zachary in here.' He waved his hand around the ICU. There were four other adult patients in the room. One was attached to a ventilator—that must have been the burring noise that she'd heard—and two others had assisted ventilation. 'There's too big a risk of exposure to infection.'

Amy knew he was being eminently sensible. But forty-eight hours' worth of post-birth hormones didn't care. 'I *need* to see my son.'

Something washed over Lincoln's face. Guilt. Why did he feel guilty? 'I know you do, Amy.' His hand was still pressed next to hers. 'Let me see what I can arrange. I promise you'll see your son soon.'

For a second she thought he was going to bend

over and kiss her. But he hesitated midway across the bed, pulling back and heading out the door in his green scrubs.

And that's when the floodgates opened.

Two hours later she was ensconced in a side room. Lincoln pushed the neonate crib into the room and Amy's breath caught in her throat. Her son.

That tiny little scrap she could see through the plastic was hers. Her baby. Wrapped in a pale blue blanket with a tiny knitted cap on his head. Fists punching angrily in the air. And a tiny plastic tube coming from his nose and taped to the side of his cheek.

Her breast ached. She wanted to feed her baby. She wanted to feel his little body next to hers. She could feel her lips tremble as Lincoln lifted him out of the crib and handed him to her.

Zachary gave a little groan and snuggled towards her—a natural response. She felt transfixed. His little eyes were screwed up, his skin pale just like hers, a few tiny strands of dark hair on his head. The wrinkled forehead smoothed out and his eyes blinked open, staring upright straight into her eyes. Her heart gave a little flutter at the blue eyes, then she realised that all babies were born with blue eyes. His eye colour could change over the next year. The thought brought a little smile to her face.

The next year. She was going to spend all that time with her son. She might have missed the first few days but there was nothing to stop her now. A little warmth spread across her chest. She lifted her finger and stroked it down her son's button nose. He was all hers. Six years she'd waited for this moment, and now she finally had her child in her arms.

Lincoln shifted his feet beside her, obviously not wanting to interrupt her first few moments with her son. She blinked back the tears forming in her eyes. 'Thank you for looking after him,' she whispered.

He looked uncomfortable. He sat down in the chair next to her bed, bringing him level with her. 'I need to tell you something.'

'What?' She couldn't take her eyes from her son.

'I couldn't do what you wanted me to.'

Cassidy's words started to float around her

brain again. This time, though, they started to register. Something about Lincoln not being her baby's doctor...

She found the little hospital band attached to his tiny wrist and rotated it. Baby Carson. Three pounds eight ounces. And his date of birth. Dr Lomax. Who was Dr Lomax?

A surge of anger struck her. Her cold stare fixed on Lincoln. 'What is it you want to tell me, Lincoln?'

She could see the pain on his face. This wasn't easy for him—but right now she didn't care. She'd asked him to do one thing for her. One thing. She'd travelled miles to find him, to find the best doctor to look after her son—and now this.

He ran his fingers through his hair the way he always did when he was nervous. 'I'm really sorry, Amy. This is all my fault. I should have kept a better eye on you—I shouldn't have taken you out to dinner. This would never have happened if I'd kept in the role I should have—as the doctor for your son.' He shook his head and lifted his eyes to meet hers. 'But I just couldn't.'

Amy took a breath. The air felt tight in her

chest. 'What do you mean, this is all your fault? How is any of this your fault? Lincoln, you let me stay in your apartment—you drove me to hospital every day, how can you possibly think this is your fault?'

'Your headache. You told me you had a headache and I ignored the signs, something a doctor on his game would never have done. I could have got you to hospital sooner. I should have been paying attention.'

She shook her head. '*I* should have paid more attention. Not you. I'd had that headache all day, but I thought it was nothing. Cassidy warned me—she gave me a list of signs and symptoms to look out for, and told me to come straight back to hospital if I developed any of them. But it seemed so mild, so subtle. It didn't even start to bother me until later in the day. I honestly thought it was just a headache. I never thought it would lead to this.' She glanced down at the bundle in her arms. 'Do you honestly think I would have put my son at risk? The headache was so mild that I hadn't even thought about taking anything until we were out. Up until then it really felt like nothing.'

The lines in his forehead were deeper than normal. She was doing nothing to alleviate his guilt. What else did he want to tell her?

Lincoln leaned forward in the chair, resting his arms on the side of her bed. 'When I saw you seizing…it was the worst five minutes of my life. By the time we got here and stabilised you then made the decision to take you to Theatre, I knew I couldn't be Zach's doctor.'

'What do you mean, you couldn't be my son's doctor?' Her voice had a cold, hard edge to it. 'It was the one thing I asked you to do for me, Lincoln. It was the *only* thing I asked you to do for me.'

'I know, I know.' The anguish in his voice was apparent, and she knew he was struggling to find the words.

'Who is Dr Lomax, Lincoln?'

'He's my colleague. My friend—someone I would trust with my child's life. As soon as I held Zach in my arms in Theatre, I knew I had to get someone else to do the job. I couldn't think straight. I couldn't think like a doctor while I was looking at him. I couldn't be the professional that I needed to be. I couldn't step back and see the wider picture. All I could see was the woman I loved lying on the operating table and her twenty-nine-week-old son in my hands. I knew I had to get someone else to do the job.'

His words hung in the air.

He loved her. He'd said it. Words that she'd been waiting to hear. So why wasn't she jumping for joy? Why wasn't she shouting it from the rooftops?

He was looking at her, waiting for her to respond. She tried to sort out her brain. She wanted to tell him that she loved him too. But something was stopping her. Something was pressing down on her chest, willing her not to say those words.

She kept her eyes on her baby. She didn't want to look at those dark-rimmed blue eyes. She didn't want them to pull her in and say something she would later regret.

Her son was staring up at her. Could he see her yet? Could he see the anguish on her face? How well could a twenty-nine-weeker see?

'Cassidy said that you'd looked after him, that you'd done kangaroo care. That you hadn't left his side for forty-eight hours.'

'I couldn't be his doctor, Amy, but that doesn't mean I don't care—it means I care too much. I didn't want anyone else to do his care. I wanted to be by his side. I wanted to watch over him. I wanted to feed him.'

A single tear slid down her face. It was just as she'd feared. He was professing not only his love for her but for Zach too. This should be what happy endings were about. But she still couldn't lift her head to meet his gaze.

Her feelings for him were so strong. Since the first time she'd seen him again, all her thoughts and memories of him had increased tenfold. He was everything she could ever want.

But what did that make her to him?

She didn't want to be his charity case. His poor ex with a baby he felt sorry for. He was feeling guilty right now. Guilt that he was confusing with love. He didn't love her. She wasn't the whole, healthy woman she'd been before.

She was damaged goods. Her body would never be the same again, even if she had the reconstruction surgery.

And Zach was it for her. She would never be able to have more natural kids. Her eggs were gone. Finished. And Lincoln...he was just starting out. He should have a whole brood of children of his own. And a happy, healthy wife who could give them to him.

She didn't want him to settle. She didn't want him to settle for her and Zachary. Even though it could make her happier than she'd thought possible, she wanted him to have the chance at life that she'd missed out on.

He stood up and moved to the side of the bed, sliding his arm around her shoulders and bending over to look down at Zach. 'Do you feel well enough to try the kangaroo care for a little while? Do you think you could manage him strapped next to your chest?'

She nodded. She couldn't speak right now. Words were just too difficult. He'd just stood up, not waiting for a response from her. He seemed to accept that she couldn't say the 'I love you' words back. What did that mean?

'Do you need some analgesia for your section wound before we start?'

She shook her head. The Caesarean section wound wasn't nearly as painful as she'd imagined. Maybe being unconscious for the first forty-eight hours had helped. The nurse had given her a couple of painkillers when she'd woken up and she felt fine.

Lincoln rummaged around in her locker. 'Let's find you something else to wear. That hospital gown won't do.'

He was right. The traditional hospital gown, with its Velcro fastenings at the back, wouldn't suit. He pulled out a pair of loose yellow jersey pyjamas, with buttons down the front. 'What about these?'

Amy nodded her head. Her tiny son was still in her arms. A nurse came into the room and between her and Lincoln they helped Amy freshen up and then secure her son next to her.

The next few hours passed swiftly. Amy tried to get her tiny son to latch onto her breast, and when that failed, she managed to express some of her milk to feed to him via the tiny tube down his nose. The nurse rechecked her vital signs and reduced some of her IV infusions.

Cassidy came and checked on her twice. She talked her through the events and her subsequent care, warning her that women could still have seizures after delivery and that she would need to be observed for the next few days.

And Lincoln floated in and out of her room all day, taking Zachary back to the nursery for a spell then bringing him back to her later.

It was almost as if the words hadn't been spoken—or never been heard. Life was beginning to tick along as normal. Why did that make her feel so empty inside?

Lincoln wheeled the cot back along the corridor to NICU. Zachary was doing well and seemed a little brighter since his mother had woken up. Although he hadn't managed to latch on today, there was every chance that he'd start breastfeeding soon and then his tube could be removed.

So why did life feel at a standstill?

For Lincoln, the instant feeling of relief when Amy had woken up had now been replaced by a feeling of worthlessness. She didn't blame him for her deterioration, she hadn't even been too angry when he'd told her he couldn't be Zachary's doctor. In fact, she'd hardly said *anything*, even after his heart had been in his throat and he'd said those words. The *I love you* words.

And there had been nothing—no response. It was almost as if he hadn't spoken.

Lincoln looked at the little baby lying in the crib beneath him. Zachary Carson. Every day he grew more attached. Every day he noticed something else about the little guy. Something new.

But what if this was a recipe for disaster? Amy had never said anything to make him think she was looking for anything else from him.

He still couldn't get to the bottom of what Amy wanted and it frustrated him beyond belief. She'd come here saying she wanted his skills and expertise as a doctor. But from the moment they'd set eyes on each other again, the tension in the air had been palpable.

He loved it that she was unpredictable. He loved it that she flirted with him. He loved it that they still seemed to fit together like pieces in a jigsaw puzzle.

But Amy was different too. Illness had changed her. A high-risk pregnancy had changed her. She wasn't as confident as she used to be. Sure, he knew that her body had changed, but something else had changed deep inside her. Was it her feelings of self-worth? He just couldn't put his finger on it. He couldn't really understand. And it was making him tiptoe around about her, something he'd never had to do before.

Then there was the guilt. Guilt that she'd come to him for help and he'd let her down. He'd let his guard down. He didn't want to be Amy's son's doctor.

One of the NICU nurses walked past and gave him a little smile. Carrie. Blonde. Cute. Nice butt. The old Lincoln would have chased her out the door. The old Lincoln would have had her number in his phone in two minutes flat.

Lincoln moved into autopilot. He lifted Zachary from the crib, strapped him to his chest and nestled him under his shirt.

He had absolutely no doubt about where he wanted to be. The effect of seeing Amy again after six years had been like a punch to the face. No woman had made him feel the way she did. He hadn't recognised love because he'd never felt it before. He didn't know what to say to her, when to back off, or when to move closer.

This was a steep learning curve.

But he'd never been one to shirk a challenge—and this was one thing he was determined to master.

CHAPTER NINE

AMY swallowed nervously as she climbed the steps towards the apartment. Her arms couldn't hide the slight tremor in them as she carried her precious bundle upstairs to the place she was currently calling 'home'.

This was nothing like she'd imagined. Zachary was six weeks old—he shouldn't even have been born yet. But his feeding and weight gain had been sufficient for him to be discharged from San Francisco's Children's Hospital. His skin had lost that translucent look and his little body had finally managed to store a tiny amount of fat and fill out a little.

His wide blue eyes had obviously started to focus and she could see him studying her face at times and reacting to her expressions. And at five pounds he was even big enough to wear some of the premature baby clothes she'd carefully folded in a drawer in Lincoln's apartment.

But all of this still unsettled her. She was in San Francisco—this wasn't home to her—but it could be. The longer she stayed here, the more she loved this city, from its quirky visitors and attractions to its deep-rooted history and traditions. She loved looking over to the Golden Gate Bridge, she loved the bustling people around Pier 39. She loved the rattle of the cable cars. And most of all she loved the staff attached to San Francisco's Children and Maternity Hospital. Unlike most hospitals, she'd yet to meet a member of staff who hadn't been warm and friendly, who hadn't made her feel at home. She was sure that being a good friend of one the consultants helped. But it was also a place she could see a future in, a place where she would be happy to go to work. So why the strange feeling in her stomach?

Lincoln had arranged for Zachary's baby items to be delivered to San Francisco from Santa Maria. Literally overnight the white wooden baby crib and chest of drawers had appeared in her bedroom in Lincoln's apartment. The zebra-print baby seat was currently sitting next to the sofa in the living room. And the red pram was parked at the bottom of the stairs. All awaiting the arrival of baby Zachary.

She thought that she would have loved this moment. To finally bring her son home from hospital was a huge step. She should be singing from the rooftops. She should be telling the whole world that Zach was well enough to come home. But she wasn't. She couldn't.

She was nervous. She felt sick. Her stomach was churning. Was this new-mother nerves? Or something else?

The patient, easily accessible staff in the NICU were no longer by her side. The emergency monitors and equipment were no longer ready to be pulled over at a moment's notice. All the little queries or insecurities she'd had in the last few weeks couldn't be answered by another person in the room. Or could they?

Because Lincoln was here with her. Lincoln hadn't left her side. Or Zachary's.

He'd done everything he could to help her. He'd bent over backwards to be accommodating. And as much as she was grateful, it was going to make it so much harder to say goodbye…

Because right now she knew that was what she had to do.

Lincoln slid his key into the lock in the door and pushed the buttons to turn off the alarm. He held the door wide for her. She gave a little smile and carried Zachary into the apartment, walking over to one of the huge windows. 'What do you think, Zach? Do you like this place?'

Because she certainly did. So why did she feel as if she had to leave? Why, when the man of her dreams was offering her love, did she feel as if she had to retreat to the distant hills? Why did she feel that she couldn't even enter into a discussion with him?

She carried Zach through to the bedroom. 'Here's your crib, right next to Mommy's bed. I'll be able to stick my hand through and hold your hand.' She held him up to look, but Zach just blinked.

Her attention was caught by something new. 'Wow, look at this.' She leaned over and touched the mobile hanging above the crib and turned on the music. The soft, multicoloured animals started to spin around to 'Nelly the Elephant'. 'Did you get this?' she asked Lincoln.

He nodded slowly, folding his arms and leaning against the doorpost. 'Colour and noise are supposed to stimulate babies.' That smile again. That smile that drew you in and held you there. Held you with those dark blue eyes.

Being around him was good. His easy way and infectious laugh made her feel comfortable. She'd fallen asleep in his arms several times over the last few weeks, resting in the chairs next to Zachary's crib in NICU, and woken to find her head on his chest and her arms wrapped around him.

The electricity between them was still there. He just wasn't acting on it.

And for some strange reason it hurt.

She knew it was all her fault. She hadn't reacted when he'd told her that he loved her. She'd stayed silent, and he must have been hurt by that. But what could she do? What could she offer him? A woman with an altered body? Someone who hadn't yet reached the golden 'five years cancer-free'? The chance to have no natural children of his own? Lincoln was a gorgeous, handsome man. He deserved to have a better future than the one she could offer him.

She already knew that he was becoming more attached to her and Zachary. If the last few weeks hadn't been so hard she might have got her act together and done something about it.

But she hadn't. And now here she was, in his apartment, with her baby son.

She felt an arm at her waist, but it was a casual movement, not an intimate one. Zachary's eyes were starting to close, so she pulled off his padded jacket and laid him down in his crib for the first time, leaning back against Lincoln to watch his eyelids finally flicker shut and his little body relax.

'It's been a big day.' His voice was warm, comforting, like a big blanket enveloping her.

'It has.' She sighed as she pressed the little night-light next to the crib. His first night home from hospital. Should she really be feeling so terrified?

'Want me to make dinner?'

All of sudden she felt exhausted. She wanted to lie down in the bed next to her son and watch him sleep. She wanted to watch his little chest rise and fall. She wanted to stretch her hand through the bars and let his little fingers wrap around her big one so they could hold each other while they slept. She shook her head. 'I'm not hungry, Linc. I just want to lie down.'

He gave her waist a little squeeze. 'You've got to keep your strength up. I have it on good authority that babies are hard work. How about I make you something light like scrambled eggs?' His hand lifted up and stroked the back of her neck in a soothing motion. 'It will take five minutes then you could soak in the bath if you wanted.'

A bath. A deep-filled bath overflowing with lavender scents and bubbles. That would be sheer bliss. She hadn't had a bath since she'd had Zachary. She always seemed to be racing in and out of the shower. It had seemed quicker, more convenient. This could be perfect.

She gave a little nod. 'Scrambled eggs would be good.' She stepped over towards the en suite bathroom and picked up the bottle of dark purple bubble bath, opening it, tipping a generous portion into the white roll-topped bath then turning the tap on full blast.

Ten minutes later, tummy full of scrambled eggs and a baby soundly sleeping, Amy stepped into the water and slid her body beneath the bubbles.

She would have a think about things tomorrow—sort everything out in her mind. Everything would seem clearer then and she would think about what to say to Lincoln. She could make plans about returning to Santa Maria and finding a paediatrician for her son. She would eventually have to think about childcare for Zachary—who would want to look after a baby that had been born premature? She would need childcare that could be flexible around her shifts. Would she be able to find anyone to do that? Maybe she should find a different job? Even the thoughts exhausted her. Tonight she just wanted to relax.

'Amy!'

The sharp knock on the door woke her with a jolt. Her brain took a few seconds to focus, obviously a few seconds too long because the door opened and Lincoln stuck his head through the gap. 'Is everything okay?'

Amy had sat bolt upright with the knock on the door, leaving her breast above the bubbled waterline and her flat side exposed. Her hands flew to her chest and she ducked beneath the bubbles again. 'Lincoln! Don't come in, I'm still in the bath!' Her cheeks flamed red. She must have dozed off as the water was now lukewarm. She leaned forward to grab a fluffy towel from beside the bath.

He must have seen her scar. He must have seen the empty side.

Lincoln pulled back. The panic on Amy's face was evident. He hadn't meant to embarrass her, he'd just wanted to check she was okay. Then he stopped. Took a deep breath, stepped into the bathroom and closed the door behind him.

'Lincoln! What are you doing?'

'Something I should have done weeks ago.'

He bent forward and picked up the towel she was grappling for, holding it open in front of him. 'Come on.'

Her flaming cheeks burned even harder. 'You've got to be joking.'

'No. I'm not.' His voice was firm and deter-mined. He gestured with the towel once more. 'Come on, Amy.'

'No.' Her voice was sharp and to the point.

He stared at her.

'Don't, Lincoln. You're making me uncomfortable.'

He knelt down next to the bath so his face was level with hers. 'I'm not trying to make you uncomfortable, Amy. But this is an issue between us—you know it is. I'm not here to upset you. I'm your friend. I'm here to support you. Now, get out the bath so we can talk about this. Take the first step.' He held the towel out again.

Her bottom lip trembled. She didn't feel ready for this. She wanted to pull her knees up to her chest, tuck her chin on top and hide her body from the world. Why couldn't he be plain? Why couldn't he be ugly? Would that make it easier? Would it be easier to bare your blemished body to someone who didn't reek of perfection?

She bit her lip, a sheen across her eyes. *Take the first step.* How did he know exactly what to say? She had to be brave. He was right. He was getting right to the heart of the matter. It was an issue. She just didn't know if she could handle this.

There was only one way to do this. She had to try. She owed it to herself to try. She closed her eyes and stood upright, stepping out the bath almost simultaneously and moving across into the comfort of the white fluffy towel. He wrapped it around her and she caught the edges of it, pulling it closer and tucking it around her before she opened her eyes.

He gestured to the side of the bath. 'Sit down.' He picked up another towel and dried her bare legs. Had he even had a chance to get a proper look at her scarred body? What had he thought?

His arm went around her shoulders, escorting her from the bathroom and into his bedroom. *His bedroom*. She hadn't set foot in this room the whole time she'd been staying here. She felt the breath catch in her throat as he guided her over towards his bed, then her heart plummeted as he stood her in front of the free-standing, full-length mirror next to his bed. He raised his hand and pulled the cream blind at the window, plunging the room into semi-darkness, with some of the early evening sun still filtering through the blind.

All of a sudden she didn't feel so exhausted. Maybe the nap in the bath had revived her, but she didn't think so. Her blood was racing around her body. Why did this feel so natural? Why wasn't she terrified?

She'd been planning to leave. She'd been think-ing about telling Lincoln a million reasons why she and Zachary shouldn't stay there. So why did this feel as though it should happen?

'Now.' He guided her in front of the mirror, standing behind her with his hands at her waist. 'What do you see?'

'What do you mean?'

His voice radiated calm. A man totally in con-trol, who knew exactly what he was doing. 'I want you to look in the mirror and tell me what you see.'

She turned to face him. 'I can't. I don't want to do this any more.'

There it was on her face again. Panic. Put her in a situation out of her control and she floun-dered. He ran his finger down her cheek, the most delicate of touches. 'Yes, yes, you can.' He gently spun her around again. 'I'll tell you what I see.' His hands crept back around her waist, his tall body right behind hers, his strength and muscles running down the length of her body, his chin resting on her shoulder, staring at their joint reflections.

He smiled into the mirror and touched her

hair. 'I see a beautiful woman, with gorgeous red tresses and magical green eyes.' He ran his finger along the skin at her neck. 'I see pale skin and a tiny splash of freckles across her nose.' His chin swapped round to the other side of her body, as if he was appreciating her from all angles. 'And I like the pale skin—because it's different. Most women here could die a death from fake tan—or a death from a real tan. I like it that your skin is completely natural and untouched by the sun. You don't need a tan. Your pure beauty radiates from your skin.'

His words danced like a song over her. Rising and falling, causing her heart to flutter in her chest one moment and her clenched stomach to flip over the next.

She looked at the reflection in the mirror. The pale face stared back at her. The tired eyes, the washed-out face. Why couldn't she see what he did?

She leaned backwards a little, relaxing into his strength. In some ways she hated this, and in others she knew that the time was right and this was exactly what she needed. And Lincoln was right—it was easier doing this with a friend.

His hands reached in front of her body to where the towel was tucked in. She flinched. No! She could see the fear in her own face in the mirror, but she was intrigued by his reflection. His fingers were gently untucking the towel, loosening it and lifting the edges, dropping the white towel to the floor and leaving her naked body exposed in front of the mirror.

And his face didn't look shocked, didn't look disgusted and didn't look repulsed. In fact, he bent and kissed the skin at the bottom of her neck, wrapping one arm around her waist, keeping her close to him.

He lifted his head again, staring at her in the mirror. 'Don't be afraid,' he whispered, a comforting smile on his face. Her hands were trembling again, she couldn't help it—she'd never felt so exposed. And although the room was warm, goose-bumps appeared all over her pale flesh.

His hand came up on one side and cupped her full breast. There was nothing sexual in his touch. Her breast was working overtime feeding her son right now and even the slightest touch could make milk leak. On the other side his fingers traced a light line up from her hip bone to under her arm, pausing for only a second before running along the flat, pale, white line of her scar—where her breast should be.

Her eyes took in her reflection. Six weeks on from giving birth and her lower body had started to return to normal. Her stomach wasn't flat. It probably never would be again and there was a small, visible red scar running along her bikini line. But it was a neat scar, well healed and already starting to retreat into her body. In a few years' time it would be pale and virtually unnoticeable. Unlike the scar at her breast. A visible marker of something missing.

He kissed her neck again whilst his fingers danced along her skin. And he kept on kissing her as his hands gently caressed her. She was caught, watching the reflection in the mirror of a handsome man touching a lover's body. There was no shame. No horror. Like a slow movie scene, with romantic music playing. Only this time, instead of music, it was one word repeating itself over and over in her head. Acceptance.

The kisses reached the bottom of her throat. The hand left her full breast—as if he knew it was too sensitive for touch right now—and reached up to tangle in her red curls. He moved, lifting up her arm on her affected side and looping it around behind his neck. Then he watched in the mirror as he ran his fingers once more down her side. Another woman might have flinched at the light, tickling sensations. But for Amy it was different. It was all about acceptance. And it wasn't about his acceptance of her. It was about her acceptance of her changed body.

She was staring at the reflection in front of her. And the old sensations were gone. And she didn't see something to be ashamed of. She didn't see something she should hide from the world. This wasn't something she would ever share. But it was something that she didn't need to hide away from any more. For the first time in six years she could look at her naked body without feeling fear or repulsion. This was a woman who had the right to be loved.

Her hand moved from behind his neck to run through his hair. The movement caused her to lean backwards, exposing even more of the sensitive flesh at the base of her neck to his lips. She wasn't looking in the mirror any more. She was losing herself in the feelings.

'This is the body of the woman that I love. This is the body of a vibrant, healthy and whole woman.' His fingers went to her flat surface again. 'This is only a tiny part of Amy. And I don't care if you decide to have reconstruction surgery or not. I will take you however you come. If it matters to you then fine. But don't change anything for me, because I love you just the way you are.'

He spun her round, hands at her waist. He looked her straight in the eye. He moved forward, pressing himself against her. She was naked and he was still fully clothed. But she could feel his hard length through his jeans, pressing against her abdomen. A smile came across her lips.

He was hard. He was very hard. It didn't matter that she felt her body was disfigured. It didn't matter that she felt she had to hide. The proof was right in front of her—literally. She turned him on. He wanted her.

She felt twenty-five again. She felt young and whole. The way she used to feel when she'd danced around his cabin naked. Her fingers moved and unfastened the buttons on his jeans, releasing him into her hands.

For the first time in five years she felt powerful. She felt sexual. It was a glimmer of what she'd felt in that hospital room the last time they'd kissed. Control. She felt in control.

He was staring at her, with those sexy, half-shut eyes. Even if she'd been on the other side of the room, those eyes alone could have turned her on. But right now his fingers were moving lower. Going from one set of red curls to another. She moved closer. She wasn't going to flinch at his touch now. This was what she wanted. She was ready.

She'd had her six-week postnatal check. Everything was as it should be. There was no reason she couldn't have sex. And from the way her body was currently responding, it was telling her it was time.

He reached his hands up to either side of her head. His eyes fixed on hers. 'Are you sure?' he whispered. 'We only do this if you want to— you're in charge.' There was a glimmer in his eye. He knew exactly what he was doing. He was giving her all the control—and it was sexy as hell.

She tilted her head to one side, her eyes glancing down at the prize possession in her hands. 'I want to see what I'm getting.' She whipped his T-shirt up and pulled it over his head, revealing his muscular torso. Her hands pressed against him. 'Not too shabby,' she whispered with a glint in her eye.

She pushed him backwards onto the bed, climbing above him. 'So *I'm* in charge?' she questioned.

His smile revealed his straight white teeth. 'Absolutely.'

'Good. Then this is what we're going to do...'

The early morning sunlight was filtering through the blind again. Amy had been up twice in the night to feed and change Zachary, and on each occasion he'd settled back down to sleep quickly.

It would have been nice to wake up in Lincoln's arms and feel his body heat next to hers, but the reality of a premature baby dictated how things would work out.

Last night had been cathartic for her. She'd finally got to the place she needed to. She'd felt desired, wanted, sexual. She'd felt loved. But the early morning light brought a whole new range of issues with it. Issues where she'd barely even scratched the surface. She threw back the white duvet and swung her legs out of the bed. Her feet padded across the dark wooden floor and she stopped in the doorway of Lincoln's room.

His long, lean naked body was entwined around his duvet cover. It looked like one of those ultra-trendy pictures you could buy in black and white and put on your wall. His chest was rising and falling and there was a dark shadow around his chin where the stubble was starting to appear. He was picture-perfect.

She moved in front of the free-standing mirror where he'd undressed her last night. She released the belt on the fluffy white dressing gown and let it fall open. She stared at her reflection. One round full breast and one flat white scar. Her finger traced along the line of the scar. Even now, after everything that had happened, it still made a little shiver go down her spine. Last night Lincoln had shown her acceptance. Acceptance for who she was now. She kept staring, her breathing and heart rate quickening. She didn't like the image in the mirror. She didn't like the person staring back at her. Lincoln may have shown her accep-tance but in the cold light of day she couldn't accept herself. She couldn't accept the reflection in the mirror.

Last night may have been wonderful, but it was only the start of the journey for her.

She could hear his breathing behind her. It could be so easy if she could just push all this aside and forget about it. It would be so easy to climb into bed next to him and snuggle into his arms. But this was never going to go away.

What was wrong? Why did her life feel like sand running through her fingers on the beach? How could she explain that to him? How could she tell him that no matter how good he was to her and Zachary, right now she needed to be on her own. How could she tell him she had to leave?

This was killing her. She'd thought that the cancer might kill her and she'd beaten that. But this was causing her more pain than the cancer ever had. More pain than the surgery and more pain than the chemotherapy and radiotherapy put together. And the worst thing about this was that she was the only person who could feel it. She wanted to feel free, she wanted to feel easy with herself. More than anything she wanted to have a happy family life. And she knew without a shadow of a doubt that Lincoln loved Zachary as if he were his own.

That's what made this so hard.

She had to step away. She didn't want to hurt him, but if she stayed without facing her demons she couldn't predict their future.

She wanted to be with Lincoln because she loved him. Not because he was the easy way for her to deal with her past illness. It wasn't true to herself and it wasn't fair to him. If she tried to deal with how she felt while staying with Lincoln, it could cloud her judgement and influence her decisions. She needed to step away. And she needed to do it before he became even more attached to Zach.

What if he met someone else? Someone who could give him a family of his own? The thought made her stomach churn. It was a risk she had to take.

She wanted to love Lincoln with her whole heart, not just the little piece she hadn't locked away.

His eyelids flickered open and a lazy smile appeared across his face. He lifted the corner of the twisted duvet. 'Wanna come in?'

She shook her head, but walked over towards him and sat on the edge of the bed. 'Morning.' Her voice was cool.

He rested his head on his hand. 'What's up? Something wrong with Zachary?'

'No, he's fine.' She smoothed her hand along the bed, focusing on the crumpled sheet rather than his face. 'He's sleeping again.'

'So why don't you come back to bed?' There was a twinkle in his eye again and it pulled at her heartstrings. She didn't want to hurt him. He'd helped her in more ways than he could ever imagine.

She took a deep breath and stood up, turning to face him. She had to be calm, she had to be in control. 'I have to leave, Lincoln.'

The words came like a bolt out of the blue, causing him to sit upright and swing his legs out of the bed. So much for a lazy morning. 'What on earth are you talking about?'

'I can't stay here any more. You've been so kind, but I need some time—some space.'

Deep lines of utter confusion furrowed

Lincoln's brow. 'We go from last night—to this?
Did I do something wrong?'

She shook her head and touched his arm. 'No,
Linc. You didn't. You did something wonderful.
But that's what's wrong. I've spent five years
avoiding this. I've spent five years not dealing
with this. And I can't move on. I can't move on
to the next stage of my life without dealing with
this first.'

'So why can't we deal with it together?'

She sighed. 'Because there can't be an "us".
There can't be a "together". I've got to take some
time to learn to accept who I am and what I've
been through. And I've got to do it on my own.
I've got to do this on my own terms.'

'Why on earth do you think you've got to do
this yourself? I told you last night that I was
happy to take you the way you are.'

She sat down next to him. 'I know you did,
Lincoln.' She looked down at the space where
her breast should be. 'You're happy to take me
the way I am…' she looked at him with tear-
glazed eyes '…but I'm not. This isn't about you.
It's about me.'

'Don't give me the "it's not you, it's me" speech. You owe me better than that.'

She bit her lip. 'I know I do, Linc. And I'm sorry. Ultimately, I truly want us to be together. I want us to be family. But I've got to be self-ish about this because right now I know I'm not ready and I've got to look after me first.'

'And you think this is the way? You think this is the answer? To go away? Hell, Amy, you're just out of hospital with a premature baby—do you really think this is the time to find your-self?' He was pacing around the room now in his white jersey shorts, agitated. She had to pull her eyes away.

But he hadn't finished. 'I've spent six weeks—*six weeks*—helping look after your son. And now you're just going to take him away from me?' His pacing grew more frenetic. 'I'm the one who's spent the most time with him, and I know I don't have any rights to him, I know Zachary isn't mine. But he feels like mine. He *feels* like my son. I can't just let you walk away. Zach knows me, he recognises me—how can this be good for him?'

Amy could feel a tear trickle from the corner

of her eye. This was harder than she'd ever imagined. Her heart was breaking. She'd never wanted this for Linc. She'd never wanted to hurt him. But that was exactly what she was doing. She'd come to him because she'd thought he'd be the best doctor for her son. But things had changed so much. This hadn't really been about healing her son, this had been about healing herself.

'This is about Zachary, Linc. This is all about Zachary. How can I be a good mother to him when I can't even look at my reflection in the mirror? How can I focus my time and attention on my son when this is hanging in the background? How can I even think about another relationship when I'm still not comfortable in my own skin?

'I want to be free to love you. I want to be free to watch you have a relationship with my son. But everything inside me is so screwed up. I need to go back home—home to Santa Maria and my friends. I need to learn to look after myself and Zach before I'm ready to do this. Don't you see what you've done for me? The best thing in the world. You've helped me realise I need to face up to my demons. I'm healthy, Linc. Physically, I'm healthy. And I hope that when I reach my five-year anniversary I'll be able to kiss my breast cancer goodbye completely. But inside?' She shook her head.

'I'm not quite there yet.' She lifted a finger and touched the side of his cheek—gently, tenderly. 'I need to take one last step. This is the final hurdle. The last thing I need to overcome. And you've given me the courage to do it. I want to have a relationship with you. I do. But right now I'm short-changing you. I'm not loving you the way I should. You need to let me go. You need to let me go and come back on my own terms.'

He stopped pacing and stared at her. She couldn't read his face. It was as if he was trying to make sense of her words. As if he was trying to rationalise what she was saying—trying to construct an argument against it. She could see the tension across the muscles in his shoulders and his abdomen. He was upset.

Then she saw his shoulders sag, his muscles relax. It was as if he'd resigned himself to the fact she wanted to leave. As if he understood her words and realised this was the only way.

And it caused her tears to flow even stronger.

He reached over and brushed a loose curl from her cheek, tucking it behind her ear. She could see a million thoughts in his eyes. He leaned forward. 'Sometimes the hardest bridge to cross is the one in your own mind.' His words were quiet, almost a whisper. 'I can't do this for you.'

'I know.' The words hung in the air between them, like a moment of suspended time.

He brushed a kiss to her cheek. 'If this is what you need, then I can't pretend to understand, but I'll always support you. You and Zach.'

He lifted his head. 'When do you want to go?' He hesitated. 'I want to say goodbye to Zach.'

She breathed a huge sigh of relief. It almost felt like a weight was lifting off her shoulders. She knew this would be killing him, but he was still giving her room to breathe, room to heal. 'I guess I should go today. I don't want to make this any more difficult.'

'Do you need a hand to move?' She could see the emotions on his face now. The pain she'd caused him bubbled beneath the surface. How could she do this to him?

'No. No, thanks. I'll make other arrangements.' She had to. She couldn't hurt him any more.

'Then let me say goodbye.' He picked up last nights discarded jeans from the floor and pulled them on. He grabbed a T-shirt from the cupboard and walked through to her bedroom. Through to where Zachary lay sleeping in his crib.

She watched as he bent over and stroked the side of Zachary's face, whispering to him for a few minutes. She had no idea what he was saying and she was glad, because her legs currently felt like jelly.

He turned to face her, striding briskly from the room but stopping just for a second beside her.

His dark-rimmed eyes caught hers. She wanted to tell him she loved him. She wanted to tell him that she ached for his touch. She wanted to tell him that she would never feel about anyone else the way she currently felt about him.

He hesitated, just for a second, as if trying to fathom if he should say the words circulating in his brain or not. Then he gave her a little smile. 'You were my One That Got Away, you know?'

'What?' His words confused her.

He moved closer. 'They say everyone has one. *The One That Got Away.* The one person that if you could turn back the clock and do something different for, you would. Anything that would have stopped them leaving. You were mine, Amy. And you always will be.'

His eyes met hers. 'Maybe this is right for us.' He glanced around him, his gaze sweeping over the apartment. 'There's something that I've wanted to do for a while—something I've been putting off. This might just give me the time to do that.' He looked thoughtful then reached over and squeezed her hand. 'Promise me you'll keep in touch.'

Her lips trembled. 'I promise,' she whispered as he kissed her cheek once more and walked out the door.

She stared down onto the San Francisco street and watched him walk briskly along the side-walk. This was hard. Harder than she could ever have imagined.

But inside she knew it was right. She'd made a decision. Out there was the man she loved. She wanted to be with him with her whole heart.

She just needed to learn how to love herself first.

CHAPTER TEN

AMY drew a deep breath before climbing the stairs. She couldn't hide the tremble in her arm as she lifted her hand to ring the bell. It was a quiet, unassuming street, with trees lining the length of it, giving it an air of suburbia in the middle of the city. The gold plaque next to the door glistened in the sun. *Donna Kennedy, Counsellor.*

Normally she would have done this kind of thing by recommendation. Taking the word of a few reliable colleagues and friends. This time she'd made an appointment with the first counsellor she'd found in the *Yellow Pages* who would see her with a baby. She only hoped the warm friendly voice on the phone lived up to reputation she'd built in her head.

The door swung open. A small round woman with grey hair lifted Zachary straight out of her arms. 'Come in, come in.' She bustled Amy into a wooden-floored room that looked out over a wide garden filled with colourful flowers, pointing her in the direction of a comfortable leather armchair.

Everything about the place was friendly and inviting. The sunlit room was spacious enough to be comfortable but not sparse and clinical and looking like so many other office spaces. Amy could hear someone clattering around in the kitchen behind her, the smell of baking inviting her stomach to rumble. This was a home.

The woman settled herself in another chair, adjusting Zach in her arms as she chattered non-stop to him. Her smile lit up her face. 'It's been a long time since I got my hands on a baby.' She stuck her pudgy finger into Zach's little fist, waiting until his tiny fingers clenched hers.

Amy sank back into the chair. A pitcher of iced water and a couple of glasses sat on the small wooden table next to the chair. The windows to the back garden were open, letting the smell of cut grass and open blooms seep in through the air. She shifted in the chair. It was a little worn in patches, the leather thinning on the arms, but was obviously well used. Always a good sign.

She caught Donna's eyes on hers and instantly understood. This was a well-rehearsed routine.

The easy, welcoming atmosphere. Taking the baby to allow her to relax, to focus on the reason she was here. She might look like a bustling grandmother, but this woman was wise.

A warm feeling swept over her. She'd come to the right place.

Donna gave Zach's head a little rub with her fingers, tracing them down his heavy eyelids— almost hypnotising him to sleep. Then, once she was satisfied with the outcome, she looked Amy straight in the eye. This woman was a professional through and through. 'So, Amy, tell me, how do you feel?'

No preamble. No 'explain why you are here'. Just straight to the point, 'how do you feel?'

Amy pressed her shoulders back into the armchair. Zach was quiet; he was sleeping. The sun was beating down on the grass outside and she could see birds pecking at the berries on the bushes next to the window. She took a deep breath. She could do this. This was easy. Everything about this felt right. But more importantly, for her, the time was right.

She looked Donna straight in the eye. 'I feel angry,' she said.

* * *

The plane circled a few times. The rain was torrential and was obviously affecting their ability to land. Time after time they swept over the darkening green rainforest as they waited for a suitable landing spot. From here, if Lincoln strained his eyes in the distance he could see the snaking Amazon, winding its way through the forest.

Home to hundreds of potential patients.

He'd successfully negotiated a variation in his contract, allowing him some extra unpaid leave from San Francisco to serve with the Amazon aid boat.

It hadn't been difficult. The hospital needed some good publicity right now, so supporting one of their best doctors on some aid missions had been an easy move for them. It helped that as the President's doctor he was still the darling of the media and could whip up some support for the people out here.

He'd managed to persuade a few colleagues at other hospitals to help out, assembling a team with a wide range of skills. Some of the best surgeons in the country were taking a few weeks out of their vacation time to come and do a series of operations on some seriously ill children. The planning had been a logistical nightmare, but at the end of the day these children would get what they needed. And the people of the world would get to see their plight as a film crew had decided to tag along for the ride.

Normally Lincoln would have avoided filming at all costs but he knew that interest in him would soon wane so he wanted to make the most of the opportunity to show the world the health-care needs in the Amazon. It might even attract a few more willing docs to join the service on a regular basis.

The staff at San Francisco had been great, helping him with fundraising activities and praising his humanitarian efforts.

But Lincoln wasn't really going to help the people of the Amazon. That had always been at the heart of his work, and had been the only reason he'd volunteered in the first place.

But this time was different. This time he was doing it for himself.

'Linc, it's your weekly call!'

Linc looked up from where he was finishing with the latest addition to their baby clinic. Alice, one of Linc and Amy's old colleagues on the boat, was brandishing the satellite phone and waving it at him furiously. He placed the newborn back in the cot and moved towards their communication room—probably the hottest room on the boat.

As usual the line was crackly. 'Hey, it's Linc,' he said as he flopped down into the nearest seat.

'Hi, Linc, how are you doing?' He leaned backwards in his chair. The weekly telephone calls from Amy had started a month after he'd started back on the boat, a few days after he'd received her letter telling him she was doing well.

'How's Zach?' He always asked about Zach first. He couldn't believe how much he missed the little guy.

'Zach's good. He was at the clinic last week. They thought he might be developing a bit of a squint, so they've referred him to an ophthalmologist.'

'Who?' The words caught his attention instantly and he leaned forward in the chair. It didn't matter that he was on the other side of the world. He wanted to know what was happening to Zach.

'Some woman called Fern Price. She specialises in kids and is supposed to be very good.'

He scribbled her name on a bit of loose paper he had in his pocket—he'd check up on her later.

'How's Alice's hair holding up?'

Lincoln laughed. Alice moaned about the state of her hair from the moment she got up until the moment she went back to bed. Lincoln leaned back in his chair and raised his voice. 'Be thankful you're on the other side of the planet, Amy.' He wrinkled his nose. 'Though looking at how frizzy Alice's hair is, I'm surprised you can't see it from there.'

'What?' The shriek came from the other room. 'I'll get you for that, Lincoln Adams.'

Lincoln smiled. That's why he was here. This was what he needed. Friendship. Companionship and a lot of distractions.

'I saw you on TV again last night.'

'What?'

'On TV. The reporters love you.'

'As long as they bring more funding I don't care. A few more recruits would be nice too.'

'I wish I was there.' Her voice sounded wistful.

He felt a tingle run down his spine. 'I wish you were here too. but we both know an Amazon aid boat isn't the right place for Zach.'

He heard her take a deep breath. 'Are you coming back soon?'

He looked around at the battered boat, with its depleted medical supplies and too few staff.

'No,' he said firmly. 'I've still got work to do here.'

'I miss you, Linc. We miss you.' She hesitated a little. 'And I've got a surprise for you when you come back.'

'Really? What is it?'

'I've applied for a new job.'

'Really? Where?'

'In San Francisco.'

His heart stopped. She hadn't wanted to stay in San Francisco. She'd wanted to stay in Santa Maria and bring her child up in a community rather than a city. The hugeness of the step wasn't lost on him. The line crackled, a sure sign it was about to disconnect.

'Linc, speak to you next week,' he could hear her shouting.

'Sure,' he said as the line fizzled and died.

He stared at the satellite phone as the little red light flickered the cut-out.

'I've got a surprise for you too,' he whispered.

The weekly calls were hard—on both of them. But at least it was a starting point. Part of him wanted to go home right now, and part of him wanted to stay here in the Amazon, where he could hold on to his heart.

He pulled his wallet from his back pocket and found the dog-eared photo he was looking for. Zach, smiling and chewing on a toy. He smiled at it then peered closely at his eyes, looking for any sign of a squint. But there was nothing he could see. And what he really wanted to do right now was pull Zach onto his lap and look at him for himself.

He looked at the calendar. Three weeks. Another three weeks then he would head home. He'd tell her nearer the time. Until then his dreams would be haunted by a pale-skinned redhead.

'Linc, we need you!'

The voice stirred him from his thoughts as he saw people dashing about next door. Another emergency. Another life at stake.

Right now he was where he needed to be.

CHAPTER ELEVEN

THE bright lights were waiting for him at the airport—again.

Lincoln sighed. He'd just flown from Iquitos airport in Peru to Lima then Mexico City and on to San Francisco. He was exhausted. He'd been travelling for more than fifteen hours and all he wanted to do was collapse into bed.

He pasted a smile onto his face. In the last few months he'd gone from being the President's doctor to being the Amazon doctor and filmed for a US television series that was now beamed around the world. For some reason unknown to Linc, the people of the world seemed to love him. Television news crews followed his every move.

'Lincoln! Lincoln!'

A crowd of teenage girls were waiting at the arrivals gate for him, all wearing T-shirts adorned with his face and thrusting autograph books towards him. He swung his rucksack onto the floor—the rest of his luggage had gone missing at Lima airport, again. He smiled and posed for photos patiently. He could do this. It was all for a good cause.

An impatient TV reporter tapped him on the shoulder, flicking her dark hair and batting her eyelashes at him. 'Can you tell us, Dr Adams, are you going back to the Amazon?'

He'd just landed. He hadn't even had a chance to get his hands on an American hot dog yet and she wanted to know when he'd be going back.

He kept his smile carefully in place. 'I'm home to do some work at San Francisco's Children Hospital—where my regular day job is. I've got a list of surgeries that need to be scheduled for some kids in the Amazon, but I'll need to take a bit of time to try and organise that. A lot of the surgeons we require have very specialised fields and tight schedules so it could take a few months.'

The TV reporter flicked her hair again. 'Can't someone else do that for you?'

Lincoln shrugged his shoulders. 'Amazon Aid is trying to arrange a co-ordinator for me, but it has to be someone who understands the types of

equipment and skills we require. It's a big job.'
Despite his tiredness he shot her a beaming smile.
'I'm sure they'll find me someone soon, but in the
meantime your viewers can donate to the charity or, if they've got a medical background, vol-
unteer to help out on one of our missions.' He
looked straight into the camera. He'd learned in
the last few months that every piece of publicity
helped. Applications for the Amazon aid boats
had shot up since the television series had been
screened. Some keen women had even tried to
lie on their CVs about their qualifications—all
in an attempt to get closer to him.

He had a whole pile of applications in his rucksack, along with some significant other paperwork that he'd had to come back to the States to
sort out. It was amazing how things could change.

But more than that, something inside him had
changed. Something deep inside. And whether
he liked it or not, he'd Amy to thank for it. First
Zach, and now another child with a pair of dark
brown eyes, currently clouded by childhood
cataracts, and a smile that could melt his heart.
Another child pulling him in. With something he
could cure. A kid whose parents had abandoned

him on the boat, thinking his damaged eyes made him worthless. A kid he fully intended to bring home with him.

The reporter batted her eyelashes again. Did she have something in her eye? She was really beginning to annoy him.

She ran her hand up his arm, looking like a leopard about to pounce. 'So, Dr Adams, all work and no play makes Linc a dull boy. What do you plan on doing now you're home?'

The way she said his name grated. He felt as if a snake was currently crawling up his arm—and he'd seen enough of them recently.

His reply was curt and to the point. 'Sleep.' Interview over. He swung his backpack over his shoulder and headed towards the door.

But something caught his attention. A flash of a red jacket with the Amazon Aid sign, topped by a mane of red curls and a set of arms clutching a squirming toddler.

A hand caught his wrist. 'Lincoln. You're back. Great. Meet your new surgical co-ordinator.'

Brian Frew, the man behind the organisation of all the Amazon Aid expeditions, looked extremely pleased with himself. 'Lincoln, meet Amy. Amy, meet Lincoln.'

He froze. He'd never seen her wearing red before. It wasn't a colour normally associated with women with red hair. But Amy looked stunning. She gave him a wide smile. 'Told you I had a surprise for you.' She stretched her hand out towards him. 'Pleased to meet you, Dr Adams.'

His eyes fixed on Zach. Now approaching his first birthday, he was obviously developing well. He still had that lean look about him—common for babies born prematurely—and would probably never be a chunky toddler.

Amy had obviously been keeping hold of him in a vise-like grip and with one arm outstretched towards Lincoln Zach was currently making a break for freedom. Lincoln clasped Amy's outstretched hand and reached with the other for Zachary, who bounced over into his arms and started tugging at the leather thong around his neck.

'Hi, little guy. How are you?' he whispered. Green. His eyes were green now—just like his mother's. And they were straight. The patch he'd worn for a few months over one eye must have worked.

Amy cleared her throat. Brian was looking frantically from side to side, obviously wondering what was wrong. 'Can you give us a minute, please, Brian?' Amy's voice was strong and determined, with only the slightest waver. Brian nodded nervously and sloped off towards the door.

She stepped forward, into Lincoln's space, her face only inches from his.

'You're my co-ordinator?'

'I told you I'd applied for a new job in San Francisco. It almost seemed as if the job description was written for me. I decided it was time for me to show how much I wanted to be here. I left you a message on the satellite phone last week.'

He shook his head. 'I never got any messages. The satellite phone died last week, that's why I didn't phone to say I was on my way home.' She was right in front of him and he had Zachary in his arms. Ten long months he'd waited for this.

She smiled. A happy smile. A healthy smile. 'Well, now you're back in the country I intend to try and keep you here for a while.' There was a wicked glint in her eyes. This was the Amy he had known. A confident woman, who knew what she wanted.

The implication was clear.

He took a deep breath. It almost felt as if his life were flashing before his eyes. Was he dreaming this? At some point on the plane he'd drifted off and his dream had definitely resembled this one. Could he still be sleeping on the plane?

No. His plane dream would never have included that obnoxious reporter. He looked at the green eyes in front of him. They were sparkling. And they were definitely there—this wasn't wishful thinking. There was only one thing he could ask her. 'How are you, Amy?'

She moved even closer, sliding one arm around behind Zach's squirming body and the other palm flat on Lincoln's chest. His eyes drifted downwards. Her chest was pressing towards him. Both sides of her chest.

She followed his gaze downwards and smiled. 'I guess I should have said I had two surprises for you. I took the steps I needed to. I figured since you already didn't object to scar tissue, you could handle a little more. I'm healed. I'm whole.'

She lifted her head, staring directly into his eyes. 'I have a wonderful counsellor—I'd like you to meet her. And I am now "officially"...' she gave a little curtsey '...five years cancer-free.'

He took a deep breath, his heart pounding in his chest. 'That's great news. I'm happy for you. But what does this mean for us?'

He watched her, waiting for her to speak. Hoping and praying she'd say the words he was looking for.

'I have some unfinished business.'

Not what he'd expected. It sounded so formal. But, then, she was Miss Unpredictable. Could he really live a life like this?

'Business? With me?' He raised his eyebrow at her.

She nodded. Her hand moved from his chest, around his waist and down to his behind. 'I've done everything I can. I've taken care of what I can. Physically, mentally, emotionally, I'm ready, Linc. I'm ready to start again. And I'm hoping you are too.' Her eyes held his. Her lips were trembling. Was she about to cry?

'I just need to ask you one question.'

'What's that?'

'Can you take me as I am? Can you live with only ever having one child? Can you live with a woman who can't give you any children? Are you ready to give me another chance? Because I can promise you I'll never hurt you again. You've given me a lot of time to think about things. Can you give me a chance again?'

He smiled. Little did she know what he held in his bag. The future he had already planned. He kissed her forehead, then her eyelids, then her cheeks. 'I think I can manage that,' he whispered. 'And I've got a little surprise for you too—one I'll tell you about later.'

She took a deep breath. 'Good.' She leaned in and wrapped her arms around his neck, with Zach between them. 'Well, in that case, I've come to get my One That Got Away.' The tears were gleaming in her eyes. 'Because it was always you, Linc.'

And this time the tears were in his eyes too.

* * * * *

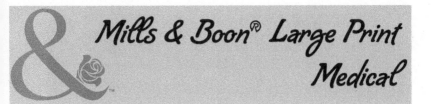

Mills & Boon® Large Print Medical

December

SYDNEY HARBOUR HOSPITAL: BELLA'S WISHLIST   Emily Forbes
DOCTOR'S MILE-HIGH FLING   Tina Beckett
HERS FOR ONE NIGHT ONLY?   Carol Marinelli
UNLOCKING THE SURGEON'S HEART   Jessica Matthews
MARRIAGE MIRACLE IN SWALLOWBROOK   Abigail Gordon
CELEBRITY IN BRAXTON FALLS   Judy Campbell

January

SYDNEY HARBOUR HOSPITAL: Fiona McArthur
MARCO'S TEMPTATION
WAKING UP WITH HIS RUNAWAY BRIDE   Louisa George
THE LEGENDARY PLAYBOY SURGEON   Alison Roberts
FALLING FOR HER IMPOSSIBLE BOSS   Alison Roberts
LETTING GO WITH DR RODRIGUEZ   Fiona Lowe
DR TALL, DARK...AND DANGEROUS?   Lynne Marshall

February

SYDNEY HARBOUR HOSPITAL: Carol Marinelli
AVA'S RE-AWAKENING
HOW TO MEND A BROKEN HEART   Amy Andrews
FALLING FOR DR FEARLESS   Lucy Clark
THE NURSE HE SHOULDN'T NOTICE   Susan Carlisle
EVERY BOY'S DREAM DAD   Sue MacKay
RETURN OF THE REBEL SURGEON   Connie Cox

Mills & Boon® Large Print
Medical

March

HER MOTHERHOOD WISH	Anne Fraser
A BOND BETWEEN STRANGERS	Scarlet Wilson
ONCE A PLAYBOY…	Kate Hardy
CHALLENGING THE NURSE'S RULES	Janice Lynn
THE SHEIKH AND THE SURROGATE MUM	Meredith Webber
TAMED BY HER BROODING BOSS	Joanna Neil

April

A SOCIALITE'S CHRISTMAS WISH	Lucy Clark
REDEEMING DR RICCARDI	Leah Martyn
THE FAMILY WHO MADE HIM WHOLE	Jennifer Taylor
THE DOCTOR MEETS HER MATCH	Annie Claydon
THE DOCTOR'S LOST-AND-FOUND HEART	Dianne Drake
THE MAN WHO WOULDN'T MARRY	Tina Beckett

May

MAYBE THIS CHRISTMAS…?	Alison Roberts
A DOCTOR, A FLING & A WEDDING RING	Fiona McArthur
DR CHANDLER'S SLEEPING BEAUTY	Melanie Milburne
HER CHRISTMAS EVE DIAMOND	Scarlet Wilson
NEWBORN BABY FOR CHRISTMAS	Fiona Lowe
THE WAR HERO'S LOCKED-AWAY HEART	Louisa George